NOLO® Products & Services

Books & Software

Get in-depth information. Nolo publishes hundreds of great books and software programs for consumers and business owners. Order a copy—or download an ebook version instantly—at Nolo.com.

Legal Encyclopedia

Free at Nolo.com. Here are more than 1,400 free articles and answers to common questions about everyday legal issues including wills, bankruptcy, small business formation, divorce, patents, employment and much more.

Plain-English Legal Dictionary

Free at Nolo.com. Stumped by jargon? Look it up in America's most up-to-date source for definitions of legal terms.

Online Legal Documents

Create documents at your computer. Go to Nolo.com to make a will or living trust, form an LLC or corporation or obtain a trademark or provisional patent. For simpler matters, download one of our hundreds of high-quality legal forms, including bills of sale, promissory notes, nondisclosure agreements and many more.

Lawyer Directory

Find an attorney at Nolo.com. Nolo's consumer-friendly lawyer directory provides in-depth profiles of lawyers all over America. From fees and experience to legal philosophy, education and special expertise, you'll find all the information you need to pick the right lawyer. Every lawyer listed has pledged to work diligently and respectfully with clients.

Free Legal Updates

Keep up to date. Check for free updates at Nolo.com. Under "Products," find this book and click "Legal Updates." You can also sign up for our free e-newsletters at Nolo.com/newsletters/index.html.

NOLO® The Trusted Name
(but don't take our word for it)

"In Nolo you can trust."
THE NEW YORK TIMES

"Nolo is always there in a jam as the nation's premier publisher of do-it-yourself legal books."
NEWSWEEK

"Nolo publications…guide people simply through the how, when, where and why of the law."
THE WASHINGTON POST

"[Nolo's]…material is developed by experienced attorneys who have a knack for making complicated material accessible."
LIBRARY JOURNAL

"When it comes to self-help legal stuff, nobody does a better job than Nolo…"
USA TODAY

"The most prominent U.S. publisher of self-help legal aids."
TIME MAGAZINE

"Nolo is a pioneer in both consumer and business self-help books and software."
LOS ANGELES TIMES

5th edition

The Corporate Records Handbook
Meetings, Minutes & Resolutions

By Attorney Anthony Mancuso

Fifth Edition	JULY 2010
Editor	DIANA FITZPATRICK
Cover Design	SUSAN WIGHT
Proofreader	ROBERT WELLS
CD-ROM Preparation	ELLEN BITTER
Index	VICTORIA BAKER
Printing	DELTA PRINTING SOLUTIONS, INC.

Mancuso, Anthony.
    The corporate records handbook : meetings, minutes & resolutions / by Anthony
Mancuso. -- 5th ed.
        p. cm.
    ISBN-13: 978-1-4133-1203-4 (pbk.)
    ISBN-10: 1-4133-1203-9 (pbk.)
    1. Corporation law--United States--Popular works. 2. Corporate meetings--Law and
legislation--United States--Popular works. 3. Business records--Law and legislation--
United States--Popular works. I. Title.
    KF1414.85.M36 2010
    346.73'0664--dc22

                            2009048204

Please note

We believe accurate, plain-English legal information should help you solve many of your own legal problems. But this text is not a substitute for personalized advice from a knowledgeable lawyer. If you want the help of a trained professional—and we'll always point out situations in which we think that's a good idea—consult an attorney licensed to practice in your state.

Acknowledgments

Many thanks to Diana Fitzpatrick for a superb job of editing this material, and to the entire Nolo crew for helping this book find its place in the world.

About the Author

Anthony Mancuso is a corporations and limited liability company expert. A graduate of Hastings College of the Law in San Francisco, Tony is an active member of the California State Bar, writes books and software in the fields of corporate and LLC law, and has studied advanced business taxation at Golden Gate University in San Francisco. He also has been a consultant for Silicon Valley EDA (Electronic Design Automation) and other technology companies. He is currently employed at Google in Mountain View, California.

Tony is the author of many Nolo books on forming and operating corporations (profit and nonprofit) and limited liability companies. Among his current books are *Incorporate Your Business*; *How to Form a Nonprofit Corporation*; *Nonprofit Meetings, Minutes & Records*; *Form Your Own Limited Liability Company;* and *LLC or Corporation?* His books and software have shown over a quarter of a million businesses and organizations how to form and operate a corporation or an LLC.

Tony has lectured at Boalt School of Law on the U.C. Berkeley campus (*Using the Law in Non-Traditional Settings*) and at Stanford Law School (*How to Form a Nonprofit Corporation*). He taught Saturday Morning Law School business formation and operation courses for several years at Nolo Press offices in Berkeley. He has also scripted and narrated several audiotapes and podcasts covering LLCs and corporate formations and other legal areas for Nolo as well as The Company Corporation. He has given many recorded and live radio and TV presentations and interviews covering business, securities, and tax law issues. His law and tax articles and interviews have appeared in the *Wall Street Journal* and *TheStreet.Com*.

Tony is a licensed helicopter pilot and has performed for years as a guitarist in various musical idioms, including jazz, Afro-Cuban, and R&B.

For links to Tony's books, go to www.nolo.com, click on "About Nolo," then "Nolo · Authors," then "Anthony Mancusco."

Table of Contents

Appendix C: Corporate Minutes Forms

Notice and Minutes Forms

Meeting Summary Sheet

Call of Meeting

Meeting Participant List

Notice of Meeting

Acknowledgment of Receipt of Notice of Meeting

Proxy

Certification of Mailing

Minutes of the Annual Meeting of Shareholders

Minutes of Special Meeting of Shareholders

Minutes of the Annual Meeting of Directors

Minutes of Special Meeting of Directors

Waiver of Notice of Meeting

Approval of Corporate Minutes

Cover Letter for Approval of Minutes of Paper Meeting

Written Consent to Action Without Meeting

Standard Corporate Business Resolutions

Authorization of Treasurer to Open and Use Accounts

Authorization of Treasurer to Open and Use Specific Corporate Account(s)

Authorization of Corporate Account and Designation of Authorized Signers

Authorization of Rental of Safe Deposit Box

Adoption of Assumed Name

Board Approval of Proposed Contract

Approval of Lease

Purchase of Real Property

Authorization of Sale of Real Property

Delegation of Authority to Corporate Employee

Director Ratification of Employee's Acts

Board Ratification of Contract

Rescission of Authority of Employee

Shareholder Ratification of Decisions or Acts

Certification of Board or Shareholder Action

Affidavit of Corporate Decision Making

Acknowledgment

Corporate Tax Resolutions

S Corporation Tax Election

S Corporation Shareholders' Agreement

Accumulation of Corporate Earnings

Qualification of Shares Under Internal Revenue Code Section 1244

Approval of Independent Audit of Corporate Financial Records

Approval of Corporate Tax Year

Payment and Deduction of Organizational Expenses

Resolutions to Amend Corporate Articles and Bylaws

Approval of Amendment to Articles of Incorporation

Approval of Restatement of Articles of Incorporation

Amendment of Articles Form

Approval of Amendment of Bylaws

Corporate Hiring and Appointment Resolutions

Approval of Hiring of Corporate Employee

Approval of Bonuses and Salary Increases

Shareholder Ratification of Employee Pay

Approval of Independent Contractor Services

Appointment of Corporate Officers

Authorization of Payment for Attending Meetings

Annual Director or Officer Stipend for Attendance at Meetings

No Compensation for Attending Corporate Meetings

Indemnification and Insurance for Directors and Officers

Director Conflict of Interest Resolutions

Board Approval of Transaction Benefiting a Director

Directors' Written Consent to Transaction Benefiting a Director

Shareholder Approval of Transaction Benefiting a Director

Shareholder Written Consent to Transaction Involving a Director

Resolutions for Loans to the Corporation

Authorization of Loan at Specific Terms

Authorization of Maximum Loan on General Terms

Unlimited Authorization of Loans for Business Needs

Authorization of Line of Credit

Authorization of Line of Credit With Cap on Each Transaction

Authorization of Loan Terms Secured by Corporate Property

Resolution Approving Loan to Corporation

Promissory Note: Installment Payments of Principal and Interest (Amortized Loan)

Promissory Note: Installment Payments of Principal and Interest (Amortized Loan) Secured by Corporate Property

Promissory Note: Installment Payments of Principal and Interest (Amortized Loan) With Balloon Payment

Promissory Note: Periodic Payments of Interest With Lump Sum Principal Payment

Promissory Note: Lump Sum Payment of Principal and Interest at Specified Date

Promissory Note: Lump Sum Payment of Principal and Interest on Demand by Noteholder

Promissory Note: Variable Schedule of Payments of Principal and Interest

Resolutions for Loans by the Corporation to Insiders

Approval of Corporate Loan to Insider

Promissory Note: Monthly Installment Payments of Principal and Interest (Amortized Loan)

Promissory Note: Installment Payments of Principal and Interest (Amortized Loan) Secured by Property

Promissory Note: Installment Payments of Principal and Interest (Amortized Loan) With Balloon Payment

Promissory Note: Periodic Payments of Interest With Lump Sum Principal Payment

Promissory Note: Lump Sum Payment of Principal and Interest at Specified Date

Promissory Note: Lump Sum Payment of Principal and Interest on Demand by Noteholder

Promissory Note: Variable Schedule of Payments of Principal and Interest

Release of Promissory Note

Employee Fringe Benefits and Business Expense Reimbursement Resolutions

Authorization of Group Health, Accident, or Disability Insurance for Employees

Adoption of Self-Insured Medical Reimbursement Plan

Purchase of Group Term Life Insurance

Authorization of Employee Death Benefit

Agreement Regarding Death Benefits

Purchase or Lease of Company Car

Authorization of Payment of Standard Mileage Allowance to Employees

Business Meal Expense Allotment for Employees

On-Premises Meals and Lodging for Employees

Authorization of Corporate Credit and Charge Cards for Employees

Reimbursement of Actual Travel and Entertainment Expenses to Employees Under Accountable Reimbursement Plan

Index

Your Legal Companion for
The Corporate Records Handbook

Forming a corporation is an important, and sometimes exhausting, task. All too often, after the new entity is established, the owners take a deep breath and get back to doing what they do best—running the day-to-day business operations. This is a big mistake. Failure to deal with the paperwork and legal formalities required to properly run your corporation can have disastrous consequences, including the loss of crucial tax benefits and limited liability protection for the owners.

With the help of this book, it's easy to take care of your corporate housekeeping responsibilities. We show you step by step how to:

- hold and document corporate meetings of shareholders and directors

- document corporate action taken without a meeting, and

- approve common ongoing corporate legal, tax, and business decisions.

The paperwork required to take care of these tasks consists of minutes and written consent forms for shareholders and directors, as well as resolution forms that you can insert into the minutes to show approval of various types of corporate actions. We have included detailed instructions and sample forms to help you fill out your forms. You will find that you can do most of the routine paperwork yourself. You may need to turn to a lawyer or accountant if you have a complicated legal or tax issue—we let you know when this might occur. All the forms you need are included on the CD-ROM and in tear-out form in Appendix C.

The material in this book is most useful for smaller businesses. By "smaller," we mean those that are privately owned, with up to about 35 shareholders and 50 employees. A typical example is a family-owned business or one in which all of the stock is owned by several people and the people who own the stock are actively involved in managing or supervising the business.

Congratulations! With the help of this book, you can rest assured that you are taking care of your corporate housekeeping responsibilities. This will allow you to focus on other important tasks—such as running your successful business venture. ●

Corporate Documents and Laws

Calling, providing notice for, holding, and voting at meetings of your directors and shareholders necessarily means becoming familiar with a bucketful of new terminology and procedures. While mastering this material isn't difficult, it does require attention to detail. In this chapter, we provide legal and practical background information about basic corporate documents and the state corporation laws on which they are based.

If you are well organized and feel you understand the purpose of your articles, bylaws, and minutes, much of the material in this chapter may seem like old hat. If so, you may wish to skip ahead to the next chapter where we present an overview of the common methods of corporate decision making, including corporate meetings and written consents.

Organize Your Corporate Records

Anyone who sets up a corporation needs to be able to quickly locate key organizational documents. Because these are really the constitution of your corporation, you'll refer to them again and again. When using this book to produce corporate minute and consent forms, we will often refer you to these documents.

If you have not already done so, the best approach is to set up a corporate records book that contains the key documents. You can do this on your own with a three-ring binder or by using a customized corporate kit designed for the purpose.

Your corporate records book should contain:

- articles of incorporation
- bylaws
- minutes of the first directors' meeting

- stock certificate stubs or a stock transfer ledger showing the names and addresses of your shareholders, as well as the number and types of shares owned by each
- minutes of annual and special meetings of directors or shareholders, if any, and
- written consents.

If someone helped you incorporate, such as a lawyer, accountant, paralegal, or financial planner, you probably received copies of these documents in a corporate records book, commonly called a corporate kit. However, some lawyers attempt to hold on to corporate records in the hope that you will have them take care of all ongoing technicalities. If so, you will need to request a copy of all corporate documents in your client file. (This is your property, so don't take "No" for an answer.)

If you can't locate a copy of your articles, write your secretary of state's corporate filing office and request a certified or file-stamped copy of your articles. (See Appendix B for contact information.) It's a good idea to call first so you can include the correct fee, which should be just a few dollars or so.

Articles of Incorporation

The first key organizing document all small business corporations must have is their articles of incorporation. (While most states use the term articles of incorporation to refer to the basic document creating the corporation, some states, including Connecticut, Delaware, New York, and Oklahoma, use the term certificate of incorporation. Washington calls the document a certificate of formation, and Tennessee calls it a charter.) A corporation comes into existence when its articles of incorporation are filed with the state corporate filing office. The articles normally contain fundamental structural information, such as the name of

The Importance of Protecting Your Corporate Status

A corporation is a legal entity that is created and regulated by state laws. For legal, practical, and tax purposes, a corporation is legally separate from any of the people who own, control, manage, or operate it. If you want the advantages of having a corporation, you must follow legal requirements for running it. If you don't abide by the rules, you could find your business stripped of its corporate status—and the benefits of that status, such as:

- **Limited liability.** Corporate directors, officers, and shareholders usually are not personally liable for the debts of the corporation. This means that if the corporation cannot pay its debts or other financial obligations, creditors cannot usually seize or sell a corporate investor's home, car, or other personal assets.

- **Business taxes and flexibility.** A corporation is a separate taxable entity. Business income can be sheltered in the corporation among the owner-employees as they see fit to reduce their overall tax liability.

- **Employee fringe benefits.** Owner-employees of a corporation are eligible for deductible fringe benefits, such as sick pay, group term life insurance, accident and health insurance, reimbursement of medical expenses, and disability insurance.

- **Commercial loans and capital investment.** Lending institutions often give the risk-conscious corporate lender special preferences. Corporations can decide to raise substantial amounts of capital by making a public offering of their shares.

- **Business credibility.** Corporations have an air of reputability about them. In other words, although placing an "Inc." after your name will not directly increase sales, it forces you to pay serious attention to the structure and organization of your business, something that is likely to improve all aspects of your business.

- **Perpetual existence.** A corporation has an independent legal existence that continues despite changeovers in management or ownership. Of course, like any business, a corporation can be terminated by the mutual consent of the owners.

- **Access to capital.** Private and public capital markets prefer the corporate form over all other business forms, giving the corporation enhanced access to private and public capital. Public offerings can be made by means of a traditionally underwritten initial public offering (IPO) or a direct public offering (DPO) of shares by the corporation itself to its client or customer base.

the corporation, names and addresses of its directors, its registered agent and his or her office address, and the corporation's capital stock structure.

For the majority of small corporations, there is no other important information in this document. However, larger corporations sometimes adopt articles containing special provisions that impact future decision-making processes of the corporation.

EXAMPLE:

The Equity Investors Capital Corporation adopts articles that contain a multiclass stock structure consisting of Class A voting shares and Class B nonvoting shares. A special article requires a vote of two-thirds of each class of stock for the approval of amendments (future changes) to the corporation's articles or bylaws.

RESOURCE

Where to get help preparing articles for a new corporation. If you have not yet formed your corporation, you can create and file your articles online through Nolo's Online Legal Forms at www .nolo.com. Or, Nolo publishes several state-specific books and software that show you how to prepare and file articles and take other incorporation steps such as issuing stock under state securities laws. If you want to incorporate in California, see *How to Form Your Own California Corporation* (Nolo). In other states, see *Incorporate Your Business* (Nolo). You can also check your state's corporate filing office for samples and instructions for drafting your own articles. Except in South Carolina, you do not need to involve an attorney. (Appendix B has information on how to find the corporate filing office in your state.)

Bylaws

The bylaws of a corporation are its second-most important document. You do not file bylaws with the state—they are an internal document that contains rules for holding corporate meetings and other formalities according to state corporate laws.

Bylaws typically specify the frequency of regular meetings of directors and shareholders and the call, notice, quorum, and voting rules for each type of meeting. They usually contain the rules for setting up and delegating authority to special committees of the board, the rights of directors and shareholders to inspect the corporate records and books, the rights of directors and officers to insurance coverage or indemnification (reimbursement by the corporation for legal fees and judgments) in the event of lawsuits, plus a number of other standard legal provisions.

TIP

Use bylaws for common or changeable rules. State law often gives corporations a choice as to whether to place corporate operating rules and procedures in the articles of incorporation or bylaws. If you have a choice, it's always best to use the bylaws, because you can change them easily without the need for filing changes with the state. For example, many states allow you to place supermajority quorum or voting rules for directors' or shareholders' meetings in either document. If you use the bylaws for this purpose, you can more easily change these provisions because less stringent vote requirements normally apply to the amendment of bylaws. In contrast, if you need to change provisions in your articles, a formal amendment to the articles must be filed with your state's corporate filing office.

Because the corporation laws of all states are subject to change, it's possible that bylaws that were valid when adopted will later go out of date. Fortunately, major changes to corporate laws happen only every decade or two, when states modernize their corporate statutes. Nonetheless, if your corporation has been in existence for a few years and you plan a major corporate decision such as the issuance of a new class of shares, declaration of a dividend, or purchase of shares from a shareholder, it's wise to make sure your bylaw provisions are up-to-date by checking your state's current business corporation act.

RESOURCE

Where to get help preparing bylaws. Some corporations may have been formed in a hurry, by filing articles of incorporation only. If that is your case, you need to take the extra step of preparing basic bylaws for your corporation. Again, if your corporation was formed in California, you can use *How to Form Your Own California Corporation* (Nolo) to prepare state-specific bylaws for your corporation. For any other state, see *Incorporate Your Business* (Nolo).

Minutes of Your First Directors' Meeting

When most businesses incorporate, they prepare minutes of the first meeting of the corporation's board of directors or of the incorporators (the person or persons who signed and filed the articles on behalf of the corporation). This meeting is usually referred to as the organizational meeting of the corporation. Minutes are simply a formal record of the proceedings of a meeting. The organizational meeting is usually held to approve standard items of business necessary for a new corporation to begin doing business.

Look through the minutes of your organizational meeting. These minutes are designed to document the essential organizational actions taken by the board or the incorporators. They typically show:

- the beginning tax elections made by the corporation—for example, the selection of the corporation's accounting period and tax year
- details of the corporation's first stock issuance
- approval of stock certificates and a corporate seal, and
- approval of other beginning business of the corporation, such as the opening of a corporate bank account.

Knowing some of this information may be essential to making informed corporate decisions later.

TIP

Don't worry if you don't have organizational minutes. Some corporations, especially those created in a rush, simply didn't prepare minutes of the first meeting of the board of directors or incorporators. If you don't have these minutes, you can recreate them as explained in "Using Paper Meetings to Create Records for Prior Undocumented Meetings," in Chapter 7.

Records Showing Stock Was Issued

A new corporation almost always issues stock to record the ownership interests of the persons who invest in the corporation. Most smaller corporations issue stock for cash, property, or the performance of services that were rendered in forming the corporation. Many states prohibit the issuance of shares in return for a promise to pay for the shares later (in return for a promissory note) or for a promise to perform future services. If a small existing business is being incorporated, the business owners are normally issued shares in return for the transfer of business assets to the new corporation.

EXAMPLE:

Just Friends, a partnership, incorporates as Just Friends, Inc. Each of the three prior business owners owned an equal one-third interest in the partnership. After the transfer of the partnership assets to the corporation, each owner is issued one-third of the shares issued by the corporation (3,000 shares are issued, so each owner receives 1,000 shares in the new corporation).

If you haven't issued stock or didn't keep written records showing who owns shares, you should do so now. Stock certificates and stock transfer ledgers are available in most office supply stores.

Once you've organized your corporate records book, remember that while a corporate records book makes it easy for you to keep all key documents in one place, it won't work unless you consistently use it.

Minutes of Meetings and Written Consents

If your corporation has been in existence for some time, you may have records of annual and perhaps special corporate meetings. This is especially likely if a lawyer helped you incorporate. Check your corporate records, or contact your attorney if you don't have copies. Again, remember that you have a right to these records.

Your State Corporate Filing Office

Each state has a corporate filing office where you pay a fee and file paperwork for creating corporations, changing the corporate structure, and dissolving corporations.

Information on how to find your state corporate filing office is provided in Appendix B. The 50 different states use slightly different names for the office where corporate filings are made. Most commonly, corporations are formed with and supervised by the secretary of state or department of state office. The department within this bureaucracy that handles corporate filings is commonly designated as the corporations division or corporations department.

Corporation filing offices are sometimes further divided into offices that oversee special areas of concern, such as corporate filings (for example, articles of incorporation or amendments to articles), corporate name availability, corporate fee information, and corporate legal counsel. Don't be put off by this seeming structural complexity. If you need information, check your state's corporate filing office website. Also, you'll normally find there is one phone number at the corporate filing office devoted to handling corporate inquiries from the public.

Throughout this book, we refer to the office that accepts corporate filings as the state corporate filing office, whether this office is formally designated as the secretary of state office or by some other title.

> ### Your State's Corporate Filing Office Website
>
> Check your state's corporate filing office website for sample forms and other useful information about forming or operating a corporation in your state. Most states have sample articles of incorporation and other forms that you can download or, in some cases, fill in and file online. Many of the state websites also contain links to your state's corporate tax office (for tax forms and information) and state employment, licensing, and other agencies. See Appendix B for information about how to locate your state corporate filing office website.

Looking Up the Law Yourself

In addition to the rules and procedures set out in corporate articles and bylaws, the organization and operation of a corporation are tightly regulated by a good-sized pile of laws adopted by each state. The primary source of laws that apply to your corporation will be found in your state's corporation laws (statutes), often titled the Business Corporation Act or designated with a similar name. Legal citations to sections of a state's business corporation laws are often listed in the following form: "Sec. 21.2 of the Business Corporation Act" or "Article 2-12, BCA."

Some readers may be reluctant to venture into what they see as the musty or mysterious realm of corporate law research. To be sure, legal research of any type may seem daunting or dry, and corporate statutes are not always models of clear, concise (let alone friendly) language. Nonetheless, be reassured: Looking up corporate rules is not akin to doing your own appendectomy. Corporate statutes are organized by subject matter and are well indexed and cross-referenced. For the most part, the statutes themselves state a fairly simple rule or requirement that, despite the inevitable lawyer jargon, can be comprehended by the average reader.

Most small business people can't afford to pay a lawyer upwards of $400 per hour every time they want access to basic legal information or help handling ongoing legal formalities and procedures. That's why we explain the importance of locating an experienced small business lawyer who is willing to act more like a legal coach, rather than a legal representative. (See Chapter 20.) For now, it's important to know that you can often look up the law yourself, without having to consult, and pay handsomely for, outside legal assistance.

Finding Your State Corporation Laws

Many routine state legal rules, such as those for holding and voting at meetings, obtaining director or shareholder written consent to action without a meeting, and conducting ongoing corporate business, are restated in your articles of incorporation and bylaws. Nevertheless, there may be times when you will want more detail on your state's corporation statutes.

Once you locate your state's corporate statutes, it usually takes only a minute or two to find a relevant corporate law requirement or procedure, or to satisfy yourself that one does not exist.

The Model Business Corporation Act

The basic corporate statutes of many states contain the same, or quite similar, rules for organizing and operating business corporations. The reason for this uniformity is that a number of states have adopted some, most, or all of the provisions of a standard law: the Model Business Corporation Act. The act undergoes periodic changes, and states are free to enact it in modified form.

The following states have enacted most, or a substantial portion, of the provisions of the Revised Model Business Corporation Act:

Arkansas	Mississippi	Tennessee
Florida	Montana	Virginia
Georgia	North Carolina	Washington
Indiana	Oregon	Wisconsin
Iowa	South Carolina	Wyoming
Kentucky		

To find your state's corporation laws, you can use any of these four easy methods:

- Check your state's corporate filing office website. Many states provide an online version of their business corporation act (or similarly titled corporation laws). Appendix B provides information on how to find your state corporate filing office website.

- Look up your state's corporations laws using Nolo's State Law Resources page at www. nolo.com/legal-research/state-law.html (under "Legal Research," then "State Law Resources").

- Type "<your state's name> Corporation Act" or "<your state's name> corporation laws" into your browser's search box. This usually leads to a link to your state's business corporation act.

- Visit a local law library, a law school library that is open to the public, or a large public library with a substantial business collection. Ask the research librarian for help looking up your state's business corporation act.

Look Up Relevant Corporate Statutes

To start, you can browse through the table of contents at the beginning of your state's corporation act or the mini table of contents often located at the beginning of each section heading in the act. Each heading covers major areas of corporate operation or procedure (for example, *Corporate Formation, Meetings, Stock Issuance, Corporate Officers, Records and Reports,* and the like). Major headings are further broken down into subheadings and sections that treat specific matters, such as *Articles of Incorporation, Bylaws,* and *Director and Shareholder Meetings*.

Or, you can usually do a search to find the statute you're interested in by entering a few key terms.

Checking Other Laws

In addition to a state's Business Corporation Act, other state laws regulate special areas of corporate activity. These include:

Securities Act or Blue Sky Law. These laws contain each state's rules and procedures for offering, issuing, selling, and transferring shares of corporate stock and other securities. (The term blue sky law was derived from the sometimes underhanded, and often colorful, practices of corporate con artists who, in return for a small investment in their latest get-rich-quick undertaking, would promise the blue sky to unsuspecting investors. The securities laws

of each state attempt, through stock offering qualification and disclosure requirements, to tone down the picture painted by stock promoters to a more realistic hue.)

Tax or Revenue Code. If a state imposes a corporate income or franchise tax, the state's tax or revenue code will typically contain these provisions.

Commercial Code. The state's commercial code contains the rules for entering into and enforcing commercial contracts, promissory notes, and other standard commercial documents.

Other state and local laws. Various state laws may impact the activities and operations of all businesses, whether or not they are incorporated. For example, state and local building codes, professional and occupation licensing, and other laws and regulations may apply to your business and its operations.

When to Consult a Professional

Holding corporate meetings and preparing standard resolutions and other corporate paperwork are usually routine tasks for corporations. However, if the decision you are facing is complex, you anticipate any complications or objections, or you simply have questions and need more information, consult with a tax or legal specialist before using the forms in this book. A consultation of this sort will be far more cost-effective than making the wrong decision and having to fix it later. Besides, the fees you incur should be relatively low, since you're not handing all the paperwork to the lawyer or tax person to do for you. For information on choosing and using a legal or tax professional to help you with ongoing corporate decisions and documentation, see Chapter 20. ●

Meetings, Minutes, and Written Consents—How to Document Corporate Action

In this chapter, we provide background information on the primary ways corporations make and formally document important decisions. These methods include holding real or paper meetings of directors or shareholders that are documented by formal minutes, and having directors or shareholders prepare and sign written paperwork (called consents) without the need to convene a formal meeting.

This chapter does not cover the detailed legal rules that affect these procedures. Instead, here we answer common questions about the use and usefulness of each of these procedures. After you go through this material, you should be able to comfortably decide when to hold formal corporate meetings or document corporate decisions without a meeting.

CAUTION

Check your bylaws for the legal rules. The legal rules and procedures for holding formal meetings or obtaining the written consents of your directors or shareholders in lieu of a meeting should be stated in your bylaws. (If you can't locate your bylaws, or you're not sure they are current, follow the suggestions in "Bylaws" in Chapter 1.)

Three Ways to Document Formal Corporate Decisions

There are three basic ways to make and document formal corporate decisions made by a corporation's board of directors or shareholders. They are:

- real meeting with minutes
- paper meeting with minutes, and
- action by written consent.

Legally, it makes no difference which way—or ways—you settle on.

Real Meeting With Minutes

For a real meeting, your directors or shareholders and all interested parties get together in person and discuss and vote on items of corporate business. During or after the meeting, written minutes are prepared showing the date, time, place, and purpose of the meeting and the decisions (resolutions) approved by the board of directors or shareholders.

Chapters 3 and 4 cover the steps necessary to hold a real meeting of directors and shareholders. Chapters 5 and 6 show how to prepare minutes to document the decisions reached at those meetings.

Paper Meeting With Minutes

With a paper meeting, the directors or shareholders informally agree to specific corporate action or actions, such as the election of new directors. Then minutes are prepared as though the decision were approved at a real meeting of directors or shareholders. We call meetings of this sort paper meetings, because the meeting takes place on paper only.

A paper meeting is often used by corporations that do not want to go to the trouble of holding a real meeting, but do want to maintain a corporate records history, complete with traditional formal minutes. While not specifically sanctioned under corporate statutes, a paper meeting with minutes is a common form of corporate documentation. It should present no problems as long as the decisions reflected in the minutes of the paper meeting represent actual decisions reached by your board or shareholders. This procedure is quite similar to taking action by written consent, discussed below, with one key difference: Formal minutes are prepared when a paper meeting is held.

Chapter 7 explains how to prepare written minutes for a paper meeting to document a decision as though it were reached at a real meeting.

Action by Written Consent

This is the quickest and least formal way of taking formal corporate action. The directors or shareholders consent to a decision or action in writing by signing a written consent form. Minutes for a real or paper meeting are not prepared. Only the written consent forms are kept in the corporate records book, to indicate that directors and shareholders made the necessary decisions.

Chapter 8 covers the procedure and forms necessary to obtain director and shareholder approval by written consent.

Questions and Answers About Meetings, Minutes, and Written Consents

The questions and answers below shed light on the advantages and disadvantages of each of the three corporate decision-making formalities. It's important to recognize that there is no one best way for all corporations to proceed. Corporations, large and small, take advantage of each of the foregoing procedures to varying degrees, depending on the nature of their business, the type of decision involved, and the amount of time available to make and document a particular decision. Your best tack is to read this material thoroughly and then consider which approach is best for you.

What Method Should You Choose?

Each of the three ways of reaching and documenting formal corporate decisions has its own advantages. You'll simply need to settle on the approach—or approaches—that best suits your corporation's needs and the temperament of its directors and shareholders.

A real meeting allows the participants to meet face to face and arrive at decisions that require the give and take of conversation, argument, or persuasion engaged in by participants. A paper meeting, like a real meeting, also results in the preparation of formal minutes that document board or shareholder decisions but does not require the time and effort involved in getting everyone together in a meeting. The written consent procedure is the quickest and simplest of all, allowing the board or shareholders to agree to an uncontested item of business with a minimum of formality and paperwork.

Sometimes it will be clear that you need to hold a formal meeting. In other situations, it would be a waste of time to do so. Sometimes, any one or two, or even all three, approaches will serve you well. In other words, you can utilize whichever method works best under the circumstances.

When Should You Hold a Formal Meeting?

Corporate statutes usually require annual board of directors' and shareholders' meetings. These meetings are usually scheduled in the corporation's bylaws. The annual shareholders' meeting is held first, in order to elect the board for the upcoming year. After the shareholders' meeting, and usually on the same day, the annual directors' meeting is held. At this meeting, the directors accept their positions for the upcoming year and tend to any business and corporate planning that is appropriate.

All other meetings of the board or shareholders are special meetings, which may be called any time during the year according to rules contained in the bylaws. Special meetings may be called to discuss urgent items of business or approve legal or tax formalities that arise from time to time. For example, a special meeting might be called to approve the adoption of a new corporate tax year recommended by the corporation's accountant, to approve the conditions of a corporate loan made to an officer of the corporation, or to approve a bank loan or real estate transaction.

Why Bother to Document Corporate Decisions?

Why bother to prepare minutes of meetings or written consents for important corporate decisions? Here are a few excellent reasons:

- Annual corporate meetings are required under state law. If you fail to pay at least minimal attention to these ongoing legal formalities, you may lose the protection of your corporate status.

- Your legal paperwork provides a record of important corporate transactions. This paper trail can be important if disputes arise. You can use this paper trail to show your directors, shareholders, creditors, suppliers, the IRS, and the courts that you acted appropriately and in compliance with applicable laws, regulations, or other legal requirements.

- Formally documenting key corporate actions is a good way of keeping shareholders informed of major corporate decisions.

- Directors of small corporations commonly approve business transactions in which they have a material financial interest. Your minutes or consent forms can help prevent legal problems by proving that these self-interested decisions were arrived at fairly, after full disclosure to the board and shareholders.

- Banks, trust, escrow, and title companies, property management companies, and other institutions often ask corporations to submit a copy of a board or shareholder resolution approving the transaction that is being undertaken, such as a loan, purchase, or rental of property.

What Decisions Need to Be Documented?

The good news is that you don't need to document routine business decisions—only those that require formal board of directors' or shareholder approval. In other words, it's not required by law or practice that you clutter up your corporate records book with mundane business records about purchasing supplies or products, hiring or firing employees, deciding to launch new services or products, or any of the host of other ongoing business decisions.

Here's our recommendation for your paper trail. At a minimum, prepare written minutes (either for real or paper meetings) for all annual meetings scheduled in your bylaws. Typically, this means preparing minutes for an annual shareholders' meeting followed by minutes for an annual directors' meeting.

Also prepare formal corporate documentation for all important legal, tax, financial, or business decisions reached by the directors or shareholders during the year. This documentation can be in the form of minutes for a special meeting—again, either real or on paper—or written consent forms signed by your directors or shareholders.

By preparing this simple paperwork, you will have prepared a paper trail of important corporate decisions, which should give your corporate records book enough girth to help satisfy courts, the IRS, and others that you attended to the necessary legal and tax niceties.

What About Written Consents?

Legally, written consents work just as well as written minutes of meetings to document director or shareholder decisions. They are, moreover, the quickest way to approve and document a formal decision by the corporation's board or shareholders, because they do not require time and effort to hold a meeting (or document a paper meeting) and prepare minutes. Directors or shareholders simply sign a consent form that states the action or business approved. The written consent form is then placed in the corporate records book as proof of the decision.

But written consents do have weaknesses. Depending on the situation, you may decide to use written consents anyway, but you should do so after careful consideration of the problems. So what's the downside?

If a number of directors or shareholders are involved (especially when some do not directly work in the business), a request to sign a written consent form may come as a surprise to an outside director or shareholder. As explained below, many corporations decide that a real meeting works best to let outsiders in on the reasons for important corporate decisions.

The IRS and the courts usually expect to see written minutes, at least for basic corporate formalities such as the annual directors' and shareholders' meetings. Most corporations decide that written minutes look better, and are more appropriate, to document the proceedings of annual directors' and shareholders' meetings, even if a real meeting is not necessary because decisions are routine and all shareholders and directors agree to the proposed decision.

All this being said, however, there is still a role for the written consent procedure in some circumstances:

- **One-person or two-people corporations.** Written consent forms are particularly useful in one-person corporations where one individual owns and manages the corporation as its only shareholder and director. The consent form procedure allows the sole corporate director-shareholder to formally approve corporate decisions without going to the trouble of preparing minutes for a pretend meeting. The same holds true for corporations where two people who work closely are the only shareholders of a corporation.

- **To document noncontroversial or time-sensitive decisions.** Particularly where time is of the essence and where a face-to-face meeting of directors or shareholders is not necessary or practical, it may make sense to take action by written consent. There shouldn't be a problem as long as minutes are kept for annual meetings and meetings where important decisions are discussed.

EXAMPLE 1:

Better Mousetraps, Inc., is advised by its accountant to pass a board resolution approving a change in tax year. After discussing this issue briefly, its directors ask the corporate secretary to prepare a written consent form for the directors to sign that shows their approval of the tax election. They see no need to meet in person to approve the decision or to prepare paper minutes for a fictitious meeting. Either of these procedures seems like overkill for this simple tax formality.

EXAMPLE 2:

The treasurer of Best Business Bureaus, Corp., a commercial furniture supplier, decides to ask directors to approve a corporate 401(k) profit-sharing plan for employees. A special meeting of directors is scheduled to discuss whether the corporation would make matching contributions for employees and to hear various corporate personnel, including the chairperson of the Employee Benefits Committee, who wish to present different opinions to the board on the advisability of adopting a plan and the level of corporate contributions to be made.

At this meeting, comments and feedback are exchanged before the board reaches decisions on the options presented under the plan. This allows the directors a chance to discuss the financial implications and pros and cons of this important piece of corporate business.

What's the Best Way for Closely Held Corporations to Meet?

A small, closely held corporation has only a few shareholders and directors. In closely held corporations, annual meetings of directors and shareholders are held mostly as a formality. At the annual shareholders' meeting, the current board of directors is usually elected, en masse, to a new term (usually one year). At the annual directors' meeting, each current director routinely accepts office for the upcoming year.

Unless the election, or reelection, of a director is contested or an important item of business needs to be raised at an annual shareholders' or directors' meeting, many small corporations dispense with holding real annual meetings. Instead, the secretary of the corporation prepares minutes for a paper meeting showing the election of the board plus any other business

the shareholders and directors agree upon in advance.

EXAMPLE:

Windows, Drapes, Sofas and Ottomans, Inc., is a closely held corporation owned and run by Saul and Barbara, a married couple. They prepare minutes for the corporation's annual shareholders' and directors' meetings, because both are required to be held annually under provisions of the bylaws of the corporation. Of course, Saul and Barbara plan to reelect each other to the board again this year, and they discuss and plan corporate operations all the time. So their annual meetings are held on paper only. They prepare minutes for each of these paper meetings and place them in the corporate records book.

Special meetings of the board and shareholders of small closely held corporations follow a similar pattern. If the resolution or business at hand is a tax or legal formality that everyone agrees must be made, special meetings are often held on paper, not in person. But if the issue that forms the basis of the special meeting requires discussion, such as the approval of competing bids for a remodeling of corporate headquarters, then the directors often decide to get together for a real meeting. At the meeting, they discuss the pros and cons of the proposed business prior to making a decision and preparing minutes.

A "Closely Held" Corporation Is Not a "Close" Corporation

A close corporation is a specific type of small corporation set up in a corporation's articles under special state corporation laws. A close corporation can dispense with a board of directors and operate under the terms of a special close corporation shareholders' agreement. Most small corporations do not bother forming this special type of corporate entity, because corporate shareholders as well as outside lenders prefer to deal with a regular corporation where the board of directors and shareholders have traditional roles and responsibilities under state law. This book does not apply to the operations of close corporations.

The term closely held corporation has a different, less legal meaning and is used loosely in the business world. Generally, it is used to refer to a corporation owned and operated by a small number of people who work in the business and who restrict the sale of their shares to outsiders. When we use the term closely held corporation, this is what we mean.

What If You Have Inactive Directors or Shareholders?

Corporations with at least one director or shareholder who doesn't work actively in the business often find it's best to hold annual and special meetings in person. Even if the business conducted is routine, this gives the outsiders a chance to ask questions before voting on the decision at hand.

Holding an in-person meeting is particularly important for annual shareholders' meetings. Even if the election of the board is a formality, holding an annual shareholders' meeting allows outside shareholders a chance to catch up on corporate business and leave the meeting satisfied that their capital investment in the corporation is in safe, capable hands. In other words, an annual shareholders' meeting can serve the same purpose as the annual report sent to shareholders in large, publicly held corporations. It both informs shareholders about and sells them on past and future corporate operations—yes, even in small corporations, a little soft-pitch self-promotion to shareholders may be necessary.

EXAMPLE:

Flexible Fliers, Inc., a round-the-clock, go-anywhere charter airline, has three main shareholders who own a majority interest in the company and act as its only directors. Two outside shareholders, having put up a portion of the capital necessary to get the business off the ground, own minority interests in the corporation.

Each year, the corporation puts out the red carpet for the outside investors, inviting them to the annual shareholders' meeting where the annual financial and business reports of the corporation are presented by the corporate secretary and president, followed by nominations and a vote for next year's board.

Although the three main shareholders obviously have the power to reelect themselves each year and make other important corporate decisions, they go out of their way to include the outside shareholders in this decision-making process. Not only does this help give the outside directors a feeling that they are taken seriously, it gives the corporation a chance to showcase its operations and plans for future expansion. It would be legal for the corporation to prepare paper minutes for a fictional annual shareholders' meeting and circulate this document (or a written consent form) to the investors for approval, but a real meeting seems like a friendlier way to interact with the investors and foster a long-term relationship. Besides, the corporation may need to ask for additional capital in the future.

By contrast, FFI's annual directors' meeting is held on paper only—the directors have just spent half a day meeting with the outside shareholders at the annual shareholders' meeting. No one sees a need to meet again so soon after this meeting. Instead, the secretary prepares minutes for a paper meeting that shows each director accepted office for the upcoming year, plus any other formalities or decisions the directors agree should be included in and approved with these minutes.

Do All Meetings Require Minutes?

No. People who work at incorporated businesses hold many scheduled and impromptu (ad hoc) meetings throughout the year to discuss and resolve items of ongoing business. In a small corporation, the directors and shareholders who also work for the corporation are likely to be in attendance in their capacity as regular corporate employees without donning their director or shareholder hats.

Normally, you do not need to prepare corporate minutes or consents to document a garden-variety business or staff meeting. However, if what starts out as a routine matter of corporate business discussed at an informal meeting takes on important legal or tax overtones, you should record those decisions by preparing corporate minutes or consents. (See the next two questions, below, for a list of the types of decisions customarily made at formal directors' meetings and shareholders' meetings.)

EXAMPLE:
Software Works Corp., a small software company, does not need to prepare minutes for its weekly product development meetings or for its sales meetings, at which it makes important price, promotion, or distribution decisions. But if important legal or tax decisions come up at the weekly staff meeting, they should be considered either at a board meeting or, if all directors are in agreement, by use of consent forms signed by the directors. The corporation should prepare formal documentation to record the proceedings.

What Decisions Should the Board of Directors Make?

The bulk of a corporation's formal decision making is done by the board of directors. The board of directors should approve important legal, tax, and financial matters or those affecting the overall management of the corporation. Typical director decisions reached at corporate meetings or agreed to by written consent include the following:

- setting officer and key employee salary amounts and fringe benefits
- amending corporate articles of incorporation or bylaws (article amendments must usually be ratified by shareholders)
- declaring dividends
- authorizing the issuance of additional shares of stock
- purchasing insurance
- approving real estate construction, lease, purchase, or sale
- appointing key corporate officers and departmental managers, and
- approving the terms of the loan of money to or from shareholders, directors, officers, and banks or other outsiders.

> **TIP**
>
> **Ready-made resolutions help you approve specific items of business at meetings.** We include instructions on preparing tear-out resolutions for these and other common types of ongoing corporate business in Chapters 9 through 19. (See the beginning of Appendix C for a list of resolution forms included with this book, with a cross-reference to the chapter of the book that contains instructions for preparing each resolution.) These resolutions are inserted in your minutes as explained in Chapters 5 and 6.

What Decisions Are Made (or Ratified) by Shareholders?

Corporate shareholders should meet annually, typically to elect the board to another term of office. If the board of directors serves for longer than one-year terms, or if the board is divided (classified) into groups, the shareholders may meet less frequently to elect the board. Or they may only elect a portion of the board at each annual shareholders' meeting.

Shareholders are asked to participate in other corporate decisions less frequently than the board. These special shareholder decisions usually consist of structural changes to the corporation or decisions that affect the stock rights or values of the shareholders. Bylaws typically set forth the major corporate decisions that shareholders are required under state law to participate in, either by ratifying (approving) a previously reached board decision or by making a decision independent from the board. Typical shareholder decisions include the following:

- electing the board of directors
- ratifying amendments to articles
- approving changes in the rights, privileges, or preferences of shares issued by the corporation
- approving the sale of substantial corporate assets, and
- agreeing to dissolve the corporation.

What Happens If Directors and Shareholders Are the Same People?

In small, closely held corporations, the shareholders and directors are very often one and the same. Obtaining shareholders' approval is really the same as obtaining directors' approval, except the directors must put on their shareholder hats prior to attending a shareholder meeting or signing a shareholder consent form. In these situations, it's common to schedule the directors' and shareholders' meetings one after the other on the same day, or pass out both directors' and shareholders' written consent forms to each director-shareholder at the same time.

Before You Hold Your Meeting —Prep Work and Notice

If you want to hold a meeting of shareholders or directors, you'll need to call and provide notice for the meeting according to the rules in your bylaws and in your state's corporation statutes. There are important premeeting procedures that you are required to follow.

In this chapter, we explain how to take these legal steps prior to holding a meeting of your directors or shareholders. We also discuss practical measures you should take to get the most out of the meeting process. This includes preparing an agenda, sending participants necessary background information, arranging for the presentation of reports, and making arrangements to keep good minutes.

Overview of Corporate Meetings

Before you dive into the mechanics of preparing for your corporate meetings, it's helpful to know where you're headed. Here are the typical steps involved in holding a meeting of directors or shareholders:

- Meeting is called (requested) by someone authorized under the bylaws or state law to do so.
- Notice of the time, place, and purpose for the meeting is given to directors or shareholders, together with any written meeting materials.
- Meeting is held; business is discussed and approved by directors or shareholders.
- Minutes of the meeting are prepared, signed, and placed in the corporate records book.

We discuss the legal requirements and normal formalities associated with each of these steps in this chapter and subsequent chapters. We also provide commonsense compliance tips designed to allow you to meet (or exceed) any state law requirements. Finally, we make a number of practical suggestions as to how to hold a productive meeting—a goal that's easy to lose sight of if you become too focused on the legal rules.

SKIP AHEAD

One-person or family-run corporations can skip these preliminary steps. As discussed in Chapter 2 and again in Chapter 7, corporations owned and operated by one person or families normally don't need to pay attention to preliminary meeting steps and can usually forgo calling and providing notice for directors' and shareholders' meetings.

Steps to Hold a Meeting

In this section, we present and discuss in sequential order the steps you normally take to prepare for an upcoming meeting of directors or shareholders. You may wish to sidestep some of the preliminaries covered below—glance through these steps at least once, then use your best judgment in deciding which steps to take prior to convening your corporate meeting.

TIP

If you don't have time to comply with the meeting call and notice requirements, you may have other options. If yours is a corporation where all shareholders or directors get along, you can simply prepare a waiver of notice form and have it signed by each director or shareholder either before, at, or after the meeting. (See Chapter 7 for instructions on using this waiver form.) However, this less buttoned-down approach is definitely not recommended if there is dissension in the ranks of your shareholders or directors, because the dissidents may simply refuse to sign.

Step 1. Prepare a Meeting Folder

You may be surprised at the number of forms and other paperwork that even the most routine meeting can generate. We suggest you set aside a blank file folder for each upcoming meeting. Put the date and type of meeting on the tab for the folder—for example, "Annual Directors' Meeting, July 2011" or "Special Shareholders' Meeting, March 15, 2011"—and keep the folder handy.

As you create each document for your meeting, place it in this file folder. After you are through with the meeting and have prepared and completed all the paperwork, you can transfer the entire contents of the file folder into the minutes section of your corporate records book.

If you're using a computer to generate documents for your meetings, another way to keep your materials organized is to place all copies of computer files from a given meeting in one directory or folder on your hard disk. For example, you may wish to create a directory named "Director Mtg 2011" on the hard disk to hold all computer files generated for the annual 2011 meeting of directors. (Appendix A contains further instructions for working with the files included on the enclosed CD-ROM.)

Step 2. Prepare Meeting Summary Sheets

When you plan and carry out the many legal and practical details necessary to make your meeting as productive as possible, paperwork and procedures can mount up fast. To help you keep track of key dates and times and when important notices are sent, we provide a Meeting Summary Sheet on the enclosed CD-ROM and in Appendix C. This form contains spaces for you to enter information summarizing what you have done and when you have done it. And if any questions are raised later, it also serves as an excellent record of meetings held by your corporation and as documentation that the meetings were called, noticed, and held correctly. Use your Meeting Summary Sheet both as a scheduler and reminder sheet for each corporate meeting you hold.

We include room for you to insert general information on the basic call and notice requirements for meetings. Giving room for you to fill in this information on the form should help remind you of the important notice requirements as you plan your yearly list of meetings.

The corporate secretary (or other person who will call or provide notice for your meetings) should keep Meeting Summary Sheets handy and refer to them often to keep track of upcoming meetings, making revisions and additions to them as necessary. When and if a director, officer, shareholder, or other authorized person calls for a special directors' or shareholders' meeting, the secretary should create a new Meeting Summary Sheet and fill in all relevant information for the meeting.

TIP

Meeting Summary Sheets can help if you are audited. Preparing Meeting Summary Sheets for your corporation can come in handy if you later need to show the IRS and others, at a glance, that you paid serious attention to the separate legal existence of your corporation by holding shareholders' and directors' meetings. Summaries of this sort are often prepared by lawyers or tax advisors when the IRS asks to see the minutes of past corporate meetings during a tax audit. Preparing your own meeting summary forms in advance may save you time and money later.

CD-ROM

Below is a sample of the Meeting Summary Sheet included on the CD-ROM at the back of the book and in tear-out form in Appendix C. Fill it out following any special instructions provided.

Special Instructions

❶ Check the type of meeting, whether it is annual (sometimes called a regular meeting in the bylaws) or special. Indicate whether it is a directors' or shareholders' meeting.

❷ If you know the meeting date and time, fill that in. If you expect to hold a special meeting but are not sure of the exact date, make a note anyway of the possible meeting date as a reminder.

❸ Show the location of the meeting. Most meetings will be held at the principal office of the corporation.

❹ Special meetings of the board or shareholders are called by those authorized to do so under the bylaws. Special meetings may usually be called by directors, the president, a specified percentage of the shares of the corporation, or others authorized under state law or established in the bylaws. (See Step 3, below, for more on calling meetings.)

Documenting Virtual Meetings

Some companies may decide to hold a meeting via a conference telephone call, a video conference (webcam) hookup, or even a virtual meeting via a conference on a local intranet. (See Chapter 4, Step 5.) If you use any of these alternate meeting methods, make sure to specify the location and method of holding these high-tech meetings on the Meeting Summary Sheet—for example, "a video conference among the following individuals located at the following video conference sites: (*name the individuals and sites*)."

---

❺ For all meetings, set forth a brief statement of the purpose of the upcoming meeting. The purpose of an annual shareholders' meeting will usually include "the election of directors of the corporation." The purpose of annual directors' meetings is normally: "acceptance by directors of their positions on the board, discussion of the past year's activities, planning of the upcoming year's operations, and the transaction of any other proper business that may be brought before the meeting." If additional items of business are on the agenda for the meeting, state them separately as well.

❻ Indicate any financial, personal, planning, or other reports you will wish to have presented at the meeting.

❼ Check the type of notice required for the meeting, whether written or verbal, and the date by which the required notice must be mailed or given to the directors or shareholders. If no notice is required—if, for example, your bylaws dispense with the requirement for notice of an upcoming annual directors' meeting— check the "Not Required" box.

❽ Many bylaws require at least ten days' prior notice for shareholders' meetings, and at least five days' prior notice for directors' meetings. Make sure you provide at least the required notice for meetings as specified in your bylaws. As a matter of courtesy and common sense, many corporations give shareholders and directors at least three or four weeks' advance notice of all annual meetings, and as much notice as possible of special meetings. (See Step 5, below, for a discussion of notice requirements.)

Enter the date by which you need to send out or personally provide notice to the meeting participants.

❾ Once notice is actually given, fill in this portion of the form to show who received notice prior to a meeting.

Meeting Summary Sheet

Name of Corporation:

_____

Year: 20_____

Type of Meeting: ☐ Annual/Regular or ☐ Special ❶

Meeting of: ☐ Directors or ☐ Shareholders

Date: _____, 20_____ Time: _____ ❷

Place: _____ ❸

Meeting Called by: _____ ❹

Purpose: ❺ _____

_____

Committee or Other Reports or Presentations: ❻ _____

Other Reminders or Notes: _____

Notice Required: ☐ Written ☐ Verbal ☐ Not Required ❼

Notice Must Be Given by Date: _____ ❽

Notice of Meeting Given to: ❾

Name	Type of Notice*	Location or Phone Number	Date Notice Given	Date Acknowledged Receipt

*Types of Notice: written (mailed, hand-delivered); verbal (in person, telephone conversation, answering machine, voice mail); email; fax

For each person given notice, show the date and manner in which notice was given for a meeting and whether the notice was acknowledged. If you have prepared or received other documentation regarding the notice (see the Acknowledgment of Receipt and Certification of Mailing forms in Step 7 and at the end of this chapter), make a note that this material has been placed in the meeting folder or corporate records.

 REMINDER

Always provide notice of meetings.
We suggest you provide prior written notice of all directors' and shareholders' meetings stating the time, place, and purpose of the meeting, even if not legally required to do so. If you are going to go to the trouble of holding a meeting, it makes sense to give all participants early and accurate notice of where and when it will occur, and why you are holding it. Our advice goes double if you plan to consider and vote on any issues for which there may be disagreement. If dissident shareholders or directors believe you are trying to take action at a "secret meeting," this will encourage controversy and tension. See Step 5, below.

Step 3. Call the Meeting

To call a meeting of shareholders or directors, someone makes an internal request within the corporation that a meeting be scheduled. Under state law or your bylaws, particular individuals may be empowered to call meetings. Typically, the bylaws allow the president, members of the board, a specified percentage of shareholders, or others to call special corporate meetings. After the meeting is called, the secretary of the corporation provides notice of the meeting to all persons entitled to attend.

Check your bylaws to determine who may call special meetings of your corporation. If you have any questions, check your state's Business Corporation Act. (See Chapter 1.)

> **Who May Call Annual and Regular Meetings**
>
> Regular or annual meetings of directors or shareholders are not legally required to be called, because they are already scheduled in the bylaws. The secretary of the corporation is normally designated to stay on top of annual meetings, but there is always a chance that he or she may forget to remind everyone that these meetings should be held. (To avoid this, the Meeting Summary Sheet should help. We discuss how to use this in Step 2, above.)

Who May Call Special Meetings

Special meetings need to be called by someone who is legally authorized to do so. Here are the rules:

- **Special meetings of directors.** Standard bylaws require that special meetings of the board of directors be called by the president of the corporation, the director who acts as chairperson of the board, or a specified number of directors. Other officers may be allowed to call special board meetings as well; check your bylaws.

- **Special meetings of shareholders.** Typically, special meetings of shareholders must be called by a majority vote of the board of directors, by a certain percentage of the voting shares of the corporation (often at least 10%), or by the president of the corporation. The corporate statutes of all states allow shareholders' meetings to be called by the board of directors. All but a few states allow a set percentage of the shares—often 10%—to call a shareholders' meeting. About half the states specifically authorize the president to call a shareholders' meeting. In most states, the corporation can authorize persons other than those specifically mentioned in the statutes to call shareholders' meetings.

Again, check your bylaws to determine the particular persons authorized to call special shareholders' meetings of your corporation.

How and When to Call Corporate Meetings

The legal requirements for the manner and timing of calling a special directors' or shareholders' meeting are normally not specified under state law or in the bylaws (but check your bylaws just to be sure). Absent specific requirements, a meeting can be called orally or in writing, and it can be made to any corporate director or officer—we suggest the corporate secretary. However made, the call should allow enough time to:

- provide shareholders or directors with ample notice of the meeting—usually a minimum of five to ten business days (see Step 5, below), and

- prepare any necessary background material and other materials for the meeting.

Smaller corporations where directors and shareholders are in close contact and on good terms can do fine calling the meeting orally. However, larger corporations, especially those with outside directors or shareholders, or those calling for a meeting at which a hot topic will be discussed, should make a written call of the meeting to create a record of the fact that the meeting was properly called well in advance.

EXAMPLE 1:

Pants de Lyon, Inc., a Miami clothing boutique, is a small, four-shareholder corporation, owned and operated by Stephanie, Claude, and their spouses. Stephanie has been working hard to set up a pension plan for the directors/employees of the corporation. At long last, they are ready to put the plan into place. Stephanie, the president, asks Claude, the secretary, to arrange for a special directors' meeting in two weeks to approve the pension plan. Stephanie and Claude inform their respective spouses of the meeting, and no formal notice is sent out.

EXAMPLE 2:

Brick-a-Bracs Corp., a closely held home remodeling and furnishing company, is owned and run by two shareholder/director/employees, Kevin and Gale. In addition, five other people hold shares in the corporation. The bylaws allow the chairperson of the board, president, vice president, secretary, or any two directors to call a special meeting of directors or shareholders. Gale wants to change the name of their corporation.

When Gale calls the special shareholders' meeting to discuss a change in the corporate name, she considers that a couple of the shareholders have not kept in close touch with Brick-a-Bracs and know nothing about the proposed corporate name change. Even though she is confident that a change of name will be approved by the inside shareholders, she decides it will be best to document every detail of the special meeting process, and therefore gives Kevin a written call of notice.

EXAMPLE 3:

Grand Plans, Inc., is a medium-size building contractor with five directors and seven shareholders. Two key shareholders conclude that the business needs more capital and, to get it, additional stock should be sold. Because doing this will affect the rights and interests of existing shareholders, the president prepares a written call of notice for a special shareholders' meeting where an amendment to increase the capital stock of the corporation will be presented to the shareholders for approval. The president gives a written notice of call form to the corporate secretary six weeks before the desired date for the meeting.

How to Prepare a Call of Meeting Form

A written Call of Meeting form is directed to the corporate secretary. It should specify the date, time, and place of the meeting, as well as the purpose of the meeting. The secretary will need ample time to prepare and send out any notices required by either the corporation's bylaws or state law for the meeting. Typically, the secretary will need to give the directors at least five business days' advance notice and shareholders a minimum of ten business days' advance notice. Your bylaws may require a longer notice period, however. (See Step 5, below.) Of course, there should always be enough time to prepare reports, presentations, and suggested resolutions for the meeting.

CD-ROM

Below is a sample of the Call of Meeting form included on the CD-ROM. Fill it out following the special instructions provided. The tear-out version is contained in Appendix C.

Special Instructions

❶ List the name of each person calling the meeting. In the columns to the right of the name, show whether the person is a director, officer, or shareholder of the corporation and, if a shareholder, the number of shares owned by the person.

❷ Fill in "special," "annual," or "regular." Annual or regular meetings do not have to be called; they're already scheduled in the corporate bylaws. However, if you want to call the meeting as a way of keeping track of the meeting date, it's fine to do so.

❸ In the blanks after the words "for the purpose(s) of," briefly state the purpose of the meeting. Here are some suggestions.

- **Annual meeting of shareholders:** "electing the directors of the corporation."

- **Annual (or regular) meeting of directors:** "review of the prior year's business, discussion of corporate operations for the upcoming year, acceptance by the directors of another term of office on the board, and transaction of any other business that may properly come before the meeting."

- **Special meetings:** state the specific purpose for which the meeting was called, for example, "approval of a stock bonus plan for employees of the corporation."

❹ If appropriate, state the specific date or general time frame you wish the meeting to be held, such as "January 15, 2012, at 10:00 a.m.," "first Monday in June," or "latter half of the month of October." If an annual meeting, specify the time and date scheduled for the meeting in the bylaws.

❺ Date the form and have each person making the call sign below the date.

When you've completed the form, place it in the folder for the upcoming meeting or in the corporate records book.

Call of Meeting

To:

Secretary: _____

Corporation: _____

Corporation Address: _____

_____

The following person(s): ❶

Name	Title	No. Shares
_____	_____	_____
_____	_____	_____
_____	_____	_____

authorized under provisions of the bylaws of ___[name of corporation]_____,

hereby make(s) a call and request to hold a(n) ____["special," "annual," or "regular"]_____ ❷ meeting

of the _____["shareholders" or "directors"]_____ of the corporation for the purpose(s) of: ❸

_____

_____

_____

_____

_____

_____.

The date and time of the meeting requested is: ❹ _____

_____.

The requested location for the meeting is ___[the principal office of the corporation or other location]____

_____,

state of _____.

The secretary is requested to provide all proper notices as required by the bylaws of the corporation

and any other necessary materials to all persons entitled to attend the meeting.

Date: ❺ _____

Signed: _____

Step 4. Prepare a Meeting Participant List

It's important that everyone who is legally entitled to be notified of an upcoming meeting receive such notice. By preparing a Meeting Participant List, you'll organize your records and make sure that no one is overlooked. In addition, many states require that shareholder lists be prepared within a few days of the date notice is first sent out for an upcoming shareholders' meeting. But some states require the list to be prepared five, ten, or 20 days before the scheduled date of the meeting itself (check your bylaws). Generally, if the list isn't available for inspection, a complaining shareholder can petition a court to have the meeting postponed. This sort of squabbling usually only occurs in large corporations where shareholders need to contact and petition other shareholders, or assess the strength of the competition prior to a shareholders' meeting. If all shareholders sign a waiver of notice form for the meeting, state law will probably dispense with the legal requirement that the list be prepared prior to the meeting (although it still may need to be made available at the meeting). The alphabetical list should show the name and address and number of shares held by each shareholder; if the corporation has issued different classes or series of shares, the names may be listed alphabetically in separate voting groups.

CD-ROM

Below is a sample of the Meeting Participant List included on the CD-ROM. Fill it out following the special instructions provided. The tear-out version is contained in Appendix C.

Shareholders List Must Be Available at Meetings

In some states, the corporation is required to prepare an alphabetical list of shareholders who are entitled to vote at upcoming shareholders' meetings, and to have this list available for inspection by any shareholder prior to and during the meeting.

Whether or not you are required to prepare a shareholders list, it makes sense for your corporate secretary to keep an up-to-date list of your corporation's directors and shareholders for all corporate meetings. By doing this, you'll keep track of shareholders entitled to receive notice of and attend all meetings, while complying with any shareholders list requirements in your state. One easy way to meet this requirement is to keep a shareholder ledger in your corporate records book, listing the names and addresses of your shareholders. Then, simply bring your corporate records book to all shareholders' meetings.

Special Instructions

Fill in, in alphabetical order, the names, addresses, and phone numbers of:

- all directors or shareholders entitled to attend the upcoming meeting, and
- others who may attend the meeting, such as officers who will present reports at the meeting.

If you need to fill in more names than the form allows, copy the paragraphs providing information about meeting participants as many times as needed.

For shareholders' meetings, you will normally list all current shareholders of the corporation, unless:

Meeting Participant List

Name of Corporation:

_____

Type of Meeting: ☐ Annual/Regular or ☐ Special

Meeting of: ☐ Directors or ☐ Shareholders

Meeting Date: _____, 20_____

Meeting Participants (*list names in alphabetical order*):

Name: _____

Address: _____

_____ Telephone: _____

☐ Director:_____

☐ Shareholder: Number and Type of Shares: _____

☐ Officer: Title: _____

☐ Other (Position and Reason for Attendance): _____

Name: _____

Address: _____

_____ Telephone: _____

☐ Director

☐ Shareholder: Number and Type of Shares: _____

☐ Officer: Title: _____

☐ Other (Position and Reason for Attendance): _____

Name: _____

Address: _____

_____ Telephone: _____

☐ Director

☐ Shareholder: Number and Type of Shares: _____

☐ Officer: Title: _____

☐ Other (Position and Reason for Attendance): _____

- some nonvoting shares have been issued to shareholders, or

- the board has set a record date (the date by which a shareholder must own stock) for the meeting that restricts the number of shareholders who can vote at the meeting.

Record Date to Participate in Meetings

Your bylaws may set a date by which a shareholder must own shares in order to be entitled to receive notice of and vote at an upcoming shareholders' meeting. This date is called a record date.

Under state law, if the bylaws do not set a record date, the board of directors may do so. Typically, however, state law also limits how far in advance a record date may be set for eligibility to vote at a meeting. Often, the board can't require shares to be held more than 50 days (some states say 60 or 70) before the meeting. Many states also specify that a record date cannot be less than ten days before a meeting. If a record date is not set by the bylaws or directors, state law may set a default record date for the meeting, typically the day the first notice of the meeting is mailed or given to a shareholder.

Watch out for multiple record dates in your bylaws: Many bylaws also specify a record date by which a person must own shares to receive dividends or other corporate benefits. The record date we are talking about is the one for the purpose of receiving notices of, and voting at, meetings.

TIP

Send notice to all current shareholders. In privately held corporations (where there is no public trading of the corporation's stock), turnovers in corporate shares occur infrequently. Record dates (the date by which a shareholder must own stock to participate in a meeting), therefore, have little significance in determining who is entitled to notice of and vote at shareholders' meetings. Further, most small corporation boards of directors do not fix a record date for shareholders' meetings. Unless shares have recently been sold or transferred, the simplest way to deal with this issue is to provide notice to all shareholders listed on the corporate books on the day the first notice is mailed or personally given to a shareholder. If shares have been sold within the previous two to three months, check to see what your bylaws or previous actions of the board of directors require. If you find nothing, include all shareholders who own stock before the meeting.

When you've completed the form, place it in the folder for the upcoming meeting or in the corporate records book.

Step 5. Prepare Notice of the Meeting

Your next step is to provide directors or shareholders with notice of the time, place, and purpose of the meeting according to the requirements in your bylaws. If your bylaws do not specify your state's notice provisions, we suggest commonsense compliance procedures for providing notice of all meetings that should satisfy even the most stringent state law requirements.

Always Give Notice

Before we summarize the state legal requirements for providing notice of directors' and shareholders' meetings, we want to make an important practical point: Even when notice of a meeting is not legally required (as is normally the case for regular annual directors' and shareholders' meetings), you should always provide it, unless you have all directors or all shareholders sign a waiver of notice form. Your directors and shareholders can't be expected to ferret these dates out of your corporate bylaws. As a matter of courtesy, they should always be informed well ahead of time of the time, place, and purpose of all meetings.

It's particularly important to provide notice when board members or key shareholders are likely to disagree on important corporate decisions. The last thing you want is for a board member or shareholder to try to set aside a key corporate decision based on a claim that a meeting was not properly noticed.

To exceed any state's legal notice requirements, simply follow these rules:

Rule 1. Provide *written* notice of all meetings.

Rule 2. Provide notice at least five business days prior to directors' meetings—unless your bylaws require a longer prior notice period for the upcoming meeting.

Rule 3. Provide notice at least ten business days prior to shareholders' meetings (unless your bylaws require a longer prior notice period for the upcoming meeting).

Rule 4. State the purpose of the meeting in the notice.

If you follow these suggestions, you should be in compliance with even the strictest statutory notice of meeting rules (and can skip the next section on state legal requirements for notice).

If a Meeting Is Adjourned With Unfinished Business

In the world of corporate legal jargon, the word adjournment has two meanings. Most commonly, adjournment of a meeting refers to the last stage of a meeting when the business of a meeting is concluded and the meeting is ended, with the person presiding announcing, "The meeting is adjourned." However, this term is also used if a shareholders' or directors' meeting is carried over to another time when unfinished business can be concluded. The second meeting, in this case, is referred to as the adjourned meeting. Statutes that refer to notice requirements for adjourned meetings use this latter meaning.

If a shareholders' meeting is adjourned to continue business at another time, there is normally no legal requirement to send out notices of the continued (adjourned) meeting. However, notice of the new meeting may be required if it will be held at a much later date—most states require a new notice if the adjourned meeting will be held more than 120 days after the date of the first meeting.

Typically, state law does not specify a rule for providing new notice to directors of an adjourned directors' meeting. There are exceptions, however. For example, California requires that new notice for an adjourned directors' meeting be given to all directors not present at the first meeting if the new meeting will be held more than 24 hours from the time of the first meeting. (Cal. Corp. Code § 307(a)(4).) Check your bylaws to be sure of the notice rules in your state.

We suggest you use common sense and send out notice for any meeting that is carried over more than a week or so from the original meeting (unless your bylaws set a shorter standard for providing notice of the adjourned meeting). Memories are short and schedules crowded with other commitments. Besides, providing a new notice gives any shareholders or directors who happened to miss the first meeting a chance to attend the second.

Requirements for Notice

Let's look at state requirements for providing notice of directors' and shareholders' meetings. Remember: Laws change and exceptions may exist. Check your bylaws, and if your bylaws do not specify a rule, check your state corporation law, to find your state's specific rules.

Directors' Meetings

State notice requirements for directors' meetings are somewhat lenient, because directors are expected to participate in corporate affairs on a regular basis.

Annual or regular directors' meetings. The laws of many states allow the corporation to set its own notice requirements for directors' meetings in its bylaws. In a number of states, it is common for bylaws to altogether dispense with notice of annual meetings of the board.

Special directors' meetings. The required notice period ranges from two to four days prior to the meeting, unless a longer or shorter notice period is stated in the bylaws.

Manner of giving notice to directors. Generally, state law allows notice to directors to be given orally or in writing. It must include the date, time, and place of the meeting. Most state laws don't require that the purpose of the directors' meeting be placed in the notice; however, we always recommend that you do so.

Shareholders' Meetings

The state law rules for providing notice of shareholders' meetings are stricter than those that apply to directors' meetings.

Regular and special meetings. In all states, written notice of the date, place, and time of all shareholders' meetings, whether annual or special, must be given to shareholders. Typically, notice must be given no more than 60 (sometimes 50) and not less than ten (sometimes less, such as five) days before the meeting.

Shareholders legally entitled to notice. Usually, all persons holding voting shares are entitled to receive written notice of a shareholders' meeting, as long as the shares were acquired at least ten to 70 days before the meeting. In the great majority of small corporations, this means all shareholders are entitled to notice of, and are allowed to vote at, shareholders' meetings.

> **CAUTION**
>
> **Nonvoting shares may be entitled to notice.** Corporations occasionally issue nonvoting shares to investors, employees, and others. Nonvoting shareholders may be required to receive notice of an upcoming shareholders' meeting if the rights, preferences, or restrictions associated with their shares will be affected or if certain fundamental corporate changes are proposed for approval at the meeting. For example, an amendment of the articles of incorporation, a merger or dissolution of the corporation, or a sale of major corporate assets that is not done in the normal course of corporate business may require notice to all shareholders, voting and nonvoting. Check your bylaws to see if special rules of this sort apply.

Notice to shareholders. All shareholder notices should be in writing. The notice should state the time, place, and date of the upcoming meeting. The purpose of the meeting should also be placed in the notice (even though some states allow any business to be approved at annual shareholders' meetings even if not stated in the notice). For special shareholders' meetings, state law generally provides that only the matters listed in the notice for the meeting can be approved by the shareholders at the meeting.

EXAMPLE:

Time Line, Incorporated, holds a special meeting of shareholders with the stated purpose of amending the articles of the corporation to increase the shares of the corporation. But during the meeting, it becomes obvious that a second class of nonvoting shares also needs to be approved. Several shareholders have strong feelings about this turn of events and refuse to address the issue in the meeting. Legally, they have the right to insist that this new issue be dealt with in another meeting called for the specific purpose of establishing a new class of nonvoting shares, because the notice for the current meeting only mentioned increasing the existing shares. A harsh result, perhaps, but it's the law under most bylaws.

When shareholders are willing to expand the scope of the meetings, it's possible to use a shareholder consent form to approve unexpected resolutions. These are ideal for on-the-spot decisions that need to be approved quickly without time-consuming notices or other formalities. (See Chapter 8.)

Fill in Notice of Meeting Form

If you have decided to provide written notice of an upcoming meeting, fill in the Notice of Meeting form included on the enclosed CD-ROM as you follow the sample form and instructions.

CD-ROM

Below is a sample of the Notice of Meeting form included on the CD-ROM. Fill it out following any special instructions provided. The tear-out version is contained in Appendix C.

Special Instructions

❶ If the meeting is scheduled in your bylaws, use the term annual or regular (some bylaws schedule more than one meeting per year for directors or shareholders; if so, these are normally called regular meetings). For all other meetings, insert special.

❷ Corporate meetings are normally held at the principal office of the corporation, although state law and corporate bylaws usually allow directors' and shareholders' meetings to be held anywhere within or outside the state.

❸ Make sure you schedule the meeting far enough in advance to comply with state law requirements. If you don't have time to give the required notice, then make sure to have each director or shareholder sign a written waiver of notice form as explained in Chapter 7. (You can still prepare and send out a Notice of Meeting form as explained here to give your directors or shareholders advance notice, but it will not be legally effective.)

❹ Succinctly state the purpose(s) of the meeting. Here are some suggestions:

- **Annual meeting of shareholders:** "electing the directors of the corporation"

- **Annual (or regular) meeting of directors:** "reviewing the prior year's business, discussing corporate operations for the upcoming year, acceptance by the directors of another term of office on the board, and transaction of any other business that may properly come before the meeting," and

- **Special meetings:** state the specific purpose for which the meeting was called, for example, "approval of a stock bonus plan for employees of the corporation."

Notice of Meeting of

_____ [name of corporation] _____

A(n) _____ ❶ meeting of the _____ ["shareholders" _or_ "directors"] _____ of

_____ [name of corporation] _____ will be held at

❷ _____ [location of meeting] _____,

state of _____, on _____, 20____ at ____:____ ___.M. ❸

The purpose(s) of the meeting is/are as follows: ❹

_____

_____

_____

_____

_____

_____

_____

_____

_____

_____

_____

_____

_____.

❺ If you are a shareholder and cannot attend the meeting and wish to designate another person to vote

your shares for you, please deliver a signed proxy form to the secretary of the corporation before the

meeting. Contact the secretary if you need help obtaining or preparing this form.

_____

Signature of Secretary

Name of Secretary: _____

Corporation: _____

Address: _____

Phone: _____ Fax: _____

RELATED TOPIC

Ready-to-use resolutions for special business. Chapters 9 through 19 contain instructions on approving various types of ongoing corporate business—see the beginning of Appendix C for a list of tear-out and CD-ROM resolution forms included with this book, with a cross-reference to the chapter of the book that contains instructions for preparing each resolution. You may want to skip ahead at this point and review any legal or tax ramifications discussed there for one or more items of special business listed in your notice form.

As discussed in Step 6, below, you will probably want to send out additional background material with your notice to help your directors or shareholders understand the issues to be discussed at the upcoming meeting.

CAUTION

Make sure to state the purposes of special shareholders' meetings in the written notice form. Under most bylaws, you can't approve any items at a special shareholders' meeting unless the general nature of the proposal was included in a written notice (or waiver of notice) of the meeting. If you follow our commonsense suggestions above, you've already got this requirement covered.

TIP

Use an agenda to give notice of all items to be considered at a meeting. One way to fully inform all potential participants of the business to be proposed at the meeting is to prepare and send out an agenda for the meeting listing all of the items and business that will be discussed or proposed for approval. We discuss the preparation of an agenda further in Step 6, below. If you decide to do this, fill in this blank as follows: "see the enclosed agenda for the meeting."

❺ This is an optional paragraph that you may wish to include in a notice for an upcoming shareholders' meeting. It alerts shareholders of their legal right to notify the secretary of the corporation prior to the meeting if they wish to have another person vote for them at the meeting. (For instructions on preparing a proxy form for an upcoming shareholders' meeting, see Step 8, below.)

Step 6. Prepare a Premeeting Information Packet

You will probably wish to include meeting materials when sending out notices of an upcoming meeting to directors and shareholders. You may wish to provide this material even if you do not send out a formal written notice of the meeting. (If you provide verbal notice of an annual shareholders' meeting or dispense with notice completely by having shareholders or directors sign a written consent, see Chapter 8.)

To prepare people adequately for a meeting, especially those who are not involved in the day-to-day management of the corporation, it normally makes sense to send out:

- **An agenda for the meeting.** This should include new business, as well as any unfinished business from a prior meeting.

- **Copies of reports, presentations, and background material.** Include all materials that may help your directors or shareholders become informed on the issues to be decided at the upcoming meeting. Doing this not only saves time at the meeting, but helps your corporation make better decisions.

- **Copies of proposed corporate resolutions.** Use one of the ready-made corporate resolutions contained on the CD-ROM. (See the beginning of Appendix C for a list of CD-ROM resolution forms included with this book, with a cross-reference to the chapter of the book that contains instructions for preparing each resolution.) If an item of business is covered by one of our resolution forms, you can prepare your own without much trouble. (See the instructions to any of the minutes forms contained in Chapters 5 and 6.)

- **Minutes of the last shareholders' or directors' meeting.** If you want to approve the minutes from the last meeting, include a copy. To save time at the meeting, you may wish to enclose an approval form with your prior minutes to allow directors or shareholders to sign off on the last meeting's minutes before the upcoming meeting. (See Chapter 7 for instructions on preparing an Approval of Corporate Minutes form.)

- **Shareholder proxies.** You may wish to enclose a blank proxy form with notice of a shareholders' meeting if you anticipate that one or more shareholders will wish to send another person to the meeting to vote his or her shares. (See Step 8, below.)

- **Proof of receipt.** If you want the shareholders or directors to acknowledge that they received notice of the meeting, send an Acknowledgment of Receipt of Notice of Meeting form to be signed and returned. (See Step 7, below.)

Step 7. Prepare Acknowledgment of Receipt Forms (Optional)

For important or controversial meetings, you may wish to dot all the "i"s and cross all the "t"s by preparing documentation that helps you establish the fact that all directors or shareholders actually received notice of the meeting. This may be particularly important if you have outside directors or shareholders and don't follow our advice to provide written notice to everyone (for example, you call or provide other oral notice instead). Below are procedures and forms you can use to create a record that notice was properly received by your directors or shareholders.

CD-ROM

Below is a sample of the Acknowledgement of Receipt of Notice of Meeting form included on the CD-ROM and as a tear-out. Note that you should fill out a separate form for each person acknowledging notice.

Special Instructions

❶ Check the box to indicate how notice was received. Fill in the recipient's telephone number or other information requested.

❷ The person who received the notice should date and sign the form. You may print his or her name on the appropriate line.

❸ To ensure that you receive the acknowledgment, fill in the secretary's name, address (include city, state, and zip), and fax number.

Place a copy of the acknowledgment in the folder for the upcoming meeting or in your corporate records book.

Acknowledgment of Receipt of Notice of Meeting

I received notice of a(n) _____ ["annual," "regular," *or* "special"] _____ meeting of the ___ ["directors" *or*

___ "shareholders"] _____ of _____ [*name of corporation*] _____ on _____

_____ [*leave date blank*] _____ , 20____ . The notice of meeting stated the date, time, place, and purpose of the

upcoming meeting.

The notice of meeting was: **❶**

☐ received by fax, telephone number _____

☐ delivered orally to me in person

☐ delivered orally to me by phone call, telephone number _____

☐ left in a message on an answering machine or voice mail, telephone number _____

_____

☐ delivered by mail to _____

☐ delivered via email, email address: _____

☐ other: _____

_____

_____

_____

Dated: _____ **❷**

Signed: _____

Printed Name: _____

Please return to: **❸**

Name: _____

Corporation: _____

Address: _____

Phone: _____ Fax: _____

Step 8. Prepare Proxies for Shareholders' Meetings (Optional)

A proxy lets a shareholder authorize another person to vote his or her shares at an upcoming shareholders' meeting. Larger corporations, or those that have shareholders scattered throughout a wide geographic region, may routinely include a blank proxy form with the notice and other premeeting materials sent to shareholders. For smaller corporations, there is no legal requirement or need to use proxy forms. This is because most of the time there is no desire on the part of a shareholder who will miss a meeting to authorize someone else to vote in his or her stead. However, in rare instances, you may be asked to provide a proxy to a shareholder prior to an upcoming meeting.

CD-ROM

Below is a sample of the Proxy form included on the CD-ROM and as a tear-out in Appendix C. Fill it out following the special instructions provided.

Special Instructions

❶ Leave a blank line here. The shareholder will insert the name of the proxyholder—this is the person who is authorized by the shareholder to vote his or her shares at the upcoming meeting of shareholders.

❷ Some corporate statutes limit the validity of a written proxy to as little as a six-month period, so the shareholder should date and sign the form less than six months prior to the scheduled date of the shareholders' meeting.

❸ Insert the date prior to the meeting for return of the proxy to the corporate secretary. This lets the secretary know in advance that a proxyholder will attend the upcoming shareholders' meeting.

❹ Normally, proxies are sent out by and returned to the corporate secretary.

Remember to place copies of all completed proxies in the folder or corporate records book for the shareholders' meeting to which they apply.

Step 9. Distribute Notice Forms and Information Packet

Have the secretary of your corporation mail or personally deliver the Notice of Meeting form to your directors or shareholders, together with any premeeting information you prepared under Step 6, above. If the information is mailed, use the exact address of the director or shareholder as shown in your corporate records. On the Meeting Summary Sheet (Step 2, above), have the secretary complete the lines at the bottom of the form indicating how and when each director or shareholder was given the notice form. Place the notated Meeting Summary Sheet in your master folder for the meeting or your corporate records book.

When to Use Certified Mail

Using first class mail for notices of meetings is all that's legally required. However, if you have dissident directors or shareholders, or have another good reason to want to be able to show that a person actually received a mailed notice, send these materials by certified mail with a return receipt requested. Place the certification number or return receipt in your meeting folder or corporate records book.

Proxy

The undersigned shareholder of _____ [*name of corporation*] _____ authorizes

_____ ❶ to act as his/her proxy and to

represent and vote his/her shares at a(n) _____ ["annual," "regular," *or* "special"] _____ meeting of

shareholders to be held at _____ [*location of meeting*] _____,

state of _____, on _____, 20____ at ____:____ __.M.

Dated: _____ ❷

Signature of Shareholder: _____

Printed Name of Shareholder: _____

Please return proxy by ❸ _____, 20_____ to:

Name: _____

Title: ❹ _____

Corporation: _____

Address: _____

City, State, Zip: _____

Fax: _____ Phone: _____

Notice by Voicemail, Email, or Fax

You may decide to provide notice of corporate meetings orally—in person, by phone, by answering machine, or by voicemail. This is particularly likely to happen in small, closely held corporations where a few people own and run the corporation and pay less attention to the procedural niceties of corporate life. If you give notice orally, it's wise to prepare documentation showing how and when the oral notice was given.

There are a number of electronic ways to provide and prove the giving of notice to directors and shareholders. For example, you may decide to email or fax notice of an upcoming meeting instead of personally delivering or mailing written notice. Although not specifically authorized under most corporate statutes, using email or a fax to send a written notice to a director or shareholder should meet the substance, if not letter, of legal notice requirements. Of course, the notice must be received by the director or shareholder within the proper number of days before the meeting.

Whatever method you use, be sure to take sensible steps to show that notice was properly sent to or received by your directors or shareholders within the proper number of days before the meeting. (In Step 7, above, we explain methods of proving receipt of notice of meeting by directors and shareholders.)

In-House Certification of Mailing Form (Optional)

If you don't want to take the time to send notices by certified mail, you can prepare an in-house certification of mailing form. In this form, your corporate secretary certifies that notice for an upcoming meeting was properly mailed to directors or shareholders.

Make sure to attach a copy of the notice prepared and mailed by the secretary to the form, and place this paperwork in your meeting folder or corporate records book.

CD-ROM

Below is a sample of the Certification of Mailing form included on the CD-ROM. Fill it out following any special instructions provided. The tear-out version is contained in Appendix C.

Certification of Mailing

I, the undersigned acting secretary of _____ [*name of corporation*] _____ ,

hereby certify that I caused notice of the _____ ["annual," "regular," *or* "special"] _____ meeting of the

_____ ["shareholders" *or* "directors"] _____ of _____ [*name of corporation*] _____ ,

to be held on _____ , 20_____ , to be deposited in the United States mail,

postage prepaid, on _____ , 20_____ , addressed to the

_____ ["shareholders" *or* "directors"] _____ of the corporation at their most recent addresses as shown

☐ on the books of this corporation

☐ as follows:

_____

_____

_____

_____

_____

_____

_____

_____

_____

_____

_____

_____

_____

_____

_____

_____

_____

A true and correct copy of such notice is attached to this certificate.

Dated: _____

Signed: _____

Printed Name: _____

How to Hold a Directors' or Shareholders' Meeting

In this chapter, we look at the basic steps necessary to hold a successful meeting of your directors or shareholders. Don't be daunted by the fact that we present a comprehensive list of possible premeeting steps below. As noted, only a few of these are legally required, and you can skip and combine the others as you see fit. Also, don't worry that you'll miss an important step—the minutes forms set out in the next two chapters remind you to take care of all legally required steps as you prepare those forms.

> **SKIP AHEAD**
>
> **If you know how to hold meetings.** If you're experienced in holding meetings of directors and shareholders and wish to get right to the task of preparing your minutes, skip to Chapter 5 or 6. Likewise, if you wish to document a directors' or shareholders' decision without holding a real meeting, skip to Chapter 7 to prepare minutes for a paper meeting or to Chapter 8 to take action by written consent.

> **TIP**
>
> **If you neglect to hold or document a meeting.** Preparing paper minutes is a good way to document past decisions. Obviously, if you failed to hold an annual meeting last year, it's too late to hold a real meeting. This can be a problem if you undergo a tax audit or simply wish your corporate records to include past directors' and shareholders' meetings that were not properly documented. The best way to catch up on corporate paperwork is to follow the paper meeting approach, which allows you to quickly document decisions after the fact. (See "Using Paper Meetings to Create Records for Prior Undocumented Meetings" in Chapter 7.)

Step 1. Call and Provide Notice of the Meeting

Before holding your meeting, it's standard procedure to call and provide notice of the meeting according to the legal requirements contained in your bylaws. The steps you'll take to accomplish these tasks are fully described in Chapter 3.

> **TIP**
>
> **You can bypass normal notice requirements.** If you wish to sidestep all legal requirements for calling and noticing your meeting, your directors or shareholders may sign a waiver of notice form. Dispensing with notice of an upcoming meeting is particularly appropriate for small corporations whose directors and shareholders are all involved in the business and maintain regular contact. (See Chapter 7.)

Step 2. Prepare Your Agenda

Especially for larger meetings, the chairperson's job will be easier if he or she has a written agenda that lists the order of business for the meeting. (See Chapter 3, Step 6, for a discussion of preparing a premeeting agenda.) An agenda can help the chairperson keep an eye on the clock, making sure that all proposed items are covered within the time allotted for the meeting.

Step 3. Prepare Your Resolutions in Advance

As a practical matter, it is usually best to prepare a draft of resolutions to be introduced at a meeting ahead of time. Drafting suitable resolutions for approval at meetings involves understanding the issues involved and using language that clearly states the business or matters approved by the board of directors or shareholders.

You don't need to use fancy or legal language for your resolution; just describe as specifically as you can the transaction or matter approved by your board or shareholders in a short, concise statement. Normally, resolutions start with a preamble of the following sort: "The (board or shareholders) resolved that…" but this is not required.

Following are some examples of resolutions:

EXAMPLE 1 (Bank Loan): "The board resolved that the treasurer be authorized to obtain a loan from (*name of bank*) for the amount of $_____ on terms he/she considers commercially reasonable."

EXAMPLE 2 (Corporate Hiring): "The board approved the hiring of (*name of new employee*), hired in the position of (*job title*) at an annual salary of $_____ and in accordance with the terms of the corporation's standard employment contract."

EXAMPLE 3 (Tax Year): "The board decided that the corporation shall adopt a tax year with an ending date of 3/31."

EXAMPLE 4 (Amendment of Articles): "The shareholders resolved that the following new article be added to the corporation's articles of incorporation: (*language of new article*)."

Each of these matters is covered in a specific resolution included with this book, and explained in the latter chapters. We offer the language above just to show you how to go about preparing your own resolution if you can't find one of our resolutions to handle the upcoming business planned for your meeting.

Step 4. Gather for Your Meeting

Your next step is to have the directors or shareholders meet at the time and place specified in your notice of the meeting. Most corporate bylaws select the principal office of the corporation as the place where meetings are held, but usually also allow meetings to be held at any location inside or outside the state as designated by the board of directors. (For a discussion of several state-of-the-art ways to hold a meeting over phone lines, on computer bulletin boards, or via videoconference hookups, see Step 5, just below.)

Step 5. Hold a Virtual Meeting

This section is not a separate, consecutive step in the corporate meeting process—rather, it is a discussion of alternative ways of convening corporate meetings. If you plan to meet in person, you can skip this step and proceed to Step 6. If you're interested in setting up a meeting without the need to get everyone together at the same physical location, we hope this step gives useful suggestions for utilizing modern technology to help streamline the corporate meeting process.

Telecommunications advances now allow a number of people to simultaneously communicate over phone lines using telephone, video (such as webcam), and computer conference hookups. The fast-widening horizons of cloud computing allow corporate and business meetings to be held from separate locations without the need for participants to be in the same physical location.

Most existing corporate statutes are worded broadly enough to allow directors and shareholders to meet using a means of telecommunication that allows the participants to hear one another simultaneously. Do the participants in an online chat "hear" each other, even though each person's comments are displayed on a computer screen? We think the answer is "yes" and that you should be safe in discussing and concluding business over a computer network this way. However, if you anticipate that any director or shareholder may object to a meeting that's not held in person, or if a matter to be resolved at a meeting is controversial, it's best to meet in person.

Here is a short review of three of the most common types of alternative meeting technologies available today.

Telephone conference call. Many modern office and home telephone systems have a built-in capability for one person to call and add additional callers in a conference call conversation.

If you don't have conference call capability, the local phone company can hook up a third party to a two-person call on a one-time basis for a special charge. If you need to link additional callers, the conference center of your local phone company can arrange a multiparty telephone conference at an additional charge (on top of local and long-distance phone charges). Of course, you will have to go through a long-distance telephone carrier if you want to link up directors or shareholders in different states or in widely separated locations.

Videoconference meetings. PCs with webcams and VOIP (voice over Internet protocol) technology allow participants to establish audio/visual conference calls. At the high end, the cost to rent a commercial video conference site typically starts at about $300 per hour. Or there is Skype, which is free for certain uses.

Online chat conference. Using the Internet or a private intranet, you can invite others to participate in a private meeting conference. The person coordinating the meeting notifies the other participants, each of whom must log onto the meeting, using a password or PIN (personal identification number). As each person signs on, the meeting coordinator, who is already logged into the meeting, invites each participant to chat, thereby linking everyone together in one online conversation. Each participant types his or her comments on a computer screen for others to view.

To avoid confusion and fast-scrolling over-lapping messages, the meeting chairperson should introduce and lead each discussion, asking each of the participants in turn for comments and votes on each matter. The secretary of the meeting can capture all dialogue on the screen by saving it to a computer file. Once the meeting is concluded and each participant has signed off, the secretary can assemble, format, and print the contents of the screen dialogue saved in the computer file, making a copy for each participant to review and approve.

Formal Rules for Running a Meeting

You can plan your meeting to be as formal or informal as you wish in raising, seconding, and voting on items of business. We do not include a guide to the many parliamentary rules and procedures (formal rules for conducting meetings) that can be used to run directors' and shareholders' meetings because we believe they are usually unnecessary. If your corporation has only a few shareholders and directors, a conversational format will probably work best. For slightly larger meetings, we have found that an agreeable, but no-nonsense, chairperson is required to keep meetings on track.

Corporations with more than about ten directors or shareholders may need to establish more detailed ground rules for meetings. For example, you may wish to call on board members or shareholders individually to elicit comments and opinions prior to a vote, setting a time limit for remarks to five minutes or so. Or directors may wish to have motions formally proposed, seconded, and discussed before the question is called and a vote taken.

If you need guidance in setting ground rules or formality, you can use formal parliamentary procedures. For a remarkably easy-to-use guide to implementing the most commonly used parliamentary procedures at meetings, see *Parliamentary Law at a Glance,* by E.C. Utter (The Reilly & Lee Co.). You can also check the ever-popular Robert's Rules of Order.

Step 6. Appoint a Chairperson and Secretary

Before the meeting begins, you'll need to find people to fulfill two important roles at the meeting:

- **Chairperson.** This person, usually the president, directs the activity at the meeting.
- **Secretary.** Someone different from the chairperson acts as secretary of the meeting. He or she takes notes of the order and outcome of business discussed and voted upon at the meeting. These notes will be used later to fill in the blanks on the minutes forms, as explained in succeeding chapters. In almost all cases, corporations choose the corporate secretary as the secretary for corporate meetings. In the minutes forms presented in later chapters, we assume you will follow this traditional practice.

Exactly how a meeting is organized and conducted and how each person does each job at the meeting is up to you. Aside from imposing quorum and voting requirements, state corporation law generally does not concern itself with parliamentary procedures used at meetings. For a discussion of practical steps to take to introduce, discuss, and vote on proposals at corporate meetings, see Step 12, below.

Step 7. Calling the Meeting to Order

The chairperson normally calls the meeting to order by announcing that it's time to begin. The chairperson then directs the order in which business will be covered at the meeting. Typically, the chairperson will introduce some items and call on others to take the lead for certain items of business. For example, the chairperson may ask the secretary of the meeting to read a proposal and take the votes after the issue is discussed.

Note-Taking Made Easy

The secretary of your meeting does not need to provide a longhand narrative of all the happenings at a corporate meeting. It is normally enough to list who is present, the nature of the proposals raised, and the outcome of votes taken. This information can then be used to complete the minutes forms on the CD-ROM (including the ready-to-use resolutions, which can be inserted in your final minutes as explained in Chapters 5 and 6). The quickest method is for the secretary to fill in final versions of the minutes forms and resolutions using a computer at the meeting and making any necessary changes on the spot.

Another workable approach is for the secretary to use a fill-in-the-blanks minutes form at the meeting, inserting ready-to-use resolutions from this book or the text of your own resolutions as the meeting progresses. You can use the completed form as your final minutes if it is prepared neatly; or, more typically, you can use it as a draft and later transfer the information to the final version of your minutes form.

Step 8. Do You Have a Quorum?

The secretary should note those present and absent from the meeting, making sure that a quorum of directors or shareholders is in attendance. If you followed our suggestion in Chapter 3, Step 5, and sent written notice of the meeting to directors or shareholders ahead of time, you should have a quorum (the minimum number of directors or shareholders needed to hold a meeting). If a quorum is not present, the chairperson should adjourn the meeting to a new time and date. (See Chapter 3, Step 5, for a discussion of the requirements for providing notice for the new meeting.)

Your bylaws should state the quorum requirements for directors' and shareholders' meetings. Below we discuss the typical quorum requirements found in most bylaws.

Establishing a Quorum at Directors' Meetings

Most bylaws, and the laws of the various states, set a quorum for directors' meetings at a majority of the authorized number of directors. The authorized number of directors is the total number of slots on your board, whether or not each board position is filled. Some states may allow business corporations to set a higher or lower quorum in their bylaws, as long as any lesser quorum requirement does not fall below a set statutory minimum (often established as one-third of the full board). For example, smaller corporations—often those with five or fewer members—may wish to ensure a significant director presence by imposing a two-thirds quorum requirement for board meetings. Conversely, larger corporations with larger boards may feel encumbered with a majority-quorum rule and decide to set a board quorum at a less-than-majority percentage or number—for example, one-third of the directors or eight out of 20 directors.

EXAMPLE:

The bylaws of Best Health Corporation state that the corporation shall have seven directors and that a majority of the authorized number of directors represents a quorum for directors' meetings. Four directors, therefore, must attend board meetings for business to be discussed and approved. This is true even if any slot on the board is currently vacant.

CAUTION

A quorum must be present to take action. For the directors to take action, a quorum must be present at the meeting. If a quorum of directors is not present at a directors' meeting, or someone leaves and the quorum is broken, the meeting must be adjourned until another time when a quorum of directors is present for the meeting.

Establishing a Quorum at Shareholders' Meetings

Bylaws usually define a quorum for shareholders' meetings as a majority of the shares (not shareholders) entitled to vote on the matters presented at the meeting. Some states permit this majority-quorum rule for shareholders' meetings to be changed in the articles or bylaws. To determine your shareholders' meeting quorum requirements, as always, check your bylaws.

For the great majority of smaller corporations that have only one class of voting shares, this means all shareholders are entitled to vote on matters presented at shareholders' meetings. Unlike the director-meeting quorum rule, this rule relates to the number of votes, not the number of people present at a meeting. Since shareholders are given one vote per share under standard bylaws, shareholders holding a majority of the shares must be present (in person or by proxy) to hold a shareholders' meeting.

Shares represented by proxies are entitled to vote at the meeting. A proxy is a signed statement by a shareholder authorizing another person to vote his or her shares at the meeting. (See Chapter 3, Step 8, for instructions on preparing the proxy form included on the CD-ROM.)

If you have issued nonvoting shares or have special classes or series of shares that are excluded from voting on particular issues, you do not normally count these nonvoting shares in determining if a quorum is present.

EXAMPLE:

Green Construction Corporation has 600 shares outstanding, but only 500 are voting shares. The corporation ignores the 100 nonvoting shares in its calculation of a quorum. If 251 out of the 500 voting shares attend a meeting, there is a majority quorum.

CAUTION

Be aware of voting rules for special classes of shares. In special cases—for example, when asking shareholders to approve an increase in one class of stock—other classes of shares, whether voting or nonvoting, may be entitled to vote on the proposal if their interests may be adversely affected by the increase. Your bylaws should alert you to any special situations where nonvoting shares or other special classes or series of shares may be entitled to vote at a shareholders' meeting.

Unlike the rule for directors' meetings, a quorum for shareholders' meetings needs to be established only once, at the beginning of the meeting. Even if shareholders owning a number of shares (or individuals holding proxies) sufficient to lose a quorum leave the meeting, the remaining shareholders can continue to take valid, legal action at the meeting. The reason for allowing continued action at shareholders' meetings is to counter quorum-busting tactics historically used at shareholders' meetings convened by larger, publicly traded corporations. There, persons holding significant numbers of shareholder votes would leave a meeting to prevent a shareholder vote on an item they opposed but didn't have sufficient votes to stop.

> **CAUTION**
>
> **Be wary when shareholders leave the meeting.** If you face a controversial decision in the context of a shareholders' meeting where you no longer have a quorum, take heed. Some states provide that the remaining shareholders can only take action by marshaling a number of votes (shares) at least equal to a majority of the required quorum. For example, let's say 1,000 shares must be present or represented at a shareholders' meeting to meet a corporation's quorum requirement. If 1,000 attend and 250 shares leave the meeting, there's no problem as long as 501 shares vote in favor of the resolution presented at the meeting. But if 500 or more shares leave, then many states prohibit any further action, since a majority of the required quorum will not be able to vote in favor of actions brought before the meeting. If your state imposes a special voting rule after the loss of a quorum at shareholders' meetings, it should be restated in your bylaws.

Step 9. Approve Minutes From Last Meeting

After determining that a quorum is present at the meeting, it is customary, but not legally required, for the secretary of the meeting to read or summarize the minutes of the last meeting, after which the minutes are approved by the participants. This is a polite and efficient way to have everyone agree that the written minutes for the prior meeting properly reflect and summarize the actions taken and decisions reached at that meeting. Often, a board member will have a small correction which can be made to the minutes. It is up to the president or chairperson to accomplish this without having meeting participants completely rehash the proceedings of the prior meeting.

> **TIP**
>
> **Save time by sending out minutes in advance.** To save the trouble and boredom of reading and discussing minutes of a prior meeting at the current meeting, you can send them out as part of the premeeting packet discussed in Chapter 3, Step 6.

Step 10. Reports by Officers and Committees

The next item on the agenda of many meetings is for the chairperson to call on committees of the board, corporate officers, department managers, and outside consultants or advisors to present or hand out presentations or reports at the meeting. Obviously, if all board members or shareholders work in the business and are fully current on its affairs, presenting formal reports may not be necessary. But when shareholders or board members are not in day-to-day contact with the business, these summaries can be extremely valuable.

> **TIP**
>
> **Do the dollars first.** In our experience, it makes sense to review the corporation's profit and loss picture first, as these are the figures everyone is most interested in.

Reports are often made to update those present at the meeting on past or projected corporate operations or a particular aspect of corporate performance, such as the corporation's net worth reflected on the latest balance sheet or upcoming plans for increasing the corporation's market share of sales in a particular area of operation. Reports can also provide shareholders or directors with the information necessary to make an informed decision on an issue. For instance, it would be helpful to have a discussion of important options associated with the adoption of a 401(k) profit-sharing plan or a report by the president explaining the reasons for the creation and issuance of a new class of shares.

EXAMPLE:

Prior to proposing a vote on a resolution to increase the coverage limits of the corporation's product liability insurance, the chief financial officer summarizes current coverage limits and options for increased coverage based upon data obtained from the corporation's insurance broker. Next, the corporation's outside legal advisor gives a report summarizing current trends and outcomes in product liability law cases in operations related to the corporation's product line.

One question that often arises when small corporations hold their annual shareholders' meeting is whether it is better to present reports at the shareholders' meeting or at the annual directors' meeting that usually follows on the same day. Our preference is to present reports at the directors' meeting, because this enhances the directors' protection from personal liability for decisions based on the reports. (See "Don't Underestimate the Importance of Reports," below.) If you have considerably more shareholders than directors, however, you'll want the reports to be heard or read by as many interested people as possible, and the shareholders to be kept fully informed of business operations and performance. One way to achieve these goals is to convene your shareholders' meeting first to elect the directors (as you would normally). Once elections are

completed, immediately adjourn the meeting and reconvene as a directors' meeting, asking all nondirector-shareholders to stay to hear the reports that will be presented at this second meeting.

EXAMPLE:

At the annual shareholders' meeting for Yolodyne Corp., the board is reelected for another term. The shareholders' meeting is adjourned, and the annual directors' meeting convened with all shareholders still in attendance. At the directors' meeting, the chairperson calls on the treasurer to report on past and projected balance sheet figures, followed by a report by the president outlining new operations planned for the upcoming year. Providing past and prospective information of this sort to shareholders (as well as directors) can be essential to keep outside investors satisfied with the work goals and performance of the corporate management and staff.

TIP

Try to avoid presenting completely new material. To save time at meetings, and to avoid surprise, we recommend that reports and background information be mailed to directors or shareholders prior to the meeting. (See Chapter 3, Step 6.) The presenters can then restrict their comments to reviewing the gist of the circulated report, emphasizing the most important points.

Don't Underestimate the Importance of Reports

In an effort to give corporate board members an additional measure of legal protection—and to increase their comfort level when discharging their managerial duties—the statutes of many states specifically immunize a director from personal liability if he or she relied on these reports when reaching a decision, unless the director knew, or should have known, that the information submitted in the report was unreliable.

Reports at shareholders' meetings can have another, broader purpose: They are an excellent way to keep shareholders informed of corporate operations and performance. Such reports not only provide a good jumping-off point for discussion at the meeting, they can also head off objections by shareholders who otherwise might claim that they hadn't been kept informed.

Step 11. Introduce and Discuss Specific Proposals

After any reports or background presentations have been made at the meeting, the chairperson or another board member will normally want to formally introduce proposals for discussion and vote by the directors or shareholders. Proposals are best introduced in the form of resolutions that clearly and legally state the item of business or matter to be approved. This allows you to include the exact language of the resolution in your minutes, with no need to reword it later.

REMINDER

Resolutions reminder. This book provides over 80 ready-to-use resolution forms that address common types of ongoing business raised at corporate meetings. If you need to prepare your own resolution, use short and simple language—avoid legalese. See the examples given in Step 3, above.

Introducing Resolutions at Directors' Meetings

The procedures used by corporations to introduce, discuss, and decide board of directors' resolutions take many forms. Typically, the chairperson or another participant at the board meeting follows a prepared agenda to introduce a proposal to be discussed, such as whether or not to increase the liability limits of the corporation's general liability insurance policy. The proposal can be introduced by way of a formal motion that is seconded by another participant and then discussed. Or a proposal can simply be introduced by the chairperson with the assumption that some discussion will occur before a formal motion is made.

Either way, a discussion of the merits and possible parameters of the proposal is likely unless all board members are already fully informed and ready to vote. For example, the president, acting as chairperson, might introduce an agenda item consisting of a resolution to increase corporate insurance coverage. The board members discuss whether and how much extra insurance coverage is necessary. Once the general discussion is over, a board member can either propose adopting the resolution if one has been introduced, or propose specific language for the resolution.

After a resolution has been introduced and discussed, it's normal to move for a voice vote on the resolution. However, experienced chairpersons, aware of the desirability of achieving a consensus, will be sensitive to divergent views and, if consistent with getting necessary business accomplished, will normally allow members to suggest modifications to the resolution prior to calling for a vote. For example, a member may propose a resolution asking for the purchase of $50,000 of additional liability coverage by the corporation. Another board member may propose that the insurance resolution be made more specific by authorizing the purchase of $50,000 of general liability insurance coverage from the lowest bidder, after getting quotes from the corporation's current insurance carrier and outside companies.

After the language of a resolution is decided, the directors vote to approve or disapprove it. (See Step 12, below.) If a resolution passes, it is inserted in the minutes for the meeting and becomes the official act of the corporation. If it fails, it normally isn't mentioned in the minutes, unless you want a record stating that the resolution didn't pass.

Introducing Resolutions at Shareholders' Meetings

The shareholders are authorized to elect the board of directors at the annual (or regular) shareholders' meeting. The board of directors performs most of the formal corporate decision making for the corporation. However, from time to time, the corporation may be required under state law, or may voluntarily decide, to seek shareholder approval of major corporate actions or structural changes to the corporation. Such decisions might include the decision to amend the articles of incorporation, a plan of merger or dissolution, and the like. When you do seek shareholder approval of a resolution, you will want to prepare shareholders in advance and allow for a full discussion of the resolution by the shareholders prior to taking a vote. (For a discussion of the decision-making roles of directors and shareholders, see "What Decisions Should the Board of Directors Make?" and "What Decisions Are Made (or

Ratified) by Shareholders?" in Chapter 2.)

The specific language of shareholders' resolutions is not normally drafted and discussed at shareholders' meetings. Instead, this language is fixed in advance by the board or officers of the corporation (various fill-in-the-blanks shareholders' resolutions are included with this book—see the beginning of Appendix C for a list of resolution forms included with this book, with a cross-reference to the chapter of the book that contains instructions for preparing each resolution). Typically, the shareholders are mailed background material and any draft resolutions prior to the meeting. At the meeting, they are simply asked to ratify the language of a resolution already proposed and approved by the directors at a directors' meeting. Of course, depending on the style of your shareholders' meetings, reports and other background material may be presented at the meeting prior to taking a shareholder vote.

EXAMPLE:

At the annual shareholders' meeting of the Rackafrax Corporation, the shareholders are asked to ratify an amendment to the articles of incorporation that increases the number of authorized shares of the corporation. The resolution presented for approval at the shareholders' meeting is a copy of a resolution approved earlier by the board of directors. This resolution, together with a written summary of the reasons for the amendment, is sent out to the Rackafrax shareholders along with notice for the meeting as part of the premeeting materials mailed in advance to each shareholder. (See Chapter 3, Step 6.)

At the shareholders' meeting, the resolution is introduced by the chairperson, then time is taken for a discussion of the resolution by the shareholders, corporate officers, and staff present at the meeting. Following this discussion, the chairperson makes a motion for a shareholder vote on the written resolution. After being seconded, the motion carries and a shareholder vote on the amendment is taken. The only other important item of business raised at the Rackafrax meeting is the election of the board of directors for another term of office. The president (chairperson) moves that all existing directors be reelected. A vote is taken and the shareholders approve the reelection of the board. The shareholders' meeting is adjourned, and the board members reconvene to hold the annual directors' meeting.

Step 12. Take the Votes of Directors or Shareholders

After resolutions have been presented in final form at a meeting, they must be voted on by the board of directors or shareholders. For most resolutions, you need the majority vote of those present at a meeting (at which a quorum is present). Below, we summarize the state law voting rules for director and shareholder approval of resolutions at meetings.

Voting Rules for Directors'

In all states, unless the articles or bylaws specify otherwise, the board of directors may legally act by the approval of a majority of the directors present at the meeting. Bear in mind, of course, that a sufficient number of directors must be present to represent a quorum of directors.

EXAMPLE:

A quorum of three directors attends a board meeting. The votes of two of the three directors present at the meeting are necessary to pass a resolution.

Following are some key issues that may arise during the voting process.

If a director abstains. When a director abstains, it often means he or she doesn't agree to a particular action, but simultaneously doesn't want to annoy others by voting "no." In short, a director may want to duck the issue by having the minutes reflect a neutral position. That's fine, but it is also important to understand that a director abstention is treated the same as a "no" vote for purposes of the vote needed to pass a resolution. Put another way, if five directors are present at a meeting, you need three "yes" votes to pass a resolution. With two "yes" votes, two "no" votes, and an abstention, the resolution fails.

Liability of silent directors. Most states specify that a director may be held liable for decisions made at meetings if the director remains silent. In other words, if the board approves a decision that later results in liability of the board (because of a grossly negligent or unlawful action approved at a board meeting), the silent directors, as well as those who voted for the proposal, may be found liable for the decision. The corporate statutes of most states contain a provision that holds silent directors to have agreed to action taken at a board meeting. Under the typical state statute, a director present at a meeting may be charged with having said "yes" to corporate action taken at a directors' meeting unless the director:

• objects to the holding of the meeting, or

• votes "no" to a proposal.

If you have doubts about a proposal submitted at your board meeting, vote "no" but don't abstain on the proposal or remain silent as a means of expressing your opinion.

Method of voting. Unless a specific request for a written vote (ballot) is presented at the meeting, voice votes are normally taken on resolutions brought before board meetings. By the time a vote occurs, often everyone is ready to say "yes." But this isn't always the case. If there is any opposition, it's usually best to poll the board by asking each member to voice his or her vote individually. Written ballots are normally only requested when the issue at hand is controversial or contested and members of the board don't wish to announce their decision at the meeting.

Voting Rules for Shareholders

Every state provides that each voting share of a corporation is entitled to one vote per share unless the articles of incorporation provide otherwise. Generally, unless otherwise specified in the articles or bylaws, resolutions must be approved by a majority of the number of shares represented at a meeting either in person or by proxy (check your bylaws).

EXAMPLE:

In a corporation that has issued 10,000 voting shares, shareholders owning 8,000 shares attend a shareholders' meeting. Action must be taken by the vote of at least 4,001 shares—a majority of the shares present at the meeting.

In unusual circumstances, the number of shares represented at a meeting may be less than a quorum. This is so because shareholders' meetings can normally continue to convene and take action despite the loss of a quorum following the departure of shareholders from the meeting. (See Step 8, above.)

REMINDER

Reminder on proxies. Shareholders can sign a proxy form that allows another person to vote shares at a meeting. (See Chapter 3, Step 8, for a discussion of proxies and instructions on preparing proxy forms for shareholder voting.)

Following are some topics that may come up in the course of a shareholder vote.

Shareholder abstentions. The traditional rule, still followed by a majority of the states, is that shareholders must approve a resolution at a meeting by a majority of shares present, with abstentions counted as "no" votes.

EXAMPLE:

In a corporation with 100 outstanding voting shares, shareholders owning 70 voting shares attend a meeting. Shareholders with 33 shares vote in favor of a proposal, 27 shares vote against, and ten shares abstain. The proposal fails because a majority of those shares present—at least 36—did not vote in favor of the matter (all shares not affirmatively voting "yes" are treated as "no" votes). Strangely, if the ten abstaining shares had not attended the meeting, the proposal would have passed—a quorum of 60 shares would have been in attendance, with a majority of the 60 shares present (33) voting in favor of the proposal.

The way shareholder abstentions are counted has begun to change. The modern shareholder approval voting requirement, adopted in Section 7.25(c) of the Model Business Corporation Act and in the corporate statutes of a substantial minority of states, requires that the number of votes cast in favor of a proposal at a meeting must exceed the number cast against it, with abstaining votes not counted either way. Of course, a quorum must be present initially at the meeting for any proposal to be submitted to the shareholders for a vote. The redefinition of the normal majority approval rule eliminates the problem of shareholder abstentions illustrated above. As always, check your bylaws to determine how to count votes in your corporation.

Check Your Articles or Bylaws for Special Voting Rules

Your articles or bylaws may require the vote of more than a majority of shares for the approval of special types of proposals. Typically, there must be approval by a majority or two-thirds of the outstanding shares of the corporation for such important matters as:

- the amendment of articles of incorporation
- the dissolution of the corporation after the issuance of shares, or
- the sale of substantially all corporate assets not in the ordinary course of business.

Very rarely, the articles or bylaws give one class or series of shares the right to a separate vote on certain proposals. So, if decisions fundamental to the organization or operation of your corporation are to be made, check your articles and bylaws for special provisions. If you find any, make sure you understand what is required, and check your conclusions with your legal advisor.

Some states specifically allow the articles to give voting rights to outsiders who hold bonds issued by the corporation. This is one method of giving control of corporate policies (by participation in board elections) to corporate creditors. Another is appointing a corporate noteholder as proxy to vote a block of shares owned by corporate shareholders. If your corporation has issued notes or bonds to outsiders, make sure you know the voting rights of these corporate bond or noteholders by checking your articles and bylaws.

EXAMPLE:

Assume the same facts as above for a corporation with 100 voting shares. Seventy voting shares attend a meeting, 33 shares vote in favor of a proposal, and 27 shares vote against it, with ten shares abstaining. The resolution would pass in a state with the modern shareholder voting rule.

This modern shareholder abstention rule normally does not apply to the election of directors, where a majority of those present at a meeting must affirmatively vote in favor of nominees to elect them to the board.

Method of voting. Shareholder votes are normally taken as voice votes, with each shareholder announcing the number of shares voted for a proposal. Of course, a particular shareholder normally votes all of his or her shares for or against a proposal, though this is not legally required. Generally, you are free to take written ballots of votes instead of voice votes if you wish; if a shareholder requests a special polled or written vote, it is customary to allow it.

Election of directors. The main job of shareholders convened at their annual meeting is to elect directors of the corporation for the next year. Normally, this is done by taking the voice votes of shareholders, with the directors receiving the highest number of votes being elected to the board—for example, the top three vote-getters from five nominees are elected to a three-person board.

Corporate bylaws sometimes contain specific provisions, based upon state statutes, that specify special voting procedures to be followed to nominate and elect directors. For example, some bylaws may provide that any shareholder may request the election of directors by written ballot.

Also, the articles or bylaws of the corporation may require or allow cumulative voting —a special type of voting process used primarily to protect minority shareholder interests in larger corporations—for directors by the shareholders. (See "Cumulative Voting by Shareholders," below.) And in some states, even if cumulative voting is not mentioned in the articles or bylaws, it may be requested by a shareholder when electing the board to another term. Although you should be aware of the existence of this special shareholder voting procedure, it rarely has relevance to small corporations with roughly proportionate share ownership, since the outcome of a cumulative and a regular election (one share, one vote) in these corporations is usually the same. Again, your articles and bylaws should alert you to when or whether cumulative voting must be used to elect directors in your state.

Although you need to pay attention to election procedures contained in your bylaws, don't obsess on them—unless, of course, a board position is contested. In such cases, you will want to be extremely careful to follow the correct procedure and may even want to double-check with a legal advisor. (See Chapter 20.) Since it's rare to have a contested director election for a small corporation, you'll normally do just fine by following our suggestions for providing shareholders with advance written notice of all shareholders' meetings, together with a list of candidates for the board. (See Chapter 3, Step 6.)

Terms of office. Corporate laws normally require the election of directors each year by the shareholders. There is, however, no limit under state law on the number of times any individual may be reelected to serve another term on the board.

TIP

Shareholders of small corporations normally reelect the entire board. Except in the case of controversy or ill will among corporate principals, or the retirement or disability of a director (state law and standard bylaws normally allow the remaining board members to elect a person to fill the unexpired term of a vacant board position), small corporations routinely reelect the corporate board to serve another term at each annual meeting of shareholders. Of course, if your state (and your bylaws) allow your corporation to elect directors for terms longer than one year, then shareholders' meetings for the election of the board may be held every other year (for two-year director terms) or at some other interval. Also, if your corporation has opted for a classified board (with some directors elected every so many years), then only a portion of the board will be elected every year.

Step 13. Handle Unfinished Business

No matter how long meetings last, an item or two of business is often carried over to the next meeting. If this happened at your last directors' or shareholders' meeting, make sure to tackle any old work. Of course, any notice (or waiver of notice) for the current meeting should have included a summary of any unfinished business to be considered at the meeting.

Step 14. Adjourn the Meeting

After all resolutions have been submitted to a vote of the directors or shareholders at a meeting, the chairperson should propose adjournment. If no further business is proposed and the motion carries, the meeting is adjourned.

If minutes were not prepared at the meeting, your next step is to prepare minutes to place in the corporate records book. We cover these and related forms in the next two chapters. For now, place all papers presented or drafted at the meeting in the folder for the meeting or directly in your corporate records book.

TIP

What to do when a meeting is adjourned with unfinished business. If a corporate meeting is carried over to another time so that unfinished business can be concluded, the second meeting is referred to as the adjourned meeting. When a meeting is adjourned to continue business at another time, we suggest you use common sense and send out notice for any meeting that is carried over more than a week or so from the original meeting, unless your bylaws set a shorter standard for providing notice of the adjourned meeting. (For details, see Chapter 3, Step 5.)

Cumulative Voting by Shareholders

Cumulative voting by shareholders in the election of directors can help protect minority shareholder interests in larger corporations. If your articles or bylaws require or permit the use of cumulative voting in an election of directors, then each shareholder can cast a total number of votes in the election equal to the number of shares owned, multiplied by the number of persons to be elected to the board. These votes can be cast all for one candidate or split up among the candidates as the shareholder sees fit.

EXAMPLE: Shareholders A and B own 2,000 shares each, and Shareholder C owns 1,000 shares. At the annual shareholders' meeting, four candidates are nominated for election to a three-person board. Under normal voting rules with one share equal to one vote, C's candidate can always be outvoted by A's or B's choice. With cumulative voting, however, C is given 3,000 votes (A and B have 6,000 votes each). While still outnumbered, if C cumulates all 3,000 votes in favor of one candidate and A and B split their votes among the other three candidates, C has a chance of electing his or her nominee to the board.

Unless required, most small corporations do not use cumulative voting at the annual shareholders' meeting to elect directors.

Preparing Minutes for Shareholders' Meetings

In this chapter, we show you how to choose and use minutes forms to document actions taken at regular and special shareholders' meetings. You will find sample minutes forms with instructions in this chapter, and ready-to-fill-in forms on the CD-ROM and in Appendix C. (Minutes for directors' meetings are in Chapter 6.)

Our minutes forms are designed to document the most common procedures and actions taken at regular and special shareholders' meetings, such as the election of directors at annual shareholders' meetings. If you wish to transact additional business at these meetings, we explain how to use one of the more than 80 ready-to-use resolutions included with this book. To transact business not covered by one of our resolutions, you need to insert your own language in the minutes describing the item of business discussed and approved at the meeting. Doing this is easy, as explained below in "How to Use Corporate Resolutions."

Preparing Minutes for Annual Shareholders' Meetings

The first form we'll cover is the minutes form for annual shareholders' meetings. Selecting and using this form is easy—just follow the instructions provided below. You'll see that all our minutes forms follow a consistent format; once you've used one, the rest will be even easier to use.

When Minutes Should Be Written Up

There are no legal requirements on when minutes must be prepared. Common sense dictates that the minutes should, however, be prepared shortly after (within a few days or so

of) the meeting being documented. If you wait longer, you may forget to prepare the minutes or be unable to remember or follow your notes about the proposals made and votes taken at the meeting. Here are some suggestions.

If you hold a real meeting. If you are preparing minutes for a meeting that really takes place, as described in Chapter 4, the secretary will normally complete the minutes form after the meeting, based upon notes taken at the meeting. Or, if you wish, a draft of the form can be prepared before the meeting and completed during or after the meeting. Some people prefer to prepare the entire minutes form during the meeting, either by using a fill-in-the-blanks minutes form (see Appendix C) or by filling in the CD-ROM form with a computer at the meeting.

If you hold a paper meeting. To prepare minutes for a paper meeting (one that doesn't actually occur), follow our instructions in Chapter 7. The secretary normally prepares this minutes form whenever it's convenient; it need not be on the meeting date. He or she then distributes a copy to all shareholders for their approval, as explained in Chapter 7, Step 5.

How to Prepare Your Minutes

Below are the instructions for the form you can use to prepare the minutes of your annual shareholders' meeting. This form specifically provides for the election of directors—the primary purpose of annual shareholders' meetings.

CD-ROM

Below is a sample of the Minutes of the Annual Meeting of Shareholders form included on the CD-ROM and as a tear-out form in Appendix C. Fill it out following the special instructions provided after the form.

How to Use Corporate Resolutions

Resolutions are inserted in the minutes of annual or special shareholders' meetings (or in written consent forms) to show formal approval of corporate legal, tax, and other business decisions.

We've included the standard language for the approval of business customarily handled at annual meetings of your shareholders in the minutes forms contained in this chapter. But for special meetings, you will want to add the language of one or more resolutions showing the approval of the particular business for which the special meeting was called.

This book provides more than 80 resolutions, which cover standard items of corporate legal, tax, and business transactions (see Chapters 9 through 19 for specific instructions on using the various resolutions forms included with this book). You can simply fill in one of these resolutions and insert it in your minutes, as explained in the special instructions to the minutes forms below.

If you need to prepare your own language for a resolution (because you want to approve an item of business at a meeting not covered by one of our resolution forms), it is easy to do. We provide examples of using your own language in the special instructions to filling out minutes forms.

Most corporate resolutions stand on their own and do not require additional documentation. However, some resolutions refer to additional backup agreements or paperwork, and you may wish to attach this supplementary material to your minutes. For example, if shareholders approve a resolution to make a loan to a director, you can prepare and attach a promissory note to your minutes. We include such backup paperwork (for example, promissory note forms) with the appropriate resolutions included with this book. But finding and adding your own supplemental forms, if necessary, is easy to do. For example, standard loan, real estate, and other business forms are available from banks, real estate brokers, legal stationers, business law libraries, and other sources.

Minutes of the Annual Meeting of Shareholders of

_____ ❶
[*name of corporation*]

An annual meeting of the shareholders of the corporation was held on ❷ _____,

20____ at ____:____ __.M., at _____ [*location of meeting*] _____ , state of _____

_____, for the purpose of electing the directors of the corporation and for the

transaction of any other business that may properly come before the meeting, including _____

_____

_____ ❸ .

❹ _____ acted as chairperson, and

_____ acted as secretary of the meeting.

The chairperson called the meeting to order.

The secretary announced that the meeting was called by _____

_____ . ❺

The secretary announced that the meeting was held pursuant to notice, if and as required under

the bylaws of this corporation, or that notice had been waived by all shareholders entitled to receive

notice under the bylaws. Copies of any certifications of mailing of notice prepared by the secretary of the

corporation and any written waivers signed by shareholders entitled to receive notice of this meeting were

attached to these minutes by the secretary. ❻

The secretary announced that an alphabetical list of the names and numbers of shares held by all

shareholders of the corporation was available and open to inspection by any person in attendance at the

meeting. ❼

The secretary announced that there were present, in person or by proxy, representing a quorum of

the shareholders, the following shareholders, proxyholders, and shares: ❽

Name	Number of Shares
_____	_____
_____	_____
_____	_____
_____	_____
_____	_____
_____	_____

The secretary attached written proxy statements, executed by the appropriate shareholders, to these minutes for any shares listed above as held by a proxyholder.

The following persons were also present at the meeting: ❾

Name   Title

_____   _____

_____   _____

_____   _____

_____   _____

_____   _____

The secretary announced that the minutes of the _____["annual," "special," or "regular"]_____

meeting held on _____, 20_____

☐ had been distributed prior to

☐ were distributed at

☐ were read at

the meeting. After discussion, a vote was taken and the minutes of the meeting were approved by the shares in attendance. ❿

The following annual and special reports were presented at the meeting by the following persons:

⓫ _____

_____

_____.

The chairperson announced that the next item of business was the nomination and election of the board of directors for another _____["one-year" or other term]_____ term of office. The following nominations were made and seconded: ⓬

Name(s) of Nominee(s)

_____

_____

_____

_____

_____

The secretary next took the votes of shareholders entitled to vote for the election of directors at the meeting, and, after counting the votes, announced that the following persons were elected to serve on the board of directors of this corporation: **13**

Names of Board Members

_____

_____

_____

_____

_____

On motion duly made and carried by the affirmative vote of [_"a majority of"_ _or other vote requirement_] shareholders in attendance at the meeting, the following resolutions were adopted by shareholders entitled to vote at the meeting: **14** _____

_____

_____

_____

_____

_____

_____

_____

_____

_____

_____

_____

_____

_____

_____

_____

_____

_____

There being no further business to come before the meeting, it was adjourned on motion duly made and carried.

15

_____

_____, Secretary

Special Instructions

❶ Most state statutes and most corporations' bylaws call for the annual election of directors by the shareholders. However, if your bylaws require election less frequently, say every two years, then delete or change the word "annual" in the heading and text of the CD-ROM form (for example, by changing all occurrences of the word "annual" to "biennial"). Similarly, if your corporation has opted for a special staggered board with only a portion of the board elected each year, make a note of this in the first paragraph. If you use tear-out forms from Appendix C, cross out material as needed and neatly write in the changes.

❷ Complete the beginning of the first paragraph by inserting the date, time, and place (street address, city, and state) of the meeting. Shareholders' meetings are usually held at the principal office of the corporation, although most bylaws allow these meetings to be held anywhere within or outside the state.

❸ If you wish, list any matters, other than the election of directors, considered at the annual shareholders' meeting. You are not legally required to do this, because the sentence already authorizes the transaction of any other business that may come before the meeting; but you may wish to do so anyway.

❹ Insert the name and title of the persons who acted as chairperson and secretary of the meeting. Often, corporate bylaws specify who should act as chairperson of shareholders' meetings. Normally this is the president or, in his or her absence, the vice president or other director. Usually, the secretary of the corporation acts as secretary of all corporate meetings. In his or her absence, another director usually assumes this task.

In the instructions for this form, we specify when we are referring to the secretary of the corporation. All other references are to the secre-tary of the meeting. Normally, the secretary of the corporation and the secretary of the meeting will be one and the same.

❺ This is an optional paragraph, which may be deleted or filled in as "not applicable" if you choose not to include it. Normally, annual shareholders' meetings are not officially "called," because they are already scheduled in the bylaws. (See Chapter 3, Step 3, for a discussion of the legal requirements for calling corporate meetings.) If your corporation follows a differ-ent practice and you wish to show that the secretary of the corporation, another officer or board member, or a number of shareholders called the meeting, include this paragraph. Indicate the name and title of each person who called the meeting.

❻ This paragraph states that each shareholder was given notice as required by your bylaws or waived notice by signing a written waiver of notice form. For shareholders' meetings, we generally recommend providing written notice prior to the meeting, because this is the best way to make sure each shareholder knows about the meeting well in advance and understands the nature of the proposals to be discussed there. If you own and run a closely held corporation, you may be able to safely use waiver of notice forms. (For an overview of state notice requirements for shareholders' meetings, see Chapter 3, Step 5.)

If notice was mailed to shareholders, attach to the minutes any Certification of Mailing of Notice or Acknowledgment of Receipt forms. (See Chapter 3, Steps 7 and 9.) Attach any written waivers of notice for the meeting that were signed by shareholders. (See Chapter 7, Step 1, for instructions on preparing waiver of notice forms.)

TIP

Use notice waiver forms with closely held corporations. Small corporations with only a few shareholders—who are almost guaranteed to attend meetings—sometimes decide to dispense with official premeeting notice formalities entirely, and, instead, informally notify all shareholders of the meeting. They then hand out written waiver of notice forms for each participant to sign. It's usually convenient to do so just prior to or at the meeting. This is perfectly legal and does no harm if you are sure each shareholder knows about the meeting and its purpose well in advance anyway. (See Chapter 7, Step 1, for instructions on preparing waiver forms.)

❼ This sentence restates a common legal requirement that an alphabetical list of shareholders be made available for inspection during the meeting. You can prepare a separate list as explained in Chapter 3, Step 4, or you can simply make your corporate records book available for inspection at the meeting if it includes a share register with a current listing of your shareholders and their shareholdings.

❽ List the names of the shareholders present at the meeting. To the right of each name, show the number of shares owned by the shareholder.

If shares are represented by proxy, list the proxyholder's name on the left, followed by the words "proxyholder for" and the name of the shareholder. Show the number of shares held by the proxyholder under the column at the right. (See Chapter 3, Step 8, for a discussion of when to use and how to prepare proxy forms for shareholders.)

EXAMPLE:

Victor Lewis attends the meeting with a written proxy signed by Margaret Billings to vote 1,000 shares for Margaret. The secretary fills out the minutes as follows:

Name	Number of Shares
Victor Lewis, proxyholder for Margaret Billings	1,000

If any proxyholders attend a meeting, attach to the minutes a written proxy statement dated and signed by the shareholder whose shares are represented by proxy. Proxy forms are included on the CD-ROM, as explained in step-by-step instructions in Chapter 3, Step 8.

REMINDER

Always check that you have a quorum. Most bylaws require that a majority of the voting shares of the corporation attend the meeting for a quorum to be in attendance. (See Chapter 4, Step 8.)

EXAMPLE:

Bioflex Weight Training Systems, Inc., holds a shareholders' meeting. The corporation's bylaws require a majority of the 2,000 issued shares as a quorum for shareholders' meetings. Because the following shareholders holding 1,500 shares show up for the meeting, a quorum is present and the meeting can be convened:

Name	Number of Shares
Robert Newquist	1,000
Rebecca Michigan	300
Samuel Thatcher	200

❾ Specify any additional persons, other than the chairperson and secretary of the meeting, who attend the meeting but do not count toward a quorum. For example, if informational reports are to be made to the shareholders by nonshareholder corporate officers, staff, or committee members, they, of course, will also be in attendance, as well as possibly the corporation's accountant or legal consultant.

❿ It is customary, though not legally necessary, for participants at an annual meeting to approve the minutes of the previous shareholders' meeting. This prior meeting may have been last year's annual meeting or a special meeting of shareholders called during the year. Mostly, this formality of approving prior minutes is undertaken to remind everyone of any special business approved at the last meeting and to allow any objections prior to placing a formal copy of the minutes in the corporate records book.

If you decide to follow this formality and wish to save time, you can send copies of the minutes of the last meeting to each participant to read prior to the meeting, as explained in Chapter 7, Steps 3–5. Otherwise, distribute copies of the minutes at the current meeting or have the secretary read or summarize them. Then ask for a voice approval. Normally, the prior meeting's minutes are routinely approved, but if there are objections, you will need to work them out before approving the minutes. You may do this either by making appropriate corrections to the prior minutes or by obtaining a majority vote to approve the minutes over the objection of one or more shareholders.

Fill in the blanks as shown in the sample form to indicate the method of distributing or announcing the minutes of the prior meeting to shareholders. If you choose not to approve the prior minutes, simply delete this reference or fill in "not applicable."

TIP

Use written approval forms to save time or obtain consent to prior decisions. You can obtain approval of minutes of prior meetings by sending written approval forms to shareholders along with the prior minutes to be signed by them

before the next meeting. Using these forms can save time and has the added advantage of providing signed consent to previous decisions reached at that meeting. This may be helpful, for example, if some shareholders did not attend the last meeting and you wish to have a record of their approval of important decisions reached at that meeting. (How to prepare a written Approval of Corporate Minutes form is covered in Chapter 7, Step 3.)

If you use an Approval of Corporate Minutes form to obtain written approval of minutes of a prior meeting, change the following paragraph in the current minutes form to read as follows:

The secretary announced that the minutes of the ["regular," "annual," or "special shareholders'"] meeting held on [date] , 20__, had been distributed prior to the meeting and that each shareholder had returned to the secretary of the corporation a signed statement showing approval of the minutes of the prior meeting. [*Delete the next sentence in the form showing a vote taken at the meeting.*]

⓫ As explained in Chapter 4, Step 10, you may wish to present annual or special reports at your meeting. For example, the president may present an annual operating report, and the treasurer may summarize the past year's financial gains or losses. List a description of the reports given, such as "treasurer's report of sales," along with the name and title of the presenter. Attach any written copies of reports to your minutes.

⓬ Here you take care of the main business of the annual shareholders' meeting—the election (or reelection) of the directors of your corporation for another term of office. Indicate the term of office of the board in the first blank. Most bylaws provide for a one-year (annual) term of office, although occasionally bylaws specify a longer term. Under "Name of Nominee(s)," fill in the names of all nominees who are to be voted upon by the shareholders. Many small corporations simply nominate (and reelect) each member of the current board for another term of office. But check your bylaws to be sure. Modern corporate statutes allow corporations to provide for a classified or staggered board in their bylaws. Typically, this means that the board is broken down—or classified—into two or more sections, with the elections for each section occurring in alternate years.

EXAMPLE:

Quark Corp. has a nine-member board, and its bylaws provide for one-third of the board to be reelected every three years. At each annual shareholders' meeting, one-third of the board is reelected to another three-year term.

⑬ In these blanks, indicate the persons who are elected to serve on the board for another term.

There are different ways ballots can be counted. Corporations usually use voice vote or written ballot. In some circumstances, your articles or bylaws may call for cumulative voting procedures. (We discuss shareholder voting rules in more detail in Chapter 4, Step 12.)

Normal voting procedures. Most corporations elect directors by voice vote or written ballot, and elect those nominees who receive the most votes.

EXAMPLE:

Ten shareholders holding 100 shares apiece vote for three of five nominees to a three-person board (each shareholder may cast 100 votes in favor of each of three candidates). There are a total of 3,000 possible votes. The results are as follows:

	Number of Votes Cast	*Result in Favor of Candidate*
Nominee 1	1,000	Elected
Nominee 2	1,000	Elected
Nominee 3	500	Elected
Nominee 4	300	Not Elected
Nominee 5	200	Not Elected

In the above example, Nominees 1 and 2 received the votes of all ten shareholders, while Nominees 3, 4, and 5 received the votes of five, three, and two shareholders respectively. The three candidates receiving the largest number of votes, Nominees 1, 2, and 3, are elected to the board.

Cumulative voting procedures. There is another way of electing directors—namely, by cumulative voting procedures. Your articles of incorporation or bylaws should state whether you are required to, are prohibited from, or have the option to use cumulative voting procedures when electing directors of the corporation. Often, the bylaws state that cumulative voting must be used to elect directors at the annual shareholders' meeting if any shareholder makes a request for cumulative voting prior to the commencement of voting for directors.

Cumulative voting differs from standard (plurality) voting in that a shareholder is given a total number of votes equal to his or her shares times the number of directors to be elected. The shareholder may vote all votes for one candidate—this is known as cumulating his or her votes—or may split them up among two or more candidates.

EXAMPLE:

Using the same ten shareholders and five nominees as in the previous example, under cumulative voting each shareholder is given a total of 300 votes to cast for one or more directors. This means that any one shareholder has a better chance of tipping the scales in favor of one candidate, since he or she is no longer limited to voting a maximum of 100 votes for a particular candidate. (Of course, a shareholder will lose a chance to vote for any other candidates by casting all votes for one nominee.) In fact, this is the purpose of cumulative voting, and a reason it is used in larger corporations: It gives minority shareholders a better shot at electing a candidate to the board, despite the voting power of the majority shareholders. (For a further discussion of cumulative voting rules, see Chapter 4, Step 12.)

14 Many small corporations use their annual shareholders' meeting simply to reelect directors and to provide progress reports to the shareholders regarding corporate operations and profits. If you decide to present other proposals for a vote by shareholders at your annual meeting, such as a ratification by shareholders of an amendment to the corporation's articles or bylaws, insert one or more resolutions that describe the matter approved in this space.

In many instances, you can insert in this space one of the ready-to-use resolutions included in this book, following the instructions for preparing the resolution from one of the later chapters (Chapters 9 through 19). See the beginning of Appendix C for a list of resolution forms included on the CD-ROM and in tear-out form with this book, with a cross-reference to the chapter of the book that contains instructions for preparing each resolution.

If you wish to approve business not covered by one of our resolutions, supply your own language for the resolution in this space in your minutes. You don't need to use fancy or legal language for your resolution; just describe as specifically as you can the transaction or matter approved by your shareholders in a short, concise statement. Normally, resolutions start with a preamble of the following sort: "The shareholders resolved that…," but this is not required.

Here are a few examples of shareholder resolution language:

EXAMPLE 1 (Amendment of Articles):
"The shareholders ratified a board of directors resolution adding the following new article to the corporation's articles of incorporation: [*language of new article*]."

EXAMPLE 2 (Amendment of Bylaws):
"The shareholders approved an amendment to the bylaws of the corporation. The text of the changed bylaws is as follows: [*language of amended bylaws*]."

If you have trouble drafting your own resolution, or if the matter has important legal or tax consequences, you may wish to turn to a lawyer or accountant for help. (See Chapter 20.)

15 This concluding adjournment paragraph and signature line should appear at the very end of your minutes after any resolutions. Fill in the name of the secretary of the meeting under the signature line.

After obtaining the signature of the secretary, file the completed minutes in your corporate records book together with all attachments.

If you prepared a separate meeting folder for the meeting (see Chapter 3, Step 1), now is the time to transfer all forms and attachments related to the meeting from the folder to your corporate records book.

Preparing Minutes for Special Shareholder Meetings

Now let's look at the form to use to document the proceedings of special meetings of your shareholders—meetings called during the year for the purpose of approving one or more items of special shareholder business.

When Minutes Should Be Written Up

Unlike regular or annual meetings of shareholders that are scheduled in your bylaws, special meetings are called during the year to discuss and vote on special items of corporate business presented for approval to the shareholders.

Special meetings of shareholders are called and held less frequently than any other kind of corporate meeting. The reason, of course, is that the great majority of corporate business is conducted by the directors, not the shareholders.

Mostly, meetings of this sort are held if required under state law to ratify action taken by the board of directors or to obtain shareholder approval of a matter on which the board cannot act independently (such as the amendment of bylaws). Generally, state corporate statutes require the approval by shareholders only of important structural changes to the corporation or of matters in which the directors have a direct financial interest. For example, a special shareholders' meeting might be called to ratify an amendment to the articles, for the authorization or issuance of additional shares of stock, or for a dissolution of the corporation. It may also be called to approve loans, guarantees, and other business favorable to the financial interests of one or more members of the board of directors.

Generally, special meetings of shareholders are called by the directors to ask for ratification of a decision already made by the board, such as an amendment of the articles or bylaws of the corporation or another major structural change to the corporation. In other words, most of the groundwork for preparing these minutes, including the drafting of resolutions to present to the special shareholders' meeting, will already have been done.

REMINDER

Quorum requirements reminder.
Your bylaws should state any special shareholder quorum or vote requirements for the ratification of amendments or approval of other business by shareholders at shareholders' meetings.

How to Prepare Your Minutes

Following is the minutes form to use to document actions taken at a special meeting of your shareholders. This minutes form is similar to the form for the annual shareholders' meeting presented above, but it eliminates the election of directors as an item on the agenda at the meeting.

REMINDER

Provide notice or waivers of notice.
Remember to call and provide notice for all special shareholders' meetings as provided in your bylaws (Chapter 3, Steps 3–5). Or, in the alternative, have each shareholder sign a written waiver of notice form prior to the meeting (Chapter 7, Step 1). Each notice or waiver of notice form should state the specific purpose(s) of the special shareholders' meeting, since state law usually prohibits the transaction of any business not specified in the notice or waiver of notice for the special shareholders' meeting.

CD-ROM

Below is a sample of the Minutes of Special Meeting of Shareholders form included on the CD-ROM and as a tear-out form in Appendix C. Fill it out following any special instructions provided.

Special Instructions

❶ Insert the date, time, and place (street address, city, and state) of the meeting. Shareholders' meetings are usually held at the principal office of the corporation, although most bylaws allow these meetings to be held anywhere.

❷ List the specific purpose(s) for which this special shareholders' meeting was called. A similar statement of purpose(s) should have been included in your notice (Chapter 3, Step 5) or waiver of notice form (Chapter 7, Step 1) used for the meeting.

Sample statements of purpose of special meetings include:

- "ratifying an amendment to the articles of incorporation that provides for the creation of a new class of shares," or

- "approving an amendment to the bylaws of the corporation that increases the minimum quorum requirement for shareholders' meetings."

❸ Insert the name and title of the persons who acted as chairperson and secretary of the meeting. Bylaws typically provide that the president or chairperson of the board presides at meetings of shareholders, and the corporate secretary acts as secretary of meetings of shareholders.

In the instructions for this form, we specify when we are referring to the secretary of the corporation. All other references are to the secretary of the meeting. Again, normally the secretary of the corporation and the secretary of the meeting will be one and the same.

❹ Indicate the person or persons who called the special meeting of shareholders, along with each person's title. Typically, bylaws and state law allow the board of directors, the president, or a minimum of 10% of the shares to call a special meeting of shareholders. (See Chapter 3, Step 3, and check your bylaws.)

❺ Proper notice or waiver of notice is particularly important for special shareholders' meetings. After all, you don't want an uninformed shareholder to complain later and challenge a decision made at a special shareholders' meeting. This paragraph states that each shareholder was given notice as required by your bylaws, or waived notice by signing a written waiver form.

TIP

Use notice waiver forms with closely held corporations. Small corporations with only a few shareholders—who are almost guaranteed to attend meetings—sometimes decide to dispense with official premeeting notice formalities entirely. Instead, they informally notify all shareholders of the meeting and then hand out written waiver of notice forms just prior to or at a meeting for each participant to sign. This is perfectly legal and does no harm if you are sure each shareholder knows about the meeting and its purpose well in advance anyway. (See Chapter 7, Step 1, for instructions on preparing the waiver of notice form.)

If notice was mailed to shareholders, attach to the minutes any Certification of Mailing of Notice or Acknowledgment of Receipt. (See Chapter 3, Steps 7 and 9.) Attach any written waivers of notice for the meeting that were signed by shareholders. (See Chapter 7, Step 1, for instructions on preparing waiver of notice forms.)

❻ This sentence restates a common requirement that an alphabetical list of shareholders be made available for inspection during

Minutes of Special Meeting of Shareholders of

_____
[*name of corporation*]

A special meeting of the shareholders of the corporation was held on _____,

20_____ at ____:____ __.M., at ❶ _____[*location of meeting*]_____,

state of _____, for the purpose(s) of ❷ _____

_____

_____

_____.

❸ _____ acted as chairperson, and

_____ acted as secretary of the meeting.

The chairperson called the meeting to order.

The secretary announced that the meeting was called by ❹ _____

_____.

The secretary announced that the meeting was held pursuant to notice, if and as required under the bylaws of this corporation, or that notice had been waived by all shareholders entitled to receive notice under the bylaws. Copies of any certificates of mailing of notice prepared by the secretary of the corporation and any written waivers signed by shareholders entitled to receive notice of this meeting were attached to these minutes by the secretary. ❺

The secretary announced that an alphabetical list of the names and numbers of shares held by all shareholders of the corporation was available and open to inspection by any person in attendance at the meeting. ❻

The secretary announced that there were present, in person or by proxy, representing a quorum of the shareholders, the following shareholders, proxyholders, and shares: ❼

Name   Number of Shares

_____   _____

_____   _____

_____   _____

_____   _____

The secretary attached written proxy statements, executed by the appropriate shareholders, to these minutes for any shares listed above as held by a proxyholder.

The following persons were also present at the meeting: ❽

Name   Title

_____   _____

_____   _____

_____   _____

_____   _____

_____   _____

The secretary announced that the minutes of the __["annual," "regular," or "special shareholders'"]__

meeting held on _____, 20_____

☐ had been distributed prior to

☐ were distributed at

☐ were read at

the meeting. After discussion, a vote was taken and the minutes of the meeting were approved by the shares in attendance. ❾

❿ The following annual and special reports were presented at the meeting by the following persons:

_____

_____

_____

_____

_____

_____

_____

_____

_____

_____

_____

_____

_____

_____ .

On motion duly made and carried by the affirmative vote of ["a majority of" *or other vote requirement*] shareholders in attendance at the meeting, the following resolutions were adopted by shareholders entitled to vote at the meeting: ⓫

_____

_____

_____

_____

_____

_____

_____

_____

_____

_____

_____

_____

_____

_____

_____

_____

_____

_____

_____

_____

_____

_____

There being no further business to come before the meeting, it was adjourned on motion duly made and carried.

⓬

_____

_____, Secretary

the meeting. You can prepare a separate list as explained in Chapter 3, Step 4, or you can simply make your corporate records book available for inspection if it includes a share register with a current listing of your shareholders and their shareholdings.

❼ List the names of the shareholders present at the meeting. To the right of each name, show the number of shares owned by the shareholder.

If shares are represented by proxy, list the proxyholder's name on the left, followed by the words "proxyholder for" and the name of the shareholder. Show the number of shares held by the proxyholder under the column at the right. (See Chapter 3, Step 8, for a discussion of when to use and how to prepare proxy forms for shareholders.)

EXAMPLE:

Victor Lewis attends the meeting with a written proxy signed by Margaret Billings to vote 1,000 shares for Margaret. The secretary fills out the minutes as follows:

Name	*Number of Shares*
Victor Lewis, proxyholder for Margaret Billings	1,000

If any proxyholders attend a meeting, attach to the minutes a written proxy statement dated and signed by the shareholder. Proxy forms, included on the CD-ROM, are discussed in step-by-step instructions in Chapter 3, Step 8.

REMINDER

Quorum requirements reminder. Most bylaws require that a majority of the voting shares of the corporation attend the meeting for a quorum to be in attendance. (See Chapter 4, Step 8.)

EXAMPLE:

Bioflex Weight Training Systems, Inc., holds a shareholders' meeting. The corporation's bylaws require a majority of the 2,000 issued shares as a quorum for shareholders' meetings. Because the following shareholders holding 1,500 shares show up for the meeting, a quorum is present and the meeting can be convened:

Name	*Number of Shares*
Robert Newquist	1,000
Rebecca Michigan	300
Samuel Thatcher	200

❽ Specify any additional persons (other than the chairperson and secretary of the meeting) who attend the meeting but do not count toward a quorum. If reports are to be submitted to the shareholders by nonshareholder corporate officers, staff, or committee members, they, of course, will be in attendance, as well as, possibly, the corporation's accountant or legal consultant.

❾ It is customary, though not legally necessary, for participants at a shareholders' meeting to approve the minutes of the previous meeting. The prior meeting may have been an annual or special shareholders' meeting. Mostly, this formality is undertaken to remind everyone of any special business approved at the last meeting and to allow any objections prior to placing a formal copy of the minutes in the corporate records book.

If you decide to follow this formality and wish to save time, you can send copies of the minutes of the last meeting to each participant to read prior to the meeting, as explained in Chapter 3, Steps 3–5. Otherwise, distribute copies of the minutes or have the secretary read or summarize them. Then ask for a voice approval. Normally, the minutes are routinely approved. If there are suggestions or corrections, you will need to work them out before voting to approve the minutes. You may do this by making appropriate corrections to the prior minutes. In the rare event this proves impossible, you'll need to obtain a majority vote to approve the minutes over the objection of one or more shareholders.

Fill in the blanks as shown to indicate the method of distributing or announcing the minutes of the prior meeting to shareholders.

TIP

Use written approval forms to save time or obtain consent to prior decisions. Written minutes approval forms can be sent out to shareholders along with the prior minutes before the meeting to obtain written approval of the prior minutes. Using this form can save time and has the added advantage of providing signed consent to previous decisions reached at meetings. This may be helpful, for example, if some shareholders did not attend the last meeting and you wish to have a record of their approval of important decisions reached at the previous meeting. How to prepare a written Approval of Corporate Minutes form is covered in Chapter 7, Step 3.

If you use an Approval of Corporate Minutes form to obtain written approval to the minutes of a prior meeting, change this paragraph in the current minutes to read as follows:

The secretary announced that the minutes of the ["regular," "annual," or "special shareholders"] meeting held on [date] , 20__, had been distributed prior to the meeting and that each shareholder had returned to the secretary of the corporation a signed statement showing approval of the minutes of the prior meeting. [*Delete the next sentence in the form showing a vote taken at the meeting.*]

❿ If reports are presented to shareholders by officers, staff, outside accountants, lawyers, or others at the meeting, specify the nature of each report, such as "treasurer's report of sales." Include the name and title of each person making or submitting a report. Attach to your minutes copies of any written reports passed out to participants at the meeting.

⓫ Here you take care of the main business of a special shareholders' meeting—the passage of one or more specific resolutions by the shareholders in attendance at the meeting. In the blank, insert the vote requirement for the resolution(s) that follow(s) this paragraph. As explained in Chapter 4, Step 12, shareholder resolutions normally must be passed by a majority of those attending and entitled to vote at a meeting—check your bylaws. If you pass a resolution that requires a different vote requirement than other resolutions under your bylaws, you should precede the text of the resolution with a statement that the resolution was passed by the appropriate number or percentage of votes.

In the space below the paragraph, insert one or more resolutions that describe the specific legal, tax, financial, or other items of business voted upon and approved at the meeting. Normally, as explained in Chapter 2, shareholders will be asked to ratify a board decision, such as an amendment of the articles already approved by the directors, although they can act independently to approve certain matters on their own, for example, the amendment of bylaws.

In many instances, you can insert one or more of the ready-to-use resolutions included in this book, following the instructions for preparing the resolution from one of the later chapters (Chapters 9 through 19). See Appendix C for a list of resolution forms included on the CD-ROM and in tear-out form with this book, with a cross-reference to the chapter of the book that contains instructions for preparing each resolution.

If you wish to approve business not covered by one of our resolutions, supply your own language for the resolution in this space in your minutes. You don't need to use fancy or legal language for your resolution; just describe as specifically as you can the transaction or matter approved by your shareholders in a short, concise statement. Normally, resolutions start with a preamble of the following sort: "The shareholders resolved that...," but this is not required.

Following are examples of standard shareholder resolution language:

EXAMPLE 1 (Amendment of Articles):

"The shareholders ratified a board of directors' resolution adding the following new articles to the corporation's articles of incorporation: [*language of new article*]."

EXAMPLE 1 (Amendment of Bylaws):

"The shareholders approved an amendment to the bylaws of the corporation. The text of the changed bylaws is as follows: [*language of amended bylaws*]."

If you have trouble drafting your own resolution language, or if the matter has important legal or tax consequences, you may wish to turn to a lawyer or accountant for help. (See Chapter 20.)

⑫ This concluding adjournment paragraph and signature line should appear at the very end of your minutes, after any resolutions. Fill in the name of the secretary of the meeting under the signature line. After obtaining the signature of the secretary, file the completed minutes in your corporate records book together with all attachments.

If you prepared a separate meeting folder for the special meeting (see Chapter 3, Step 1), now is the time to transfer all forms and attachments related to the meeting from your folder to your corporate records book. ●

Preparing Minutes for Directors' Meetings

The key to documenting the actions of your board of directors is to prepare accurate minutes of your meetings. In this chapter we show you how to prepare and use minutes forms for regular and special directors' meetings. (To fill in minutes forms for annual and special meetings of shareholders, see Chapter 5.)

At this point, we assume you have followed the preliminary steps set out in Chapter 3 to call, provide notice, and get ready for your upcoming directors' meeting.

Minutes of directors' meetings are most often prepared by the corporate secretary shortly after the meeting, based upon notes taken at the meeting. But you can opt to prepare minutes during the meeting by filling in a draft minutes form from Appendix C or the CD-ROM. You may also consider using a computer at the meeting to fill in the CD-ROM form.

TIP

If you're holding a paper meeting. You can use the minutes forms set out in this chapter to prepare minutes for a meeting that occurs only on paper. This paper meeting procedure works well for small businesses with only a few directors, who agree on all major points but who want to prepare a professional-looking record of their actions. (See Chapter 7.)

The minutes forms covered in this chapter contain the language necessary to document standard items normally dealt with at annual and special meetings of your directors. For example, the annual meeting minutes form shows acceptance by the directors of their election for another term, as well as other routine items of business such as establishing that a quorum is present and approving the minutes of prior meetings.

Skipping Minutes Altogether

Corporations with very few directors who usually agree on all major points may not want to deal with meetings or minutes forms at all. It's legal to have directors take action by unanimous written consent without a meeting and without formal minutes, as explained in Chapter 8.

But even with a tiny corporation, there is a downside. Written consents provide minimal documentation of corporate action and may not be as official looking to the IRS and other agencies as meeting minutes.

At some annual meetings and all special meetings of directors, you will want your directors to approve items of business not specifically listed in the body of our minutes forms. For example, at a special meeting of directors, you might want to authorize a bank loan or the purchase of real property. To document these more specialized actions, you will need to insert the necessary resolution in your minutes showing the acceptance of these terms by the board. This book provides more than 80 ready-to-use resolutions, any one or more of which can be prepared and inserted in your minutes form to show the approval of specific additional items of corporate business transacted at a directors' meeting.

To transact business not covered by one of our resolutions, you need to insert your own language in your minutes describing the item of business discussed and approved at the meeting. Doing this is easy, as explained below in "How to Use Corporate Resolutions."

How to Use Corporate Resolutions

Resolutions are inserted in minutes of annual or special directors' meetings (or in written consent forms) to show formal approval of corporate legal, tax, and other business decisions.

We've included the standard language for the approval of business customarily handled at annual meetings of your board in the minutes forms contained in this chapter. But for special meetings, you will want to add the language of one or more resolutions showing the approval of the particular business for which the special meeting was called.

This book provides more than 80 resolutions, which cover standard items of corporate legal, tax, and business transactions (see Chapters 9 through 19 for specific instructions on using the various resolutions forms included with this book). You can simply fill in one of these resolutions and insert it in your minutes, as explained in the special instructions to the minutes forms below.

If you need to prepare your own language for a resolution (because you want to approve an item of business at a meeting not covered by one of our resolution forms), it is easy to do. We provide examples of using your own language in the special instructions to filling out minutes forms.

Most corporate resolutions stand on their own and do not require the preparation of additional documentation. However, some resolutions refer to additional backup agreements or paperwork, and you may wish to attach this supplementary material to your minutes. For example, if shareholders approve a resolution to make a loan to a director, you can prepare and attach a promissory note to your minutes. We include such backup paperwork (for example, promissory note forms) with the appropriate resolutions included with this book. But finding and adding your own supplemental forms, if necessary, also is easy to do. For example, standard loan, real estate, and other business forms are available from banks, real estate brokers, legal stationers, business law libraries, and other sources.

Choosing the Correct Minutes Form

We've already touched upon the basic differences between annual (sometimes called "regular") and special meetings of the board of directors. (See Chapters 2 and 4 for more information.) Here's a recap of a few essential points:

When to hold annual directors' meetings. The annual directors' meeting is normally held on the same day as or shortly after the annual shareholders' meeting. At this meeting, the directors accept their election to the board by the shareholders and transact any additional business brought before the meeting.

EXAMPLE:

All officers, directors, and shareholders attend the annual shareholders' meeting of WIZ-E-WIG Computer Graphics, Inc. Reports are given by the corporate president and treasurer, summarizing the business operations and results of the preceding year and outlining plans for the future. The shareholders then reelect the five-person board for another one-year term.

Next, the shareholders leave, and the newly constituted board stays behind. First, the board members accept their reelection to the board; then they discuss business plans for the upcoming year. Of course, if corporate shareholders also serve as board members when the shareholders' meeting ends, the shareholders simply don their directors' hats and reconvene to transact the business of the annual directors' meeting.

What is covered in annual directors' meetings. Routine items of business that are typically taken up at the annual directors' meeting include the appointment of officers for another year by the directors, the announcement of important salary increases or bonuses approved for the past or upcoming year, and reports of past or upcoming corporate business of importance to the directors. We include each of these items of business in the annual minutes form below. Our annual minutes form also contains space to add special resolutions to show the completion of any nonroutine business taken up and approved at the annual meeting, such as the approval of a 401(k) profit-sharing plan.

When to hold special meetings. Special meetings of directors are called during the year to discuss and approve specific items of corporate business as the need arises. In fairly rare circumstances, a special meeting of shareholders is called shortly after the special directors' meeting to obtain shareholder ratification of the directors' decision. For example, this would be appropriate if the directors approved a structural change to the corporation (such as authorizing a new class of shares), which requires shareholder approval.

CAUTION

Remember to give advance notice. Your bylaws should specify the date and time of your annual (or regular) meeting of directors. As we emphasize in Chapter 3, Step 5, it is important to provide directors with notice of upcoming meetings well in advance of the proposed meeting date. This is particularly important for special meetings of directors that are not scheduled in the corporation's bylaws—you want to make sure to inform all directors that a special meeting has been called by the president, a board member, or another person authorized to do so.

Preparing Minutes for Annual Directors' Meetings

Following is a sample annual minutes form for an annual directors' meeting. For help in completing it, refer to the special instructions which immediately follow this annual meeting form.

CD-ROM

Below is a sample of the Minutes of the Annual Meeting of Directors form included on the CD-ROM. Fill it out following any special instructions provided. The tear-out version is contained in Appendix C.

Special Instructions

❶ Your bylaws should specify the date, time, and place of annual directors' meetings (also called regular directors' meetings). Most annual meetings are held at the principal office of the corporation, although any meeting place, whether within or outside the state, typically is permitted under corporate bylaws and state corporate statutes.

Minutes of the Annual Meeting of Directors of

_____ [_name of corporation_] _____

An annual meeting of the directors of the corporation was held on _____,

20_____ at _____:_____ ____.M., at ❶   [_location of meeting_] _____

___, state of _____, for the purpose of reviewing the prior year's business

and discussing corporate operations for the upcoming year, and for the transaction of any other business

that may properly come before the meeting, including: ❷

_____

_____

_____

_____.

_____ acted as chairperson, and

_____ acted as secretary of the meeting. ❸

The chairperson called the meeting to order.

The secretary announced that the meeting was called by _____

_____. ❹

The secretary announced that the meeting was held pursuant to notice, if and as required

under the bylaws of this corporation, or that notice had been waived by all directors entitled to receive

notice under the bylaws. Copies of any certificates of mailing of notice prepared by the secretary of the

corporation and any written waivers signed by directors entitled to receive notice of this meeting were

attached to these minutes by the secretary. ❺

The secretary announced that the following directors were present at the meeting: ❻

Name of Director

_____

_____

_____

_____

_____

_____

The above directors, having been elected to serve on the board for another [*"one-year" or other term*]

term by the shareholders at an annual meeting of shareholders held on _____,

20_____, accepted their positions on the board. The secretary then announced that the presence of these

directors at the meeting represented a quorum of the board of directors as defined in the bylaws of this

corporation.

The following persons were also present at the meeting: ❼

Name   Title

_____   _____

_____   _____

_____   _____

_____   _____

_____   _____

The secretary announced that the minutes of the __[*"annual," "regular," or "special" directors'*]__

meeting held on _____, 20_____

☐ had been distributed prior to

☐ were distributed at

☐ were read at

the meeting. After discussion, a vote was taken and the minutes of the meeting were approved by the

directors in attendance. ❽

The following reports were presented at the meeting by the following persons: ❾

_____

_____

_____.

The chairperson announced that the next item of business was the appointment of the officers

and of standing committee members of the corporation to another __[*"one-year" or other term*]__

term of office. After discussion, the following persons were appointed to serve in the following capacities

as officers or committee members or in other roles in the service of the corporation for the upcoming

year: ❿

Name	Title
_____	_____
_____	_____
_____	_____
_____	_____

The next item of business was the determination of compensation or fringe benefits to be paid or awarded for services rendered the corporation by employees and staff. After discussion, the following employee compensation amounts were approved by the board to be paid for the upcoming fiscal year to the following employees of the corporation: **⓫**

Name	Type and Amount of Compensation or Benefit
_____	_____
_____	_____
_____	_____
_____	_____

On motion duly made and carried by the affirmative vote of [_"a majority of" or other vote requirement_] directors in attendance at the meeting, the following resolutions were adopted by directors entitled to vote at the meeting: **⓬**

_____

_____

_____

_____

There being no further business to come before the meeting, it was adjourned on motion duly made and carried.

⓭

_____

_____, Secretary

❷ Even though this paragraph includes the approval of "the transaction of any other business that may properly come before the meeting," it makes sense to mention all special resolutions to be presented at the annual meeting and that you will insert at the end of your minutes form. (See Special Instruction 12, below.) As explained in Chapter 3, Step 5, notice is normally not required for annual directors' meetings, and the directors may normally transact any business at the meeting whether or not it was stated in a notice or waiver of notice for the meeting. Do not mention standard agenda items and matters of routine business here, such as acceptance by the board of their elected positions or the reappointment of officers at the annual meeting, which are already built into the minutes form.

❸ Insert the name and title of the persons who acted as chairperson and secretary of the meeting. Normally, the president acts as chairperson of the board and board meetings, and the secretary of the corporation usually acts as secretary of corporate meetings. Under most bylaws, anyone may serve in any of these capacities, so you are normally free to appoint another director, officer, or staff person to take over if the person normally delegated to perform one of these tasks is absent.

In the instructions for this form, we specify when we are referring to the secretary of the corporation. All other references are to the secretary of the meeting. Normally, the secretary of the corporation and the secretary of the meeting will be one and the same.

❹ This is an optional paragraph, which may be deleted or filled in as "not applicable" if you choose not to include it. Normally annual directors' meetings are not called, since they are scheduled in the bylaws. (See Chapter 3, Step

3, for a discussion of the legal requirements for calling corporate meetings.) If your corporation follows a different practice, you may wish to show the corporate secretary as the person who called the annual directors' meeting.

❺ This statement indicates that notice, if required, was given to or waived by each director. As explained in Chapter 3, Step 5, although notice is usually not legally required for annual directors' meetings under most bylaws, we suggest that you do provide it or have each director sign a waiver of notice form. After all, if you are going to the trouble of holding (or at least documenting) an annual meeting, why not make sure everyone knows about the meeting? If notice is mailed to directors, your corporate secretary may wish to prepare and attach a Certification of Mailing of Notice to the minutes. (See Chapter 3, Step 9.) Also attach any written waivers of notice for the meeting that have been signed by directors. (See Chapter 7, Step 1, to prepare the waiver of notice form.)

❻ List the names of the directors present at the meeting. There must be a sufficient number of directors present to represent a quorum for a directors' meeting under your bylaws. (See Chapter 4, Step 8.)

Before announcing the achievement of a quorum in the next paragraph, the minutes indicate that all board members accepted their election to the board for another year. Most corporations hold their annual meeting of shareholders just before the annual board meeting to reelect the board to another one-year term. Fill in the date of the annual meeting of shareholders in the blank provided. If your directors were not reelected at the recent annual shareholders' meeting (for example, if they are elected biennially), insert "not applicable" in this blank.

EXAMPLE:

The bylaws of Supple Shoe Corp. authorize five directors and specify that a quorum for directors' meetings consists of a majority of the full board. Three directors, therefore, must attend the meeting in order for a quorum to be in attendance. If fewer than three attend the meeting, it must be adjourned until another date and time when a quorum can attend. (For the rules on providing notice of the adjourned meeting, see Chapter 3, Step 5.)

⚠ **CAUTION**

Directors don't act by proxy. Corporate statutes normally allow shareholders, but not directors, to designate another person to vote at a meeting by proxy. Even if allowed, letting someone vote for a board member is risky: The absent board member could be held liable for another person's negligent or ill-advised board decisions. Bottom line for board of directors members: Directors should take an active, personal interest in the decisions discussed and voted upon at board meetings, or consider resigning from the board.

---

❼ Specify any additional persons (other than the chairperson and secretary of the meeting) who attend the meeting but do not count toward a quorum. If reports are to be submitted to the directors, additional corporate officers, staff, or committee members may be in attendance, as well as the corporation's accountant or legal consultant.

List the president and treasurer here if you plan to follow our format in Special Instruction 9, below, indicating that these officers presented annual reports to the board. Also list the names of any other officers or committee members who will report to the board at the meeting.

❽ It is customary, though not legally necessary, for participants at an annual meeting to approve the minutes of the previous directors' meeting. Mostly this formality is undertaken to remind everyone of any special business approved at the last meeting and to allow any objections prior to placing a formal copy of the minutes in the corporate records book.

If you decide to follow this formality and wish to save time, you may send copies of the minutes of the last meeting to each participant to read prior to the meeting, as explained in Chapter 7, Steps 3–5. Otherwise, distribute copies of the minutes or have the secretary read or summarize them. Then ask for voice approval. Normally, the minutes are routinely approved, but if there are objections, you will need to work them out before approving the minutes. You may make appropriate corrections to the minutes or obtain a majority vote to approve the minutes over the objection of one or more directors. Fill in the blanks as shown to indicate the method of distributing or announcing the minutes of the prior meeting to directors. If you choose not to address prior minutes at your meeting, either delete this entire paragraph or fill in "not applicable."

💡 **TIP**

Use written approval forms to save time or obtain consent to prior board decisions. Written minutes approval forms can be sent out to directors along with the prior minutes before the meeting to obtain signed approval of those minutes. Using this form can save time and has the added advantage of providing signed consent to previous decisions reached at meetings. This may be helpful, for example, if directors did not attend the last meeting and you wish to have a record of their approval of important decisions reached at that meeting. (How to prepare Approval of Corporate Minutes forms is covered in Chapter 7, Step 3.)

If you use an Approval of Corporate Minutes form to obtain written approval of minutes of a prior meeting, change this paragraph in the current minutes to read as follows:

The secretary announced that the minutes of the ["regular," "annual," *or* "special directors'"] meeting held on [date] , 20__, had been distributed prior to the meeting and that each director had returned to the secretary of the corporation a signed statement showing approval of the minutes of the prior meeting. [*Delete the next sentence in the form showing a vote was taken at the meeting.*]

❾ If officers, staff, outside accountants, lawyers, or others present written or oral annual reports to directors, specify the nature of each report and the name of each presenter. We recommend that you use the following language to at least show annual reports by the corporate president and treasurer: "an annual financial report by the treasurer and an annual operations report by the president."

You may also want to show standing or ad hoc committee reports presented or distributed at the meeting.

EXAMPLE:

"report by the chairperson of the corporation's standing New Building Committee; report by the secretary of the Insurance Committee on the availability and cost of general liability and directors' and officers' errors and omissions insurance coverage."

❿ A standard item of business at an annual meeting of the board is the reappointment of the officers of the corporation and members of standing committees of the board. For small corporations, the president, vice president, secretary, and treasurer are normally reappointed for another term, and

all current standing committee members are also redelegated to their committees. However, this is a good time to make changes if officers, committee members, or board members think it makes sense to do so.

Most smaller corporations do not set up separate committees of the board, because the board is small to start with. Instead, the board sets up one or more nondirector committees composed of officers, department managers, and staff to tend to particular aspects of corporate activity.

EXAMPLE:

Hare and Tortoise, Inc., a small publishing company, appoints a workers' benefits committee to meet throughout the year to discuss suggestions for improvements to workers' health and pension coverage. The board has also set up a building improvement committee that negotiates with the landlord for improvements to corporate headquarters. At the annual directors' meeting, the board reestablishes the authority for each committee for another year and fills any vacancies and makes any replacements requested by each committee.

⓫ Another standard item of business at annual directors' meetings is the award of annual salary increases, bonuses, or additional fringe benefits to employees for work performance or results achieved during the preceding fiscal year. Use this paragraph for this purpose if you wish; leave it blank or delete it if it doesn't apply.

Either specify the name of each employee separately, or specify groups or categories of employees, if you'd prefer. In the blanks at the right of the name of each employee (or group of employees), specify the amount and type of compensation or benefit approved by the directors.

EXAMPLE:

The Middle Road Management Corporation decides to award three of its VPs an additional bonus for their outstanding work performance during the preceding year. The corporation also rewards its entire customer service department for excellent work:

Name	Type and Amount of Compensation or Benefit
Mark Fuller	$5,000 annual bonus
Tricia Mueller	$5,000 annual bonus
Benjamin Bailey	$5,000 annual bonus
Customer Service	10% annual bonus

⑫ You may wish to take action at annual directors' meetings on extraordinary items not built into the minutes form. This section of the annual minutes allows you to document these additional decisions by inserting one or more resolutions in the space following this paragraph.

In the first blank, show the vote required for passage of the resolution, normally a majority of directors present at the meeting. (See Chapter 4, Step 12.) Then include the language of the resolution passed by the board.

In the space below the paragraph, insert one or more resolutions that describe the specific legal, tax, financial, or other items of business voted upon and approved at the meeting. Describe the matter approved in this space.

In many instances, you can insert in this space one of the ready-to-use resolutions included in this book, following the instructions for preparing the resolution from one of the later chapters (Chapters 9 through 19). See the beginning of Appendix C for a list of resolution forms included on the CD-ROM and in tear-out form with this book with a cross-reference to the chapter of the book that contains instructions for preparing each resolution.

If you wish to approve business not covered by one of our resolutions, supply your own language for the resolution in this space in your minutes. You don't need to use fancy or legal language for your resolution; just describe as specifically as you can the transaction or matter approved by your board in a short, concise statement. Normally, resolutions start with a preamble of the following sort: "The board resolved that…," but this is not required.

Here are several examples of director resolution language:

EXAMPLE 1 (Bank Loan):

"The board resolved that the treasurer be authorized to obtain a loan from [*name of bank*] for the amount of $_____ on terms he/she considers commercially reasonable."

EXAMPLE 2 (Corporate Hiring):

"The board approved the hiring of [*name of new employee*], hired in the position of [*job title*] at an annual salary of $_____ and in accordance with the terms of the corporation's standard employment contract."

EXAMPLE 3 (Tax Year):

"The board decided that the corporation shall adopt a tax year with an ending date of 3/31 and directed the appropriate officers to file the required IRS forms."

EXAMPLE 4 (Amendment of Articles):

"The board of directors resolved that the following new article be added to the corporation's articles of incorporation: [*language of new article*]."

If you have trouble drafting your own resolution, or if the matter has important legal or tax consequences, you may wish to turn to a lawyer or accountant for help. (See Chapter 20.)

13 This adjournment paragraph and concluding signature line should appear at the very end of your minutes after any specialized resolutions adopted by your board. Fill in the name of the secretary of the meeting under the signature line.

After obtaining the signature of the secretary, file the completed minutes in your corporate records book, together with all attachments. If you prepared a separate meeting folder to include material having to do with your meeting (such as reports, notice forms, and the like—see Chapter 3, Step 1), now is the time to transfer this material, along with your completed minutes, to your permanent corporate records book. This paperwork can come in handy later to show that your meeting was called, noticed, and held properly. With respect to reports, the minutes will serve as a reminder of the reasons for decisions reached at your meeting.

Preparing Minutes for Special Directors' Meetings

Unlike regular or annual meetings of directors scheduled in advance in your bylaws, special directors' meetings are called during the year to discuss and vote on important items of corporate business.

Typical resolutions presented and approved at special meetings of the board are usually legal or tax-related decisions, such as:

- approval of a lease or real estate purchase agreement

- approval of a bank loan or line of credit

- approval of a standard employment or

independent contractor hiring policy to be used by the corporation

- approval of an amendment to articles or bylaws, or

- authorization of the issuance of shares to new or existing shareholders.

Following is the minutes form to use to document the actions taken at a special meeting of your directors. This form is similar to the annual directors' meeting form presented just above, but it does not contain the annual agenda items included in the preceding form.

CD-ROM

Below is a sample of the Minutes of Special Meeting of Directors form included on the CD-ROM and as a tear-out form. Fill it out following any special instructions provided.

Special Instructions

1 Insert the date, time, and place (street address, city, and state) of the meeting. Directors' meetings usually are held at the principal office of the corporation, although most bylaws allow meetings to be held anywhere.

2 List the specific purpose(s) for which this special directors' meeting was called. A similar statement of purpose(s) should have been included in your notice or waiver of notice form used for the meeting. (See Chapter 3, Step 5, and Chapter 7, Step 1.)

3 Insert the name and title of the persons who acted as chairperson and secretary of the meeting. Bylaws typically provide that the president or chairperson of the board presides at meetings of directors, and that the corporate secretary acts as meeting secretary.

In the instructions for this form, we specify when we are referring to the secretary of the corporation. All other references are to the secretary of the meeting. Normally the secretary of the corporation and the secretary of the meeting will be one and the same.

❹ Indicate the person or persons who called the special meeting of directors, along with each person's title. Typically, bylaws allow one of the directors, the president, or another corporate officer to call a special meeting of directors; see Chapter 3, Step 3, and check your bylaws.

❺ Proper notice or waiver of notice is important for special directors' meetings. You want all directors to be fully informed of the time and purpose of all specially called board meetings. We describe the legal requirements and practical procedure for preparing a notice in Chapter 3, Step 5. Instead of providing notice, it's legal to have each director sign a written waiver of notice, as explained in Chapter 7, Step 1. Make sure to attach any written waivers of notice to your minutes. If you mailed actual notice to your directors before the meeting, you may wish to have your corporate secretary prepare and attach a Certification of Mailing of Notice as explained in Chapter 3, Step 9.

❻ List the names of the directors present at the meeting. Normally, the bylaws specify that a majority of the full number of directors represents a quorum for a directors' meeting. Remember, if you don't have a quorum, you must adjourn the meeting. (See Chapter 4, Step 8.)

❼ Specify any additional persons (other than the chairperson and secretary of the meeting) who attend the special board meeting but do not count toward a quorum. If reports are to be submitted to the directors, then additional corporate officers, staff, or committee members may be in attendance, as well as the corporation's accountant or legal consultant.

❽ It is customary, though not legally necessary, for participants at a special meeting to approve the minutes of the previous directors' meeting. Mostly this formality is undertaken to remind everyone of any special business approved at the last meeting and to allow any objections prior to placing a formal copy of the minutes in the corporate records book.

If you decide to follow this formality and wish to save time, you may send copies of the minutes of the last meeting to each participant to read prior to the meeting as explained in Chapter 7, Steps 3–5. Otherwise, distribute copies of the minutes or have the secretary read or summarize them. Then ask for voice approval. Normally, the minutes are routinely approved, but if there are objections, you will need to work them out before approving the minutes. You may make appropriate corrections to the minutes or obtain a majority vote to approve the minutes over the objection of one or more directors. Fill in the blanks as shown to indicate the method of distributing or announcing the minutes of the prior meeting to directors. If you choose not to address prior minutes at your meeting, either delete this entire paragraph or fill in "not applicable."

TIP

Use written approval forms to save time or obtain consent to prior board decisions. You can send approval forms to directors along with the minutes of the prior meeting to obtain approval of those minutes before the next meeting. Using this form can save time and has the added advantage of providing signed consent to decisions reached at previous meetings. This may be helpful, for example, if directors did not attend the last meeting and you wish to have a record of their approval of important decisions reached at that meeting. (How to prepare Approval of Corporate Minutes forms is covered in Chapter 7, Step 3.)

Minutes of Special Meeting of Directors of

_____ [name of corporation] _____

A special meeting of the directors of the corporation was held on _____,

20_____ at ____:____ __.M., at ❶ _____ [location of meeting] _____,

state of _____, for the purpose(s) of ❷ _____

_____

_____

_____.

_____ acted as chairperson, and

_____ acted as secretary of the meeting. ❸

The chairperson called the meeting to order.

The secretary announced that the meeting was called by ❹ _____

_____.

The secretary announced that the meeting was held pursuant to notice, if and as required under the

bylaws of this corporation, or that notice had been waived by all directors entitled to receive notice under

the bylaws. Copies of any certificates of mailing of notice prepared by the secretary of the corporation and

any written waivers signed by directors entitled to receive notice of this meeting were attached to these

minutes by the secretary. ❺

The secretary announced that the following directors were present at the meeting, representing a

quorum of the board of directors: ❻

Name of Director

_____

_____

_____

_____

_____

_____

The following persons were also present at the meeting: ❼

Name   Title

_____   _____

_____   _____

_____   _____

_____   _____

_____   _____

The secretary announced that the minutes of the ____["annual," "regular," *or* "special" directors]____

meeting held on _____, 20_____

☐ had been distributed prior to

☐ were distributed at

☐ were read at

the meeting. After discussion, a vote was taken and the minutes of the meeting were approved by the

directors in attendance. ❽

The following reports were presented at the meeting by the following persons: ❾

_____

_____

_____

_____

The secretary announced that the next item of business was the consideration of one or more

formal resolutions for approval by the board. After introduction and discussion, and upon motion duly

made and carried by the affirmative vote of [__"a majority of" *or other vote requirement*__] directors in attendance

at the meeting, the following resolutions were adopted by directors entitled to vote at the meeting: ❿

_____

_____

_____

There being no further business to come before the meeting, it was adjourned on motion duly

made and carried.

⓫

_____

_____, Secretary

If you use an Approval of Corporate Minutes form to obtain written approval of minutes of a prior meeting, change this paragraph in the current minutes to read as follows:

> The secretary announced that the minutes of the ___["regular," "annual," or "special" directors']___ meeting held on ___[date]___ , 20__ , had been distributed prior to the meeting and that each director had returned to the secretary of the corporation a signed statement showing approval of the minutes of the prior meeting. [*Delete the next sentence in the form showing a vote was taken at the meeting.*]

❾ If officers, staff, outside accountants, lawyers, or others present written or oral reports to directors, specify the nature of each report and the name and title of each presenter. For example, this might be: "a presentation by Tasha Browne, corporate vice president, on plans to expand the company's current product line, and a report by the treasurer, Dan Woo, on the amounts of additional bank loan funds that will be required to fund this expansion."

❿ This section shows the main business of special directors' meetings: The consideration and approval of one or more formal resolutions. In the first blank, show the vote required for passage of the resolution—normally a majority of directors present at the meeting. (See Chapter 4, Step 12.) Then include the language of each resolution passed by the board in the space shown.

In many instances, you can insert one or more of the ready-to-use resolutions included in this book, following the instructions for preparing the resolution from one of the later chapters (Chapters 9 through 19). See the beginning of Appendix C for a list of resolution forms included on the CD-ROM and in tear-out form with this book, with a cross-reference to the chapter of the book that contains instructions for preparing each resolution.

If you wish to approve business not covered by one of our resolutions, supply your own language for the resolution in this space in your minutes. Again, you don't need to use fancy or legal language for your resolution; just describe as specifically as you can the transaction or matter approved by your board in a short, concise statement. Normally, resolutions start with a preamble of the following sort: "The board resolved that…," but this is not required.

Following are examples of standard director resolution language:

EXAMPLE 1 (Bank Loan):

"The board resolved that the treasurer be authorized to obtain a loan from [*name of bank*] for the amount of $_____ on terms he/she considers commercially reasonable."

EXAMPLE 2 (Corporate Hiring):

"The board approved the hiring of [*name of new employee*], hired in the position of [*job title*] at an annual salary of $_____ and in accordance with the terms of the corporation's standard employment contract."

EXAMPLE 3 (Tax Year):

"The board decided that the corporation shall adopt a tax year with an ending date of 3/31 and directed the appropriate officers to file the required IRS forms."

EXAMPLE 4 (Amendment of Articles):

"The board of directors resolved that the following new article be added to the corporation's articles of incorporation: [*language of new article*]."

If you have trouble drafting your own resolution language, or if the matter has important legal or tax consequences, you may wish to turn to a lawyer or accountant for help. (See Chapter 20.)

⓫ Put this concluding adjournment paragraph and signature line at the very end of the minutes, after any resolutions. Fill in the name of the secretary of the meeting under the signature line.

After obtaining the signature of the secretary, file the printed minutes in your corporate records book, together with all attachments.

If you prepared a separate meeting folder to include material having to do with your meeting (such as reports, notice forms, and the like—see Chapter 3, Step 1), now is the time to transfer this material, along with your completed minutes, to your permanent corporate records book. This paperwork can come in handy later to show that your meeting was called, noticed, and held properly. With respect to reports, the minutes will serve as a reminder of the reasons for decisions reached at your meeting. ●

Paper Meetings

In this chapter, we present the few simple steps necessary to document a paper meeting of your directors or shareholders. With a paper meeting, shareholders or directors don't actually hold a meeting; instead, they arrive at necessary decisions informally. To make a clear record of these decisions, you must prepare minutes and have them approved by the directors or shareholders.

When Is It Appropriate to Hold a Paper Meeting?

We've already touched upon the advantages and disadvantages of preparing minutes for a paper meeting in Chapter 2. Here we will make a few key points related to their use. The paper meeting procedure works best for corporations with only a few directors or shareholders who work together or know each other well and agree to most corporate decisions. Of course, paper meetings also work fine for a one-person corporation, where the sole shareholder-director really doesn't need to sit down and talk to himself or herself (or if so, then perhaps it's time for a two-week vacation).

In such small corporations, the paper meeting procedure allows corporate principals to elect officers and conduct other routine corporate business without going through the motions of holding a meeting. Legally, preparing and ratifying paperwork for a fictional corporate meeting will not present problems for your corporation as long as every shareholder or director agrees to the procedure and, of course, approves the decisions reflected in the minutes of the paper meeting.

! **CAUTION**

Avoid paper meetings if there is conflict or disagreement. Even for small, closely held corporations, we suggest you only use paper meetings for corporate decisions where everyone is in agreement. If there is even a whiff of dissent in the wind, or if the decision requires additional discussion, it is far better to hold a real meeting.

Using Paper Meetings to Create Records for Prior Undocumented Meetings

If you failed to properly document past annual and special meetings of your directors and shareholders, you are not alone. Many, if not most, smaller corporations that do their own paperwork forget to document important legal and tax decisions as they occur, putting off the task of preparing the paperwork until later. Often, this failure to document properly is overlooked until there is an IRS audit or a request for minutes of a meeting from a bank or other financial institution.

As long as all directors and shareholders mutually agreed to the past actions when they were taken, using the paper meeting approach to recreate corporate records after the fact should work well for your corporation.

EXAMPLE:

Small Systems, Inc., is a small, closely held corporation with six shareholder-directors who work in the business. They have been in operation for five years when they are notified of an IRS audit of their last two years' corporate income tax returns. For the audit, they need to produce corporate records for the years in question. Like many other small corporations, the daily grind of business has consumed the energies of each of the co-owners, and procedural niceties, such as annual meetings, have been skipped. Informally, and by mutual agreement, the initial directors named in the articles of incorporation have stayed on the board since the beginning of corporate existence, and the only special items of formal legal or tax paperwork executed during the first five years were the signing of a lease by the corporate president and treasurer and the signing by the shareholders of an IRS S corporation tax election form.

The directors decide it is best to memorialize these past decisions by preparing minutes for the annual directors' and shareholders' meeting for the last five years. They also decide to prepare minutes of a special directors' meeting (approving the corporate lease) and a special shareholders' meeting (approving the S corporation tax election).

To make clear that the records have been recreated, the secretary puts a note at the beginning of each document:

These documents have been recreated "after-the-fact" to the best recollection of the parties as of the date noted at the end of this document.

Signed: _____

Typed Name: _____ , Secretary

These minutes of paper meetings are placed in the corporate records book, and copies of the minutes of meetings for the two years in question are given to the IRS.

Comparison of Paper Meetings and Written Consents

For those who don't want to hold a formal directors' or shareholders' meeting, or missed holding one, there are two alternative procedures:

- preparing minutes of a paper meeting, or
- acting by written consent.

If you prepare minutes for a paper meeting, you are, in essence, doing the same thing as approving corporate business by the unanimous written consent of your directors or shareholders, a procedure sanctioned by the corporate statutes of the various states. However, minutes of a paper meeting often look better in the corporate records and carry more weight, at least from a practical standpoint, than written consent forms.

Here are a few important points if you're not sure whether paper meetings or written consents best meet your needs.

Use paper meetings for annual business. Paper meetings with minutes approved by the board or shareholders work better than written consents to show the discussion and approval of standard items of business taken up annually by the board or shareholders. Such business includes the annual review and discussion of past and present corporate business, the annual election of the directors, and acceptance by directors of another term on the board. The reason to use minutes of paper meetings for routine decisions is simple: The IRS, courts, financial institutions, and others generally expect corporate records to contain standard minutes for annual meetings. Written consent forms with no supporting documentation normally aren't enough to convince others that you paid attention to the ongoing formalities of corporate life.

Written consents may be used for special business. Written consent forms are generally adequate to document actions that would normally be approved at special meetings of your board or shareholders. These isolated decisions, approved during the year between annual directors' or shareholders' meetings, are commonly approved and documented with written consent forms rather than more formal minutes of a paper meeting.

Corporate records may contain minutes and consent forms. It's fine to prepare minutes of paper meetings for some decisions and written consents for others.

EXAMPLE:

Bertrand and Jackie are a married couple and the only two shareholder-directors of a small consulting business. They both work for the corporation and routinely reelect themselves to the board each year. After a few years of operation, they realize that they haven't kept up their corporate records. Bertrand prepares minutes of annual shareholders' meetings for the past two years showing the reelection of each director to the board. He accompanies these with minutes of annual directors' meetings showing the directors' acceptance of their reelection to the board each year. These minutes forms also show the discussion and approval of standard agenda items and business normally taken up at these meetings, such as reading and approval of past minutes and the approval of annual raises or bonuses to employees.

To save time, Bertrand prepares written consent forms showing two special transactions—a change of corporate tax year recommended by the corporation's accountant and the approval of a ten-year lease for the corporate main office premises—approved by the directors between the dates of the annual meetings. Approval could also have been documented by preparing minutes of special meetings, but consent forms seem adequate, especially given the fact that the annual meetings are fully documented.

How to Prepare Minutes for Paper Meetings

If you've decided to hold a paper meeting, follow the steps below to prepare the necessary paperwork.

Step 1. Prepare a Waiver of Notice Form

If you're going to prepare minutes for a meeting that has not occurred or will not occur, you'll obviously want to sidestep any formal call and notice requirements for holding the meeting. (See Chapter 3, Steps 3 to 5 for an overview of call and notice requirements contained in most bylaws and state corporate statutes.) The best way to do this from a legal perspective is to have each director or shareholder sign a written Waiver of Notice of Meeting form, dated before or on the same date of the meeting.

We strongly advise you to always summarize the purposes of the upcoming meeting in your Waiver of Notice of Meeting form. In some cases, it is legally required; we recommend it anyway to make sure all directors and shareholders appreciate the nature of the business to be taken up at the meeting. (State laws usually prohibit the transaction of any business not specified in the waiver of notice for a special shareholders' meeting.)

TIP

Other reasons to use a Waiver of Notice of Meeting form. You may use a Waiver of Notice of Meeting form even if you're planning to hold a real meeting. As discussed earlier in Chapters 3 through 6, you should use a Waiver of Notice of Meeting form whenever you wish to hold a meeting of your board or shareholders and do not have or do not choose to take time to provide everyone with advance verbal or written notice.

Waivers of Notice May Be Used for Real Meetings Too

State corporate laws usually allow waivers of notice to be used for directors' and shareholders' meetings.

Directors' meetings. Most states specifically allow directors to sign a written waiver of notice of meeting. The standard form used for this purpose is called, in legal slang, a waiver of notice form. Typically, state laws also provide that even if a director didn't get proper formal notice of a meeting, but hears about it and attends, by the act of showing up the director legally waives notice to any meeting unless he or she speaks up at the beginning of the meeting and objects to not having received proper notice of the meeting.

Shareholders' meetings. Most states specifically allow shareholders to sign a written Waiver of Notice of Meeting form, and, as with directors, most states provide that shareholders who attend a meeting without objection are assumed to have agreed to the notice or lack of notice for the meeting.

Check your bylaws to determine the waiver of notice rules that apply to your corporation.

Following is a sample of the Waiver of Notice of Meeting form included on the CD-ROM and in Appendix C. By signing this form, the director or shareholder waives any notice requirements for the meeting otherwise required under state law and any additional or alternative notice rules set in your bylaws.

You can prepare one Waiver of Notice of Meeting form for multiple directors or shareholders to sign, or you can prepare one form for each person.

CD-ROM

Below is a sample of the Waiver of Notice of Meeting form included on the CD-ROM and as a tear-out. Fill it out following any special instructions provided.

Special Instructions

❶ Under state corporate statutes, for certain important corporate decisions such as the election of directors or amendment of bylaws, a waiver of notice form must contain a description of the matter presented and approved at a meeting. When preparing a waiver of notice form, whether for a real or paper meeting, you should always state the purpose of the meeting. Be as specific as you can regarding the proposals presented at the meeting.

EXAMPLE:

A meeting is held on paper to approve an amendment to increase the authorized voting shares of the corporation. The purpose of the meeting stated in the waiver reads as follows: "amending Article III of the Articles of Incorporation to increase the authorized voting shares of the corporation from 100,000 to 200,000 shares."

❷ If more than one person will sign the form, the date inserted here should be the date the first person signs the waiver form. This date should be on or before the meeting date.

TIP

Pass out all paperwork at once. In Steps 2 through 5, below, we recommend that you have directors or shareholders approve the minutes of a paper meeting. So, to avoid contacting directors or shareholders twice, prepare this extra paperwork first, then pass out all forms together.

Waiver of Notice of Meeting of

_____ [*name of corporation*] _____

The undersigned ___[*name(s) of director(s) or shareholders(s)*]___ waive(s) notice of and consent(s) to the

holding of the _____ [*"annual," "regular," or "special"*] _____ meeting of the

_____ [*"shareholders" or "directors"*] _____ of _____ [*name of corporation*] _____

held at _____ [*location of meeting*] _____,

state of _____, on _____, 20____ at ____:____ __.M.,

for the purpose(s) of: ❶ _____

_____

_____.

Dated: _____ ❷

Signature   Printed Name

_____   _____

_____   _____

_____   _____

Step 2. Prepare Minutes of the Paper Meeting

Your next step is to prepare the minutes for your paper meeting of directors or shareholders. Usually, the secretary of the corporation prepares and distributes this paperwork, but the task can be assigned to anyone.

To prepare minutes for an annual or special paper meeting of shareholders, follow the corresponding minutes form covered in Chapter 5. To prepare minutes for an annual or special paper meeting of directors, follow the appropriate form covered in Chapter 6.

Place your minutes of the paper meeting in your corporate records book, and make copies of the minutes for each director or shareholder to review prior to signing the Approval of Corporate Minutes form discussed in the next step.

Step 3. Prepare Approval of Corporate Minutes Form

After preparing minutes for your paper meeting, we recommend that you get each director or shareholder to specifically sign off on the decisions approved in the minutes. This step is essential when you use the paper meeting procedure to document past corporate decision making; because a real meeting was not held, you need to be sure everyone agrees to your summary of the decisions reflected in your minutes.

Following is a sample of the Approval of Corporate Minutes form that is included on the enclosed CD-ROM and in Appendix C. Use this form to obtain approval of minutes of a paper meeting. You can prepare one Approval of Corporate Minutes form for multiple directors or shareholders to sign, or you can prepare one form for each person.

TIP

When to use an approval form for minutes of real meetings. The Approval of Corporate Minutes form can come in handy if you need to obtain approval of the past minutes of real meetings. For example, as we suggest in Chapters 5 and 6, prior to holding annual shareholders' and directors' meetings, you may wish to send the minutes of previous meetings to directors or shareholders to read before the meeting. Instead of waiting for the next meeting to approve these minutes, you may wish to ask them to sign an approval form—assuming, of course, they do not have corrections or additions to make. Doing this can save time at the meeting, as well as provide a signed document showing that the directors or shareholders specifically approved actions taken at a prior meeting. Especially if a director or shareholder missed a previous meeting, it's a good idea to make a written record of his or her signed approval to important decisions reached at that earlier meeting.

CD-ROM

Below is a sample of the Approval of Corporate Minutes form included on the CD-ROM and as a tear-out in Appendix C. Fill it out following any special instructions provided.

Approval of Corporate Minutes of

_____
[*name of corporation*]

The undersigned _____ ["shareholders" *or* "directors"] _____ consent(s) to the minutes of the

_____ ["annual," "regular," *or* "special"] _____ meeting of the _____ ["shareholders" *or* "directors"] _____

of _____ [*name of corporation*] _____

held at _____ [*location of meeting*] _____,

state of _____, on _____, 20____ at ____:____ __.M.,

attached to this form, and accept(s) the resolutions passed and decisions made at such meeting as valid

and binding acts of the _____ of the corporation.

Dated: _____

Signature   Printed Name

_____   _____

_____   _____

_____   _____

Special Instructions

If this is an approval of minutes for a paper meeting, we suggest you date the approval on or before the date set for the paper meeting.

Step 4. Prepare a Cover Letter

Following is a sample of the cover letter included on the CD-ROM and in Appendix C. You may wish to send this letter with the approval form you mail out to directors or shareholders. This letter explains why you are asking for approval of paper minutes and can come in handy if your directors or shareholders are not corporate insiders or are unfamiliar with corporate procedures and formalities.

CD-ROM

Here is a sample of the Cover Letter for Approval of Minutes of Paper Meeting form included on the CD-ROM and as a tear-out in Appendix C. Fill it out following any special instructions provided.

Step 5. Get Directors' and Shareholders' Approval

After you've completed the forms (Steps 1–4, above), make copies. Then distribute the forms to each director or shareholder. If it's easier, you may send around one copy of the forms to be signed; this is particularly efficient when shareholders or directors all work at the business.

Remember to include:

- Waiver of Notice of Meeting form
- Minutes, which include resolutions for the approval of special items of business—see Chapters 9 through 19, along with any reports, attachments, or resolutions describing special items of business approved, and
- Approval of Corporate Minutes.

After you've completed your paperwork and obtained signed copies, place the signed documents in your corporate records book.

Cover Letter for Approval of Minutes of Paper Meeting

Date: _____

Name: _____

Mailing Address: _____

City, State, Zip: _____

Re: Approval of Minutes

Dear _____:

I am enclosing minutes of a meeting of the _____["shareholders" or "directors"]_____ of
_____[name of corporation]_____ that show approval of one or more
specific resolutions. Each resolution contains the language of an item of business approved by the
_____["shareholders" or "directors"]_____.

Since these items were agreeable to the _____["shareholders" or "directors"]_____, we did not
hold a formal meeting to approve these decisions. We are now finalizing our corporate records and
preparing formal minutes that reflect prior corporate decisions.

To confirm that these minutes accurately reflect the past decisions reached by the _["shareholders"_
or "directors"], please date and sign the enclosed Approval of Corporate Minutes form and
mail it to me at the address below. If you have corrections or additions to suggest, please contact me so
we can hold a meeting or make other arrangements for formalizing and documenting these changes.

Sincerely,

_____

Enclosures: Minutes and Approval of Corporate Minutes Form

Please return to:

Name: _____

Corporation: _____

Mailing Address: _____

City, State, Zip: _____

Phone: _____   Fax: _____

CHAPTER

8

Action by Written Consent

State statutes allow directors and shareholders of a corporation to take action without holding a meeting by signing written consent forms. Basically, all of the shareholders or directors sign a piece of paper that contains the language of the decision (resolution) to be approved.

Using written consents for corporate decision making is often appropriate for small corporations with only a few shareholders or directors. It's sometimes even suitable for slightly larger organizations that have a deadline for making a decision and don't have time to assemble the board of directors or shareholders at a special meeting.

Action by written consent is most appropriate if the issue at hand is a routine tax or financial formality; for instance, the approval of standard loan terms offered by the corporation's bank or the approval of a tax election recommended by the corporation's accountant. It is not appropriate where a decision may engender debate or disagreement among directors or shareholders.

In the steps below, we discuss the legal rules related to taking action by written consent. We provide a sample form with instructions that you can follow as you fill out the Written Consent to Action Without Meeting form included on the CD-ROM. You'll see that it only takes a minute or two to fill out this form, which must then be distributed to your directors or shareholders for signing.

TIP

Provide written consents to absent directors or shareholders. Written consent forms also come in handy when a director or shareholder is not able to attend an important corporate meeting. Even if you obtain a quorum and therefore legally approve decisions at a meeting, it's wise to get the written consent of any nonattending directors or shareholders, especially where important resolutions are adopted. Doing this ensures that all directors

---

When to Use Minutes of Paper Meetings Instead of Written Consents

Even small corporations usually prepare minutes of a real or paper meeting to document the decisions made at annual directors' and shareholders' meetings. These take a little more time to prepare but look more convincing and official in the corporate records book. (See Chapters 5 and 6 for instructions on preparing minutes of directors' and shareholders' meetings. Chapter 7 covers how to hold paper meetings.)

You can safely use written consents to show the approval of the type of decisions that would otherwise be documented by preparing minutes of a special directors' or shareholders' meeting.

---

or shareholders are informed of actions taken at the meeting, and it provides clear evidence of their assent to the action taken.

Step 1. Check Your Bylaws for Your Written Consent Rules

Start by checking your bylaws to determine your corporation's rules for taking action by written consent. Your bylaws should mirror state law rules for written consents. The most common requirement is that directors and shareholders can take action without a meeting only by the *unanimous* written consent of directors or shareholders. Some states do, however, allow fewer than all shareholders to approve decisions by written consent as explained below.

Rules for Directors

Most states have a corporate statute specifically authorizing director action by written consent (without a meeting). Usually, the written consent of all directors is required. Therefore, if you think that one or more directors may object to the director action or resolution, you need to hold a meeting to approve the matter.

Rules for Shareholders

Most states allow shareholder action by written consent. A majority of states require unanimous shareholder consent to the action—in other words, all shareholders entitled to vote on a matter must sign the consent form. Some states allow approval by less than the unanimous written consent of shareholders. For example, some states say that the number of shareholders required to sign the consent form is the same number of shareholders owning or representing the number of shares required for passage of the action at a meeting at which all shareholders are present. But even in these states, unanimity for special shareholder actions, such as an increase in the stock or indebtedness of the corporation, may be required. As always, check your bylaws for the shareholder written consent rules in your state. If you're not sure your bylaws have all the state rules, then check your state laws as well.

You may live in a state with other rules, such as one that allows less than unanimous written consent by shareholders in all matters except the election of directors. Again, check your bylaws (and state laws if necessary) for the specific shareholder written consent rule in your state.

> **CAUTION**
>
> **Have all directors or shareholders sign a consent form.** We recommend that you always obtain the unanimous written consent of all directors or shareholders. Doing so not only ensures that you will meet the most stringent bylaw and state law requirements for director or shareholder

written consents but also gives notice to every director and shareholder of the decision. Regardless of the legal requirements, if you expect opposition by one or more directors or shareholders to a decision, it makes sense to hold a meeting to discuss these differences and obtain a vote on the issue instead.

Step 2. Prepare the Written Consent Form

Following is a sample of the Written Consent to Action Without Meeting form included on the enclosed CD-ROM and in Appendix C.

> **CD-ROM**
>
> Below is a sample of the Written Consent to Action Without Meeting form included on the CD-ROM and as a tear-out form in Appendix C. Fill it out following the special instructions provided.

Special Instructions

❶ Indicate whether you are preparing this consent form to show action taken without a meeting by either your directors or shareholders. If you want both the directors and shareholders to approve a given action, prepare separate forms.

❷ Insert a description of the actions or decisions agreed to by the directors or shareholders, in the form of a resolution. Chapters 9 through 19 contain instructions for preparing the ready-to-use resolutions included with this book (see Appendix C for a list of these resolutions, with a cross-reference to the chapter of the book that covers each one). If you wish to approve a matter not covered by one of our resolutions, insert your own resolution language in the consent form. You don't need to use fancy or legal language for your resolution; just describe as specifically as you can the transaction or matter approved by your board or shareholders in a short, concise statement. Normally, resolutions start with a preamble of the following sort: "The (board *or* shareholders) resolved that…," but this is not required.

The following are examples of resolution language:

EXAMPLE 1 (Bank Loan):

"The board resolved that the treasurer be authorized to obtain a loan from [*name of bank*] for the amount of $_____ on terms [*he/she*] considers commercially reasonable."

EXAMPLE 2 (Corporate Hiring):

"The board approved the hiring of [*name of new employee*], hired in the position of [*job title*] at an annual salary of $_____ and in accordance with the terms of the corporation's standard employment contract."

EXAMPLE 3 (Tax Year):

"The board decided that the corporation shall adopt a tax year with an ending date of 3/31 and directed the appropriate officers to file the required IRS forms."

EXAMPLE 4 (Amendment of Articles):

"The shareholders resolved that the following new article be added to the corporation's articles of incorporation: [*language of new article*]."

If you need to draft your own resolution language and have trouble doing so, or if the matter has important legal or tax consequences, you may wish to turn to a lawyer or accountant for help. (See Chapter 20.)

❸ Date the consent form and have your directors or shareholders sign their names. If you have only a few directors or shareholders, it may be easiest to prepare one master consent form to be passed around to each of your directors or shareholders to sign. In this case, date the form as of the date of the first signature by a director or shareholder. Another method, more appropriate when you have a larger number of directors or shareholders, is to prepare a separate consent form for dating and signing by each director or shareholder to date and sign. Either method works.

REMINDER

Signing reminder. We recommend that you have all directors or all shareholders sign the consent form. However, if your bylaws allow your shareholders to take the action at hand by less than unanimous written consent, you can have a lesser number of the group sign the form if you are comfortable doing so.

Written Consent to Action Without Meeting

The undersigned _____ ["shareholders" *or* "directors"] _____ ❶ of _____ [*name of corporation*] _____

hereby consent(s) as follows: ❷ _____

_____

_____

_____

_____

_____

_____

_____

_____

_____

_____

_____

_____

_____

_____

_____

_____

_____

_____

_____

_____

Dated: _____ ❸

Signature   Printed Name

_____   _____

_____   _____

_____   _____

_____   _____

Step 3. Place Signed Consent Forms in Your Corporate Records Book

After distributing your Written Consent to Action Without Meeting forms and obtaining the signatures of your directors or shareholders, make sure to place each completed form in your corporate records book. It's common to place these papers in the minutes section of the corporate records book, arranged according to the date of the action by written consent. ●

CHAPTER

9

Resolutions for Authorizing Business Transactions

This chapter has resolutions that authorize the transaction of standard items of ongoing corporate business: opening corporate bank accounts, adopting a fictitious corporate name, approving corporate contracts, and purchasing or leasing real property. We also provide forms that can be used to delegate, approve, rescind, or certify corporation decision-making authority. Where appropriate, we give relevant legal and tax information to help you select and use the resolutions.

If you don't see a resolution you need for a standard item of corporate business, scan the index or table of contents—it's quite possible you'll find it in a later chapter.

When to Use Business Corporate Resolutions

Much of the paperwork covered in this chapter may not be required legally or practically to consummate a corporate business deal. In fact, many smaller corporations forgo the formality of passing board resolutions for all but the most important items of ongoing corporate business, such as the purchase or sale of corporate real estate or the approval of long-term business or financial commitments. Of course, any business deal that has major tax or legal consequences should be approved by the board.

How to Select and Use Corporate Resolutions

- Scan the table of contents at the beginning of the chapter to find resolutions of interest to you.

- Read the background material that precedes each pertinent corporate resolution.

- Follow the instructions included with the sample resolution and complete a draft using your computer, or fill in the tear-out version included in Appendix C. If you need guidance on selecting and using the CD-ROM files, see Appendix A.

- Complete any needed attachment forms, such as account authorization forms or lease agreements.

- If a resolution involves complex issues that will benefit from expert analysis, have your legal or tax advisor review your paperwork and conclusions.

- Prepare minutes of a meeting or written consent forms as explained in Chapter 1, and insert the completed resolution(s) in the appropriate form. If you're seeking shareholder approval in addition to board approval, prepare two sets of minutes or written consent forms—one for your directors and one for your shareholders.

- Have the corporate secretary sign the printed minutes or have directors and/or shareholders sign any written consent forms and waivers. Then place the signed forms, together with any attachments, in your corporate records book.

But even small corporations sometimes decide to prepare formal paperwork for less critical business matters. For example, before entering into a business deal with the corporation, an outsider may want to know there was full board approval of the deal. Or, a vendor may want board approval of a long-term purchase order before agreeing to grant a hefty long-term discount for goods or services.

> **TIP**
>
> **Corporate business resolutions require board approval only.** The corporate resolutions in this chapter need only be approved by the board of directors. Of course, you may choose to have shareholders approve (ratify) any decision made by the board. Normally, you will not wish to take this extra step unless shareholder approval is legally required or the decision is important enough to warrant the extra time and effort.

Bank Account Resolutions

One of the first items of business for any corporation is to open a corporate checking account. Checks may be drawn against a standard bank checking account, a stock brokerage money market account, or other type of interest-bearing account set up to provide a reasonable return on the corporation's funds.

Opening and maintaining financial accounts in the name of the corporation is not just a practical nicety, it's a legal necessity. If you, as an owner of a corporation, intermingle corporate funds with your own personal account, a court or the IRS may hold you personally liable for corporate debts and bills. One of the reasons you incorporated was to gain personal protection from legal liability for your business. You don't want to let sloppy financial habits destroy the benefit of this important corporate attribute.

Often, personal checks from shareholders who paid cash for their initial shares of stock are the first money deposited into a corporate bank account. In small, closely held corporations, the first deposit may be money advanced by the incorporators to help pay initial corporate organizational and operational costs.

> **RELATED TOPIC**
>
> **Repaying personal advances.** If personal funds are advanced, the board should authorize their repayment when the corporation begins taking in cash receipts from the sale of products or services. The board also should make a tax election to amortize these start-up costs. For a resolution you may use to accomplish both tasks, see "Resolution for Payment and Deduction of Corporate Organizational Costs" in Chapter 10.

Now, let's look at the resolutions provided with this book that show board of director authorization for the opening of one or more corporate financial accounts at banks and other financial institutions. These resolutions vary as to where accounts may be opened and who may sign checks or withdraw funds.

Start-Up Money: Funding Your Corporate Bank Account

When you should deposit operating funds into your corporate checking account, and how much you should deposit, is often a matter of common sense. In most states, you can fund ("capitalize" in legal jargon) your corporation with as little or as much money as you wish (but a handful of states require that you deposit a minimum of $500 or $1,000 into the corporate coffers before the corporation begins doing business).

Take heed, however. If you fail to pay into your corporation at least enough money to cover foreseeable short-term debts and liabilities of your corporation and you're later sued, a court may decide to "pierce the corporate veil" and hold the owners personally liable for corporate debts. This is particularly likely to occur if a court sees this personal liability solution as a way to prevent fraud or injustice to creditors or other outsiders.

EXAMPLE: The principals of Think Thin, Inc., begin doing business with no money or assets, hoping to obtain initial receipts by franchising a national chain of hypnotherapy weight reduction clinics. A few outsiders buy initial franchises in the mistaken belief (reinforced by the Think Thin sales force) that the corporation has sufficient operating capital to advertise and otherwise actively promote the franchise chain. In a later lawsuit brought by the franchisees, a court holds the corporate business owners personally liable for monetary damages to the franchise purchasers, stating that, under these circumstances, it would be unfair to let the corporate structure protect corporate principals from personal liability.

General Resolution to Open Corporate Bank Account

This resolution will work well for most small corporations with a treasurer who handles the corporation's day-to-day finances, such as writing checks and making deposits. The resolution authorizes the treasurer to open one or more unspecified accounts in the name of the corporation. The treasurer alone is permitted to withdraw funds or write checks from these accounts, although anyone authorized by the treasurer may make deposits.

In this, as well as other resolutions below, you can change the title of the officer if you wish to designate a different person to deal with corporate funds. For example, you may substitute the title "vice president of corporate finance" for the word "treasurer" wherever the latter title occurs.

CD-ROM

Use the resolution titled Authorization of Treasurer to Open and Use Accounts to authorize the treasurer to open corporate accounts. The tear-out version is contained in Appendix C.

Authorization of Treasurer to Open and Use Accounts

The treasurer of the corporation is authorized to select one or more banks, trust companies, brokerage companies, or other depositories, and to establish financial accounts in the name of this corporation. The treasurer and other persons designated by the treasurer are authorized to deposit corporate funds in these accounts. However, only the treasurer is authorized to withdraw funds from these accounts on behalf of the corporation.

The treasurer is further authorized to sign appropriate account authorization forms as may be required by financial institutions to establish and maintain corporate accounts. The treasurer shall submit a copy of any completed account authorization forms to the secretary of the corporation, who shall attach the forms to this resolution and place them in the corporate records book.

Specific Corporate Account Resolution

The next resolution authorizes the treasurer to open an account with specific banks or other institutions. Only the treasurer is allowed to withdraw funds or write checks drawn against the funds in this account, although anyone authorized by the treasurer may make deposits. Again, you may delegate this authority to someone other than the treasurer.

CD-ROM

Fill in the resolution titled Authorization of Treasurer to Open and Use Specific Corporate Account(s) as you follow the sample and special instructions below. The tear-out version is contained in Appendix C.

Special Instructions

If you wish to authorize only one account, delete the remaining lines designating another account. For three or more accounts, add additional information about the type of account and financial institution.

**Authorization of Treasurer to Open
and Use Specific Corporate Account(s)**

The treasurer of this corporation is authorized to open the following account(s) in the name of the corporation with the following depositories:

Type of account: ["checking," "petty cash," *or other*]

Name, branch, and address of financial institution:

_____

_____

_____

Type of account: ["checking," "petty cash," *or other*]

Name, branch, and address of financial institution:

_____

_____

_____

The treasurer and other persons authorized by the treasurer shall deposit the funds of the corporation in this account. Funds may be withdrawn from this account only upon the signature of the treasurer.

The treasurer is authorized to complete and sign standard authorization forms for the purpose of establishing the account(s) according to the terms of this resolution. A copy of any completed account authorization form(s) shall be submitted by the treasurer to the secretary of the corporation, who shall attach the form(s) to this resolution and place them in the corporate records book.

Corporate Account Resolution With Multiple Signatories

This corporate account authorization resolution allows you to authorize one or more persons, such as officers and staff personnel, to sign corporate checks. You also can specify how many persons from this list are required to sign each corporate check.

CD-ROM

Fill in the resolution titled Authorization of Corporate Account and Designation of Authorized Signers on the CD-ROM as you follow the sample and special instructions below. The tear-out version is contained in Appendix C.

Special Instructions

The board may designate two or more persons to sign corporate checks. One or more—or all—may be required to sign each check. Especially with all but the smallest corporations, it may make sense to permit one of a number of trustworthy individuals to sign corporate checks.

EXAMPLE 1:

"All checks, drafts, and other instruments obligating this corporation to pay money shall be signed on behalf of this corporation by any one of the following: Janice Spencer, President; James Williams, Treasurer; William Yarborough, Assistant Treasurer."

EXAMPLE 2:

"All checks, drafts, and other instruments obligating this corporation to pay money shall be signed on behalf of this corporation by any two of the following: Janice Spencer, President; James Williams, Treasurer; William Yarborough, Assistant Treasurer."

TIP

Add terms or conditions if you wish. You may customize this resolution to add other conditions or requirements for check writing. For example, an additional sentence could be added to the above paragraph to require the approval of the president for all checks written for amounts above $1,000, $5,000, $10,000, or any amount you choose.

EXAMPLE OF ADDITIONAL TERMS:

"All checks, drafts, and other instruments obligating this corporation to pay money shall be signed on behalf of this corporation by any one of the following: Janice Spencer, President; James Williams, Treasurer; William Yarborough, Assistant Treasurer. However, the verbal or written approval of the president shall be required prior to the signing by the Treasurer or Assistant Treasurer for checks with a face amount of or above the amount of one thousand dollars ($1,000)."

**Authorization of Corporate Account and
Designation of Authorized Signers**

The treasurer of this corporation is authorized to open a [*type of account, such as "checking" or "petty cash"*]
account in the name of the corporation with ___[*name and branch address of bank or other institution*]___

_____.

Any officer, employee, or agent of this corporation is authorized to endorse checks, drafts, or other
evidences of indebtedness made payable to this corporation, but only for the purpose of deposit.

All checks, drafts, and other instruments obligating this corporation to pay money shall be signed
on behalf of this corporation by ___[*number*]___ of the following: ___[*names and titles of persons*
_authorized to sign checks*]_____

The above institution is authorized to honor and pay any and all checks and drafts of this
corporation signed as provided herein.

The persons designated above are authorized to complete and sign standard account authorization
forms, provided that the forms do not vary materially from the terms of this resolution. The treasurer shall
submit a copy of any completed account authorization forms to the secretary of the corporation, who
shall attach the forms to this resolution and place them in the corporate records book.

Certification of Bank Account Resolution by Corporate Secretary

Banks usually provide their own account authorization form(s) to be completed by the corporate secretary or treasurer. The form will show the signature(s) of the person(s) authorized to sign corporate checks according to the terms of one of the above bank account resolutions.

Some banks may ask you to attach a copy of your board of director's bank account resolution to its authorization form, certified as authentic by your corporate secretary. If required, complete a certification form and submit it to the bank with your completed bank account authorization form.

Authorization of Corporate Safe Deposit Account

Some corporations decide to open a safe deposit box at a local bank or other financial institution to store important corporate documents or assets, such as stock certificates, promissory notes, or trade secrets. Your board can use the resolution shown below to authorize this item of business.

CD-ROM

Fill in the resolution titled Authorization of Rental of Safe Deposit Box as you follow the sample below. The tear-out version is contained in Appendix C.

Authorization of Rental of Safe Deposit Box

The treasurer of the corporation is authorized to rent a safe deposit box in the name of the corporation with an appropriate bank, trust company, or other suitable financial institution, and to deposit in this box any securities, books, records, reports, or other material or property of the corporation that he or she decides is appropriate for storage and safekeeping in this box.

Resolution to Adopt Assumed or Fictitious Business Name

Sometimes a corporation wishes to do business under a name different from the one stated in its articles, although it doesn't want to give up its full corporate name.

EXAMPLE:

The Accelerated Business Computer Corp. decides to advertise and otherwise do business under the abbreviated name ABC Corp.

The easiest solution is to register the new, shortened name as a fictitious or assumed business name. You may need to file the assumed name with a state and/or local office. In most states, the filing is made in the county clerk's office for the counties in the state where the assumed name will be used. For example, a corporation that sells goods and services locally would file assumed name documents in the office of the county where the principal office of the corporation is located.

To find out how to register your assumed business name, call the state corporate filing office first. The office will provide forms if you must register the name at the state level, and refer you to a local government office (county clerk) if the assumed name must be registered locally instead of at the state level. To register locally, you may be required to publish a notice of assumed name and file a proof of publication with the local county clerk's office; your local county clerk's office can provide instructions for any publication requirements.

If you must file the assumed name with the state office, the name may have to be different from names of other corporations registered in the state. For local filings, the new name is not usually checked against other names already in use.

RELATED TOPIC

Changing the corporate name. If the corporation wishes to change to a completely new name that it will use exclusively to conduct business, changing the formal name in the articles of incorporation makes more sense. In that case, an amendment to the articles showing the new corporate name must be filed with the corporate filing office; see "Amending Your Articles of Incorporation" in Chapter 11.

CD-ROM

Use the resolution titled Adoption of Assumed Name on the CD-ROM to adopt an assumed or fictitious name. The tear-out version is contained in Appendix C.

Adoption of Assumed Name

It was decided that the corporation should do business under a name that is different from the formal name of the corporation stated in its articles of incorporation. The assumed name selected for the corporation is _____ [*assumed name*] _____.

The secretary of the corporation was instructed to register the assumed corporate name locally and/or with the secretary of state or similar state or local governmental offices as required by law.

Do a Trade Name and Trademark Search Before Adopting or Changing a Name

Selecting and registering an assumed name, just like registering a formal corporate name by filing articles of incorporation, does not guarantee that you have the absolute legal right to use the name. If another business in your area has been using this name or a similar name in connection with its business, products, or services, a court can award the other business the right to the name and hold you liable for damages, including profits the other business lost because you used the name.

If your business involves interstate commerce, you will want to make sure that another business is not using the name in other states in which you plan to do business. (Also, an out-of-state business using a name similar to yours could decide to start setting up branch offices or selling franchises in your area—this too can cause problems.) The U.S. Patent and Trademark Office can help you locate these out-of-state names.

Private businesses listed in the telephone directory under "Trade names" will perform searches of business, trademark, and service mark names in use by others in your county and state, in other states, and registered with the federal Patent and Trademark Office. If you have access to the Internet, you can perform your own preliminary name search for less expense by searching the Patent and Trademark Office's database at www.uspto.gov or by using trade name and trademark search services found on commercial database bulletin boards. (For more information on performing your own trade name search, see *Trademark: Legal Care for Your Business & Product Name*, by Stephen Elias (Nolo).)

Resolution to Approve a Contract

You can use this resolution to show board approval of a negotiated or proposed contract, and to delegate to an officer the authority to enter into the contract on the corporation's behalf.

It's a good idea to obtain specific board approval of a contract ahead of time if the contract concerns an important undertaking by the corporation or obligates it to spend substantial funds. Other types of contracts that are appropriate for board approval include:

- business deals that extend over a period of time, such as a five-year purchase-option contract on a building

- complicated business arrangements that would benefit from formal board review and approval, and

- contracts where the other party wants the board to approve the decision—for example, an outsider who is to provide long-term services or products requests the board to approve the contract before fulfilling the order.

RELATED TOPIC

Sometimes you'll want to specifically authorize an officer to sign a contract. For a discussion of resolutions specifically geared to authorizing or ratifying the authority of officers to transact business for the corporation, before or after the fact, see "Authorization or Ratification of Employee's Authority," below.

CD-ROM

Fill in the resolution titled Board Approval of Proposed Contract on the CD-ROM as you follow the sample below. The tear-out version is contained in Appendix C.

Board Approval of Proposed Contract

The board was presented a proposed contract to be entered into between the corporation and

_____[name of outside party]_____ for the purpose of [subject matter of contract

____such as "the renovation of corporate offices"]_____

together with the following attachments:

[specify additional material submitted with contract for approval by the board, such as "building plans"]

Next, a report on the proposed contract was given by [name of corporate officers or other employees]

_____, who made the following major points and concluded with

the following recommendation: ____[if applicable, cite major points provided in oral or

____written reports given at meeting and the conclusions of the reports]_____

After discussion by the board, __[if you wish, you may add: "including discussion by the____

following directors with respect to the following point:" and cite specific statements or conclusions

given by individual board members]____, it was decided that the transaction of the business covered by the

contract was in the best interests of the corporation, and the proposed contract and attachments were

approved by the board.

The _____[title of corporate officer]_____ was instructed to execute the contract submitted

to the meeting in the name of and on behalf of the corporation, and to see to it that a copy of the

contract executed by all parties, together with all attachments, be placed in the corporate records of the

corporation.

Real Property Resolutions

These resolutions address the lease, purchase, or sale of real property by the corporation.

Resolution Approving Lease

The board may pass a formal resolution to approve a lease of corporate business premises. Some lease arrangements are routine and need not be given to the board to approve. However, those that involve a long-term lease commitment or substantial deposits may benefit from board discussion and approval by way of a formal resolution.

Commercial leases generally specify either a fixed rental amount or rent calculated as a percentage of gross or net profits earned by the business. Of course, lease terms vary depending upon market conditions, bargaining positions, and state law requirements.

Use the following resolution to show board approval of lease terms negotiated with a property owner or manager. Attach a copy of the lease to the resolution and file both documents in your corporate records book.

CD-ROM

Fill in the resolution titled Approval of Lease on the CD-ROM as you follow the sample below. The tear-out version is contained in Appendix C.

Consider a Lease-Back of Property to Your Corporation

An owner of a small corporation may wish to lease property to the corporation to get cash out of the corporation and obtain favorable tax benefits. Of course, the IRS will expect the rent charged to be reasonable. The corporation deducts rent payments as business expenses, and the shareholder-lessor reports the rent payments as ordinary income on his or her tax return. These rent payments, in turn, can be offset by depreciation deductions, at least to some extent.

For an owner of a closely held corporation, there may be tax advantages of a lease-back arrangement rather than an outright sale of property to the corporation. For example, the tax law provides that an individual who owns more than a 50% interest in a corporation cannot claim a loss on the sale of property to the corporation unless it is part of a liquidation plan. This is true even if the sale is for a reasonable amount and is based upon fair market value. In this circumstance, a lease of the real estate probably would be a better idea, with the owner holding title to the building until he or she can sell at a gain to another buyer, or until death. (At death, the property gets a stepped-up basis, meaning that its basis (value for tax purposes) will be the value on the date of death; less taxes will ultimately be paid upon a sale of the property.)

When a corporation sells or liquidates appreciated property that it owns, a double tax on appreciation may be owed—by the corporation *and* the shareholders. This is another reason corporate owners may decide to keep real estate out of the corporation.

Talk to your tax adviser about your options if you own real estate used in your business.

Approval of Lease

A proposed lease agreement between _____[name of corporation]_____ and _____[name of lessor]_____ for the premises known as _____[address of property]_____ was presented to the board for approval.

The lease covered a period of _____[term of lease]_____, with _____[period of lease payments, such as "monthly" or "quarterly"]_____ rental payments of $_____[dollar amount or formula used to compute rent payments]_____.

After discussion, it was decided that the lease terms were commercially reasonable and fair to the corporation and that it was in the best interests of the corporation to enter into the lease.

The board approved the lease and all the terms contained in it, and the secretary of the corporation was instructed to see to it that the appropriate officers of the corporation execute the lease on behalf of the corporation and that a copy of the executed lease agreement be attached to this resolution and filed in the corporate records book.

Resolution Authorizing Purchase of Real Property

The board should authorize any purchase of real estate by the corporation. This is not only a significant business transaction that warrants extra formality, but title and trust companies also routinely require a board resolution before escrow papers are finalized.

The purchase of real property gives rise to significant mortgage interest and depreciation deductions for the corporation and, if a building or other property is purchased from a shareholder, a source of cash to the selling shareholder. Of course, to ward off IRS attacks (and possible challenges from outside shareholders), any land sold to the corporation by an inside shareholder should be priced at fair market value (or less).

> **TIP**
>
> **Consider a lease-back option.** Owners of a small corporation who hold title to business property may wish to lease, rather than sell, business property to their corporation. (See the discussion in "Resolution Approving Lease," above.)

> **CD-ROM**
>
> Below is a sample of the resolution titled Purchase of Real Property to use to approve the purchase of real property by the corporation. The tear-out version is contained in Appendix C.

Purchase of Real Property

The board discussed the purchase of real property commonly known as ___*[street address of property]*___.

The president announced that the property had been offered to the corporation for sale by the owner

at a price of $___*[listed or seller's asking price]*___. After discussing the value of the property to

the corporation and comparable prices for similar properties, it was agreed that the corporation should

___*["accept the offer"* or *"make a counteroffer for the property at a price of $(counteroffer price)"]*___

_____.

It was also agreed that the corporation shall seek financing for the purchase of the property on the

following terms:___*[insert, if applicable, the term and interest rate of financing the corporation will seek for*

financing the purchase of the property, for example, "This offer shall be contingent on the corporation's ability to

obtain financing for the purchase under a 30-year note carrying an interest rate not to exceed 10%"]___.

The president was instructed to see to it that the appropriate corporate officers prepare all financial

and legal documents necessary to submit the ___*["offer"* or *"counteroffer"]*___ to the seller and to seek

financing for the purchase of the property according to the terms discussed and agreed to by the directors.

Resolution Authorizing Sale of Corporate Real Property

The sale of real estate owned by the corporation is an important corporate transaction that should be formally approved by the directors. As with the purchase of real estate, this type of business transaction warrants a little extra formality, and title and trust companies routinely require a board resolution before the escrow papers are finalized.

CD-ROM

Fill in the resolution titled Authorization of Sale of Real Property on the CD-ROM as you follow the sample below. The tear-out version is contained in Appendix C.

Authorization of Sale of Real Property

After discussion, the board agreed that the president of the corporation is authorized to contract to sell real

property of the corporation commonly known as _____ [*street address of the property to be sold*] _____

on the following general conditions and terms: [*provide price and other terms that the president should*

_____ *seek to obtain; for example:* "at a sales price of no less than $100,000, with no less than 10% down _____

_____ and the balance carried through a 10-year or less note at current commercial interest rates"] _____.

The president of the corporation and any other officers of the corporation authorized by the president

are empowered to execute all instruments on behalf of the corporation necessary to effectuate and record a

sale of the above property according to the terms approved by the board in this resolution.

Authorization or Ratification of Employee's Authority

Major actions or business undertaken by key corporate employees (including officer-employees of the corporation) should be specifically approved by the board. There's no test for what's considered "major"—simply use your own business and common sense.

Sometimes it makes sense to give an employee a formal grant of authority before the employee makes a significant decision. For example, if an employee may commit significant funds or handle a critical area of corporate operations—such as a decision to commit substantial corporate resources to a new product or service—it makes sense to have the board officially delegate authority to the employee for these actions. This type of official delegation is often required by third parties, such as banks, title companies, and insurance companies, and it can be useful internally to emphasize to the employee the limits of his or her authority. It also provides a paper trail of decisions if they are later questioned by others.

Passing this type of resolution, either before or after the fact, also helps assure the employee that he or she is not personally liable for or bound by the transaction or contract. Rather, the employee is simply performing corporate business as an employee or agent of the corporation.

In the next sections, we provide resolutions your board can use to approve the authority of corporate officers, key employees, or other corporate workers to undertake corporate business or enter into corporate contracts, either before or after the fact.

Resolution Delegating Authority to Corporate Employee

The following resolution can be used by the board to delegate specific authority for one or more contracts, decisions, or business matters. This resolution can help make the employee aware of his or her role in the upcoming business transaction, as well as let others know how far the employee can go in acting on behalf of the corporation. This resolution is to be used before the employee makes decisions or authorizes contracts on behalf of the corporation.

EXAMPLE:

Tired Treads, Inc., a car leasing company, wants an employee to negotiate and sign a long-term car rental agreement with another corporation. Before the other corporation will close the deal, however, it wants to see a corporate resolution from Tired Treads that sets out the employee's authority.

CD-ROM

Fill in the resolution titled Delegation of Authority to Corporate Employee as you follow the sample and special instructions below. The tear-out version is contained in Appendix C.

Special Instructions

You can limit the authority of the employee to specific business transactions, to specific monetary or time limits, or in any other way you wish.

Delegation of Authority to Corporate Employee

After discussion, it was agreed that the following employee shall be granted authority to perform the tasks or transact business by and on behalf of the corporation, or to see to it that such tasks are performed for the corporation under his or her supervision as follows:

_____ [state name and title of employee and general or specific nature of authority granted to employee,

including any limitations to his or her authority]   .

The employee also shall be granted the power to perform any and all incidental tasks and transact incidental business necessary to accomplish the primary tasks and business described above.

EXAMPLE:

The board of GyroCopter Tours Corp. uses this resolution to help define the authority of a corporate vice president to negotiate the renewal of lease terms for the corporation. Specific monetary and time limits are set in the resolution, which specifies: "Sharon Hammond, the vice president of the corporation, has authority to renegotiate the renewal of the lease for the corporation, provided the the lease amount does not exceed $4,000 per month and the lease term does not exceed five years in duration. If a new lease is not negotiated by the vice president within the following 90 days, this authority shall automatically terminate, and the vice president shall request additional approval from the board in order to proceed with lease negotiations on behalf of the corporation."

Resolution Ratifying Employee's Acts

When a business decision needs to be made in a hurry, a corporate employee sometimes does not have time to check with the board to obtain prior approval of a transaction. If the transaction is important or potentially controversial—or if some directors may object or wish to debate the outcome of the employee's decision—it is wise to show that a majority of the board approved the decision and agreed that the employee had a right to enter into the business on the corporation's behalf. An after-the-fact approval by the directors of the employee's decision is called a ratification.

The following board resolution can be used to obtain a ratification by the board of prior business actions taken on behalf of the corporation by an employee. (If you wish to obtain board ratification of a *contract* entered into by an employee, see the next sample resolution.)

CD-ROM

Fill in the resolution titled Director Ratification of Employee's Acts as you follow the sample below. The tear-out version is contained in Appendix C.

Director Ratification of Employee's Acts

After discussion, it was agreed that the following acts, business, or transactions are hereby adopted, ratified, and approved as acts of the corporation and are accepted as having been done by, on behalf of, and in the best interests of the corporation:

_____ *[insert the name and title of the employee and date and nature of the business performed]* _____

_____ .

Resolution Ratifying Employee's Contract

Sometimes an employee may sign a contract on behalf of the corporation without obtaining prior approval from the board. In many cases, this is perfectly fine and no followup ratification or documentation is required. But in important instances—for example, when an employee signs a contract that commits the corporation to a major business deal—it's wise to provide documentation in the corporate records book showing that the corporation accepted the terms of the contract. Here, we present a resolution that can be used to ratify a contract that was signed by an employee on behalf of the corporation.

 CD-ROM

Fill in the resolution titled Board Ratification of Contract on the CD-ROM as you follow the sample and special instructions below. The tear-out version is contained in Appendix C.

Special Instructions

This resolution assumes that the employee signed the contract in the proper fashion—in the name of the corporation. (See "The Right Way for Officers and Other Employees to Sign Corporate Contracts," below.)

Board Ratification of Contract

After discussion, it was agreed that the contract dated _____[date of contract]_____ entered into between

_____[name of third party]_____ and _____[name and title of employee]_____,

in the name and on behalf of the corporation, for the purpose of ____[state nature of contract]____ is

hereby adopted, confirmed, and ratified, and is approved as being in the best interests of the corporation

and its business.

The Right Way for Officers and Other Employees to Sign Corporate Contracts

Whenever an employee signs a contract for the corporation—whether before or after obtaining board authority for the contract—the document should always be signed as follows:

_____[name of corporation]_____

by ___[signature of employee]___

_____[name and title of employee]_____

If an employee fails to do this and signs a contract in his or her own name instead, a third party may be able to hold the employee personally responsible for performance under the contract, even if the corporation ratifies it later. This is particularly true for officers. Outsiders are entitled to rely on the "apparent authority" of officers to act for and bind the corporation unless they know that the officer is not empowered to act—for example, an outside businessperson was told that the officer's ability to bind the corporation was rescinded or limited.

Resolution Rescinding Employee's Authority

A corporation may wish to cancel an employee's authority to transact business or negotiate the terms of a contract previously allowed by the board. This may be the case, for instance, if the board passed an open-ended resolution giving the employee the authority to negotiate a lease, without specifying a time limit, and business conditions now render the delegation of authority to the employee unnecessary. For example, the board may want to rescind the authority of the treasurer to seek loan funds, because the treasurer borrowed sufficient funds under the prior authority.

CD-ROM

Below is the resolution the board may use to revoke previously approved authority to an employee to enter into corporate business or contracts, titled Rescission of Authority of Employee on the CD-ROM. Fill in the resolution as you follow the sample below. The tear-out version is contained in Appendix C.

Rescission of Authority of Employee

After discussion, it was agreed that prior authority granted to _____ [name and title of employee] _____

on _[date of approval of authority]_ for the purpose of _[describe the authority granted to the employee]_

was no longer necessary to the interests of the corporation and that any and all authority granted

under this prior approval of authority is hereby rescinded and no longer in effect.

Resolution by Shareholders Ratifying Directors', Officers', or Employees' Acts

This handy resolution can be used to show shareholder approval and ratification of business approved and undertaken by corporate directors, officers, and other corporate personnel.

It may make sense to ask for shareholder ratification of a director's decisions or an officer's or key employee's acts—for example, after the settlement of a lawsuit or payment of substantial severance benefits to a departing executive. There is no legal requirement to do this, but it may help everyone rest a little easier.

CD-ROM

Fill in the resolution titled Shareholder Ratification of Decisions or Acts as you follow the sample below. The tear-out version is contained in Appendix C.

Shareholder Ratification of Decisions or Acts

After discussion, it was agreed that the following decisions, acts, resolutions, and proceedings of the board

of directors and/or employees of this corporation as specified below, are approved and affirmed by the

shareholders of this corporation as necessary to the business of and in the best interest of this corporation:

[insert date and nature of decisions and acts and names and titles of directors,

officers, or other employees who approved or implemented them]   .

Certification, Affidavit, or Acknowledgment of Corporate Decision Making or Document

Your corporate employees (including officers) or directors may need to certify to others that a given corporate decision, act, or document was approved by your board or shareholders in accordance with state law and the operating rules of the corporation. For example, prior to obtaining a loan, a bank may require the secretary to certify that the board of directors approved the loan.

We provide three forms a director or employee may use to make this showing. None of the forms is a resolution. The first two forms are ways to validate or certify a resolution that is attached to or quoted in the form; the third is a legal statement that can be added to the end of another legal document, such as a contract.

Certification of Board or Shareholder Action

The following form is used by the corporate secretary to certify to outsiders that an act by the board or shareholders was properly made. This is the least formal of the three forms in this section, and the most common way this type of action is taken.

CD-ROM

Fill in the form titled Certification of Board or Shareholder Action on the CD-ROM as you follow the sample and special instructions below. The tear-out version is contained in Appendix C.

Special Instructions

❶ Although it is most common for the secretary to sign this form, any officer or director can do so. Show the title of the officer or director who is certifying the corporate decision.

❷ Attach a copy of the board or shareholder resolution or written consent form to this form before submitting it to the bank or other institution that has requested the certification. Remember to place copies in your corporate records book.

Certification of Board or Shareholder Action

The undersigned, duly elected and acting _____ ["secretary" *or title of other officer*] ❶ _____ of

_____ [*name of corporation*] _____, certifies that the attached resolution was ❷

adopted by the _____ ["directors" *or* "shareholders"] _____ as follows:

[ ] at a duly held meeting at which a quorum was present, held on _____
[*if the resolution was approved at a meeting, check the above box and insert date of meeting*]

[ ] by written consent(s) dated on or after _____
[*if the resolution was approved by written consent, check above box and insert date of first written consent obtained for approval of resolution*]

that it is a true and accurate copy of the resolution, and that the resolution has not been rescinded or modified as of the date of this certification.

Dated: _____

Signed: _____   Name/Title: _["Secretary" *or title of other officer*]_

Affidavit of Corporate Decision Making

A more formal way for the corporate secretary to certify that a particular corporate decision was approved by the board or shareholders is through the use of an affidavit. This is a sworn statement, signed in the presence of a notary, that attests to the truth of statements made in the affidavit. The language for affidavits varies from state to state, but a typical affidavit follows the format of the form shown below.

 CD-ROM

Fill in the form titled Affidavit of Corporate Decision Making on the CD-ROM as you follow the sample below. The tear-out version is contained in Appendix C.

 CAUTION

Check your state's notarization form. Before using this form, ask a notary in your state for a copy of your state's affidavit language. To make sure this form conforms to your state's notarization language, make any necessary modifications to the notary sections of the form before using it. Normally, you won't have to make many changes.

Affidavit of Corporate Decision Making

STATE OF _____

COUNTY OF _____

Before me, a Notary Public in and for the above state and county, personally appeared _[name of corporate_
_secretary or other officer or director]_____ who, being duly sworn, says:

　　1. That he/she is the duly elected and acting _____[title]_____ of __[name of corporation]_____
_____, a __[name of state]_____ corporation.

　　2. That the following is a true and correct copy of a resolution duly approved by the
___["directors" or "shareholders"]_____ of the corporation, as follows:

　　[ ] at a duly held meeting at which a quorum was present, held on _____,
　　[if the resolution was approved at a meeting, check the above box and insert date of meeting]

　　[ ] by a sufficient number of written consents dated on or after _____
　　[if the resolution was approved by written consent, check above box and insert date of first written
　　consent obtained for approval of resolution]

　　　____[insert language of resolution here]_____

　　3. That the above resolution has not been rescinded or modified as of the date of this affidavit.

Signed: _[signature of officer or director taken in the presence of Notary]___

Name/Title: _____[title]_____

Sworn to and subscribed before me this _____ day of _____, 20__.

Notary Public: __[signature of Notary Public]_____

My commission expires: _____

NOTARY SEAL

Acknowledgment of Corporate Document

A corporate employee or director may be asked to acknowledge a legal document, such as a lease or deed. An acknowledgment states that the person is who he or she claims to be and that he or she actually signed the document in question. Acknowledgments, like affidavits, are often required to be given in the presence of a notary.

Following is a sample of the acknowledgment form that can be attached to the end of a legal document signed by a corporate employee or director.

CD-ROM

Fill in the form titled Acknowledgment on the CD-ROM as you follow the sample below. The tear-out version is contained in Appendix C.

Acknowledgment

STATE OF _____

COUNTY OF _____

I hereby certify that on _____[date]_____, before me, a Notary Public, personally appeared _____[name of employee, officer, or director]_____, who acknowledged himself/herself to be the _____[title]_____ of _____[name of corporation]_____ and that he/she, having been authorized to do so, executed the above document for the purposes contained therein by signing his/her name as _____[title]_____ of _____[name of corporation]_____.

Notary Public: ___[signature of Notary Public]___

My commission expires: _____

NOTARY SEAL

Corporate Tax Resolutions

This chapter contains some of the most common corporate tax resolutions approved by a corporation's board of directors. Often, the corporation's tax advisor provides the impetus to consider and approve these matters. For example, he or she may call the treasurer while preparing the corporation's year-end tax returns and recommend the election of S corporation tax status to help save taxes in future years.

TIP

The board should approve tax resolutions. The corporate resolutions contained in this chapter need to be approved by the board of directors. Of course, you may choose to have shareholders approve or ratify any decision made by the board. Normally, you will not wish to take this extra step unless shareholder approval is legally required or the decision is important enough to warrant the extra time and effort.

S Corporation Tax Election

Deciding whether to elect federal S corporation tax status should be an important part of each small corporation's initial and ongoing tax planning. We focus our discussion on the steps necessary to make this election. If you're considering S corporation tax election, you'll need to get information outside of this book.

In case you're confused about the significance of S corporation tax election, let's clear that up now. An S corporation is not a special type of corporate legal entity but simply an existing corporation that has made a special tax election with the IRS, and sometimes with a state corporate tax agency. When you incorporate (file your articles of incorporation with your state), you do not address this special tax status, and your state's corporate filing office is not interested in whether you plan to do so. In

---

How to Select and Use Corporate Resolutions

- Scan the table of contents at the beginning of the chapter to find resolutions of interest to you (for a full list of resolutions included with this book, see Appendix C).

- Read the background material that precedes each pertinent corporate resolution.

- Follow the instructions included with the sample resolution and complete a draft on the computer or using the tear-out version. If you need guidance on selecting and using the CD-ROM files, see Appendix A.

- Complete any needed attachment forms, such as account authorization forms or lease agreements.

- If a resolution involves complex issues that will benefit from expert analysis, have your legal or tax adviser review your paperwork and conclusions.

- Prepare minutes of a meeting or written consent forms as explained in Chapters 5 through 8, and insert the completed resolution(s) in the appropriate form. If you're seeking shareholder approval in addition to board approval, prepare two sets of minutes or written consent forms—one for your directors and one for your shareholders.

- Have the corporate secretary sign the printed minutes or have directors and/or shareholders sign any written consent forms and waivers. Then place the signed forms, together with any attachments, in your corporate records book.

other words, the S corporation election is made with tax authorities after you incorporate.

Here's how an S corporation tax election works. When a corporation elects S corporation tax status, corporate profits and losses are said to "pass through the corporation," to be reported on the individual tax returns of the shareholders. As a result, S corporation profits are subject to individual—not corporate—tax rates. In effect, the S corporation tax election provides corporations with the ability to live in two different worlds: Enjoying a corporate legal life (which includes limited liability status for its owners) and partnership-like tax status.

 RELATED TOPIC

Resource for S corporation tax election. For a longer discussion of S corporations, see *Incorporate Your Business* (Nolo), or *How to Form Your Own California Corporation* (Nolo).

Pros and Cons of S Corporation Tax Election

For some corporations, having profits and losses pass through to the individual shareholders can result in a net tax savings: Less taxes may be paid overall if profits are taxed on individual tax returns.

EXAMPLE 1:

In start-up businesses that expect initial losses, S corporation tax status can pass these initial losses to the individual tax returns of shareholders who actively participate in the business. This allows the business owners to offset income from other sources with the losses of their corporation.

EXAMPLE 2:

If corporate taxable income is so high that corporate profits are taxed at rates that are higher than the marginal (top) rates of its shareholders, S corporation tax election allows these profits to be taxed at the individual tax rates of the corporation's shareholders instead.

Even if S corporation tax election can save shareholders tax dollars, it may not be the best move for your corporation. For some corporations, the disadvantages of S corporation tax status outweigh the benefits. Consider the following:

- **S corporations must generally choose a calendar year as their corporate tax year.** To have the flexibility of choosing a fiscal tax year that corresponds to the business cycle of the corporation, you must have a C corporation (a regular corporation—one that has not made the special S corporation tax election with the IRS).

- **S corporations, like partnerships or LLCs (limited liability companies), cannot provide tax-deductible fringe benefits to shareholder-employees owning more than 2% of the S corporation's stock.**

- **A technical disadvantage of this tax election is that the amount of S corporation losses that a shareholder can use to offset income on his or her individual tax return is limited by technical provisions of the Internal Revenue Code.** Partnerships and LLCs have greater flexibility in deducting business losses on their individual tax returns.

Requirements for Making an S Corporation Tax Election

To qualify for S corporation tax status, a corporation must meet the following requirements:

- It must be a U.S. corporation, and its shareholders must all be U.S. citizens or residents.

- There must be only one class of stock. This means that all shares must have equal rights, such as dividend and liquidation rights, although differences as to voting rights are permitted.

- All shareholders must be individuals, estates, certain qualified trusts, or tax-exempt organizations (including tax-exempt charities and pension funds).

- There must be no more than 100 shareholders. Shares that are jointly owned by a husband and wife (and other designated family members) are considered to be owned by one person.

Steps to Elect S Corporation Tax Status

A corporation making an S corporation tax election will need to take the following steps:

- **Get board approval.** The directors must consent to the S corporation tax election at a meeting recorded with minutes or by using written consents. The resolution provided below is designed for either approval procedure. (Shareholders also must consent to the election, but they do so by signing the S corporation tax election form itself.)

- **File IRS Form 2553.** To make its federal S corporation tax election, the corporation must complete and file Form 2553 with the IRS. To obtain the latest version of this form, go online to www.irs.gov or call 800-TAX-FORM. The election must be made on or before the 15th day of the third month of the corporation's tax year for which the S corporation status is to be effective, or any time during the preceding tax year.

- **Make state S corporation tax election if required.** If your state has a corporate income tax, it may implement its own state version of S corporation tax election. In some states, a state S corporation tax election is automatically made when the federal election is made; in other states, you must file a special state S corporation tax election. To find out about any S corporation tax rules in your state, check with your state's department of revenue and taxation, corporations division, or similar state agency. (See "State Tax Information" under your state in Appendix B for your state tax agency's website address.)

- **File S corporation tax returns.** Although S corporations are not taxed on corporate income, they must prepare and file annual informational returns with the IRS (Form 1120S). This form must have an attached Schedule K-1 for each shareholder, which shows the shareholder's pro rata share of corporate income, losses, deductions, and credits. Shareholders of an S corporation report their shares of corporate income and losses on Schedule E, which is filed with their annual 1040 individual tax returns. (Under IRS rulings, S corporation shareholders may also be required to estimate and pay taxes during the year on their expected pro rata share of corporate income; check with your accountant.)

Similar state tax return filings also may be required in states that have implemented a state version of the S corporation tax election.

TIP

Some states don't recognize S corporation status. Most states with corporate income taxes recognize the federal S corporation tax election or implement their own version at the state level. But some states don't recognize S corporation status—in these states you'll be taxed as a regular corporation. Check your state tax agency's website (see Appendix B for contact information) to see if your state recognizes the S corporation tax election.

Revoking or Terminating Federal S Corporation Tax Status

After a corporation elects S corporation tax status, it remains in effect until it is formally revoked or terminated.

To revoke S corporation tax status, you must file written shareholder consents to the revocation with the IRS. Shareholders who collectively own at least a majority of the shares in the corporation must consent to the revocation.

S corporation status is automatically terminated if the corporation fails to continue to meet any of the requirements listed in "Requirements for Making an S Corporation Tax Election," above—for example, if the corporation issues a second class of shares, which gives the holders preferred dividend rights.

S corporation tax status cannot be reelected until at least five years have elapsed following a revocation or termination.

Resolution for S Corporation Tax Election

Use the following resolution to show board discussion and approval of S corporation tax election for the corporation. Note that the treasurer is directed to prepare and file Form 2553 with the IRS.

CD-ROM

Fill out the resolution titled S Corporation Tax Election on the CD-ROM as you follow the sample and special instructions below. The tear-out version is contained in Appendix C.

Special Instructions

❶ If you are unsure whether your state recognizes the federal S corporation tax election or requires a separate state filing, call the corporate income tax section of your state department of revenue and taxation, or similar state tax agency located in the state capital. If appropriate, include this bracketed phrase and insert the name of your state if you wish to elect S corporation tax status at the state level as well.

❷ In the blank, specify the first tax year for which the S corporation tax election is to be effective, such as "2011."

❸ Once you complete IRS Form 2553, remember to make a copy and attach it to this resolution and place it in your corporate records book. Also attach any separate state tax election forms to your resolution.

S Corporation Tax Election

The board of directors considered the advantages of electing S corporation tax status for the corporation under Section 1362 of the Internal Revenue Code. After discussion, which included a report from the treasurer that the corporation's accountant had been consulted and concurred with the board's decision, it was agreed that the corporation shall elect S corporation tax status with the IRS _["and with the (*name of state corporate tax agency, such as* "Department of Revenue and Taxation") for the State of (*name of state*)"]_ ❶ .

It was further agreed that the treasurer of the corporation be delegated the task of preparing and filing IRS Form 2553 and any other required forms in a timely manner so that the S corporation tax election will be effective starting with the _[tax year]_ ❷ tax year of the corporation. The treasurer was further instructed to have all shareholders and their spouses sign the shareholder consent portion of IRS Form 2553. ❸

S Corporation Shareholders' Agreement

Sometimes corporations take steps to make reliance on S corporation status a safer bet by requiring all shareholders and their spouses to sign an S corporation shareholders' agreement. Typically, this agreement provides that the shareholders and spouses will not transfer their shares in such a way as to jeopardize the corporation's S corporation tax election. In other words, shareholders and their spouses are prevented from selling part of their shares to a new shareholder if it would bring the total number of shareholders above 100 or to someone who doesn't qualify as an S corporation shareholder, such as a non-U.S. resident.

Below is a sample of a simple S corporation shareholders' agreement that restricts future transfers of shares: It allows only transfers that do not jeopardize the corporation's S corporation tax status. Corporations with only a few shareholders won't be too concerned with this extra precaution, but it makes sense if your number of shareholders approaches the maximum shareholder limit for S corporations (currently 100), or if you want to prevent other shareholders from selling their shares to an unqualified person or entity. Have each of your current shareholders and their spouses sign this agreement, and require any new shareholders and their spouses to do so prior to receipt of their new shares. Note that this agreement is a document that stands on its own; it is not a resolution. Make sure to have this agreement reviewed by your tax adviser.

CD-ROM

Fill out the form titled S Corporation Shareholders' Agreement on the CD-ROM as you follow the sample and special instructions below. The tear-out version is contained in Appendix C.

Special Instructions

State corporation laws often require that share certificates indicate if shares are subject to restrictions on future transfer. Usually, you do not have to spell out the restrictions; a statement that these restrictions exist and short

S Corporation Shareholders' Agreement

The undersigned shareholders and spouses of shareholders of _____ [*name of corporation*] _____
represent and agree as follows:

The board of directors has approved a resolution authorizing the corporation to elect S corporation
tax status with the IRS under Section 1362 of the Internal Revenue Code, to be effective for the corporate
tax year beginning _____ [*start date of first S corporation tax year*] _____ .

To help preserve and maintain the effectiveness of this S corporation tax status, the undersigned
agree that they shall not transfer, sell, assign, convey, or otherwise dispose of their shares, or any interest in
these shares, if such disposition would result in the corporation no longer being eligible for S corporation
tax status with the IRS.

The undersigned further agree to sign any consent forms or other documents necessary to elect
and obtain S corporation tax status with the IRS in a timely matter as requested by the treasurer of the
corporation.

The undersigned further agree that, even if a proposed transfer or other disposition of shares does
not jeopardize the corporation's S corporation tax status, no such transfer or disposition shall take place
until the proposed shareholder and the proposed shareholder's spouse consent to the corporation's
S corporation tax status, and sign an agreement that contains substantially the same terms as this
agreement.

This agreement may be terminated by the consent of a majority of the outstanding shareholders of
this corporation. Any person who breaches this agreement shall be liable to the corporation, its officers,
directors, shareholders, spouses of shareholders, and any transferees of shareholders or their spouses, for
all losses, claims, damages, taxes, fines, penalties, and other liabilities resulting from the breach of this
agreement.

This agreement shall bind all parties, their successors, assigns, legal representatives, heirs, and
successors in interest. The undersigned shall ensure that any such successors and representatives shall
be given a copy of this agreement prior to, or at the same time as, the delivery of any share certificates
to them. A conspicuous legend shall be placed on all share certificates of the corporation indicating that
the shares are subject to restrictions on transferability and that the holder may obtain a copy of these
restrictions at any time from the secretary of the corporation.

Dated: _____

Signature   Printed Name

_____   _____

_____   _____

_____   _____

instructions on how to get a copy of them will suffice. Here is a sample of a legend found on a share certificate:

> THESE SHARES ARE SUBJECT TO RESTRICTIONS ON TRANSFER. SHAREHOLDERS MAY OBTAIN, UPON REQUEST AND WITHOUT CHARGE, A STATEMENT OF THE RIGHTS, PREFERENCES, PRIVILEGES, AND RESTRICTIONS GRANTED TO OR IMPOSED UPON EACH CLASS OF SHARES AUTHORIZED TO BE ISSUED, AND UPON THE HOLDERS THEREOF, FROM THE SECRETARY OF THE CORPORATION AT *[address of corporation]* .

A copy of the shareholders' agreement should be placed in your corporate records book and be made available to any existing or prospective shareholder for inspection and copying.

Accumulation of Earnings

In this section, we look at another aspect of corporate taxation—accumulation of corporate earnings. Larger corporations often decide to keep substantial sums of money in the corporation from one year to the next. They may do so simply because they must pay bills; sometimes, the purpose is to split income between their business and themselves to achieve the benefit of lower corporate tax rates on business profits.

TIP

Accumulation of earnings rules don't apply to S corporations. The rules discussed in this section do not apply to S corporations, as earnings cannot accumulate in an S corporation. All income of an S corporation is treated, and taxed, as though it had been distributed to shareholders in proportion to their shareholdings each year, and taxed on their individual tax returns.

Section 535(c) of the Internal Revenue Code allows corporate business owners to keep money in the corporation, within limits. Most corporations are allowed an automatic accumulated earnings credit of $250,000 ($150,000 for professional corporations, such as incorporated lawyers, doctors, accountants, or engineers). That is, the IRS will allow you to retain this amount of earnings in your corporation, no questions asked. If the IRS determines that a corporation has sheltered more than the amount of this automatic accumulated earnings credit, the IRS will apply a penalty tax (equal to the highest individual income tax rate) to this excess retained income unless it's for reasonable business needs. The penalty tax is above and beyond the normal corporate income tax rate.

TIP

Invest excess cash in stock of U.S. corporations. Corporations often invest excess funds in the stock of other U.S. corporations to take advantage of one of the nicer corporate perks provided in the Internal Revenue Code (IRC). Under IRC Sections 243 to 246, the corporation can deduct 70% or more of the dividends received from an unaffiliated U.S. domestic corporation against its yearly corporate taxable income. (See IRS Publication 542, *Tax Information on Corporations*.)

Valid Reasons to Accumulate Earnings

If you decide to retain earnings and profits in your corporation in excess of the accumulated earnings credit, you should normally have little difficulty showing that the money is being held for the reasonable needs of the business. IRS regulations give a number of examples of valid reasons to accumulate funds, such as the need to:

- replace or expand the physical facilities of the business (add office, manufacturing, or inventory space)

- acquire a business enterprise through the purchase of stock or assets

- pay off debts in connection with the trade or business of the corporation (such as establishing a sinking fund to retire corporate bonds)

- provide necessary working capital for the business, such as for the purchase of inventory

- provide for the payment of reasonably anticipated product liability losses, including legal judgments that may be entered against the corporation, and

- redeem stock included in the estate of a deceased shareholder.

These are not the only valid reasons to accumulate earnings. As long as the corporation can show that the funds are being held for reasonably anticipated business needs, the IRS should not object. The income tax regulations provide additional insight on this point, as follows:

"(b) Reasonable anticipated needs. (1) In order for a corporation to justify an accumulation of earnings and profits for reasonably anticipated future needs, there must be an indication that the future needs of the business require such accumulation, and the corporation must have specific, definite, and feasible plans for the use of such accumulation. Such an accumulation need not be used immediately, nor must the plans for its use be consummated within a short period after the close of the taxable year, provided that such accumulation will be used within a reasonable time depending upon all the facts and circumstances relating

to the future needs of the business. Where the future needs of the business are uncertain or vague, where the plans for the future use of an accumulation are not specific, definite, and feasible, or where the execution of such a plan is postponed indefinitely, an accumulation cannot be justified on the grounds of reasonably anticipated needs of the business." (See Income Tax Regulation §§ 1.537-1 through 1.537-3.)

Resolution for Accumulation of Earnings

The best way to help establish the validity of accumulations above the automatic accumulated earnings credit (generally $250,000, or $150,000 for professional corporations) is through the use of a board resolution that specifies the reasons for holding excess earnings within the corporation.

CD-ROM

Fill out the resolution titled Accumulation of Corporate Earnings on the CD-ROM as you follow the sample and special instructions below. The tear-out version is contained in Appendix C.

Special Instructions

Any time your board makes a financial decision with major tax consequences, you should consult your accountant to ensure that you stand to achieve the desired favorable tax treatment. This resolution is no exception. Make sure your accountant agrees that your expected accumulations of corporate earnings will pass muster under IRS income tax rules and regulations for accumulated earnings.

Accumulation of Corporate Earnings

After discussion, the board resolved that it was necessary to retain the following earnings in the corporation to provide for the following reasonably anticipated needs of the business:

[*insert schedule of anticipated accumulations of corporate earnings and reasons for these accumulations*]

_____

      The treasurer of the corporation reported that the corporation's accountant had been consulted and agreed that the above accumulations should qualify as reasonable needs of the business under Internal Revenue Code Section 537(a).

      The above accumulations of corporate earnings were approved, and the treasurer was instructed to see to it that these accumulations of corporate earnings are made.

Section 1244 Stock Plan

Under Section 1244 of the Internal Revenue Code, many smaller corporations may provide shareholders with the benefit of treating future losses from the sale, exchange, or worthlessness of their stock as ordinary rather than capital losses on their individual federal tax returns. A maximum of $50,000 for an individual, or $100,000 for a husband and wife filing a joint return, may be claimed each tax year. Stock issued by a corporation that qualifies for this ordinary loss treatment is known as Section 1244 stock.

Section 1244 stock provides a tax advantage because ordinary losses are fully deductible against individual income, while capital losses are only partially deductible. Normally, capital losses may be deducted to offset a maximum of $3,000 of individual income in a given tax year.

TIP

State tax note. State tax statutes sometimes incorporate the federal Section 1244 provisions in their state tax scheme to allow you to claim a larger portion of stock losses on your individual state income tax return. Ask your accountant about state requirements for claiming future stock losses on state individual income tax returns.

Qualifications for Section 1244 Stock

You are not required to file a special election form with the IRS or adopt a formal Section 1244 stock plan to be eligible for this special tax treatment. However, you must meet these requirements:

- **Size of corporation.** The corporation must be a small business corporation as defined in Section 1244 of the Internal Revenue Code. Generally, a corporation qualifies if the total amount of money or property received by the corporation for stock does not exceed $1 million.

- **Issuance of shares.** The shares must have been issued for money or property other than corporate securities.

- **Gross receipts.** More than 50% of the corporation's gross receipts during the five tax years preceding the year in which the loss occurred must have been derived from sources other than royalties, dividends, interest, rents, annuities, or gains from sales or exchanges in securities or stock. If the corporation hasn't been in existence for the five tax years preceding the year in which the loss occurred, the five-year period is replaced either by: (a) the number of tax years the corporation has been in existence prior to the loss year, or (b) the fraction of the present tax year if it hasn't been in existence for a full tax year.

- **Notice to IRS.** When a loss occurs, the shareholder must submit a timely statement to the IRS electing to take an ordinary loss pursuant to Section 1244.

- **Original shareholder.** The shareholder claiming the loss must be the original shareholder to whom the stock was issued.

CAUTION

Watch out for future transfers. Section 1244 ordinary loss treatment is only available to the original owner of shares, so think twice (and check with your accountant) before making transfers of your shares to family members for tax purposes or before making any disposition of your shares to other persons or entities—including living trusts. The price of such transfers may be a loss of a shareholder's ability to deduct losses on shares as ordinary, rather than capital, losses.

Resolution for Section 1244 Stock Plan

A formal board resolution indicating the corporation's intent to fall under the Section 1244 provisions is a helpful reminder to the board and other corporate insiders of the importance of this tax provision and the requirements that must be met to rely on it. Note, however, that shareholders may elect Section 1244 stock treatment without passing a resolution, as long as they meet the requirements set out above. Make sure to talk with your tax adviser if you wish to be certain that you qualify under Section 1244.

CD-ROM

Use the resolution titled Qualification of Shares Under Internal Revenue Code Section 1244 on the CD-ROM to show the corporation's intent to fall under Section 1244. The tear-out version is contained in Appendix C.

Qualification of Shares Under
Internal Revenue Code Section 1244

The board discussed the advisability of qualifying the shares of this corporation as Section 1244 stock as defined in Section 1244 of the Internal Revenue Code, and of operating the corporation so that it is a small business corporation as defined in that section.

It was agreed that the president and treasurer of the corporation are, subject to the requirements and restrictions of federal and state securities laws, authorized to sell and issue shares of stock in return for the receipt of an aggregate amount of money and other property, as a contribution to capital, and as paid-in surplus, which does not exceed $1,000,000.

It was also agreed that the sale and issuance of shares shall be conducted in compliance with Section 1244 so that the corporation and its shareholders may obtain the benefits of that section.

The above officers are directed to maintain such records pursuant to Section 1244 so that any shareholder who experiences a loss on the transfer of shares of stock of the corporation may determine whether he or she qualifies for ordinary loss deduction treatment on his or her individual income tax return.

Another Tax Break for Small Business Stock

The Internal Revenue Code contains another tax break on the sale of some small business corporation stock. Specifically, persons who own shares in a qualified small business can be eligible for a special tax rate of one-half of the capital gains tax rate when they report gains from the sale or other disposition of their shares.

To qualify for this tax break, a number of requirements must be met, including the following:

- The corporation must have gross assets of no more than $50 million on the date of stock issuance.
- The corporation must be engaged in the operation of an active business. The practice of an incorporated profession such as a medical, accounting, or engineering practice, and other types of businesses such as investing, farming, and mining are specifically excluded and do not qualify under this tax provision.
- The stock must be acquired when newly issued by the corporation, and after August 10, 1993 (the date of enactment of this federal tax legislation).
- With some exceptions, the shares must be held for at least five years.
- The stock must have been purchased with money or property other than shares in the corporation and must not have been payment to an employee as compensation.

This special tax rate for small business stock gains may be an important one for your shareholders. Check with your tax adviser for the complete rules on this tax break.

Resolution for Approval of Independent Audit

As a preliminary to or part of the corporation's annual tax accounting procedures, a tax audit of the corporation's books may be necessary. A special audit may be requested by the IRS or required by a bank prior to approval of a loan or credit application. An audit may also be required under state corporate or securities laws before declaring a dividend or approving the issuance of stock.

Audits of this sort are called independent audits, and they are usually done by an outside accounting firm that does not handle ongoing tax or bookkeeping chores for the corporation.

 TIP

Alternatives to independent audits. To avoid the expense and hassles of a full-blown outside audit, financial institutions sometimes allow corporations to submit financial statements that have been reviewed by the corporation's accountant, using standard auditing rules. If this alternative is available when you are preparing financial statements that will be examined by others, you will likely wish to take it.

CD-ROM

The resolution titled Approval of Independent Audit of Corporate Financial Records on the CD-ROM may be used by the board to authorize the undertaking of an independent audit of the corporation's financial records and transactions. Fill out the resolution as you follow the sample below. The tear-out version is contained in Appendix C.

Approval of Independent Audit of Corporate Financial Records

After discussion, it was agreed by the board that the accounting firm of _[name of accountant or firm]_

_____ was selected to perform an independent audit of the financial records of the corporation for the _____[year]_____ fiscal year and to prepare all necessary financial statements for the corporation as part of its independent audit.

The treasurer was instructed to work with the auditors to provide all records of corporate finances and transactions that may be requested by them, and to report to the board on the results of the audit upon its completion.

Selection of Corporate Tax Year

The choice of a tax year for a corporation is an important tax decision, best arrived at with the guidance of the corporation's accountant. The deadlines for preparing and filing corporate tax returns, and the tax consequences of specific transactions made during the year, will hinge on the determination of this important tax decision. Further, the corporation's accounting period (the period for which the corporation keeps its books) must correspond to its tax year.

Choosing Your Corporation's Tax Year

A corporation's tax year, and its accounting period, may be:

- the calendar year from January 1 to December 31
- a fiscal year consisting of a 12-month period ending on the last day of any month other than December—for example, from July 1 to June 30, or
- a "52-53 week" year that ends on a particular day closest to the end of a month—for example, the last Friday of March—instead of the last day of the month. This means that some tax years will be 52 weeks long and others will be 53 weeks long.

Almost all corporations choose either a calendar year or a fiscal year as their tax year. For many corporations, a calendar tax year proves easiest because it is the tax year period used by its shareholders. Others, because of the particular business cycle of the corporation—or simply because December is a hectic month—choose the end of a different month to wind up their yearly affairs. Moreover, having the corporation's tax year end after that of the individual shareholders (after December 31) may allow special initial and ongoing tax advantages, such as the deferral of income to employee-shareholders of a small corporation. Also, since accountants are busy preparing individual and corporate tax returns at the end of the calendar year, some accounting firms encourage the selection of a noncalendar tax year by providing reduced fees for corporate income tax return preparation for fiscal-year corporations.

Resolution for Selection of Corporate Tax Year

Below is a sample resolution that your board can use to approve the selection of a tax year for the corporation. The language of the resolution assumes that the corporation has consulted the corporation's accountant prior to making this decision.

CD-ROM

Fill out the resolution titled Approval of Corporate Tax Year on the CD-ROM as you follow the sample below. The tear-out version is contained in Appendix C.

Tax Year Rules for S Corporations and Personal Service Corporations

Under IRS rules, S corporations and personal service corporations—those whose principal activity is the performance of personal services rendered by legal, accounting, health care, and certain other licensed professionals—are required to elect a calendar tax year with the IRS, subject to several exceptions. Here is a summary of the two principal areas:

- **Natural business cycle.** S corporations and personal service corporations can elect a fiscal year for their corporation if they can show that the fiscal year requested represents the natural business year of the corporation. One way to make this showing is if 25% or more of the corporation's gross receipts from services or sales are obtained during the last two months of the requested fiscal year. For example, an S corporation would qualify for a fiscal tax year ending on June 30th if at least 25% of its income from services is earned during the months of May and June. (See IRS Revenue Procedure 87-32 (1987).)

- **Three-month deferral of income.** S corporations and personal service corporations can adopt a noncalendar tax year if it results in a deferral of income of three months or less. For example, if a fiscal year ending September 30th is requested, this tax year will generally be allowed since this results in a three-month deferral of income when compared to the normal calendar tax year ending December 31. Use of this three-month deferral exception comes at a price: S corporations relying on this rule have to make an extra tax payment to the IRS each year; personal service corporations are limited in the amount of corporate deductions they can take for amounts paid to employee-shareholders. (See Section 444 of the Internal Revenue Code.)

For further information on these technical tax year rules and exceptions, check with your accountant.

Approval of Corporate Tax Year

The chairperson informed the board that the next order of business was the selection of the corporation's tax year. After discussion and a report from the treasurer, which included advice obtained from the corporation's accountant, it was resolved that the accounting period of this corporation shall end on the
___[*ending date, usually the "31st of December" or the last date of another month*]___ of each year.

Resolution for Payment and Deduction of Corporate Organizational Costs

Many of the initial organizational expenses associated with forming a corporation are advanced by the incorporators or other persons instrumental in setting up the corporation. These include state incorporation fees as well as accountant and attorneys' fees.

The board of directors may authorize the reimbursement of these expenses by the corporation. Further, federal tax law allows a corporation to deduct up to $5,000 of organizational expenses (plus up to $5,000 of start-up expenses) in the first corporate tax year. The corporation can elect to amortize and deduct remaining organizational (and start-up) expenses over the next 15 years.

RESOURCE

Useful IRS publication. For information on the importance of and requirements for the deduction and amortization of corporation organizational and start-up costs, see IRS Publication 535, *Business Expenses*, Chapter 9, "Amortization."

To implement this federal tax election, you must attach a statement to your first federal corporate income tax return indicating that you are choosing to deduct and amortize organizational expenses, providing a description of the expenses and giving other required details.

SEE AN EXPERT

See your tax adviser. This is a technical tax resolution. Check with your tax adviser before using it. Your advisor can also help you decide which organizational and start-up costs to deduct and amortize and help you prepare the statement to send to the IRS.

CD-ROM

Use the resolution titled Payment and Deduction of Organizational Expenses on the CD-ROM to authorize the reimbursement and amortization of organizational expenses. The tear-out version is contained in Appendix C.

Special Instructions

Start-up costs related to the qualification and issuance of shares or the transfer of assets to the corporation cannot be amortized—they can only be deducted when particular assets are sold or when the corporation goes out of business.

Payment and Deduction of Organizational Expenses

The board considered the question of paying the expenses incurred in the formation of this corporation. A motion was made, seconded, and unanimously approved, and it was resolved that the president and treasurer of this corporation are authorized and empowered to pay all reasonable and proper expenses incurred in connection with the organization of the corporation, including, among others, filing, licensing, and attorney and accountant fees, and to reimburse any directors, officers, staff, or other persons who have made or do make any such disbursements for and on behalf of the corporation.

It was further resolved that the treasurer is authorized to elect to deduct and amortize the foregoing expenses, pursuant to, and to the extent permitted by, Section 248 of the Internal Revenue Code of 1986, as amended.

Resolutions for Amending Articles or Bylaws

Many, if not most, corporations eventually must undertake the commonplace legal procedure of amending their articles of incorporation and bylaws. To do so, the corporation must follow rules in their state's corporation laws.

TIP

Various names for articles of incorporation. While most states use the term articles of incorporation to refer to the basic document creating the corporation, some states use the term certificate of incorporation, certificate of formation, or charter.

TIP

Shareholder approval is advised. Unlike most other corporate formalities which are approved by the board alone, shareholders often play a role in approving changes to articles and bylaws. As you'll see below, shareholder approval is normally required for amendments to articles, but not bylaws. Whether legally required or not, we think amendments to both articles and bylaws are important enough to warrant discussion and approval by the board and shareholders. (Of course, if you run a one-person corporation, putting on your shareholder hat to approve a board amendment is silly, unless separate shareholder approval is legally required.)

How to Select and Use Corporate Resolutions

- Scan the table of contents at the beginning of the chapter to find resolutions of interest to you (for a full list of resolutions included with this book, see Appendix C).

- Read the background material that precedes each pertinent corporate resolution.

- Follow the instructions included with the sample resolution and complete a draft using your computer or by filling out the tear-out version included in Appendix C. If you need guidance on selecting and using the CD-ROM files, see Appendix A.

- Complete any needed attachment forms, such as account authorization forms or lease agreements.

- If a resolution involves complex issues that will benefit from expert analysis, have your legal or tax advisor review your paperwork and conclusions.

- Prepare minutes of a meeting or written consent forms as explained in Chapters 5 through 8, and insert the completed resolution(s) in the appropriate form. If you're seeking shareholder approval in addition to board approval, prepare two sets of minutes or written consent forms—one for your directors and one for your shareholders.

- Have the corporate secretary sign the printed minutes or have directors and/or shareholders sign any written consent forms and waivers. Then place the signed forms, together with any attachments, in your corporate records book.

Decide Whether to Amend Articles or Bylaws

If you want to add something to your articles of incorporation, it's possible that your state law allows you to place new provisions in either your articles or bylaws. When you have the choice, it is best to add new provisions to your bylaws, rather than your articles. Bylaws can be amended more easily and inexpensively than articles because amendments are not filed with the state's corporate filing office.

EXAMPLE:

The board of Qui Vive Sentry Alarms Systems, Inc., wishes to impose a requirement that all shareholders be at least 18 years of age. In their state, shareholder qualifications are not required to be placed in the articles. The board decides to amend the bylaws to add this requirement.

To find out what provisions must be included in your articles of incorporation, take a look at your state's corporation law (see Appendix B for information about how to find your state's corporation laws). Typically, one section of the law lists the provisions that must be included in articles. Another section usually lists provisions that may be placed in articles; these are called optional article provisions and may be placed in either your articles or bylaws. All other provisions may be placed in a bylaws amendment.

Amending Your Articles of Incorporation

From time to time, corporations may need to amend their original articles of incorporation to add, change, or delete provisions. Like the original articles, amendments to the articles

must be filed with the state's corporate filing office, accompanied by a filing fee. (See Appendix B for information on how to find your state's corporate filing office.)

Reasons to Amend Articles of Incorporation

Corporations often amend their articles of incorporation because they wish to:

- authorize additional shares of an existing class or series of stock
- authorize the creation of a new class or series of stock
- change the name of the corporation
- add additional provisions to the articles, such as limitations on the personal liability of directors and officers, or
- delete provisions that the corporation wishes to repeal or that list outdated information— for example, the name of the corporation's initial registered agent.

Let's look at each of these areas in detail.

Adding Shares

When you incorporate, you authorize at least enough shares to issue to your initial shareholders. Incorporators with foresight authorize additional shares, which are available to issue to new shareholders later. Of course, 20-20 foresight is not always achievable, so you may find that you need to amend your articles to issue additional shares to new investors or to permit shares to be issued as part of an employee stock bonus or option plan.

EXAMPLE:

Sonic Sound Systems Corp.'s original articles of incorporation stated: "The aggregate number of shares that the corporation shall have authority to issue is 100,000 shares of common stock." A total of 80,000 shares were issued to the corporation's four shareholders, but the corporation now wishes to sell an additional 10,000 shares to each shareholder. Before issuing the shares, this article must be amended to authorize the issuance of at least 120,000 shares altogether. It would be prudent to provide an extra cushion of shares, this time by authorizing the issuance of a total of 300,000 shares.

If you wish to issue more shares than the amount currently authorized in your articles, you must amend your articles to authorize the additional shares. (We provide a resolution to amend your articles and sample language below.)

Creating a New Class of Shares

If you decide to authorize a new class or series of shares that is not currently authorized in your articles—such as Class B nonvoting shares that will be issued to employees as part of a stock option plan or shares that will be issued to nonvoting investors who will contribute additional capital to your corporation—you'll need to add additional language to an existing article or add a new article that authorizes the new class or series of shares. (We provide a resolution to amend your articles and sample language below.)

Do You Need a Permit to Issue New Shares?

The offering and issuance of new shares in your corporation are regulated by the securities laws of your state and by the federal Securities Act. You will typically either need to qualify for an exemption from these securities laws or obtain a permit from your state securities office or the federal Securities and Exchange Commission prior to issuing new shares.

Fortunately, federal rules and most state administrative regulations provide exemptions (usually called small offering exemptions) that allow small corporations to issue shares privately to a limited number of people. Typically, these exemptions allow shares to be offered and issued privately (without advertisement) to a limited number of investors, typically 35 or fewer.

For information on qualifying for small offering exemptions, see *Incorporate Your Business*, by Anthony Mancuso (Nolo).

Changing Your Corporate Name

The formal name of a corporation is specified in its articles of incorporation. When a corporation changes its focus, product line, or primary business activity, it sometimes decides to change its corporate name. The business corporation laws of all states allow corporations to do this, although most corporations opt to retain their original corporate name and simply do business under a fictitious or assumed name, as explained in "An Easier Way to Change a Corporation's Name," below.

Under corporate laws, your new proposed corporate name must be available for your use with the state corporate filing office. Mostly, this means it must not be the same or similar to a name already on the state's corporate filing list of existing corporations formed in the state or registered to do business in the state. In many states, the availability of the new name can be checked over the phone by calling the state corporate filing office or by going online to the state corporate filing office's website (see Appendix B). In other states, you must send a name availability letter to that office asking if the proposed new name is available for use. We recommend that you request a name reservation (and provide the required fee)—if the name is available—at the same time that you inquire on a name's availability. This way, you can be sure that the name will not be grabbed by someone else between the time of your name availability check and the time you file an amendment to your articles. (We provide a resolution to amend your articles and sample language for changing a corporation's name below.)

TIP

Make sure the new corporate name is not a trademark or service mark. Don't forget that you may also need to check state and federal trademarks and service marks to make sure that the new name is not registered as a state or federal trademark or service mark. For an explanation of trademark and service mark law, and the steps to take to search for existing trademarks or apply for one of your own, see *Trademark: Legal Care for Your Business & Product Name*, by Stephen Elias (Nolo).

An Easier Way to Change a Corporation's Name

If you're planning to amend your articles to change your corporation's name, either to better identify your business or to benefit from a name that has become associated with your corporation's products or services, there's an easier way to change the name.

In most states, a corporation wishing to do business under a name different from that specified in its articles may file a fictitious or assumed business name statement with the state corporate filing office or local county clerk's office. This simple procedure allows the corporation to use the name locally without having to file a formal articles amendment with the state corporate filing office. (A resolution for adopting an assumed or fictitious corporate name is covered in Chapter 9.)

Adding Provisions to Your Articles

Under state law, a short list of provisions must always be included in a corporation's articles, such as the name of the corporation, the number of shares it is authorized to issue, and the name and address of the corporation's registered agent.

After incorporation, the directors may decide to amend the articles to include one or more additional provisions. Amendments to articles are normally technical in nature—for example, adding a provision that makes shareholders liable to pay annual assessments on their shares or a redemption provision that allows the corporation to buy back a special class of shares at its option. You will probably wish to check your language with your legal or tax adviser before approving the amendment.

The following are typical optional provisions that may be added to articles of incorporation:

- limitation of the liability of directors in lawsuits brought by or in the name of the corporation (in shareholder lawsuits)
- addition of greater-than-majority quorum or voting requirements for directors or shareholders
- authorization of assessments (special monetary charges) against shares
- addition of special qualifications for shareholders
- limitations on the duration, business, or powers of the corporation, and
- granting of voting rights to creditors of the corporation.

> ### You Can't Change Certain Article Provisions
>
> In most states, you can delete—but cannot change—article provisions that specify the initial agent, initial registered office, or initial directors of the corporation. The reason is simple: These people and this address always remain the *initial* agent, directors, or registered office. You may delete any reference to them—for example, if you are amending your articles to increase the number of authorized shares and decide to take out the reference to your first registered agent, who has been replaced.
>
> To notify the corporate filing office of any change in your registered agent or registered office, file a statement of change of agent or registered address. If you request it, most states provide a form to use for this purpose.

Deleting Provisions in Your Articles

You may decide to repeal a provision in your articles—for example, one that requires directors to pass resolutions at meetings by a three-quarters vote of the full board. Or you may wish to delete outdated information, such as the name of the corporation's initial registered agent and office (if a new agent with a new office has recently been named and the directors are amending the articles for another reason). Deletions, like additions or changes to articles, must be made by formal amendments to the articles and must be approved by the board and shareholders and filed with the corporate filing office, as explained below.

Overview of How to Amend Articles of Incorporation

Here are the general rules for proposing and approving amendments to articles of incorporation.

Who Proposes Amendments to Articles

Under most bylaws, the directors propose and vote on amendments to the articles of incorporation; after the directors approve the amendment, it is passed along to the shareholders for their ratification. Under other bylaws, the shareholders propose and vote on the amendment first, then the board ratifies the shareholder amendment. Check your bylaws to determine the procedure you should follow.

Who Must Approve Amendments to Articles

For most amendments to the articles, you'll generally need to obtain approval of both the board of directors and the shareholders. We always recommend this approach, even when it is not legally required.

Under many bylaws and state laws, the board alone may approve certain routine article amendments without obtaining shareholder approval. Here are some of the routine board-only article amendments that many state laws and bylaws allow:

- deletion of names and addresses of the directors of the corporation (note that in a small number of states, the names of the initial directors named in the articles may not be deleted from the articles until the corporation has filed its first annual report with the state corporate filing office)

- deletion of the name and address of the initial registered agent of the corporation

- if the corporation has only one class of shares, conversion of each share of the corporation into a greater number of whole shares (in other words, a stock split, where each share is converted into a greater number of shares—in a two-for-one stock split, 100 shares become 200 shares)

- change of only the corporate or geographical designator in the corporate name—for example, changing "Specialty Tools of Chicopee, Inc." to "Specialty Tools of Chicopee Corp." or to "Specialty Tools of Pittsfield, Inc.," and

- approval of restatements of the articles. These restatements simply consolidate the original articles plus all past amendments into one final document.

TIP

Take the easy way out. If your bylaws are unclear, or you want to avoid having to look up or ask a lawyer about the legal rules for amending articles, have both directors and shareholders approve all amendments to your articles. This is the normal rule anyway under state law, and, by doing this, you'll keep everyone informed about changes to the articles of incorporation, your corporation's primary legal document.

Approval of Amendments If Shares Have Not Been Issued

If shares have not yet been issued, take note of these common rules:

- Most states allow the directors alone to approve an amendment to the articles.

- If directors have not been named in the articles or appointed by the incorporators (the persons who signed the articles), normally the incorporators may approve an amendment to the articles.

As always, check your bylaws (and state law) for the rules that apply to your corporation.

Special rules may apply if your corporation has more than one class of shares, as would be the case if you issued Class A voting shares to the founders and Class B nonvoting shares to employees under a stock bonus or profit-sharing plan. Under state law, separate approval by any special class of shares (including nonvoting shares) is often required if a proposed amendment to the articles would affect the class of shares separately—for example, increase, decrease, or change the rights or restrict the classes of shares.

EXAMPLE:

An amendment to Quotidian Time Management Consulting Corporation's articles would add restrictions on the transferability of Class B nonvoting shares of the corporation by requiring unanimous approval of shareholders prior to the transfer of a portion of shares by an exiting shareholder to an outsider. A majority (or, in some states, two-thirds) of all of the Class B shares must approve the proposed amendment.

The types of proposed changes to a class of shares that will trigger a separate class vote by the shareholders vary from state to state.

Separate voting procedures also may be required for amendments that:

- create a new class of shares having preferences or privileges that supersede those of an existing class, or

- increase the preferences of a class that already has preferences over another class of shares.

EXAMPLE:

Yer Blues and Cappuccino Corp., a franchiser of espresso cafes featuring live musical entertainment, decides to issue a new class of preferred shares to an investment group in return for an infusion of cash. The new shares entitle their holders to preference in receiving dividends that may be declared by the board and a first right to any remaining corporate assets if the business is liquidated. Because the new preferred shares are being granted rights that supersede the rights of existing shareholders, the existing shareholders must approve the resolution authorizing the new shares.

Notice Required to Amend Articles

Most bylaws require that a notice of shareholders' meeting must contain a description of the articles of incorporation amendment to be presented at the meeting. To prepare notice for a shareholders' meeting, see Chapter 3, Step 5.

Votes Required to Amend Articles

Voting requirements for amendments to articles vary from state to state. We discuss the basic rules below, but remember: In the typical small corporation, most or all shareholders normally concur in any article amendment brought up for passage.

- **Board of directors.** Most states allow the board to approve amendments to the articles by normal board voting rules—that is, by a majority of those present at a board meeting at which a quorum is present.

- **Shareholders.** A majority of states require amendments to be approved by at least a majority of all the shares of the corporation entitled to vote on the amendment.

A lesser number of states require the approval of two-thirds of all the shares of the corporation entitled to vote on the amendment.

A handful of other states require a two-thirds shareholder vote for amendments to the articles but allow certain corporations—for example, those with a large number of shareholders or those listed with a securities exchange—to pass an amendment by a majority vote of all shareholders.

TIP

In some states, the two-thirds vote requirement may be lowered in the articles. Some states that specify a two-thirds vote approval by the corporation's shareholders allow the articles to lower this requirement to a majority shareholder vote. Again, check your articles and bylaws to see if your corporation has adopted any special voting requirements for amendments to the articles.

Resolution to Amend Articles of Incorporation

It's easy to prepare a resolution to amend your articles, which you'll then insert in your minutes or written consent form. The resolution can show approval of:

- only the specific language that you wish to change ("Aproval of Amendment to Articles," below), or

- a restatement of your entire articles—which, of course, includes any changes you are making ("Approval of Restatement of Articles of Incorporation," below).

Remember, most article amendments must be approved separately by the board and the shareholders. To obtain this approval, you'll need to hold separate directors' and shareholders' meetings (see Chapters 5 and 6) or obtain separate director and shareholder written consents (see Chapter 8).

Resolution to Amend Articles

You may use the form shown below to make one or more specific amendments to your articles of incorporation. Because you are not changing the entire text of your articles, make sure you attach a copy of the new approved resolution to the current articles in your corporate records book.

CD-ROM

Fill out the resolution titled Approval of Amendment to Articles of Incorporation on the CD-ROM as you follow the sample and special instructions below. The tear-out version is contained in Appendix C.

Special Instructions

Here are a few examples of ways to complete the information in these blanks. For background information on each of these areas, see "Reasons to Amend Articles of Incorporation," above.

EXAMPLE 1 (Adding Shares):

"RESOLVED, that Article FIVE of the articles of incorporation be amended to read as follows: The aggregate number of shares that the corporation shall have authority to issue is 150,000 shares of common stock."

EXAMPLE 2 (Creating a New Class of Shares):

"RESOLVED, that Article EIGHT of the articles of incorporation be amended to read as follows: The corporation shall be authorized to issue 200,000 Class A voting common shares and 100,000 Class B nonvoting common shares."

EXAMPLE 3 (Changing the Corporate Name):

"RESOLVED, that Article ONE of the articles of incorporation be amended to read as follows: The name of this corporation is Atlanta Big Wheels, Inc."

EXAMPLE 4 (Adding a New Article):

"RESOLVED, that Article TEN of the articles of incorporation be added as follows: One member of the corporation's board of directors shall be elected annually by the Hingham Investment Group, with the initial election date to be determined by the board of directors."

EXAMPLE 5 (Deleting an Article):

"RESOLVED, that Article B of the articles of incorporation be deleted as follows: ~~The initial registered agent and registered office of this corporation is: Paul Winslow, 55 Pomme Rouge Boulevard, Lafayette, Kentucky.~~"

Approval of Amendment to Articles of Incorporation

RESOLVED, that Article ___[number or letter of article that is being amended, added, or deleted]___ of the articles of incorporation be ___["amended to read," "added," or "deleted"]___ as follows:

___[insert the language of the changed or new article, or show a struck-through version of the wording to be deleted]___.

Resolution to Restate Articles

To avoid confusion, directors and shareholders sometimes decide to approve a restatement of the articles, which contains all old and new provisions (minus any deletions also being made).

 CD-ROM

Below is a sample of the Approval of Restatement of Articles resolution included on the CD-ROM. Fill out the resolution as you follow the sample below. The tear-out version is contained in Appendix C.

Approval of Restatement of Articles of Incorporation

RESOLVED, that the articles of incorporation be amended and restated to read as follows:

[insert the entire text of your articles, including any new or changed provisions that are being _____

incorporated into your articles and omitting any provisions that are being deleted] _____ .

File Your Certificate of Amendment With the State

Following approval of a resolution to amend your corporate articles, you'll need to file an amendment of articles form with your state's corporate filing office. A sample, specimen, or printed form for this purpose should be available from the corporate filing office in your state, or you can download one from your state's filing office website. (See Appendix B for information on how to find your state's corporate filing office website.) Typically, the amendment form is referred to as an amendment of articles or certificate of amendment form. A nominal fee is usually charged for the filing.

The sample form below contains the basic information normally required in an amendment of articles. It shows the text of the amended or restated articles and how, when, and by whom the amendment was approved.

After filing your amendment form with your state's corporate filing office, remember to place a copy in your corporate records book, along with a copy of the written consents or minutes of the meeting used to show approval of your amendment resolution.

 CD-ROM

We include a specimen statutory amendment form titled Amendment of Articles Form on the CD-ROM—although you should use the form provided by your state's corporate filing office, if one is available. The tear-out version is contained in Appendix C.

Amendment of Articles Form

To: _____ [corporate filing office name and address] _____

Articles of Amendment

of

_____ [name of corporation] _____

One: The name of the corporation is _____ [name of corporation] _____.

Two: The following amendment to the articles of incorporation was approved by the board of directors

on ____ [date of board meeting or written consent] _____ and was approved by the shareholders on

__ [date of shareholder meeting or written consent] _____:

_____ [language of amendment to one or more articles here] _____.

Three: The number of shares required to approve the amendment was __ [total number of shares

__ required for approval] _____, and the number of shares that voted to approve the amendment was

__ [number of shares voting in favor of the amendment] _____.

Date: _____

By:

__ [signature of president] _____

__ [typed name] _____, President

__ [signature of secretary] _____

__ [typed name] _____, Secretary

Amending Your Bylaws

Corporations sometimes wish to add, delete, or change provisions in their bylaws. This is easy to do, because bylaws amendments simply need to be approved by the appropriate number of director or shareholder votes (as explained below), then filed in the corporate records book. Unlike articles, amendments to bylaws do not need to be filed with the state's corporate filing office.

You may wish to amend your existing bylaws to accomplish one or more of the following items:

- change the date, time, or place of the annual directors' or shareholders' meeting specified in the bylaws

- specify special notice, call, or voting rules for annual or special meetings of directors or shareholders—for example, your directors may wish to require written notice well in advance of all meetings, even if not required under state law

- change the authorized number of directors of the corporation (the total number of positions on the board)

- change the duties and responsibilities of one or more corporate officers, or

- add provisions to the bylaws that specify when and for how much shares may be sold by existing shareholders to other shareholders or to outsiders (called buy-sell provisions).

Overview of Bylaws Amendments

Now, let's review what requirements normally must be met to amend corporate bylaws.

Who Must Approve Bylaws Amendments

In most states, certain amendments to the bylaws need to be approved by directors only.

But, even if ratification (approval) by shareholders is not required, we think this extra step is well worth the time and trouble. After all, the bylaws are an important operational document, and shareholders—as well as directors—will have to abide by the rules contained there. Unless you are pressed for time (or you run a small corporation where all shareholders are directors), have your shareholders ratify all amendments approved by the board.

While not common, it's possible that your articles or bylaws may reserve the power to amend bylaws exclusively for the shareholders (either in general or for specific types of amendments). As always, check your articles, bylaws, or state corporation laws to determine your state's rules. (Appendix B contains information on how to find your state's corporation laws.)

Notice Required to Amend Bylaws

Because bylaws amendments may represent a major change in corporate regulations or procedures, we recommend that all notices of meetings at which a bylaws amendment will be proposed state that a purpose of the meeting is to amend the bylaws. In addition, it's helpful to provide a copy or summary of the amendment that will be brought before the meeting.

Generally, no special notice is required to be given to directors when a bylaws amendment is proposed—amendments can be made at any directors' meeting. Of course, we recommend you give directors advance notice of any proposals to make important bylaw amendments.

Under typical state corporate laws, written notice of all special shareholders' meetings must state the nature of the business to be proposed for approval at the meeting. Because bylaws amendments are normally taken up at special meetings called during the year, this statement of purpose will be a legal requirement. To prepare notice for a shareholders' meeting, see Chapter 3, Step 5.

Votes Required to Amend Bylaws

Normal voting rules apply to bylaws amendments unless other provisions are specifically required by law or the corporation's articles or bylaws. Amendments generally are approved by a majority of directors or shares present at a meeting or by the written consent of all directors or all shareholders.

Resolution to Amend Bylaws

To approve an amendment to your bylaws by directors, shareholders, or both, insert the amendment of bylaws resolution into your minutes of meeting or written consent forms. Include in the resolution the language of the new or changed bylaws provision, as shown in the sample below.

CD-ROM

Fill out the resolution titled Approval of Amendment of Bylaws on the CD-ROM as you follow the sample and special instructions below. The tear-out version is contained in Appendix C.

Special Instructions

For deleted provisions, indicate that the bylaw is "deleted as follows," then insert a struck-through version of deleted language. To add or amend provisions, fill in the appropriate language.

Supermajority Quorum and Voting Rules in Bylaws

To increase the consensus for major decisions, some smaller corporations adopt a rule that requires a greater-than-majority—for example, two-thirds—director or shareholder quorum or vote to approve specific changes to the corporation's bylaws (and article of incorporation changes as well). For example, a two-thirds director and shareholder vote at meetings may be required to authorize a new class or series of shares or to decrease the number of directors on the board. These provisions are known as supermajority quorum or voting rules.

Typically, states allow the bylaws to increase director or shareholder quorum or voting requirements. However, exceptions do exist, particularly with respect to raising the quorum or voting requirements for shareholders. In some states, supermajority shareholder quorum or voting rules may only be included in the bylaws if the articles of incorporation specifically allow it.

Once enacted, it is typical to require a corresponding supermajority shareholder quorum or vote to repeal or change a supermajority shareholder quorum or voting rule (for example, a two-thirds shareholder vote would be necessary to repeal a two-thirds shareholder voting rule in the bylaws). Check your articles and bylaws carefully if you wish to add, delete, or change shareholder supermajority quorum or voting rules.

Approval of Amendment of Bylaws

RESOLVED, that __[number and/or letter designation of amended bylaw]__ of the bylaws of the corporation

is _____["added," "amended," or "deleted"]_____ as follows:

[insert language of new or changed bylaw or show a struck-through version of the wording to be deleted]

_____ .

EXAMPLE 1:

"RESOLVED, that Article TWELVE of the bylaws of the corporation is added as follows: "Article TWELVE: Nontransferability of Shares. All shares of this corporation shall be nontransferable, except with the written approval of all existing shareholders.""

EXAMPLE 2:

"RESOLVED, that Article II, Section A (3) of the bylaws of the corporation is amended as follows:

"Article II: Meetings of the Board of Directors

"Section A (3): The board of directors of this corporation shall meet annually on the first Wednesday of June of each year, and shall also meet on the same day as, and immediately following, the annual shareholders' meeting provided for by other provisions of these bylaws."

Place Approved Resolution in Your Corporate Records Book

After your directors (and, if you wish, shareholders) have approved the resolution amending your bylaws, place a copy of the resolution in your corporate records book. Also attach a copy of the resolution to the back of your current bylaws (also in your corporate records book).

As an alternative, you may have the corporate secretary prepare an updated copy of your bylaws that contains the old and new language of the current bylaws. Of course, this updated copy should replace the old copy of the bylaws in your corporate records book. You can keep the old version in your corporate records book, but mark it clearly as "AMENDED" or with other language that indicates it has been superseded by new provisions. ●

Corporate Hiring and Appointment Resolutions

An important part of any corporation's business is to hire corporate personnel and set salaries for those who work for the corporation. This is true for small, closely held corporations as well as big businesses with a large payroll.

Another increasingly important issue is when and how to contract for services offered by outside individuals and companies (independent contractors). Hiring independent contractors can be a cost- and tax-effective strategy for obtaining help with a corporate project without having to place a worker or workers on the payroll.

Finally, corporations may decide to pass special compensation resolutions for approving year-end salary increases and bonuses for officers and employees, payment to directors or officers for attending meetings, and indemnification for costs assessed against directors, officers, and employees. This chapter covers these issues and provides instructions for selecting and using resolutions to approve these and related matters.

TIP

These resolutions usually require board approval only. The corporate resolutions contained in this chapter usually need to be approved by the board of directors only. We flag any resolutions that may require shareholder ratification. Of course, you may choose to have shareholders approve or ratify any decision made by the board. Normally, you will not wish to take this extra step unless shareholder approval is legally required or the decision is important enough to warrant the extra time and effort.

How to Select and Use Corporate Resolutions

- Scan the table of contents at the beginning of the chapter to find resolutions of interest to you (for a full list of resolutions included with this book, see Appendix C).

- Read the background material that precedes each pertinent corporate resolution.

- Follow the instructions included with the sample resolution and complete a draft using your computer. (You'll have to fill in the tear-out resolution included in Appendix C if you don't have a computer.) If you need guidance on selecting and using the CD-ROM files, see Appendix A.

- Complete any needed attachment forms, such as account authorization forms or lease agreements.

- If a resolution involves complex issues that will benefit from expert analysis, have your legal or tax advisor review your paperwork and conclusions.

- Prepare minutes of a meeting or written consent forms as explained in Chapters 5 through 8, and insert the completed resolution(s) in the appropriate form. If you're seeking shareholder approval in addition to board approval, prepare two sets of minutes or written consent forms—one for your directors and one for your shareholders.

- Have the corporate secretary sign the printed minutes or have directors and/or shareholders sign any written consent forms and waivers. Then place the signed forms, together with any attachments, in your corporate records book.

Hiring and Paying Corporate Employees

Resolutions are sometimes used to document the hiring of key corporate personnel, particularly if they will receive substantial corporate salaries. In closely held corporations, the corporate principals (the shareholder-executives) may want to set the terms of their employment in writing for the board to approve, so everyone will know what is expected of them.

This paperwork also can come in handy if you will be paying a shareholder-executive a hefty, perhaps above-average salary, and you want some documentation of the special skills and responsibilities that go along with this person's position. This can help head off IRS objections of "unreasonable compensation" if your corporation is audited.

RESOURCE

Employment laws. For an excellent resource in understanding the employment law requirements, see *The Employer's Legal Handbook*, by Fred S. Steingold (Nolo). It contains a wealth of information, including rules on hiring and firing.

Resolution Approving Corporate Hiring

While this resolution can be an excellent means of formalizing the hiring of a corporate insider (the corporate principals, or shareholder-executives, in a closely held corporation), think twice before putting the terms of any employment relationship in writing—whether in this resolution, an employment contract, or other corporate paperwork. State law will most likely impose requirements on terminating the employment relationship of any worker who is hired for a set employment term (as opposed to an "at-will" worker hired for an unspecified period).

How to Back Up Substantial Salaries Paid to Shareholder-Employees

The IRS sometimes challenges the compensation paid to shareholder-employees of closely held corporations, especially if it seems inordinately high. To bolster your case for high salaries paid to yourself and other business owners of your corporation, you can make and substantiate one or more of the following points in your resolution:

- The employee's expertise, energy, or know-how is vital to the success of the business.

- The employee has significant responsibility within the corporation and is charged with overseeing or implementing critical areas of corporate operation.

- The employee has special training, knowledge, or skills that are indispensable to the operation of the corporation or to a particular area of operations.

- The employee is expected to achieve, or has achieved, significant increases in corporate profits or productivity.

CD-ROM

Fill out the resolution titled Approval of Hiring of Corporate Employee on the CD-ROM as you follow the sample and special instructions below. The tear-out version is contained in Appendix C.

Special Instructions

Generally, you won't want to specify job duties in your resolution or use the optional paragraph below. If you include this paragraph, a court may decide your language gives an employee permanent rights to work for your corporation. But you may want to use this clause for an executive you know will be around for a while—for example, one of the founders and key shareholder-employees of your closely held corporation.

Approval of Hiring of Corporate Employee

After discussion, the directors approved the hiring of _____ [*name of employee*] _____

to the position of _____ [*job title*] _____ in the employ of the corporation.

It was agreed that this employment would be subject to the following terms and conditions and would be compensated with the following amounts and benefits:

[*OPTIONAL—see Special Instructions:* "It was agreed that this employment would be subject to the following terms and conditions and would be compensated with the following amounts and benefits: (*specify job duties and compensation*)"]_____ .

It was agreed that the above individual is particularly qualified for employment and entitled to the compensation associated with this position with the corporation for the following reasons:

[*specify education, experience, and other qualifications and factors that support the amount of compensation to be paid to the employee*]_____ .

Resolution for Salary Increases or Bonuses

It is customary for corporations to increase the pay of top executives from time to time and to award annual bonuses to employees. If the increase or bonus is substantial, you may wish to pass a resolution showing board approval of the additional payment. Doing so helps show that the additional expenses were approved after due consideration by the board, a formality that may help if the IRS or outside shareholders question whether the increases were warranted.

 **CD-ROM**

Fill out the resolution titled Approval of Bonuses and Salary Increases on the CD-ROM as you follow the sample below. The tear-out version is contained in Appendix C.

Approval of Bonuses and Salary Increases

The board considered the question of salary increases and bonuses to employees of the corporation. After discussion, the board approved the following salary increases and bonuses, to be paid for the upcoming fiscal year to the following persons:

Name and Title   Salary or Bonus

_____ $_____

_____ $_____

_____ $_____

_____ $_____

_____ $_____

The above salary amounts or bonuses shall be paid as follows:

[specify when bonuses will be paid or the calendar year when salary increases are effective] _____

_____

Resolution for Shareholder Approval of Employee Compensation

In corporations with nonemployee shareholders, it may make sense to have the shareholders approve compensation paid to top executives. This keeps outside shareholders satisfied that they are being consulted on important corporate pay decisions. The form below can be used to obtain shareholder approval of a previously passed board resolution to pay corporate employees.

CD-ROM

Fill out the resolution titled Shareholder Ratification of Employee Pay on the CD-ROM as you follow the sample below. The tear-out version is contained in Appendix C.

Shareholder Ratification of Employee Pay

After discussion, the following annual compensation, increase in annual compensation, or authorization of bonus amount(s), paid to the following corporate _____ ["employee(s)" *and/or* "executive(s)"] _____ , was ratified by the shareholders of this corporation:

Name and Title

Salary or Bonus

_____ $_____

_____ $_____

_____ $_____

_____ $_____

_____ $_____

The above salary amounts or bonuses shall be paid as follows:

[specify when bonuses will be paid or the calendar year when salary increases are effective] _____ .

Using Independent Contractors

As a way to keep costs down, corporations often hire outside individuals to perform work for their corporation, thus saving on payroll taxes, workers' compensation, health insurance, disability insurance, and other employment costs.

Even though you do not need to withhold or pay employment taxes for independent contractors, you must prepare and file IRS Form 1099-MISC for each independent contractor to whom you pay $600 or more during the tax year. Keep tabs on the 1099 requirements if you hire independent contractors; the threshold amount for this filing may increase at some point. Also, at some future date, regulations may require income and employment tax withholding to be made for independent contractors by companies using their services.

The IRS and state tax agencies are becoming increasingly stubborn and aggressive about the misclassification of employees as independent contractors. These agencies routinely perform employment audits that result in independent contractors' being reclassified as employees, with back taxes and penalties being assessed against the employer.

CAUTION

The IRS may assess substantial penalties if you misclassify workers. If you misclassify an employee as an independent contractor, unpaid payroll taxes and withholding amounts can easily equal from 20% to 40% of compensation paid to the worker. Once additional penalties and interest are added, the total employer liability resulting from an employment tax audit can exceed the amount of compensation paid to the worker. The corporation can be responsible to pay these amounts even if the person who was improperly treated as an independent contractor filed tax returns and paid income and self-employment taxes on the earnings. Fortunately, the Internal Revenue Code provides some relief from these harsh penalties as long as the

violations are not shown to be due to intentional disregard. (See IRC § 3509.)

Board approval of the use and terms of an independent contractor relationship is really only necessary in situations where the independent contractor asks the corporation for formal board approval of the terms of his or her work agreement. In other situations, your normal outside contracting procedures will work best—a corporate purchase order for work to be performed, or simply an invoice for services provided by the independent contractor.

Resolution Approving Independent Contractor Services

Our resolution gives a quick and general way to obtain board approval of the use of outside services.

CD-ROM

Fill out the resolution titled Approval of Independent Contractor Services on the CD-ROM as you follow the sample and special instructions below. The tear-out version is contained in Appendix C.

Special Instructions

If the outside firm or individual has submitted a schedule of services or agreement for approval, you can refer to it and attach it to your resolution after it is approved by the board. In the second blank, fill in "see schedule/ agreement submitted to and approved by the board, which is attached to this resolution."

TIP

When to prepare an independent contractor agreement. An agreement with an independent contractor can help specify the terms of the work to be performed. This can be particularly useful if work is to be performed and payments are to be paid according to a performance

IRS Independent Contractor Classification Criteria

The IRS looks to a number of tests when deciding whether a worker is an independent contractor or employee. Here are some of the more important independent contractor (IC) tests:

- **If the IC looks like a business.** One of the most heavily weighted factors the IRS uses to determine IC status is whether the person who provides the services has a substantial investment in his or her own business and facilities and is pursuing personal profit motives in performing the work. If so, the person is more likely to be treated as an IC.

- **Other outside work.** Does the worker or firm work for other companies while working for your corporation? If so, this helps establish IC status.

- **Supervision.** If the worker must account for his or her actions on an ongoing basis or is directed not just as to the results of the work, but when and how it must be done, the worker looks more like an employee.

- **Importance of the work.** If the success or failure of the corporation's business hinges in a major way on the outcome of the work, or if the type of work being performed is the primary business of the company, this will weigh heavily toward a finding of employee status.

- **Frequent contracting.** If you constantly employ the same person to perform the same task over an extended period of time, this factors against IC status.

- **Training required.** If you must give the worker extra help or training to perform the task, this figures in favor of employee tax status.

- **Incorporation.** If the outside worker has incorporated his or her business, this is often persuasive evidence that the person should be treated as an independent contractor. In fact, more and more companies that utilize or arrange for the services of outsiders—for example, firms that contract for programmer services—are requiring individuals to be incorporated (or have formed an LLC) to help dispose of any employment tax issues that would otherwise arise.

Approval of Independent Contractor Services

After discussion, the board authorized and approved the services specified below to be performed by

___[name of independent contractor firm or individual]___ according to the following terms:

___[specify services and payment schedule for services to be performed]___

_____.

schedule (although, typically, the outside person or company will submit their invoice or contract for the performance of services and payments). Written independent contractor agreements also can help make it clear that the arrangement qualifies for independent contractor status with the IRS—standard independent contractor agreements reference many of the tax factors used by the IRS for classifying the worker as an outside contractor, such as making the service provider liable for his or her own employment taxes, withholding, and the like.

RESOURCE

Make sure you understand the rules before you hire independent contractors. To prepare an independent contractor agreement and understand the various tax criteria used by the IRS in classifying workers as employees and independent contractors, you'll need outside help. One excellent resource is *Working With Independent Contractors*, by Stephen Fishman (Nolo).

Appointing and Paying Corporate Officers

Your corporate documentation should include a formal resolution by the board appointing the corporation's president, secretary, treasurer, and other officers required or allowed under your state's corporation laws.

You may also designate any salaries to be paid to the officers. Officers are normally not paid for performing their statutory duties as officers, but instead are paid in other capacities under different job titles.

EXAMPLE:

Betty Bidecker is a 75% shareholder as well as the president and treasurer of her incorporated software publishing company. Her husband, Bix Bidecker, is a 25% shareholder and the vice president and secretary of the corporation. Rather than being paid for serving in officer capacities, both are paid annual salaries as executive employees of the corporation: Betty as the publisher, Bix as the associate publisher.

RELATED TOPIC

Compensation for attending meetings. Individuals normally serve on the board without being paid a salary for acting as directors, although many are paid a per meeting allotment, advanced or reimbursed necessary travel expenses to attend meetings, or paid per diem meeting fees. We cover resolutions to handle pay arrangements of this sort for directors and officers below (see "Resolution Authorizing Payment for Attending Meetings").

Officer Requirements Under State Law

Below is a summary of state corporation law rules on designating corporate officers. As always, your bylaws are your best source of information for any special or self-imposed officer requirements that apply to your corporation.

- **Mandatory positions.** A corporation must usually fill the officer positions of president, treasurer, and secretary. Additional officer positions, such as vice president or assistant officers, are optional.

- **Officers who are directors or shareholders.** An officer is not required to be a director or shareholder in your corporation. But in small corporations, it's common sense that the officer usually will be both.

- **Officer titles.** Some states use or allow different designations for some offices. For example, the president may be called the chairman of the board, the secretary may be referred to as the clerk, and the treasurer may be called the chief financial officer.

- **Specific officer appointments.** In a number of states, a corporation may appoint as many or as few officers as its bylaws require or as its board of directors directs.

- **Serving in more than one position.** In many states, one person may serve in one, more than one, or all officer positions. However, in several states, the same person cannot act as both president and secretary.

- **Record-keeping responsibilities.** In most states, a corporation is required to delegate at least one officer—usually the secretary—with the specific responsibility of keeping corporate minutes and other records for the corporation.

Resolution for Appointment and Compensation of Officers

Use the resolution shown below to appoint officers and set their salaries if they are to be paid as officers. Generally, officers are appointed en masse as shown in the resolution presented here.

RELATED TOPIC

Hiring officers as employees. If you want the board to approve the hiring of officers as salaried nonofficer employees as well, see "Resolution Approving Corporate Hiring," above. You may use that resolution in addition to the resolution presented here.

CD-ROM

Fill out the resolution titled Appointment of Corporate Officers on the CD-ROM as you follow the sample and special instructions below. The tear-out version is contained in Appendix C.

Special Instructions

If officers will not receive salaries in their capacities as officers, fill in "N/A" or "none" in the salary blanks.

In the unusual case where officers will be paid for serving as officers, fill in the amount. If salaries have not yet been set, insert "to be determined by board of directors" in the appropriate salary blanks.

Appointment of Corporate Officers

The board of directors appoints the following individuals to serve in the following corporate offices, at the annual salaries shown next to their names.

Name   Salary

President: _____[*name of officer*]_____ $___[*salary*]_____

Vice President: _[*name of officer*]_____ $___[*salary*]_____

Secretary: _____[*name of officer*]_____ $___[*salary*]_____

Treasurer: _____[*name of officer*]_____ $___[*salary*]_____

Each officer shall have such duties as are specified in the bylaws of the corporation and as may be designated from time to time by the board of directors. An officer shall serve until his or her successor is elected and qualified to replace him or her as officer.

Compensation for Attending Meetings

Your corporation may authorize the payment of compensation to directors, officers, and employees for attending corporate meetings, as well as for incurring travel and other expenses in the process. All types of special compensation paid to these individuals are taxable income to the individual, and are deductible as business expenses by the corporation on its tax return.

RELATED TOPIC

Reimbursement for travel. We cover separate resolutions to approve the reimbursement of expenses incurred while corporate employees are traveling on business away from the corporation in Chapter 16.

Resolution Authorizing Payment for Attending Meetings

Directors and officers are often paid a per diem payment for attending corporate director or shareholder meetings. In addition, directors or officers who must travel to attend these meetings are sometimes reimbursed for additional reasonable travel expenses. This occurs most often where closely held corporations have outside directors or officers—perhaps even an out-of-state relative who fills an officer or board position and who must travel to the corporation once or twice a year to attend corporate meetings. Below is a sample of the resolution your board can use to approve each or both types of this special compensation.

CD-ROM

Fill out the resolution titled Authorization of Payment for Attending Meetings on the CD-ROM as you follow the sample below. The tear-out version is contained in Appendix C.

Authorization of Payment for Attending Meetings

After discussion, it was agreed that all of the following __["directors" *and/or* "officers"]_____ be paid the following amounts for each day, or fraction of a day, during which they attend a meeting of the board of directors or shareholders of the corporation.

Name and Title	Per Diem Amount
_____	$_____
_____	$_____

It was also discussed and agreed that the following __["directors" *and/or* "officers"]_____ be __["advanced" *or* "reimbursed"]_____ the following reasonable and necessary travel expenses incurred to attend meetings of the board of directors and/or shareholders of the corporation:

Name and Title	Per Meeting Travel Expense Allotment
_____	$_____
_____	$_____

Resolution Authorizing Stipend for Attending Meetings

You can also compensate directors and officers for attending corporate meetings by authorizing the payment of an annual amount, regardless of the number of meeting days per year or the actual travel expenses incurred. Below is the sample resolution to use for this purpose.

CD-ROM

Fill out the resolution titled Annual Director or Officer Stipend for Attendance at Meetings on the CD-ROM as you follow the sample below. The tear-out version is contained in Appendix C.

**Annual Director or Officer Stipend
for Attendance at Meetings**

After discussion, it was agreed that the following ___["directors" *and/or* "officers"]___ be paid the following annual amounts, which include a yearly travel allotment, for traveling to and attending regular and special meetings of the ___["board of directors" *and*/or "shareholders"]___ of this corporation:

Name and Title   Annual Stipend and Travel Allotment

_____ $_____

_____ $_____

Resolution Approving No-Pay Policy for Directors Attending Corporate Meetings

Some corporations may wish to establish a formal corporate policy of not paying directors to attend meetings or perform other chores associated with their director position. Especially if your corporation will bring in new outside directors, it's a good idea to make it clear that it's a no-pay proposition. Your current board may wish to approve this measure, then provide a copy to prospective board members so they can read this no-pay policy before accepting a board position with your corporation.

The language of the resolution makes it clear that directors may be paid for serving as officers or employees or in any other nondirector corporate capacity. Of course, this is normally the case for "inside directors" serving on the boards of smaller corporations.

CD-ROM

Use the resolution titled No Compensation for Attending Corporate Meetings on the CD-ROM to establish a no-pay policy for directors. The tear-out version is contained in Appendix C.

**No Compensation for Attending
Corporate Meetings**

After discussion, it was agreed that no salary, commission, per diem fee, travel allotment, or other amount shall be paid to the directors of this corporation for traveling to or attending meetings of this corporation or for furnishing services to the corporation in their capacity as directors. However, no director shall be prevented from receiving compensation, fees, or other payment for services or work performed for the corporation as an officer, employee, independent conractor, agent, or in any other nondirector capacity for the corporation.

Approval of Indemnification for Corporate Directors, Officers, and Employees

Indemnification refers to the promise to pay fines, settlements, awards, judgments, attorneys' fees, penalties, or other amounts that are personally assessed against a director, officer, or other person because of their decisions or omissions made while performing services for the corporation. In other words, indemnification is a corporation's way of guaranteeing corporate directors and officers that the corporation will pay certain costs and amounts that may be assessed against them as a result of working for the corporation.

EXAMPLE:

The directors of the Lox Box Corporation approved the use of wholesalers who turned out to be lax in their refrigeration procedures. A customer sued director Tosh Imato for medical bills resulting from a food-poisoning incident. Tosh wins the suit, after a finding by the court that the directors could not have reasonably known of or foreseen the inferior food-processing procedures used by the wholesaler. The victory is not complete, since Tosh is liable for hefty lawyers' fees incurred in his own defense. Because the corporation has authorized indemnification for all legal costs associated with lawsuits that are resolved in favor of directors, the corporation—not Tosh—pays these fees.

The extent and amount of indemnification that can or must be paid by corporations to directors and officers vary under state corporate statutes. Most states require indemnification of a corporate director, officer, employee, or agent of the corporation for legal expenses, including attorneys' fees, if that corporate representative is sued and wins the lawsuit.

Other types of indemnification may be authorized by a corporation if certain conditions are met. Under state statutes, additional indemnification generally can be approved only if the board determines that the person acted in good faith and in the best interests of the corporation and, in criminal cases, he or she did not believe his or her conduct was unlawful.

Your articles or bylaws may have a synopsis of the permissible indemnification rules in your state and may already explicitly authorize the payment of one or more types of indemnification for your directors and officers. If you need more information, check your state's corporation laws or ask a small business lawyer for guidance.

Why Director and Officer Liability Insurance Is Important

Even if your corporation wants to indemnify you to the maximum extent possible under state corporate statutes, this may not be enough. State law may not allow indemnification if a director or officer *loses* a lawsuit unless an independent committee of the board or a judge finds that the person acted in good faith. Moreover, even if indemnification can be authorized in a particular case, the corporation may not have the funds to pay indemnification.

For reasons such as these, many corporations decide that the best way to protect directors and officers from personal liability for their acts or omissions is to purchase a special directors' and officers' liability policy (called a D & O liability policy). These policies can be used in conjunction with indemnification—they can pick up the cost of legal expenses not paid directly by the corporation—or they can pay in addition to any indemnification made. D & O policies may be costly, or they may contain too many exclusions to be worthwhile. So shop around and check with different business insurance brokers to find a suitable and affordable policy if you want this type of coverage.

Resolution Authorizing Maximum Statutory Indemnification

The general purpose resolution provided below can be used by the board to authorize the maximum indemnification for corporate directors and officers permitted by state law. It also authorizes the corporation to purchase director and officer liability insurance (D & O insurance) to cover legal expenses, settlements, fines, and other costs not covered by indemnification.

TIP

There's more to indemnification than meets the eye. This general resolution is not tailored to meet the details of your state's indemnification scheme. Normally, this shouldn't be necessary; authorizing the maximum possible indemnification should be adequate. However, if director indemnification is of crucial concern to you—perhaps because your particular line of business or the legal climate in your field means that you can expect lawsuits directed against your directors and officers—check with a small business lawyer to explore just how helpful your state's indemnification statutes really are. Also check into buying a D & O liability policy to cover any nonindemnified legal costs. (See above, "Why Director and Officer Liability Insurance Is Important.")

CD-ROM

Fill out the resolution titled Indemnification and Insurance for Directors and Officers on the CD-ROM as you follow the sample below. The tear-out version is contained in Appendix C.

Indemnification and Insurance for
Directors and Officers

The corporation shall indemnify its current directors and officers [*if desired, add:* "and other

employees and agents"] to the fullest extent permitted under the laws of this state. Such

indemnification shall not be deemed to be exclusive of any other rights to which the indemnified person

is entitled, consistent with law, under any provision of the articles of incorporation or bylaws of the

corporation, any general or specific action of the board of directors, the terms of any contract, or as may

be permitted or required by common law.

The corporation may purchase and maintain insurance or provide another arrangement on behalf of any

person who is a director or officer [*add if appropriate:* "or other employee or agent of the corporation"]

against any liability asserted against him or her and incurred by him or her in such a capacity or arising

out of his or her status as a director or officer, whether or not the corporation would have the power to

indemnify him or her against that liability under the laws of this state.

Conflict of Interest Resolutions

This chapter contains resolutions to be used when a director has business dealings with the corporation. They cover conflict of interest rules that arise when a director is involved in a transaction with the corporation in which he or she has a financial interest.

RELATED TOPIC

Resolutions to approve fringe benefits, adopt a retirement plan, or borrow money from/lend money to officers, directors, and shareholders are covered in other chapters. For employment-related tax and fringe benefit resolutions that can be used to compensate corporate employee-directors, see Chapter 16. For retirement plan resolutions, see Chapter 17. For resolutions to lend money to or borrow money from directors, officers, and shareholders, see Chapters 14 and 15.

CAUTION

If you have outside shareholders, resolutions should be approved by both the board and shareholders. The conflict of interest resolutions presented in this chapter should be approved by both the board and the shareholders. This double approval is not always legally necessary, but we think an extra measure of safety is important if your corporation has outside investors who may wonder what your board is up to when it agrees to business that personally benefits board members.

Approval of Business Between the Corporation and Its Directors

It is common for directors of a small or closely held corporation to decide matters in which they have a personal financial interest. The corporation laws of each state provide special rules covering business deals between a director and a corporation, such as the sale of a piece of land or a patent. Typically, these self-interested transactions involve at least one director who has a personal financial interest in—and stands to benefit from—a transaction with the corporation. Sometimes these rules are referred to as conflict of interest rules.

Not all self-interested decisions by the board require special approval. In fact, state law normally allows the board to set compensation for board members and to approve similar items of routine business even when one or more members of the board may personally benefit from the transaction.

For the most part, corporate laws enacted to deal with conflict of interest decisions are geared toward disclosure: Corporate insiders can engage in these transactions as long as other board members or shareholders know about the insiders' financial interests before they agree to the transactions. In addition, the directors who have a personal interest in a transaction should abstain from voting on the approval of the transaction.

TIP

There is no need to avoid self-serving decisions. Should you be contemplating business matters in which one or more directors has a personal financial stake, don't feel guilty—this is standard business practice, particularly in small corporations. Just get the requisite approvals to be on safer ground. As you'll see below, you should always use common sense when deciding whether to take the extra time and trouble of having directors and shareholders formally approve a transaction.

How to Select and Use Corporate Resolutions

- Scan the table of contents at the beginning of the chapter to find resolutions of interest to you (for a full list of resolutions included with this book, see Appendix C).

- Read the background material that precedes each pertinent corporate resolution.

- Follow the instructions included with the sample resolution and complete a draft using your computer. (You'll have to fill in the tear-out resolution included in Appendix C if you don't have a computer.) If you need guidance on selecting and using the CD-ROM files, see Appendix A.

- Complete any needed attachment forms, such as account authorization forms or lease agreements.

- If a resolution involves complex issues that will benefit from expert analysis, have your legal or tax advisor review your paperwork and conclusions.

- Prepare minutes of a meeting or written consent forms as explained in Chapters 5 through 8, and insert the completed resolution(s) in the appropriate form. If you're seeking shareholder approval in addition to board approval, prepare two sets of minutes or written consent forms—one for your directors and one for your shareholders.

- Have the corporate secretary sign the printed minutes or have directors and/or shareholders sign any written consent forms and waivers. Then place the signed forms, together with any attachments, in your corporate records book.

Overview of State Laws on Conflict of Interest

The corporation laws of each state address director conflict of interest rules. If these rules aren't followed, any shareholders, creditors, or others with a stake in the corporation can later seek to hold the directors personally liable for any personal gain or unfair financial advantage they receive or approve in a transaction between themselves and their corporation.

In most states, to be safe from attack, a decision or transaction that financially benefits a director must meet at least one of the following tests. We recommend that you meet all three tests to avoid future conflicts or controversy:

- After disclosure of how the decision would benefit one or more directors, the matter is approved by the vote of a majority of the board who do not have a financial interest in the decision (with the interested directors abstaining from the vote).

- After disclosure of how the decision would benefit one or more directors, the matter is approved by a majority of disinterested shareholders—that is, shareholders who have no financial stake in the decision (and who are not also directors).

- The transaction is fair to the corporation at the time it is entered into.

EXAMPLE:

The three-member board of Foam and Futon, Inc., wishes to approve the sale by one of the directors to the corporation of a plastic injection molding machine for use in creating castings for futon frames. The price asked by the director is competitive in view of current industry pricing. The deal is approved by the other two disinterested directors and by all shareholders of the corporation after disclosure of the details of the deal and a discussion of similar prices sought by outsiders for the sale of similar machinery. In these circumstances, and after approvals of the directors and shareholders are placed in the corporate records, it is unlikely that any nondirector-shareholder, creditor, or other outsider with a stake in the financial affairs of the corporation would decide to challenge this "self-serving" decision later.

> **CAUTION**
>
> **Director conflict of interest rules vary from state to state.** To be absolutely sure of the laws in your state, you should consult your bylaws for the procedures and vote requirements to approve business transactions involving a director. If your bylaws don't have your state's conflict of interest rules (or you're not sure if they follow the state rules), look them up in your state's corporation laws. (See Appendix B for information on how to find your state's corporations laws.) Conflict of interest rules are typically listed in the law's table of contents under "Directors" and contained in a provision typically titled "Approval of Self-Dealing Transactions." As an alternative, ask your legal adviser for your state's conflict of interest approval rules.

Small Corporations and Disinterested Voters

What if you run a small corporation, say with three directors, and two directors will benefit from a proposed business deal? How can you obtain a quorum to hold the directors' and shareholders' meeting to approve the business? Generally, state law allows the interested directors, or those directors' shares, to be counted for purposes of determining if a quorum is present at a meeting held to approve the transaction, even though these directors should abstain from voting.

This also raises the question of how to seek approval if you don't have a disinterested majority—for example, if two of the three directors will benefit from the deal. In such cases, it's of utmost importance to make sure the deal is fair—this is the third alternative under the normal tests listed above, and is the one you will need to fall back on in case of a dispute later.

Approval in Very Small Corporations

As a practical matter, if yours is a small, closely held corporation, it's possible that a majority of your board or shareholders will have a financial interest in the transaction. Even though you may be able to get the approval of all disinterested directors or shareholders, their number may not be sufficient to pass the resolution by normal voting rules.

EXAMPLE: Two members of Threadbare Sofa Reconditioners Corp.'s three-director board will benefit from a transaction. Even though the sole remaining director votes "yes" to the deal, her vote is insufficient to pass the resolution because the bylaws require a majority vote of the three-person board.

In these situations, make sure the resolution reflects that the transaction is fair to your corporation. To support this position, list facts or state the basis as to why the deal is fair in the resolution—for example, by stating that the contract price is commercially competitive with other bids currently being offered for similar work in the geographical area, or stating that the property is being sold for fair market value (to support this conclusion, include current comparable real estate listings in your area for similar properties or businesses).

Commonsense Approval Procedures

Here's our practical advice for dealing with transactions involving the financial interests of directors—including when to use resolutions and what kind of approval to get:

- **Prepare resolutions if one or two directors will benefit financially.** If a director is going to benefit from a business deal that doesn't benefit other directors or shareholders, it's best to prepare a conflict of interest resolution that shows you took extra precautions before approving the transaction.

- **Prepare resolutions if there are secondary benefits to directors.** This applies if one or more directors will clearly receive a collateral financial benefit as a secondary effect of the transaction. For example, the directors approve an increase in the stock bonus plan to employees, but two directors also work for the corporation and, as the highest-paid employees, they will receive 90% of the additional bonus shares.

- **Get unanimous approval.** If possible, have every transaction in which a director stands to receive a financial benefit approved by all disinterested directors and all disinterested shareholders after full disclosure of the details of the transaction and the director's potential interest in it. By taking these steps, you can help avoid future controversy and claims against the corporation and directors.

- **If unanimous approval is not available, get majority approval.** If it's impossible to get full approval by all disinterested directors and shareholders, have the transaction approved by a majority of the disinterested board and shareholders.

- **Make sure the transaction is fair.** If it's not, you are unjustly benefiting directors at the expense of the corporation, and asking for trouble, particularly if you have nondirector-shareholders.

EXAMPLE:

AB Corp.'s five-person board is asked by the president to approve a contract for the furnishing of supplies to AB Corp. by a company in which one director has a part-ownership interest. Three of the four disinterested board members—a majority—vote to approve the transaction only after making sure that the cost of supplies is at least as good as the lowest price available from independent suppliers. A statement that this determination was made by the board is placed in the resolution. Because of these precautions, it is unlikely that shareholders will challenge the transaction later.

Resolutions to Approve Director Conflict of Interest Transactions

We provide different versions of conflict of interest resolutions, for approval by directors or shareholders at a meeting or by written consent. Remember, to satisfy state corporation law standards, we suggest that both your board and your shareholders approve business of this sort after full written disclosure of all material facts. If doing so is impractical or seemingly not necessary in a particular case, obtain the approval of the board or shareholders. (Approval by written consent, rather than calling a special meeting, is often the easier of the two proceedings in small, closely held corporations.)

The conflict of interest resolutions that follow can normally be used to approve and validate a wide variety of business transactions. In some instances, you may wish to give specific details on the terms of the business being approved. For example, you might wish to include all the particulars of a real estate purchase transaction. There are two good ways to provide such detailed information:

- If you have adopted another resolution to actually approve the transaction (such as a resolution to approve purchase of real property), you can simply refer to that resolution and attach a copy.

- If, for some reason, the board hasn't approved a particular transaction in detail, you can refer to and attach any other documents (such as a purchase contract) that accomplish this.

Resolution by Directors Approving Conflict of Interest Transaction (for Minutes)

Below is a sample of the resolution to show board approval of a director conflict of interest transaction at a meeting of directors.

CD-ROM

Fill out the resolution titled Board Approval of Transaction Benefiting a Director on the CD-ROM following the special instructions provided. The tear-out version is contained in Appendix C.

Special Instructions

❶ Describe the business transaction or contract to be approved. If the terms of the transaction can be documented with another resolution or form contained in this book (or by a separate contract such as a loan to a director or a lease of property from a director), you can describe it generally in a sentence or two and then refer to the additional resolution,

form, or contract. Then, attach a copy of the other resolution, form, or contract to this resolution and have both approved when you insert them together in your minutes of meeting form.

EXAMPLE:

Shake and Rake Tree Trimmers, Inc., wishes to obtain board approval of a loan made to a director. The loan itself is described in a separate board resolution and evidenced with a separately prepared promissory note. Instead of describing the loan and the terms of the note in this conflict of interest resolution, the secretary fills in: "loan transaction approved by separate board resolution with terms as described in a promissory note, both of which are attached to this resolution." (Chapter 15 covers sample resolutions and promissory note forms for insider loans.)

❷ This language helps strengthen your showing that the decision was proper, because, as explained above, you can usually validate conflict of interest decisions simply on the basis that they were fair to the corporation.

❸ In the vote column, insert the word "approved," "against," or "abstained" next to each board member's name to show how each person voted. Remember, it is best to get approval by all disinterested directors, but approval by a majority of disinterested directors will work in a pinch. Self-interested directors should normally abstain from voting, unless their vote is necessary to obtain a majority vote—as may be the case, for example, in a small, closely held corporation.

Board Approval of Transaction Benefiting a Director

The next item of business considered by the board was:

[*state nature of transaction or contract*] ❶ _____.

It was understood that the following directors have a material financial interest in this business as follows: [*state the name(s) of the director(s) and the scope of their personal financial interest in the transaction or contract with the corporation*]

Name   Scope of Personal Interest

_____   _____

After discussion, it was agreed that the approval of this business was fair to the corporation. ❷

Therefore, it was approved by the votes of the directors present at the meeting as follows:

Name of Director   Vote ❸

_____   _____

_____   _____

Written Consent of Directors Approving Conflict of Interest Transaction

In this section, we show a sample of the written consent form that can be used by the board to approve a transaction where one board member has a conflict of interest. To accommodate the written consent procedure, the language in this form is slightly different from that of the previous resolution.

This is a complete written consent form that stands on its own. Unlike the resolutions in this book, you don't need to insert this language into written minutes. Simply fill it in, have it signed, then place a copy in your corporate records book.

CD-ROM

Fill out the form titled Directors' Written Consent to Transaction Benefitting a Director as you

follow the sample and special instructions below. The tear-out version is contained in Appendix C.

Special Instructions

❶ Describe the business transaction or contract to be approved. If the terms of the transaction can be documented with another form or resolution contained in this book, such as a loan to a director or a lease of property from a director, you can refer to the additional documentation here (for instance, by saying "transaction approved by separate board resolution that is attached to this resolution"). Then, attach a copy of the other form or resolution to this written consent form prior to having it signed by your directors.

❷ This language helps strengthen your showing that the decision was proper because, as explained earlier, you can usually validate conflict of interest decisions simply on the basis that they were fair to the corporation.

❸ If possible, obtain the written consent of all disinterested board members. Have every director sign on a separate signature line, and print or type each name below the signature. If more than one director signs a single consent form, show the earliest date on which a director signed the form.

Resolutions for Shareholder Approval

In addition to getting the approval of all (or a majority of) disinterested directors, we also recommend that you obtain the approval of all shareholders who do not stand to gain financially from a decision that personally benefits board members. We provide resolutions for obtaining approval both at a meeting and by written consent.

Directors' Written Consent to Transaction Benefiting a Director

The undersigned approve the following item of business:

[*state nature of transaction or contract*] ❶ _____

Prior to signing this form, the undersigned understood that the following director(s) had a material financial interest in this business as follows: [*state the name(s) of the director(s) and the scope of their personal financial interest in the transaction or contract with the corporation*]

Name of Director   Scope of Personal Financial Interest

_____   _____

It was agreed that the approval of this business was fair to the corporation. ❷

Date: _____ ❸

Signature: ___[*signature of director*]_____

Name: ___[*printed name of director*]_____, Director

Date: _____

Signature: ___[*signature of director*]_____

Name: ___[*printed name of director*]_____, Director

Date: _____

Signature: ___[*signature of director*]_____

Name: ___[*printed name of director*]_____, Director

Resolution by Shareholders Approving Conflict of Interest Transaction (for Minutes)

Here's the sample of the resolution to use to show approval at a shareholders' meeting of a transaction that financially benefits one or more directors.

CD-ROM

Fill out the form titled Shareholder Approval of Transaction Benefiting a Director on the CD-ROM as you follow the sample and special instructions below. The tear-out version is contained in Appendix C.

Special Instructions

❶ Describe the business transaction or contract to be approved. If the terms of the transaction can be documented with another resolution or form contained in this book (such as a loan to a director or a lease of property from a director), you can refer to the additional resolution or form here. Then, attach a copy of the other form or resolution to this resolution before you insert it in your minutes of the shareholders' meeting.

❷ State the names and financial interests of directors who stand to benefit from the transaction being approved. Make sure to indicate whether any directors also are shareholders; as explained below, you normally do not count the vote of these director-shareholders when seeking approval of a self-interested transaction or decision.

EXAMPLE:

Robin and Lauren, two of the five shareholders of a corporation, are also the corporation's only two board members. As board members, they have already approved the terms of loans to be made by their corporation to each of them. The board now goes to the shareholders to obtain approval of the transaction. Because Robin and Lauren are director-shareholders who stand to benefit from the deal, they abstain from voting at the shareholders' meeting. A description of the transaction and of each director-shareholder's interest is inserted in this blank, as follows: "Robin Kemani, director and shareholder, and Lauren Steingold, director and shareholder, seek personal loans of cash from the corporation for the amounts of $5,000 each, with terms as contained in promissory notes that are attached to this resolution."

❸ You can usually validate conflict of interest decisions simply on the basis that they were fair to the corporation. This language helps strengthen your showing that the decision was proper.

❹ Fill in the names of all shareholders. In the "votes" column, show the number of shares voted by each and whether the shares were voted "approved" or "against" the proposal, or whether a shareholder "abstained" from voting the shares. Again, if possible, get the approval of all or a majority of disinterested shareholders.

**Shareholder Approval of Transaction
Benefiting a Director**

The next item of business considered by the shareholders was: _[state nature of transaction or contract]_ ❶.

It was understood that the following person(s) has/have a material financial interest in this business as follows:

[state the name of each such director, followed by each person's position as "director" or "director and

shareholder" and the nature and extent of each person's personal financial interests in the

transaction or contract] ❷

After discussion, it was agreed that the approval of this business was fair to the corporation. ❸
Therefore, it was approved by the votes of the shareholders present at the meeting as follows:

Name of Shareholder   Vote ❹

_____   _____

_____   _____

Written Consent of Shareholders Approving Conflict of Interest Transaction

As an alternative to having shareholders approve director self-interested business at a meeting, you can use a written consent form. Note that this is a complete written consent form that stands on its own. Unlike the resolutions in this book, you don't need to insert this language into written minutes. Simply fill it in, have it signed, then place it along with any attachments in your corporate records book.

CD-ROM

Fill out the Shareholder Written Consent form as you follow the sample and special instructions below. The tear-out version is contained in Appendix C.

Special Instructions

❶, ❷, and ❸ See the corresponding special instructions to the previous shareholder form (Shareholder Approval of Transaction Benefiting a Director), above.

❹ If you can, obtain the written consent of all disinterested shareholders. Have each shareholder sign on a separate signature line, and print or type each name below the signature. If more than one shareholder signs a single consent form, show the earliest date on which a shareholder signed the form.

**Shareholder Written Consent to Transaction
Involving a Director**

The undersigned approve the following item of business:

[state nature of transaction or contract] ❶ _____ .

      Prior to signing this form, each of the undersigned understood that the following person(s) has/ had a material financial interest in this business as follows: _[state the name of each director, followed by each person's position as "director" or "director and shareholder" and the nature and extent of each person's personal financial interests in the transaction or contract]_ ❷

Name of Director/Shareholder	Position	Personal Financial Interest
_____	_____	_____
_____	_____	_____

      It was agreed that the approval of this business was fair to the corporation. ❸

Date: _____ ❹

Signature: ___[signature of shareholder]_____

Name: _____[printed name of shareholder]_____, Shareholder

Date: _____

Signature: ___[signature of shareholder]_____

Name: _____[printed name of shareholder]_____, Shareholder

Resolutions for Loans to the Corporation

When a corporation needs to borrow money, it typically applies to a bank for a loan or asks its shareholders for additional funds. Small corporations often prefer to borrow funds from shareholders, and the shareholders are usually active in the business and willing to help out when cash is tight.

Of course, there are other ways corporations can raise funds—such as by going to venture capitalists or even by making a private or public issuance of shares to obtain capital. Less formally, the owner-employees of small, closely held corporations are sometimes fortunate enough to be able to borrow money from friends or relatives with cash reserves.

In this chapter, we focus on the most common sources of funds for small corporations. The resolutions in this chapter show board approval for corporate borrowing from financial institutions or from existing shareholders (or their family and friends). We also show you how to select and use different types of promissory notes included on the CD-ROM to help you document the payback terms of your corporation's loans. (If your corporation wishes to lend money to—rather than borrow from—a corporate director, officer, employee, or shareholder, see Chapter 15.)

SEE AN EXPERT

Tax and legal considerations. Corporate borrowing is serious business, even if the lender is a shareholder, director, or other corporate insider. We suggest you use the information gleaned from this chapter to discuss the tax, legal, and practical considerations with your tax adviser or business lawyer before approving any sizable corporate loan.

TIP

For loans, board approval is required; shareholder approval is optional. Normally, only the board needs to approve loan transactions. Nonetheless, if the amount of the loan is substantial, or if your corporation has outside investors who might raise eyebrows at a loan transaction you plan to engage in, we recommend you have your shareholders ratify the board decision to approve the loan. This should be done prior to signing the loan or receiving the corporate loan proceeds.

When to Use Corporate Loan Resolutions

If you plan to borrow money from or establish a line of credit with a bank or other financial institution, check with its loan department before preparing any of the resolutions provided in this chapter. You may find that much, or all, of the paperwork will be done for you. All banks will provide you with a promissory note to sign, and some use their own loan resolution form for directors' approval.

If you are borrowing from a shareholder or other individual, you should get board approval of a formal resolution, backed up by a promissory note that spells out the terms for repayment. As discussed below, this type of paperwork may help you avoid unfavorable tax consequences if the IRS looks at your borrowing transactions later.

But more than this, documenting the loan provides a paper trail that the corporation and the individual lender can refer to later to handle any disputes. It's surprising how often undocumented loans can lead to trouble, with lenders and borrowers remembering the terms of the deal differently, or walking away from the transaction with different expectations. If you put it in writing, you can resolve

How to Select and Use Corporate Resolutions

- Scan the table of contents at the beginning of the chapter to find resolutions of interest to you (for a full list of resolutions included with this book, see Appendix C).

- Read the background material that precedes each pertinent corporate resolution.

- Follow the instructions included with the sample resolution and complete a draft using your computer. (You'll have to fill in the tear-out resolution included in Appendix C if you don't have a computer.) If you need guidance on selecting and using the CD-ROM files, see Appendix A.

- Complete any needed attachment forms, such as account authorization forms or lease agreements.

- If a resolution involves complex issues that will benefit from expert analysis, have your legal or tax adviser review your paperwork and conclusions.

- Prepare minutes of a meeting or written consent forms as explained in Chapters 5 through 8, and insert the completed resolution(s) in the appropriate form. If you're seeking shareholder approval in addition to board approval, prepare two sets of minutes or written consent forms—one for your directors and one for your shareholders.

- Have the corporate secretary sign the printed minutes or have directors and/or shareholders sign any written consent forms and waivers. Then place the signed forms, together with any attachments, in your corporate records book.

later controversies with a quick look at your corporate records.

Here's an example of a loan arrangement that went bad because the sole owner of a small corporation failed to properly document his corporate loan transaction: The owner of a corporation took out a personal loan of $60,000 from his personal bank account, then loaned the money to his corporation. When the money was repaid by the corporation, the IRS said the payback was not a tax-free repayment of the loan to the owner, but a taxable salary payment that had to be reported on his 1040 form. The IRS gave three reasons: The loan was not properly reflected on the corporation's income tax return, a promissory note for the loan was not prepared and placed in the corporate records book, and no interest was charged on the loan by the lender. This case points out the importance of following the formalities discussed in this chapter for documenting loans by corporate insiders to a corporation.

Finally, keep in mind that some of the resolutions below, whether for borrowing from banks or individuals, are preliminary in nature—that is, they grant board authority to officers to seek a loan, sometimes with a limit placed on the maximum amount they may borrow or with other restrictions on the terms of the financing being sought. In many instances, you will not need to use these preliminary resolutions. Instead, to cut down on approvals and paperwork, have the board approve the actual terms of the loan once it is obtained from either an individual or institution.

Loans by Banks and Other Lending Institutions

Corporations borrow funds from time to time from banks and other commercial institutions, such as savings and loans institutions and credit unions. In this chapter, we generally refer to all of these institutions as banks.

There are two common ways corporations borrow from banks:

- **Lump sum loan.** The corporation receives the funds all at once and repays them over time, usually within two to five years. Banks often charge the prime interest rate currently in effect plus two or three points (a point is 1% of the face amount of the loan) or, as interest rates fluctuate, variable rates that change in step with a preselected financial index. Especially at the start of your relationship with a bank, you also should expect to be asked to pay a point or two as a loan fee, and to pledge personal assets, accounts receivable, and corporate inventory to guarantee repayment of the loan. As your credit history develops with the bank, you should be able to negotiate lower points on future loans.

- **Revolving line of credit.** Funds may be borrowed, paid back, and reborrowed over a period of time (usually one year) on an as-needed basis, up to the credit limit. Interest rates and fees are similar to those for a loan, but for the credit limit to be renewed for another year, the bank may require that the line of credit be paid off at least for part of the year. "Out of debt for thirty days once in each 12 months" is a typical requirement for renewal.

EXAMPLE:

The Hinterland Campwear Corporation finds it needs additional funds to take up the slack in cash flow during lull periods of its yearly business cycle. It applies for and obtains a $75,000 line of credit at a local bank. Throughout the year, authorized officers may call the bank and ask to have funds transferred to the corporate account. Requests for funds may be made as often as needed, as long as cumulative borrowing under the line of credit does not exceed the credit line limit of $75,000 in a fiscal year. Hinterland may pay back as little or much of the amount borrowed as it chooses, which allows the corporation to save on interest payments when it has extra cash.

Interest the corporation pays on a bank loan is deductible as a corporate business expense. Also, the money it borrows is not considered business income on which taxes must be paid. After all, the principal amount of a loan must be repaid—the corporation doesn't get to keep this money.

Banks often require that you attach a copy of a resolution that shows approval by the board of the loan or line of credit. If the bank doesn't provide its own resolution form, you may use the forms presented in this chapter to prepare this sort of documentation.

RELATED TOPIC

A bank may require a loan approval resolution to be certified by your corporate secretary. This means the secretary signs a statement at the bottom of the resolution stating that it was approved by the board and is still in effect. For a certification form the corporate secretary may use to show approval of a resolution by the board, see "Certification of Board or Shareholder Action" in Chapter 9.

Understanding Loan Terms

A bank will usually lend money to a smaller, less-established corporation only if its primary shareholders cosign, or personally guarantee, repayment of the corporate promissory note. Make sure you fully understand the terms of any corporate loan *before* you sign on the dotted line. Here are some loan terms to read carefully:

- **Security pledge.** Depending on the primary shareholders' net worth and credit history, as well as the amount of the corporate loan, the bank may ask primary shareholders to pledge personal assets as collateral for the note—such as equity in a house (in the form of a second or third mortgage). If the corporation defaults on repayment of the note, the bank may legally foreclose on the house or other property and sell it to satisfy the delinquent debt.

- **Right of setoff.** In case of default, the bank will have the right to reach all of the money, securities, and other property the corporation and its guarantors have deposited with the bank.

- **Subordination agreement.** If the corporation is in default, the bank has a legal right to be paid before the lenders listed in the subordination clause. In other words, if you previously loaned your corporation money, either as part of the incorporation or at a later date to supply operational funds, the bank has a right to be paid before you. And if the corporation declares bankruptcy, the bank will be entitled to be paid ahead of you.

Resolutions for Loans by Lending Institutions

Below, we present samples of various resolutions that show board approval of loans to the corporation from banks and other outside lending institutions. Pick the one that applies best to your situation.

Resolution Authorizing Bank Loan at Specific Terms

Use this resolution if you are seeking approval of a loan already negotiated with a local bank or other lender. This resolution shows approval of the specific terms of the loan.

CD-ROM

Fill in the resolution titled Authorization of Loan at Specific Terms on the CD-ROM as you follow the sample and special instructions below. The tear-out version is contained in Appendix C.

Special Instructions

❶ As a shortcut, you can use the words "terms according to the attached promissory note" and attach a copy of the promissory note form to your resolution.

❷ Normally, either or both the president and treasurer are authorized by the board to borrow loan funds on behalf of the corporation, but you may specify other officers or employees if you wish.

Authorization of Loan at Specific Terms

It was announced that the officers of the corporation have received a loan commitment from the following bank, trust company, or other financial institution on the following terms:

Name of Lender: _[name of bank or other financial institution]_

Loan Amount: $ _[principal amount of the loan—amount you plan to borrow, not including interest]_

Terms of the Loan:

[state the terms of the loan, including rate of interest, the full repayment period, number and amount of installment payments and date, and amount of final payment if different from other payments] ❶

It was resolved that the proposed terms of the loan are fair and reasonable to the corporation and that it would be in the best interests of the corporation to borrow the funds on the terms stated above.

It was further resolved that the following officers are authorized to execute the notes and documents on behalf of the corporation necessary to effect the above loan:

Officer Name   Title ❷

_____   _____

_____   _____

Resolution Authorizing Maximum Loan on General Terms

The next resolution shows general approval of a loan that has not yet been arranged with a lender. The resolution allows your officers to seek financing from a bank or other financial institution for a maximum loan amount on currently available terms, without limiting them to a specific interest rate or other repayment limitations.

CD-ROM

Fill in the resolution form titled Authorization of Maximum Loan on General Terms on the CD-ROM as you follow the sample and special instructions below. The tear-out version is contained in Appendix C.

Special Instructions

Normally, either or both the president and treasurer are authorized by the board to borrow loan funds on behalf of the corporation, but you may specify other officers or employees if you wish in the blanks at the bottom of the form.

Authorization of Maximum Loan on General Terms

It was resolved that it was in the best interests of the corporation to borrow up to the following amount of funds from the following bank, trust company, or other financial institution:

Name of Lender: ___[name of bank]_____

Loan Amount: $ _[principal amount of the loan not including interest]_

The following officers were authorized to sign the appropriate notes and documents on behalf of the corporation necessary to borrow an amount that does not exceed the amount noted above on terms reasonable to the corporation:

Officer Name   Title

_____   _____

_____   _____

Resolution Giving General Authorization of Loans for Business Needs

You may use this resolution to give one or more corporate officers unlimited authority to borrow money on behalf of the corporation. The delegation of this much financial leeway by the board to a corporate officer is predicated on a significant amount of personal trust—the type most typically found in small corporations where the officers in question and the directors are in very close touch.

CD-ROM

Fill in the resolution titled Unlimited Authorization of Loans for Business Needs as you follow the sample and special instructions below. The tear-out version is contained in Appendix C.

Special Instructions

Normally, either or both the president and treasurer are authorized by the board to borrow loan funds on behalf of the corporation, but you may specify other officers or employees if you wish.

Unlimited Authorization of Loans for Business Needs

It was resolved that the following officers of the corporation are authorized to borrow on behalf of the corporation from one or more banks or other financial institutions such amounts as they decide are reasonably necessary to meet the needs of the business of the corporation:

Officer Name   Title

_____   _____

_____   _____

Resolution Authorizing Line of Credit

The next resolution authorizes one or more officers to arrange for and utilize an ongoing line of credit at a bank. It's important to realize that, once granted, an authorized officer may tap the line at any time without returning to the board; but of course he or she won't be able to borrow more than the bank authorized. (If you are looking for a resolution that places a cap on the amount of money that an officer may borrow in any one transaction under a line of credit, see the resolution that follows.)

The authority granted under this resolution is different from the grant given under the previous resolution just above. Here, the designated officers may enter into repeated borrowing transactions after the corporation obtains a line of credit. The result is the officers can't borrow more than the maximum amount authorized by the line. By contrast, in the previous resolution, officers are given the power to apply repeatedly for different bank loans, with no maximum overall limit established.

CD-ROM

Fill in the resolution titled Authorization of Line of Credit on the CD-ROM as you follow the sample and special instructions below. The tear-out version is contained in Appendix C.

Special Instructions

❶ Normally, either or both the president and treasurer are authorized by the board to borrow loan funds on behalf of the corporation, but you may specify other officers or employees if you wish.

❷ You can use this optional provision to restrict the amount and frequency of credit limit borrowing by corporate officers.

EXAMPLE:

The board of Execuflex Time Management Systems, Ltd., authorizes its treasurer and president to establish and borrow against a corporate line of credit as they see fit, subject to an annual borrowing limit of $100,000, or up to $50,000 in a given quarter. Here's how this blank is filled in: "It was further decided that the authority granted by this resolution be limited and that the officers not be allowed to borrow funds against the line of credit that exceed $100,000 per year or that exceed $50,000 in any calendar quarter."

If you don't wish to limit the borrowing authority of officers, simply delete this optional paragraph from your final resolution.

Authorization of Line of Credit

It was resolved that it would be in the best interests of the corporation to obtain a line of credit for

borrowing funds from ___[name of bank]_____.

The following officers were authorized to complete all necessary forms, documents, and notes and to

pledge as security corporate assets necessary to obtain and utilize the line of credit:

Officer Name   Title ❶

_____   _____

[OPTIONAL: It was further decided that the authority granted by this resolution be limited and that the ❷

officers not be allowed to borrow funds against the line of credit that exceed (*credit line limit and period*).]

Resolution Authorizing Line of Credit With Cap on Each Transaction

The sample resolution below authorizes a line of credit and restricts the amount that may be borrowed in any given transaction under this line of credit.

CD-ROM

Fill in the resolution titled Authorization of Line of Credit With Cap on Each Transaction on the CD-ROM as you follow the sample and special instructions below. The tear-out version is contained in Appendix C.

Special Instructions

Normally, either or both the president and treasurer are authorized by the board to borrow loan funds on behalf of the corporation, but you may specify other officers or employees if you wish.

Authorization of Line of Credit With Cap on Each Transaction

It was resolved that it would be in the best interests of the corporation to obtain a line of credit for the

borrowing of funds from ___[name of bank]_____.

The following officers were authorized to complete all necessary forms, documents, and notes necessary

to obtain and utilize the line of credit to allow borrowing by the corporation in an aggregate amount

that does not exceed $___[credit line limit: specify total borrowing limit and period if you wish—for

example, "$50,000 per fiscal year"]_____.

Officer Name   Title

_____   _____

_____   _____

It was further resolved that the amount borrowed under the line of credit in one transaction shall not

exceed $ ___[maximum amount that can be borrowed against the line of credit in one transaction]_____

unless any excess amount is specifically approved by further resolution of the board of directors.

Resolution Authorizing Specific Loan Terms Secured by Corporate Property

You may use the following resolution to approve and document a corporate loan that is secured by property owned by the corporation. While the earlier loan resolutions can be modified to allow you to do this, here you can specifically list the corporate assets pledged as security in the resolution itself. This extra bit of detail makes sense if the corporation is pledging significant corporate assets, such as corporate real estate, accounts receivables, or inventory. Having the board specifically approve this pledge of security is just one more way of showing full authority for the loan in your corporate records.

CD-ROM

Fill in the resolution titled Authorization of Loan Terms Secured by Corporate Property on the CD-ROM as you follow the sample and special instructions below. The tear-out version is contained in Appendix C.

Special Instructions

❶ Normally, either or both the president and treasurer are authorized by the board to borrow loan funds on behalf of the corporation, but you may specify other officers or employees if you wish.

❷ Describe the corporate property pledged for the loan. For personal property (individual items of movable property such as an auto or equipment), provide serial or ID numbers and a description of the property. An example might be "2011 Jeep Grand Cherokee, ID # XXX0099." For real estate, a street address (rather than a legal description) will do fine.

❸ Spell out the terms of the loan, such as the rate of interest and the number and amount of monthly payments. If terms have not been arranged, insert the following statement: "on best terms available from lender."

If you prepare a promissory note, you can attach it to the resolution and refer to it here as follows: "See the terms of the promissory note between _____ [*name of corporation*] _____ and _[*lender*]_ attached to this resolution."

TIP

Get permission from shareholders before pledging substantial corporate assets. To avoid shareholder discontent if the corporation can't repay the debt and the security for the loan is liquidated by the lender, we suggest you have the shareholders separately approve the loan transaction after it is approved by the board. You may do this by shareholder written consent or at a shareholders' meeting reported with written minutes, as discussed in Chapters 5 and 8.

Authorization of Loan Terms Secured
by Corporate Property

It was resolved that the following officers of the corporation are authorized to borrow the sum of

$ _[principal amount of loan]_ on behalf of the corporation from _[name of bank]_ :

Officer Name   Title ❶

_____   _____

_____   _____

      The above officers are authorized to execute a promissory note for the above amount under the

following terms together with a mortgage, deed of trust, or security agreement and other documents

necessary to secure payment of the note with the pledge of the following property:

Property Used as Security for Note:

[insert a description of the property] ❷

Terms of Note:

[specify loan terms or refer to and attach promissory note] ❸

Loans by Shareholders and Other Insiders

A corporation's shareholders or a shareholder's family or friends may lend money to the corporation—usually to increase the corporation's cash reserves or to cover operational expenses. Shareholder loans of this sort mostly occur in the context of smaller, closely held corporations where there is considerable overlap between the fortunes of the corporation and the personal finances of its main shareholders. If this isn't the case, it may be difficult to find shareholders or other individuals willing to come up with additional funds to help finance the corporation, unless the corporation is doing well and needs the extra money to expand.

EXAMPLE:

Larry's Reality, Inc., is a one-person corporation that runs a computer arcade and virtual reality parlor in the Westmont Mall complex. To keep his adolescent clientele interested in making return visits to the arcade, Larry must purchase the latest in expensive computer and virtual reality game gear, regardless of the current condition of his shop's bottom line. As a result, he finds that he must occasionally make short-term (one- to three-month) personal loans to his corporation.

It is essential to document all insider loan transitions with corporate resolutions. If, for example, you routinely lend your one-person or small corporation operational funds by writing checks out of your personal checking account without any extra paperwork, the courts or the IRS may well decide that your corporation is simply your alter ego and hold you personally liable for corporate debts or taxes.

EXAMPLE:

For each of the personal loans Larry makes to his corporation, he prepares a corporate loan resolution and a basic promissory note in his capacity as director and places them in the company's corporate records book. These should stand Larry in good stead in case his individual tax return or Larry's Reality, Inc.'s, corporate tax return is audited by the IRS. It also will protect him if he ever lands in court with a disgruntled creditor claiming that his operation is nothing more than an incorporated checking account that should be disregarded by the court.

TIP

Shareholder loans to S corporations have additional benefits. A technical—but important—tax advantage of a loan that an S corporation shareholder makes directly to the corporation is that the shareholder gets to increase his or her tax basis in the shares by the amount of the loan. (Remember, the S corporation shareholder is taxed at the individual, not corporate, level.) Should the business lose money, this qualifies the shareholder to write off a larger amount of corporate losses against personal income on his or her individual tax return. (For more information on S corporation taxation, see Chapter 10.) Always check with your tax adviser before making a loan to your corporation to ensure favorable tax treatment.

How Shareholders May Contribute to the Corporation

Money paid into a corporation by incorporators and investors is known as capital, and the process of paying this money to the corporation is called "capitalization." In small, closely held corporations, the shareholders often have a choice on how to capitalize their business—that is, money may be paid in as equity or debt. This choice applies whether the funds are obtained at the start-up of the corporate enterprise or after the corporation has been in business for a while. Let's distinguish between these two ways of putting money into a small corporation.

Buying Shares and Income Tax Basis

Buying shares in a corporation is usually a tax-neutral proposition—neither the corporation nor the purchaser is subject to income tax on account of the transaction. The amount paid for the shares is used as the tax basis of the shares. If the shareholder later sells the shares, he or she will have to pay taxes on any profit realized over and above his or her tax basis in the shares.

EXAMPLE: Dianne capitalizes her one-person advertising consulting corporation with $50,000 and receives 50 shares valued at $1,000 each. She sells her corporation—and her shares—seven years later for $150,000. Her taxable profit on the sale is $100,000 ($150,000 minus her $50,000 tax basis in the shares).

Equity Investments (Shares)

Equity investors receive shares of stock in the corporation and corporate assets in proportion to their stockholdings when the corporation is dissolved or sold. They are also allowed to receive profits during the life of the corporation when and if the board declares dividend payments. (See Chapter 18 for dividend declaration resolutions.) In small corporations, dividends are rarely paid, since they are subject to double taxation, with taxes due both at the corporate and shareholder level. Instead, funds are typically distributed to shareholders in ways that subject them to single taxation only—for example, as salaries or fringe benefits that are taxed to the shareholders but deducted by the corporation as business expenses.

Debt Investments (Loans to the Corporation)

When money is paid into a corporation as debt, the lender should receive a promissory note back from the corporation entitling him or her to repayment of the principal plus interest over time. The creation of debt instead of equity has tax advantages, since repayment of the principal amount of the loan is tax free to the lender who receives it, and payment of interest is deductible by the corporation. Of course, the lending person (shareholder) must report and pay income taxes on interest payments received from the corporation. (By contrast, a distribution of profits—a dividend—paid to a shareholder is 100% taxable to the shareholder and nondeductible by the corporation.)

It's common practice for shareholders, and sometimes their friends or relatives, to lend money to their corporation. For example, shareholders of a small corporation may decide to lend additional funds to their three-year-old corporation to help it meet expenses. They pay in $10,000, taking back a $10,000 note that will be repaid with interest over a five-year period.

Other Ways to Capitalize

There are a number of other ways a corporation can tap shareholders to help solve the problem of a cash shortage. In fact, sometimes a corporation can receive money or property in a way that benefits both the corporation and its shareholders. Here are a few examples:

- The corporation may not need to go to the trouble of raising money to buy property that is currently owned by shareholders. Instead, the shareholders can lease property to the corporation and receive rental income in return. Rent payments, like interest paid under a note, are deductible by the corporation. And like interest income, rental income is taxed to the shareholders who own the property.

- In some circumstances, it may be more advantageous for a shareholder to purchase property (real property or personal property, such as equipment or automobiles) and lease it to the corporation. (For more on leasing property to the corporation, see Chapter 9.)

- If the corporation needs funds, it can borrow them from a bank, using the personal collateral of the shareholders as a way to qualify for the corporate loan. In other words, the shareholders pledge personal assets to guarantee repayment of the loan if the corporation defaults on the loan.

Avoiding Shareholder Loan Problems With the IRS

The IRS commonly scrutinizes shareholder loan transactions when auditing small corporations, particularly those that are closely held. The IRS wants to make sure the loans are not really sham transactions designed for the purpose of generating favorable tax consequences to the shareholders, without any bona fide commercial reason for the loan.

If the IRS thinks a shareholder loan looks more like a capital investment in the corporation, it has the power to recharacterize loan repayments by the corporation to the shareholder as dividends paid by the corporation. If this happens, the corporation will not be entitled to deduct interest payments made under the loan. In addition, the shareholder will be responsible for paying individual taxes on the principal repayments, as well as on interest received.

Fortunately, you should avoid this unwanted tax result if your loan transaction carries commercially reasonable terms and is backed up by corporate resolutions and promissory notes, all of which should be placed in your corporate records book.

Below are other primary considerations you should keep in mind to try to ensure that the IRS will treat loans made by your shareholders as legitimate lending transactions, rather than as equity contributions. Don't overemphasize these additional points—they are mostly meant as signposts to point out paths that can lead to trouble if you lend way too much money at ridiculously low rates to your own corporation.

Debt-to-Equity Ratio

The IRS may attack the validity of loans made by shareholders if the overall ratio of the corporation's debt to its equity is extremely high. Highly leveraged corporations—those with much more debt than equity—are known as thin corporations and are potential targets of the IRS under the theory that new money should be contributed in the form of equity.

Accepted debt-to-equity ratios depend somewhat on the particular industry. For example, some types of businesses are more likely to have

stable, long-term business cycles or sufficient cash flows so that they don't usually carry lots of debt, while other types of businesses with seasonal cycles or high demands for start-up or R&D funds may require large amounts of initial and ongoing debt. (If this issue concerns you, a financial advisor, trade journal, or publication of industry financial standards in your field of operations may be able to provide specific advice to help you arrive at a standard debt-to-equity ratio for your business.)

Many IRS practitioners recommend that, to be safe from IRS attack, corporate debt should not exceed corporate equity by more than 3 to 1.

EXAMPLE:

Kevin's Kitchen, Inc., starts up with $60,000 in shareholder loans and $30,000 in equity—this results in a debt-to-equity ratio of 2 to 1. This company should not be considered thinly capitalized by the IRS.

Loan Documentation

Let us again emphasize that the IRS is likely to challenge a loan transaction if it is not set up and documented properly. To reap the tax benefits of a corporate loan transaction, a valid debtor-creditor relationship should exist between the corporation and the shareholder or other individual making the loan. Each loan should be documented by:

- a promissory note. All loan terms should be specified in a written promissory note, and
- corporate minutes. These documents should contain resolutions that show approval of the note by the board.

Loan Terms Favored by the IRS

To be sure your loan passes possible IRS audit scrutiny, make certain it is commercially reasonable. A note that will be repaid in ten or fewer years and that carries a commercially reasonable rate of interest and repayment schedule will normally pass scrutiny. The note should include:

- an unconditional promise by the corporation to repay the loan amount

- a fixed maturity date (short-term notes are preferable to long-term notes, but repayment terms as long as ten years are usually considered acceptable), and

- interest payments at or close to the prevailing commercial rates to help show that the loan transaction is commercially reasonable. For small businesses, this hovers around, or perhaps a little above, the prime rate. If payments are contingent on earnings of the corporation, the IRS is more likely to disregard the loan.

TIP

What interest rates to charge. Commercial banks commonly charge variable interest rates that float two or three points above prime, but shareholder loans are less likely to be set up with fluctuating rates because it's too much trouble to do all the calculations. However, charge an amount of interest that is less than the usury (unlawful interest) rate in your state. Depending on the state, individuals are usually restricted from charging interest of more than 10% to 12%. Check with your accountant, your local bank, or another financial institution if you're not sure of the usury regulations in your state.

How to Make a Note Negotiable

Most loans made by shareholders or other individuals to a small corporation are not negotiable—that is, they cannot be sold or transferred to others by the lender. As a practical matter, outsiders rarely are interested in buying these notes even at a substantial discount; for example, paying $5,000 for a corporate note with a current outstanding principal balance of $10,000.

Legally, for a promissory note to be negotiable—that is, capable of being bought and sold by persons not parties to the original note—it must contain the following:

- names of the lender and borrower

- the borrower's address

- a statement that the debt is payable "to the order of" the lender (the lender can sign the debt to be paid over to another person)

- a specified interest amount and a specified, fixed interest rate (although states are changing this requirement to allow variable interest rate notes to be negotiable)

- the address where payments are to be made

- the location (city or county and state) where the note is signed, and

- the signature of the borrower.

Resolution for Loan by Shareholder or Other Individual

Here's a resolution that shows acceptance by the board of a loan of funds to the corporation from one or more shareholders or other individuals (friends or family). This resolution uses language designed to remind the board and assure the IRS that the loan is properly documented by a written promissory note, is being made on commercially acceptable terms, and is capable of being paid without jeopardizing the financial viability of the corporation. These recitals help establish the loan as a valid debt transaction.

> ⚠ **CAUTION**
>
> **Use a separate conflict of interest resolution if a director is a party to the loan transaction.** Especially in smaller, family-run corporations, it's common for shareholders who propose to make a loan to the corporation to also be members of the board of directors. If so, we suggest you do not count the vote of any financially interested directors when approving the loan. To do this, prepare and use a director conflict of interest resolution to approve the shareholder loan transaction. As explained in Chapter 13, where we cover director conflict of interest rules, you can insert the specific loan approval language resolution into your conflict of

interest resolution or refer to the loan resolution. This may sound complicated, but it's easy to do when you follow the instructions in Chapter 13. Using a conflict of interest resolution this way to approve a loan from a director-shareholder makes it clear that the vote of an interested director is not being counted to approve the loan transaction.

> 💿 **CD-ROM**
>
> Fill in the resolution titled Resolution Approving Loan to Corporation as you follow the sample and special instructions below. The tear-out version is contained in Appendix C.

Special Instructions

Specify the amount being loaned along with the name of each shareholder or other individual making the loan to the corporation.

Resolution Approving Loan to Corporation

It was resolved that it is in the best interests of the corporation to borrow the following amount(s) from the following individuals:

Amount   Name of Lender

$_____   _____

$_____   _____

The terms of ___["each" *or* "the"]_____ loan were included in a promissory note presented for approval at the meeting. The board determined that these terms were commercially reasonable. The board also determined that corporate earnings should be sufficient to pay back the loan(s) to the lender(s) according to the terms in the note(s), and that such repayment would not jeopardize the financial status of the corporation.

Therefore, the board approved the terms of ___["each" *or* "the"]_____ note and directed the treasurer to sign ___["each" *or* "the"]_____ note on behalf of the corporation. The secretary was directed to attach a copy of _____["each" *or* "the"]_____ note, signed by the treasurer, to this resolution and to place the resolution and attachment(s) in the corporate records book.

Promissory Notes Overview

Before looking at the various promissory note forms included with this book, let's explore the different ways promissory notes are commonly structured. This discussion will help you select the note form most appropriate for your particular loan.

Simple Versus Compound Interest

The promissory notes provided in this chapter call for simple, rather than compound, interest. With simple interest, interest is charged on the remaining unpaid principal due under the note, but not on any unpaid interest.

As a practical matter, compound interest should not be an issue for most insider loans. If the loan is paid off in installments, the borrower will usually pay off all accrued interest with each installment. For long-term loans that don't call for any payments for quite a while (perhaps a year or more), it's possible to compound the interest due, although most smaller corporations won't choose to do so. If you want to figure out compound interest, use Nolo's financial loan calculators at www.nolo.com or you may use a future value table; check with your tax person, bank, or real estate broker.

Lump Sum Repayment With Interest

If your promissory note provides for a lump sum repayment, both principal and interest must all be repaid at the end of the agreed repayment period. (We provide sample lump sum promissory note forms below.)

To compute the interest due with the repayment, multiply the full amount of principal owed under the note times the annual interest rate times the number of years (and/or fraction of a year) the loan is outstanding.

EXAMPLE:

Kyle will lend $10,000 to his corporation at an annual interest rate of 6%. Under the terms of the promissory note, repayment of principal plus interest is due in one lump sum at the end of a five-year period. To compute the simple interest due with the lump sum payment, Kyle multiplies $10,000 x .06 x 5 to arrive at an interest payment of $3,000. The total lump sum payment due at the end of the loan period will be $13,000.

It may be necessary to calculate the interest on a monthly basis, such as when a note calls for a 15- or 30-month repayment period. In that case, you should figure out the monthly interest and multiply it by the appropriate number of months. Finally, add that amount to the principal.

EXAMPLE:

Kyle will lend $10,000 to his corporation at an annual interest rate of 6%. Repayment of principal plus interest is due in one lump sum at the end of an eight-month period. To compute the interest due, Kyle multiplies $10,000 x .06 to arrive at an annual interest payment of $600. He then divides that by 12, to get a monthly interest of $50. He multiplies the monthly payment by 8, for a total of $400. Finally, he adds the interest to the principal to calculate the total lump sum payment due at the end of the loan period: $10,400.

Periodic Payments of Interest Only

If your promissory note provides for periodic payments of interest only with a lump sum (or balloon) payment of principal at the end, the corporation will pay the same amount of interest as it would if it repaid the entire amount (principal and interest) at the end of the loan term, as in the example discussed just above. (We provide a sample interest-only note with a balloon payment of principal at the end of the loan term later in this chapter.)

To compute the total interest charged under the note, multiply the principal amount times the annual interest rate times the number of years (and/or fraction of a year) of the note term. Then, divide this total interest amount by the number of periodic payments under the note. The result is the amount of each interest-only payment to be made by the corporation each period.

EXAMPLE:

> Maria lends $15,000 to her corporation. The note provides for quarterly interest-only payments at the rate of 6% over the three-year life of the note (12 payments). Total due on the $15,000 over the three-year period is $2,700 ($15,000 x .06 x 3). The amount of each quarterly interest payment is $225—the total $2,700 interest amount divided by 12, the number of quarterly payments under the note.

If your loan period does not easily fit into years or fractions of years, you'll need to figure out the monthly interest and multiply it by the appropriate number of months.

Periodic Payments of Interest Plus Principal (Amortized Loans)

When both principal and interest are paid in periodic installments under a promissory note, the total interest due under the note changes with each payment. This is so because the outstanding principal balance declines with each payment. The total monthly payment—principal plus interest—remains the same each month. (We provide installment notes with interest and principal payments below.)

Fortunately, it's not difficult to figure out the amount required for each payment. To help you do this, we provide an amortization schedule below. If you can't find the interest rate and time period you want, there are amortization schedule calculators available on the Internet, or real estate brokers, banks, credit unions, financial publications, and books have amortization schedules that show amortization multipliers for other interest rates and periods. Standard computer spreadsheets such as Microsoft *Excel* can also compute interest due on notes.

To use the amortization schedule, you need to know the annual interest rate and term of the note in years. Find your interest rate percentage in the left-hand column of the schedule, and the number of years for the term of your note in the upper row. Then, extend this column and row until they intersect. Multiply this number by the total principal amount of your loan. The result is the monthly principal and interest payment under the note that will pay off the principal in the specified number of years.

EXAMPLE:

> Martina, a shareholder, plans to lend her corporation $20,000 at 6% over a period of ten years, with equal monthly principal and interest payments. She finds the 6% row

Amortization Schedule for Monthly Payments

Interest Rate	\ Number of Years →	1	1.5	2	2.5	3	4	5	6	7	8	9	10	11	12	13	14	15	20
3.0%		.0847	.0569	.0430	.0346	.0291	.0221	.0180	.0152	.0132	.0117	.0106	.0097	.0089	.0083	.0077	.0073	.0069	.0055
3.5%		.0849	.0571	.0432	.0349	.0293	.0224	.0182	.0154	.0134	.0120	.0108	.0099	.0091	.0085	.0080	.0075	.0071	.0058
4.0%		.0851	.0573	.0434	.0351	.025	.0226	.0184	.0156	.0137	.0122	.0110	.0101	.0094	.0088	.0082	.0078	.0074	.0061
4.5%		.0854	.0576	.0436	.0353	.0297	.0228	.0186	.0159	.0139	.0124	.0113	.0104	.0096	.0090	.0085	.0080	.0076	.0063
5.0%		.0856	.0578	.0439	.0355	.0300	.0230	.0189	.0161	.0141	.0127	.0115	.0106	.0099	.0092	.0087	.0083	.0079	.0066
5.5%		.0858	.0580	.0441	.0358	.0302	.0233	.0191	.0163	.0144	.0129	.0118	.0109	.0101	.0095	.0090	.0085	.0082	.0069
6.0%		.0861	.0582	.0443	.0360	.0304	.0235	.0193	.0166	.0146	.0131	.0120	.0111	.0104	.0098	.0092	.0088	.0084	.0072
6.5%		.0863	.0585	.0445	.0362	.0306	.0237	.0196	.0168	.0148	.0134	.0123	.0114	.0106	.0100	.0095	.0091	.0087	.0075
7.0%		.0865	.0587	.0448	.0364	.0309	.0239	.0198	.0170	.0151	.0136	.0125	.0116	.0109	.0103	.0098	.0094	.0090	.0078
7.5%		.0868	.0589	.0450	.0367	.0311	.0242	.0200	.0173	.0153	.0139	.0128	.0119	.0111	.0106	.0101	.0096	.0093	.0081
8.0%		.0870	.0591	.0452	.0369	.0313	.0244	.0203	.0175	.0156	.0141	.0130	.0121	.0114	.0108	.0103	.0099	.0096	.0084
8.5%		.0872	.0594	.0455	.0371	.0316	.0246	.0205	.0178	.0158	.0144	.0133	.0124	.0117	.0111	.0106	.0102	.0098	.0087
9.0%		.0875	.0596	.0457	.0373	.0318	.0249	.0208	.0180	.0161	.0147	.0135	.0127	.0120	.0114	.0109	.0105	.0101	.0090
9.5%		.0877	.0598	.0459	.0376	.0320	.0251	.0210	.0183	.0163	.0149	.0138	.0129	.0122	.0117	.0112	.0108	.0104	.0093
10.0%		.0879	.0601	.0461	.0378	.0323	.0254	.0212	.0185	.0166	.0152	.0141	.0132	.0125	.0120	.0115	.0111	.0107	.0097
10.5%		.0881	.0603	.0464	.0380	.0325	.0256	.0215	.0188	.0169	.0154	.0144	.0135	.0128	.0122	.0118	.0114	.0111	.0100
11.0%		.0884	.0605	.0466	.0383	.0327	.0258	.0217	.0190	.0171	.0157	.0146	.0138	.0131	.0125	.0121	.0117	.0114	.0103
11.5%		.0886	.0608	.0468	.0385	.0330	.0261	.0220	.0193	.0174	.0160	.0149	.0141	.0134	.0128	.0124	.0120	.0117	.0107
12.0%		.0888	.0610	.0471	.0387	.0332	.0263	.0222	.0196	.0177	.0163	.0152	.0143	.0137	.0131	.0127	.0123	.0120	.0110

on the left side of the schedule and extends it to the right to meet the ten-year column extended down from the top of the schedule. She multiplies the resulting number, .0111, by $20,000 to arrive at the monthly principal plus interest payment amount of $222.

Securing Loans With Interests in Property

Sometimes, although not often, individual lenders (shareholders, their friends, or family) may ask for the repayment of the loan to be secured. This means property owned by the corporation is pledged as security or collateral for the loan. In the event the corporation defaults on the loan, the lender may take the property and keep it or sell it as repayment for the debt.

Collateral for loans typically consists of interest the corporation holds in real estate or personal property—such as land or a building, a boat, a car or truck, or computers. The accounts receivable of the corporation—amounts owed to the corporation and carried on the corporate books as assets—also may be pledged for a loan. Product inventory owned by the corporation is another likely source of collateral for loans. In all cases, you must make sure that the property has not already been pledged for the repayment of another corporate loan, such as a bank loan secured with accounts receivable or inventory.

It's often desirable to prepare paperwork to put third parties on notice that property is being used to secure a note. This is routinely done when real estate is used as security: A mortgage or deed of trust is prepared and recorded at the office of the county recorder of deeds. For personal property (as opposed to real

estate), the corporation should sign and file a financing statement—a Uniform Commercial Code form called Form UCC-1.

We provide a basic secured amortized promissory note below, to which you can attach copies of any security and disclosure agreements necessary in your state. A legal stationer who carries legal forms, a local real estate broker, a bank officer, or your legal or tax adviser may have copies of these forms available for your use. You can also find a security agreement online through Nolo's Online Legal Forms at www.nolo.com.

Sample Promissory Note Forms

Let's look at the promissory note forms included with this book. As discussed earlier, we suggest you prepare a promissory note for each loan transaction made by an individual to your corporation and attach it to your board of directors resolution approving the loan.

SEE AN EXPERT

When to get outside help. It's always a good idea to have your tax person or lawyer give a corporate promissory note the once-over before using it, to ensure favorable legal and tax treatment. This is particularly important if you decide to add additional provisions to your note or wish to make any of the changes discussed below in "Changing Note Form Provisions."

Changing Note Form Provisions

There are a great many terms and variations of terms that may be included in promissory notes, including interest rates, maturity dates, the type of property pledged to secure the loan (if any), default provisions, and periodic payments of interest, principal, or both. The promissory notes included with this book contain the most common terms used by smaller corporations, but you may wish to add, delete, or change provisions on these forms to suit your own loan transaction. Here are some examples:

- **Acceleration clause.** All of the promissory notes we present contain an acceleration clause that allows the lender to declare the entire unpaid amount of the loan due if the corporation misses a payment for a specified number of days after its due date. While it's unlikely that an individual lender closely associated with the corporation will actually enforce this provision if one payment is missed, the fact that he or she has the right to do so

helps show that parties to the note intend to create a valid creditor/debtor relationship. If, however, you don't want your corporation to be obligated for a loan with this type of instant repayment provision, you can delete the provision.

- **Collection costs.** Another provision we include in our promissory notes allows the noteholder to recover collection costs in the event the corporation defaults on the loan. These costs of collection include reasonable attorneys' fees. Some readers may wish to define or place a limit on these fees, perhaps limiting the attorneys' fees that the corporation will pay in the event of a default to 10% to 15% of the principal amount of the loan. While this type of provision is also unlikely to be used by a lender closely associated with the corporation, including this provision helps establish the commercial reasonableness of the loan transaction.

Promissory Note: Installment Payments of Principal and Interest (Amortized Loan)

Most smaller corporations will prefer to use this type of promissory note—one that provides for periodic payments of principal plus interest until the principal amount of the loan is paid off.

CD-ROM

Fill in the note titled Promissory Note: Installment Payments of Principal and Interest (Amortized Loan) as you follow the sample and special instructions below. The tear-out version is contained in Appendix C.

Special Instructions

❶ Use an amortization schedule to calculate the monthly payment. (See "Amortization Schedule for Monthly Payments," above.) Payments are usually made on a monthly basis, but you can establish a different interval if you choose. If you do, you'll need to use an amortization table based on your repayment schedule, such as quarterly or bimonthly. Check with a library, bookstore, bank, or on the Internet for other amortization tables.

❷ This paragraph specifies that the loan may be repaid by the corporation at any time without triggering a penalty (known in the loan trade as a prepayment penalty). This allows your corporation to pay back the loan whenever it makes economic sense to do so.

The loan is also made assumable with the permission of the noteholder (the shareholder or other individual), but it is unlikely that another person or corporation will wish to assume payment obligation under the loan. Finally, the note is nontransferable—the individual lender may not transfer the note to another person. This provision is normal for insider loans in a small corporation, but you can easily change this sentence to allow transfers if you wish (this is probably academic, as it would be difficult to find anyone to buy this type of note, even at a discount).

Promissory Note:
Installment Payments of Principal and Interest
(Amortized Loan)

For Value Received, _____[*name of corporation*]_____, the borrower, promises to pay to the order of __[*name of shareholder or other individual lender*]__, the noteholder, the principal amount of $ __[*principal amount of loan*]__, together with simple interest on the unpaid principal balance from the date of this note until the date this note is paid in full, at the annual rate of ___[*annual rate of interest*]___ %. Payments shall be made at ___[*address of lender*]_____.

Principal and interest shall be paid in equal installments of $ __[*amount of each payment*]__, beginning on __[*date of first payment*]__, 20___ and continuing on ___[*day for ongoing payments, for example, "the fifteenth day of each month"*]___ ❶ until the principal and interest are paid in full. Each payment on this note shall be applied first to accrued but unpaid interest, and the remainder shall be applied to unpaid principal.

This note may be prepaid by the borrower in whole or in part at any time without penalty. This note is not assumable without the written consent of the noteholder, which consent shall not be unreasonably withheld. This note is nontransferable by the noteholder. ❷

If any installment payment due under this note is not received by the noteholder within __[*number of days*]__ of its due date, the entire amount of unpaid principal and accrued but unpaid interest due under this note shall, at the option of the noteholder, become immediately due and payable without prior notice from the noteholder to the borrower. In the event of a default, the borrower shall be responsible for the costs of collection, including, in the event of a lawsuit to collect on this note, the noteholder's reasonable attorneys' fees as determined by a court hearing the lawsuit.

Date of Signing: _____

Name of Borrower: ___[*name of corporation*]_____

Address of Borrower: __[*address of principal office of corporation*]_____

City or County and State Where Signed: _____

Signature of Borrower: [*signature of treasurer*]__, Treasurer on Behalf of __[*name of corporation*]___

Promissory Note: Installment Payments of Principal and Interest (Amortized Loan) Secured by Property

This promissory note is the same as the previous note form, but adds a clause that pledges corporate property as security for repayment of the loan. Again, loans individuals make to your corporation are not normally secured, but this may be necessary in some cases to help make the lender feel more comfortable.

TIP

How to use the security clause in other note forms. You may copy the security clause—the last paragraph in the text of this promissory note—to any of the other promissory note forms in this chapter to pledge property as security for the repayment of a note.

CD-ROM

Fill in the note titled Promissory Note: Installment Payments of Principal and Interest (Amortized Loan) Secured by Corporate Property as you follow the sample and special instructions below. The tear-out version is contained in Appendix C.

Special Instructions

❶ Use an amortization schedule to calculate the monthly payment. Payments are usually made on a monthly basis, but you can establish a different interval if you choose. If you do, you'll need to use an amortization table based on your repayment schedule, such as quarterly or bimonthly. Check with a library, bookstore, or bank for other amortization tables.

❷ See Special Instruction ❷ to the previous note form for additional information on the first paragraphs of this note form.

❸ This is the security clause. Specify the security agreement used to pledge the property as repayment of the loan, together with a description of the property. Again, for real property, you will want to complete and record a mortgage deed or deed of trust with the county recorder. For personal property, under state law, you'll normally need to complete and file a security agreement to enforce the security clause in your note. A legal forms stationer may have these forms on hand, or you can contact a real estate broker, tax advisor, or lawyer to obtain these forms and/or have them prepared for you. In addition, you can find a security agreement online at Nolo's Online Legal Forms (www.nolo.com). Attach a completed copy of the security document to the resolution.

EXAMPLE (Real Property as Security):

"Deed of Trust to real property commonly known as _____ [*address*] _____, owned by _____ [*name of corporation*] _____, executed on _____ [*date of signing of deed of trust*] _____, at _____ [*city/state where signed*] _____, and recorded at _____ [*place recorded*] _____, in the records of _____ [*name of recording office*] _____, _____ [*name of county and state*] _____."

EXAMPLE (Corporate-Owned Automobile as Security):

"Security Agreement signed by _____ [*name of officer*] _____, on behalf of _____ [*name of corporation*] _____, on _____ [*date of signing*] _____, pledging title to _____ [*make and model and year of automobile with Vehicle ID #*] _____."

Promissory Note:
Installment Payments of Principal and Interest
(Amortized Loan) Secured by Corporate Property

For Value Received, _____ [name of corporation] _____, the borrower, promises to pay to the order of __[name of shareholder or other individual lender]__, the noteholder, the principal amount of $ [principal amount of loan] , together with simple interest on the unpaid principal balance from the date of this note until the date this note is paid in full, at the annual rate of __[annual rate of interest]__ %. Payments shall be made at ___[address of lender]_____.

Principal and interest shall be paid in equal installments of $ [amount of each payment] , beginning on __[date of first payment]__, 20___ and continuing on _[day for ongoing payments, for example, "the fifteenth day of each month"]_ ❶ until the principal and interest are paid in full. Each payment on this note shall be applied first to accrued but unpaid interest, and the remainder shall be applied to unpaid principal.

This note may be prepaid by the borrower in whole or in part at any time without penalty. This note is not assumable without the written consent of the noteholder, which consent shall not be unreasonably withheld. This note is nontransferable by the noteholder. ❷

If any installment payment due under this note is not received by the noteholder within _____ [number of days] _____ of its due date, the entire amount of unpaid principal and accrued but unpaid interest due under this note shall, at the option of the noteholder, become immediately due and payable without prior notice from the noteholder to the borrower. In the event of a default, the borrower shall be responsible for the costs of collection, including, in the event of a lawsuit to collect on this note, the noteholder's reasonable attorneys' fees as determined by a court hearing the lawsuit.

Borrower agrees that until such time as the principal and interest owed under this note are paid in full, the note shall be secured by the following described mortgage, deed of trust, or security agreement: _[describe security agreement or deed of trust or mortgage used to pledge security of the property, including a description of the property]_ ❸ .

Date of Signing: _____

Name of Borrower: _____[name of corporation]_____

Address of Borrower: ___[address of principal office of corporation]_____

City or County and State Where Signed: _____

Signature of Borrower: _[signature of treasurer]_, Treasurer on Behalf of __[name of corporation]__

Promissory Note: Installment Payments of Principal and Interest (Amortized Loan) With Balloon Payment

This next promissory note specifies a balloon payment (large, final payment), which consists of all remaining unpaid principal and interest due under the note. Use this note if the lender wishes to receive regular payments of principal and interest for a period of time, but then wants to cut short the time it would take to finish paying off the note by requiring a final payment of all remaining principal and interest on a specific date. You will need to use a special amortization table that allows you to calculate the balloon payment.

CD-ROM

Fill in the note titled Promissory Note: Installment Payments of Principal and Interest (Amortized Loan) With Balloon Payment as you follow the sample and special instructions below. The tear-out version is contained in Appendix C.

Special Instructions

❶ You start by figuring the amount of principal and interest payments under a balloon note the same as for any amortized loan. The major difference is that you will amortize the loan for a longer period than the loan will be outstanding (the balloon payment date will occur before the end of the full amortization term). For example, if you plan to provide for a balloon payment in seven years, you may wish to amortize monthly payments over ten or 15 years, which will allow you to make relatively low payments.

First, choose an amortization term for the loan, then find the monthly payment amount under the interest rate on the amortization schedule (see the "Amortization Schedule for Monthly Payments," above). Payments are usually made on a monthly basis, but you can establish a different interval if you choose. (If you do, you'll need to use an amortization table based on your repayment schedule, such as quarterly or bimonthly.)

Next, you'll need to figure the amount of the balloon payment—the balance owed on the note—on the scheduled date for the balloon payment. An easy way to do this is to use a table called a remaining loan balance table that is included in standard loan amortization pamphlets and books. This table will show the percentage of the principal remaining in a given year of a loan. These percentages vary according to the interest rate and the full amortization term of the loan, as well as the year in which the balloon payment is made.

RESOURCE

Remaining loan balance table. *McGraw-Hill's Interest Amortization Tables,* by Jack Estes and Dennis Kelley (McGraw-Hill), gives remaining loan balance tables for five- to 30-year loans.

Our promissory note form does not require you to insert the amount of the balloon payment—just the date it is due—but you will probably wish to calculate this amount for your own information anyway. That way you can figure out exactly how much you'll end up paying in principal and interest.

EXAMPLE 1:

Sheryl Shore, a shareholder of Ship to Shore Electronics, Inc., proposes to lend $10,000 to her corporation at a 5% interest rate, with the loan amortized over 15 years and a balloon payment date set for seven years from the original loan date. Using the Amortization Schedule for Monthly Payments, above, Sheryl multiplies the principal amount of the loan by .0079 to arrive at a monthly payment amount of $79. Next,

Promissory Note:
Installment Payments of Principal and Interest
(Amortized Loan) With Balloon Payment

For Value Received, _____ [*name of corporation*] _____, the borrower, promises to pay to the order of ___ [*name of shareholder or other individual lender*] ___, the noteholder, the principal amount of $ __ [*principal amount of loan*] __, together with simple interest on the unpaid principal balance from the date of this note until the date this note is paid in full, at the annual rate of ___ [*annual rate of interest*] ___ %. Payments shall be made at _____ [*address of lender*] _____.

Principal and interest shall be paid in equal installments of $___ [*amount of each payment*] ___, beginning on ___ [*date of first payment*] ___, 20___ and continuing on the [*day for ongoing payments, for example, "the fifteenth day of each month"*] ___ except that a final payment of the remaining unpaid principal amount, together with all accrued but unpaid interest, shall be paid on ___ [*date of final (balloon) payment*] ❶. Each payment on this note shall be applied first to accrued but unpaid interest, and the remainder shall be applied to unpaid principal.

This note may be prepaid by the borrower in whole or in part at any time without penalty. This note is not assumable without the written consent of the noteholder, which consent shall not be unreasonably withheld. This note is nontransferable by the noteholder. ❷

If any installment payment due under this note is not received by the noteholder within _____ [*number of days*] _____ of its due date, the entire amount of unpaid principal and accrued but unpaid interest due under this note shall, at the option of the noteholder, become immediately due and payable without prior notice from the noteholder to the borrower. In the event of a default, the borrower shall be responsible for the costs of collection, including, in the event of a lawsuit to collect on this note, the noteholder's reasonable attorneys' fees as determined by a court hearing the lawsuit.

Date of Signing: _____

Name of Borrower: _____ [*name of corporation*] _____

Address of Borrower: ___ [*address of principal office of corporation*] _____

City or County and State Where Signed: _____

Signature of Borrower: __ [*signature of treasurer*] ___, Treasurer on Behalf of __ [*name of corporation*] __

Sheryl looks at a remaining loan balance table. She finds that the percentage of the original principal amount owed on a loan amortized over 15 years at a 5% interest rate if paid off after seven years is 62.464% (the same as .62464). Sheryl multiplies .62464 by $10,000, and comes up with $6,246.40. This is the amount of the balloon payment that must be paid in seven years. The corporation will end up paying a total of $12,882.40—($79 x 12 x 7) plus $6,246.40.

EXAMPLE 2:

Let's say Sheryl's corporation wants to amortize the monthly interest and principal amounts over ten years instead of 15. The loan payments will be $106 per month ($10,000 x .0106) according to the loan amortization table above. A loan balance table shows that the remaining loan balance after seven years is 35.390% of the original principal amount. In this case, $3,539 ($10,000 x .35390) will be owed on the seven-year anniversary balloon payment date. This payment is less than the balloon payment in the previous example because here the loan is paid off more quickly ($106 per month instead of $79 per month). The corporation will end up paying a total of $12,443—($106 x 12 x 7) plus $3,539.

❷ See Special Instruction ❷ for "Promissory Note: Installment Payments of Principal and Interest (Amortized Loan)," above, for an explanation of the prepayment and nontransferability provisions in this note.

Promissory Note: Periodic Payments of Interest With Lump Sum Principal Payment

This promissory note provides for monthly payments of interest only. After a designated period of interest-only payments, a lump sum payment of the entire principal amount of the loan is due. This form of loan makes sense if the loan amount is not excessive and the corporation will be able to come up with the entire principal amount of the loan funds at the end of the loan period.

EXAMPLE:

Gerard, as sole shareholder, lends his corporation $10,000 at a 7.5% rate for five years. Total interest for these funds is $3,750 ($10,000 x .075 x 5). The amount of each monthly interest installment under the note is $62.50 (total interest for the five-year loan period divided by the 60 installments made in this period). At the end of the five-year period in which the corporation pays monthly interest only, it must pay Gerard the entire $10,000 amount plus any interest that has accrued on this sum since the last interest payment.

CD-ROM

Fill in the note titled Promissory Note: Periodic Payments of Interest With Lump Sum Principal Payment as you follow the sample and special instructions below. The tear-out version is contained in Appendix C.

Special Instructions

❶ Calculate the monthly payments of interest as discussed above. Payments are usually made on a monthly basis, but you can establish a different interval if you choose.

❷ See Special Instruction ❷ presented in "Promissory Note: Installment Payments of Principal and Interest (Amortized Loan)," above, for an explanation of the prepayment and nontransferability provisions in this paragraph.

Promissory Note:
Periodic Payments of Interest
With Lump Sum Principal Payment

For Value Received, _____ [name of corporation] _____, the borrower, promises to pay to the order of __[name of shareholder or other individual lender]___, the noteholder, the principal amount of $_[principal amount of loan]___, together with simple interest on the unpaid principal balance from the date of this note until the date this note is paid in full, at the annual rate of __[annual rate of interest]___%. Payments shall be made at ___[address of lender]_____.

Interest shall be paid in equal installments of $_[amount of each interest payment]___, beginning on ___[date of first payment]_____, and continuing on the ____[day for ongoing payments, for example, "the fifteenth day of each month"] ❶ until ___[ending date of loan period]_____ 20__, on which date the entire principal amount, together with total accrued but unpaid interest, shall be paid by the borrower.

This note may be prepaid by the borrower in whole or in part at any time without penalty. This note is not assumable without the written consent of the noteholder, which consent shall not be unreasonably withheld. This note is nontransferable by the noteholder. ❷

If any installment payment due under this note is not received by the noteholder within _____[number of days]_____ of its due date, the entire amount of unpaid principal and accrued but unpaid interest due under this note shall, at the option of the noteholder, become immediately due and payable without prior notice from the noteholder to the borrower. In the event of a default, the borrower shall be responsible for the costs of collection, including, in the event of a lawsuit to collect on this note, the noteholder's reasonable attorneys' fees as determined by a court hearing the lawsuit.

Date of Signing: _____

Name of Borrower: _____[name of corporation]_____

Address of Borrower: ___[address of principal office of corporation]_____

City or County and State Where Signed: _____

Signature of Borrower: _[signature of treasurer]___, Treasurer on Behalf of _[name of corporation]____

Promissory Note: Lump Sum Payment of Principal and Interest at Specified Date

This note is similar to the previous note in that the entire amount of principal is paid in one lump sum at the end of the loan period. However, unlike the previous promissory note form, where interest payments are made in installments during the loan period, here the entire interest amount is paid along with the entire principal amount at the end of the loan term.

EXAMPLE:

Ubiquity Movers Corporation borrows $10,000 for three years at 6% interest. Under the terms of the promissory note, a one-time payment of $11,800 ($10,000 principal plus the entire $1,800 interest amount) is due at the end of the three-year loan term.

CD-ROM

Fill in the note titled Promissory Note: Lump Sum Payment of Principal and Interest at Specified Date as you follow the sample and special instructions below. The tear-out version is contained in Appendix C.

Special Instructions

❶ See "Lump Sum Repayment With Interest," above, for how to calculate the lump sum payment due. You do not need to insert this lump sum payment into the promissory note.

❷ See Special Instruction ❷ presented in "Promissory Note: Installment Payments of Principal and Interest (Amortized Loan)," above, for an explanation of the prepayment and nontransferability provisions in this paragraph.

Promissory Note:
Lump Sum Payment of Principal and Interest
at Specified Date

For Value Received, _____ [name of corporation] _____, the borrower, promises to pay to the order of __[name of shareholder or other individual lender]__, the noteholder, the principal amount of $_[principal amount of loan]_, together with simple interest on the unpaid principal balance from the date of this note until the date this note is paid in full, at the annual rate of _[annual rate of interest]_ ❶ %. Payments shall be made at _____[address of lender]_____.

The entire principal amount of the loan, together with total accrued but unpaid interest, shall be paid by the borrower on __[due date for payment of all principal and interest]_____. Any payment made by the borrower prior to the due date specified above shall be applied first to accrued but unpaid interest, and the remainder shall be applied to unpaid principal.

This note may be prepaid by the borrower in whole or in part at any time without penalty. This note is not assumable without the written consent of the noteholder, which consent shall not be unreasonably withheld. This note is nontransferable by the noteholder. ❷

In the event of a default, the borrower shall be responsible for the costs of collection, including, in the event of a lawsuit to collect on this note, the noteholder's reasonable attorneys' fees as determined by a court hearing the lawsuit.

Date of Signing: _____

Name of Borrower: ___[name of corporation]_____

Address of Borrower: ___[address of principal office of corporation]_____

City or County and State Where Signed: _____

Signature of Borrower: _[signature of treasurer]___, Treasurer on Behalf of _[name of corporation]___

Promissory Note: Lump Sum Payment of Principal and Interest on Demand by Noteholder

Here is a classic demand note that allows the noteholder (lender) to call the promissory note due at any time. Rather than specifying a particular date in the future for repayment, the lender is given the power to call the loan due and payable by making a written demand for payment.

The promissory note specifies how much time the corporation has to pay off the loan after receiving the demand by the noteholder. This period will vary depending on the negotiating power of the parties and taking into consideration factors such as the amount due under the loan and the cash flow requirements of the corporation and the lender. Thirty days is often specified as the period, but if the loan amount is substantial, up to three months or more may be allowed for repayment after demand. A longer period would be appropriate if the corporation may need to seek a bank loan to satisfy the demand on the promissory note by the noteholder.

You can, if you wish, add language to the note setting forth or limiting conditions or circumstances that may trigger a demand for repayment. For example, you can prohibit the lender from demanding repayment on the loan until at least three years have elapsed from the date of signing of the loan. In addition, you might make an exception to such a prohibition by allowing an employee-lender to make a demand for repayment at any time during the life of the note if he or she no longer owns shares or works in the employ of the corporation.

! CAUTION

Proceed cautiously with a demand note. Although your corporation and the lending shareholder (or a family member or friend) may be getting along now, it's possible that there could be a falling out, with the lender deciding to get even by making an unexpected demand for a large loan amount set out in a demand note. Don't use a demand note if you think there's a reasonable chance that this may happen and the corporation may not have the cash necessary to fulfill the loan repayment demand.

CD-ROM

Fill in the note titled Promissory Note: Lump Sum Payment of Principal and Interest on Demand by Noteholder as you follow the sample and special instructions below. The tear-out version is contained in Appendix C.

Special Instructions

See Special Instruction presented in "Promissory Note: Installment Payments of Principal and Interest (Amortized Loan)," above, for an explanation of the prepayment and nontransferability provisions in the next to last paragraph.

Promissory Note:
Lump Sum Payment of Principal and Interest
on Demand by Noteholder

For Value Received, _____ [name of corporation] _____ , the borrower, promises to pay to the

order of ___ [name of shareholder or other individual lender] ___ , the noteholder, the principal amount of

$ __ [principal amount of loan] __ , together with simple interest on the unpaid principal balance from the

date of this note until the date this note is paid in full, at the annual rate of __ [annual rate of interest] __ %.

Payments shall be made at _____ [address of lender] _____ .

    The entire principal amount of the loan, together with total accrued but unpaid interest, shall be paid

within ___ [period, for example "30 days"] ___ of receipt by the corporation of a demand for repayment by

the noteholder. A demand for repayment by the noteholder shall be made in writing and shall be delivered

or mailed to the borrower at the following address: __ [address of principal office of corporation] __ .

If demand for repayment is mailed, it shall be considered received by the borrower on the third business

day after the date when it was deposited in the U.S. mail as registered or certified mail.

    Any payment made by the borrower prior to the due date specified above shall be applied first to

accrued but unpaid interest, and the remainder shall be applied to unpaid principal.

    This note may be prepaid by the borrower in whole or in part at any time without penalty. This note

is not assumable without the written consent of the noteholder, which consent shall not be unreasonably

withheld. This note is nontransferable by the noteholder.

    In the event of a default, the borrower shall be responsible for the costs of collection, including, in the

event of a lawsuit to collect on this note, the noteholder's reasonable attorneys' fees as determined by a

court hearing the lawsuit.

Date of Signing: _____

Name of Borrower: _____ [name of corporation] _____

Address of Borrower: ___ [address of principal office of corporation] _____

City or County and State Where Signed: _____

Signature of Borrower: ___ [signature of treasurer] ___ , Treasurer on Behalf of __ [name of corporation] ____

Promissory Note: Variable Schedule of Payments of Principal and Interest

This promissory note form allows you to specify a custom-made schedule for repayments of principal and interest under the loan. For example, your schedule may show changes in principal and/or interest payments over the life of the note, often ending with a final balloon payment of the remaining principal and all accrued and unpaid interest due. The options here are almost unlimited, but here's one example to give you the general idea.

EXAMPLE:

On July 1, Laura lends her corporation $10,000 for five years at 8% interest. They agree that Laura will receive nothing until the end of the second year. She'll then receive $1,600 in interest-only payments for the first two years of the loan ($10,000 x .08 x 2). The corporation will also make an interest-only payment of $800 at the end of the third year. At the end of the fourth year, it will make an $800 interest payment, along with a payment of $4,000 in principal, leaving a principal balance of $6,000. Finally, at the end of the fifth year, the corporation will make its last payment, which consists of the balance of $6,000 principal along with $480 in interest ($6,000 x .08). Here is the customized repayment schedule:

On June 30 of 2nd year:	$1,600	(interest)
On June 30 of 3rd year:	$800	(interest)
On June 30 of 4th year:	$4,800	($4,000 principal; $800 interest)
On June 30 of 5th year:	$6,480	($6,000 principal; $480 interest)
Total Payments:	$13,680	($10,000 principal; $3,680 interest)

TIP

A corporation may pay less with an amortized loan. In the above example, if the same loan had been amortized, Laura's corporation would have paid $203 per month—or $2,436 per year—for a total of $12,180 over five years. In that case, the corporation would have paid only $2,180 in interest

CD-ROM

Fill in the note titled Promissory Note: Variable Schedule of Payments of Principal and Interest as you follow the sample and special instructions below. The tear-out version is contained in Appendix C.

Special Instructions

See Special Instruction ❷ presented in "Promissory Note: Installment Payments of Principal and Interest (Amortized Loan)," above, for an explanation of the prepayment and nontransferability provisions in the next to last paragraph.

Promissory Note:
Variable Schedule of Payments
of Principal and Interest

For Value Received, _____ [*name of corporation*] _____ , the borrower, promises to pay to the

order of __ [*name of shareholder or other individual lender*] __ , the noteholder, the principal amount of

$ __[*principal amount of loan*]__ , together with simple interest on the unpaid principal balance from the

date of this note until the date this note is paid in full, at the annual rate of __[*annual rate of interest*]__ %.

Payments shall be made at _____ [*address of lender*] _____ .

   Principal and interest shall be paid as follows:

[*include schedule of payments here. For the last payment, you can insert the following:*

"The borrower shall make a final payment in the amount of all remaining principal and all accrued but

unpaid interest on __[*date*]__ ."]

   This note may be prepaid by the borrower in whole or in part at any time without penalty. This note

is not assumable without the written consent of the noteholder, which consent shall not be unreasonably

withheld. This note is nontransferable by the noteholder.

   If any installment payment due under this note is not received by the noteholder within

_____ [*number of days*] _____ of its due date, the entire amount of unpaid principal

and accrued but unpaid interest of the loan shall, at the option of the noteholder, become immediately

due and payable without prior notice by the noteholder to the borrower. In the event of a default, the

borrower shall be responsible for the costs of collection, including, in the event of a lawsuit to collect on

this note, the noteholder's reasonable attorneys' fees as determined by a court hearing the lawsuit.

Date of Signing: _____

Name of Borrower: _____ [*name of corporation*] _____

Address of Borrower: _____ [*address of principal office of corporation*] _____

City or County and State Where Signed: _____

Signature of Borrower: ____ [*signature of treasurer*] ____ , Treasurer on Behalf of ____ [*name of corporation*] ____

Resolutions for Loans to Insiders

It's fairly common for small business corporations to make loans to corporate insiders—directors, officers, employees, or shareholders of the corporation. This chapter covers legal and tax information concerning these insider loans. And of crucial importance, we also provide a corporate resolution and promissory note forms to help you set the terms of each loan transaction.

State law usually permits insider loans of this type. As long as the loan benefits the corporation in some way and is approved by the board (and preferably the shareholders as well), it generally will be safe from legal attack. However, to ensure that this is true, the terms of an insider loan should always be commercially competitive—or at least reasonable—and the disbursal of loan funds should not impair the financial condition of the corporation.

EXAMPLE:

A small semiconductor chip fabrication corporation, MegaChips, decides to entice corporate officers to relocate close to its main headquarters by lending funds to newly hired officers for the purchase of residential housing in the vicinity of the corporation's principal office. Doing this benefits the corporation by making it easier to attract key employees. As long as the loans do not impair the corporation's ability to pay its ongoing bills, carry a reasonable rate of interest (which may be slightly lower than the rates charged by commercial lenders), are secured by the property purchased by the officers (a second deed of trust on the purchased property), and are approved by the board and/or shareholders, they should be considered fair to the corporation.

If you're thinking of lending money to insiders, the following tips should guide you in the right direction:

- **Rules aren't as rigid for very small corporations.** In corporations that are owned and operated by one or just a few director-shareholders who agree to the loan, you can be more relaxed when deciding to lend money to corporate principals. After all, if there are no outside shareholders, who's to complain that the interest rates are noncompetitive (but you still need to think about the IRS—more on this later) or that the corporation could invest its money more productively elsewhere?

- **Avoid making loans during hard times.** Even if you meet all legal requirements for an insider loan, if your corporation is on a shaky financial footing at the time of your loan or you suspect it soon may be, we suggest you wait until the corporation is more solvent before making the loan. Making an insider loan when your corporation is cash-poor risks legal, as well as financial, trouble.

- **Get outside help if you need it.** Any time your corporation makes a loan, you will want to make sure that it can afford to do so. You should discuss any special tax, legal, or practical considerations that may cause making a loan to be problematic with your tax adviser or business lawyer. The information below should help you be a knowledgeable participant in any such discussions.

TIP

Consider getting approval from both the board and shareholders. It is often a good idea to have loans to corporate insiders approved by both the board and shareholders, even if not legally required. This gives you the best chance of avoiding any problems with disaffected shareholders later on.

How to Select and Use Corporate Resolutions

- Scan the table of contents at the beginning of the chapter to find resolutions of interest to you (for a full list of resolutions included with this book, see Appendix C).

- Read the background material that precedes each pertinent corporate resolution.

- Follow the instructions included with the sample resolution and complete a draft using your computer. (You'll have to fill in the tear-out resolution included in Appendix C if you don't have a computer.) If you need guidance on selecting and using the CD-ROM files, see Appendix A.

- Complete any needed attachment forms, such as account authorization forms or lease agreements.

- If a resolution involves complex issues that will benefit from expert analysis, have your legal or tax advisor review your paperwork and conclusions.

- Prepare minutes of a meeting or written consent forms as explained in Chapters 5 through 8, and insert the completed resolution(s) in the appropriate form. If you're seeking shareholder approval in addition to board approval, prepare two sets of minutes or written consent forms—one for your directors and one for your shareholders.

- Have the corporate secretary sign the printed minutes or have directors and/or shareholders sign any written consent forms and waivers. Then place the signed forms, together with any attachments, in your corporate records book.

Insider Loan Restrictions Under State Law

In most states, insider loans are allowed, although they are usually subject to special approval procedures.

Most states allow a majority of disinterested board members to approve a loan to directors or officers if the loan is expected to benefit the corporation. (See "When Do Loans Benefit the Corporation?" below, for more on what constitutes a corporate benefit.) If the loan is not approved in this manner, the directors can be held personally liable to corporate shareholders or creditors for the unpaid portion of the loan. Check your bylaws and state corporation laws for the specific loan approval rules in your state.

Over and above your state's laws, your articles and bylaws may impose conditions on insider loans. Before approving an insider loan, always make sure loans to directors, officers, shareholders, and others are not prohibited or limited by your articles or bylaws.

Loans to Outsiders

This chapter deals with loans to insiders (directors, officers, shareholders, and employees). Extra precautions are in order here, if for no other reason than to head off charges of favoritism. Your corporation also may decide to make loans or extend credit to outsiders—customers, clients, purchasers, and others. Arm's length transactions of this sort are governed by the credit and consumer loan laws in your state. We do not cover these laws here, since there is normally no need to observe these extra precautions when making loans to insiders.

Also keep in mind that your corporation probably will have to be organized and operated under special laws if it seeks to make loans as a regular part of its business (as a bank, credit or finance company, real estate agency, and the like). This commercial lending and credit area is a broad one—obviously, if you plan to set up shop as a commercial lender or finance company, you will need to check the legal resources at your law library, and consult a knowledgeable lawyer or tax person who specializes in your area of operation.

When Do Loans Benefit the Corporation?

Court cases defining when loans benefit the corporation are few and far between. Generally, cases say that a deal or contract benefits the corporation when it is both commercially reasonable (for example, a purchase of land at a price close to fair market value) and reasonably likely to further the business operations of the corporation (the corporation needs to purchase the land to build a plant essential to business operations).

When applied to loans made by the corporation, the few court cases that have looked at this issue have mostly clarified the definition by circumscription—that is, by ruling against loans that fall outside the limits of appropriate lending/borrowing. For example, one such case struck down interest-free loans made by a closely held corporation to a person who was a director and majority shareholder and who admitted he did not intend to repay them. (*Oberhelman v. Barnes Investment Corporation*, 690 P. 2d 1343, 236 Kan. 335 (1984).) Another case disallowed loans made by a corporation to the president and majority shareholder; the minority shareholders sued to set aside the loans. (*Milam v. Cooper Co.*, 258 S.W.2d 953 (1953).) The court held that the loans were made primarily to benefit the president to allow him to buy additional shares of corporate stock and increase his ownership percentage.

Another case set aside loans as unfair where an unsecured corporate loan was made to a director at less-than-market interest rates (4%). (*Washington National Trust Co. v. W.M. Dary Co.*, 116 Ariz. 171, 568 P.2d 1069 (1977).)

Loans that are struck down as invalid or unfair will be treated as dividends to the shareholder or other insider who receives the loan funds.

Tax Considerations and Consequences of Insider Loans

A corporate loan to an insider usually has minimal tax consequences. On the lender's (corporation's) side of the transaction, the corporation does not report the repayment of principal from the borrower as income. The corporation does, however, report interest paid to it by the borrower as income on its corporate tax return. Loans made at below-market interest rates can lose some of their tax advantages.

The borrower (director, officer, employee, or shareholder) need not report the loan proceeds as income, because, of course, they must be paid back. The borrower cannot deduct interest payments made on the loan for federal income tax purposes unless the borrower legitimately uses the income for business or investment purposes (in which case, it's a normal business expense) or secures it with an interest in the borrower's residence. (See "Interest and federal tax returns" just below.)

TIP

Interest and federal tax returns. Interest paid on a personal loan may be deducted on federal income tax returns when the loan is secured by a first or second residence of the borrower. If the loan funds will not be used to purchase or improve the residence, the loan amount is limited to $100,000. (This amount may change—check IRS publications for current ceiling amount.) Interest deductions are itemized on the borrower's Form 1040 income tax return and are subject to a floor amount—they can only be deducted in a given tax year to the extent that they exceed a percentage of the taxpayer's adjusted gross income. Interest may also be deducted if charged on a loan made for business or investment by the taxpayer in certain circumstances. For the latest interest deductibility rules, check IRS publications or see your tax advisor.

No matter how straightforward and sound your insider loan may appear, the IRS often scrutinizes insider loans as part of business audits, which are fairly common. Below, we summarize major tax issues that can arise, especially if an interest-free or low-interest loan is made by a corporation to an insider.

The following discussion is technical and, of course, the tax code contains even more fine print on these and related concerns. Our advice is simple: Don't get overwhelmed or bogged down in this material, but treat it as a useful overview of a technical area. The information provided here should make it easier to discuss these tax considerations with your tax adviser.

Invalid Shareholders' Loans Treated as Dividends

One big problem area with insider loans is that if the IRS decides that a loan to a corporate shareholder is not a bona fide debt, it will reclassify the loan payment as a dividend paid to that shareholder. If this happens, the shareholder must report the disallowed loan funds as income on his or her tax return and pay individual taxes on this income. The loan proceeds will be subject to double taxation: once at the corporate level when the income is earned by the corporation, and a second time at the individual level when the shareholder receives the money in the form of a dividend because the loan was disallowed.

To avoid dividend treatment of a shareholder loan, the loan transaction should include as many of the following features as possible:

- **A promissory note should be prepared to document the loan.** The promissory note should carry a rate of interest and specify a maturity date—either on a specific date or in specified installments or payable on demand by the corporation. The rate of interest should be commercially reasonable.

- **The loan transaction should be formally approved by the board and, unless the corporation is very small, by the shareholders.** The loan approval should be documented in corporate minutes or written consents, which are placed in the corporate records book. Advances of money to directors, officers, or shareholders without a written note or other formal documentation should be strictly avoided.

- **The loan should be carried on the corporate financial books and shown on the corporation's income tax returns.**

- **The insider-borrower should make interest and principal payments according to the terms of the promissory note.**

- **If the promissory note is a demand note (as opposed to one with a due date or payment schedule), demand for payment should be made by the corporation within a reasonable time.** In other words, the loan should not be carried on the books indefinitely.

- **Repeated loans to shareholders should not be made (and paid off) on a regular schedule.** Making repeated loans to shareholders on a regular basis makes the loans look more like dividend payments to the IRS. In particular, avoid having loans paid off at year-end, then renewed at the start of the next year.

- **Avoid issuing loans to shareholders in proportion to stockholdings.** This makes the loan transactions look like taxable dividends.

Below-Market Loans and Imputed Interest Payments

The IRS doesn't like to see corporate loans to insiders that call for inadequate interest, or no interest at all. Why? Because the IRS loses taxes on interest income that the corporation would normally receive in connection with the loan

transaction. As a result, if the IRS determines that a loan of this type, called a below-market loan, has been made by the corporation to an employee or shareholder, it will claim taxes are owing.

TIP

You may want to charge competitive interest on insider loans anyway. Even though the IRS has reasons for objecting to low-interest loans by a corporation to an insider, you may want to charge competitive interest rates for your own reasons. For example, you may decide to make a corporate loan to shareholders at the current prime interest rate plus two percentage points to provide your corporation with interest income on the loan amounts and to encourage a timely payback by borrowing shareholders (the longer they take to repay the loan, the more interest they end up paying to the corporation).

What Is a Below-Market Loan?

The IRS applies very specific rules to determine if a below-market loan was made by a corporation to an insider. Basically, except for small loans discussed in the next section, the IRS establishes minimum interest rates for different types of loan transactions (such as demand loans, term loans, and installment loans) and then looks to see if they have been met. If the interest rate charged is lower than the applicable federal rate for a transaction, the loan will be considered a below-market loan.

How to Find Federal Loan Rates

To obtain the current month's applicable federal rates, go to www.irs.gov and search for "applicable federal rate." The federal rates are announced each month by the Treasury and are specified for various loan terms:

- The short-term federal rate applies when the loan is due or paid off in full in three years or less, or when the loan is based upon a demand note that can be called due and payable at any time.

- The midterm rate applies to loans with a term of more than three but no more than nine years.

- The long-term rate applies to loan terms of more than nine years.

The Small Loan Exception

There is a handy exception to the rule that loans may not be below market. If you plan to lend relatively small amounts ($10,000 or less) to corporate insiders, you'll fall under the small (called the de minimus) loan exception. This exception says that the below-market loan rules do not apply (taxable interest will not be imputed) for loan transactions if the cumulative amount of funds loaned to a person by a corporation does not exceed $10,000. (See Internal Revenue Code § 7872(c)(3)(A).)

In other words, even if your corporation makes loans to an insider at interest rates below the then-current federal rate, interest income will not be imputed to the insider and the corporation if the outstanding balance of all loans to the insider does not exceed $10,000.

TIP

Other below-market loan exceptions. There are other exceptions to the below-market loan rules—for instance, loans by an employer to help an employee relocate can be at below-market rates as long as they are secured by the employee's new residence. Ask your tax adviser about this and other below-market loan rule exceptions.

If Your Loan Is Below-Market

To claim taxes on a below-market loan, the IRS presumes that the corporation gave the borrower the additional funds necessary to pay what would have been a fair market interest rate. This extra interest income is normally taxable both to the borrower and to the corporation (although the corporation may be able to get around it). These are some pretty strange assumptions, we know, but the result is that at least one taxpayer—the borrower—has to pay taxes on the amount of interest that should have been charged if the transaction weren't between insiders.

Remember, the IRS charges penalties and interest on owed and unpaid taxes. If you and your corporation owe taxes in prior years because of these below-market loan rules, penalties and interest on the unpaid amounts will be charged as well.

TIP

The difference between dividend treatment of a loan and the below-market loan rules. Notice that if the IRS asserts that a below-interest loan has been made, the principal amount of that below-market loan is not taxed to the shareholder, as would be the case if the entire loan is disallowed and treated as a dividend. Instead, because other proper formalities were followed, just the amount of interest the IRS says must be charged on the principal amount of the loan, less any amount that was charged, must be reported by the shareholder as income.

Employment-Related Loan Exceptions

A corporation can deduct the imputed interest income it is assumed to have received (under the below-market rules discussed above) as a compensation-related business expense if:

- the corporation makes the below-market loan to a shareholder who works for the corporation, and
- the loan is tied to the employment relationship (for example, lower interest is charged to reward an employee for past service or to help purchase a residence close to corporate headquarters).

The result is that the corporation's tax consequences end up as a wash—the imputed interest income is offset on its tax return with a corresponding deduction for compensation paid to an employee. The shareholder-employee must still report the imputed interest as income on his or her individual tax return.

Of course, the IRS anticipates and attempts to curtail strategies of this sort. Under proposed Treasury Regulation 1.7872-4 (d), in effect, below-market loans from a privately held corporation to an employee who is also a shareholder owning more than 5% of the shares of the corporation are presumed to be corporation to shareholder (not corporation to employee) loans. By the way, some corporations do not worry about the extra tax cost of below-market loans to employees—some simply set up a low-interest loan program for persons in their employ, and decide to pick up the tax cost of any imputed interest charges under the IRS rules.

> **TIP**
>
> **Tie insider loans to an employment relationship.** You may wish to characterize any loans made to corporate insiders as related to the employment relationship in your corporate loan

resolutions. This way, even if the loan is treated as a below-market loan, your corporation may end up saving taxes. This is a technical exception to a technical rule—see your tax adviser before using this tax strategy.

Resolution for Approval of Corporate Loan to Insider

Use the following resolution to show approval of a loan made by the corporation to a director, officer, employee, shareholder, or other corporate insider. Again, unless you operate a closely held corporation with no outside shareholders, we recommend that you have the resolution approved separately by both your board of directors and by your shareholders. You'll need minutes of meetings for shareholders and for directors or separate written consents.

Get the approval of all directors and shareholders who are not parties to the transaction if you can. In all cases, make sure the loan terms are fair to the corporation and that the corporation can afford to make the loan.

> **CD-ROM**
>
> Fill in the resolution titled Approval of Corporate Loan to Insider as you follow the sample and special instructions below. The tear-out version is contained in Appendix C.

Special Instructions

❶ You may insert the specific terms of the loan in the blanks, or you can simply refer to the terms of a promissory note that you complete and attach to your resolution as explained in "Supporting Documentation—Promissory Notes," below. If you're attaching a promissory note, delete all loan terms from the resolution.

❷ Here's an example of a repayment schedule for a five-year $10,000 shareholder loan carried

---

Approval of Corporate Loan to Insider

It was resolved that the _____["board" or "shareholders"]_____ approved the following loan to

the following person under the following terms:

Name and Title of Borrower: ___[name and title of director, officer, employee, or shareholder
who is borrowing the funds]___

Principal Amount of Loan: $___[principal amount of the loan—or refer to promissory note: "see attached ❶
note for terms of loan" and leave all loan terms below blank]___

Rate of Interest: ___[interest rate]___ %

Term of Loan: ___[number of months or year if a term loan, or "payable on demand
by corporation" if a demand loan]___

Payment Schedule:

[specify number and amount of payments, whether they consist of interest or principal and

interest, and date and amount of final payment] ❷

_____

_____

It was further resolved that the above loan could reasonably be expected to benefit the corporation
and that the corporation would be able to make the loan payments without jeopardizing its financial
position, including its ability to pay its bills as they become due.

[If you are making the loan to a shareholder/employee and you wish to have the loan considered
employment-related, add the following paragraph: "It was further resolved that the loan approved by
the board was being made solely in connection with the performance of services rendered (or 'to be
rendered') the corporation by the borrower (and add any additional details, such as 'in particular, as a
reward for increasing the productivity of the corporation during the preceding fiscal year in her position
as assistant sales manager')."]

---

at a 7% annual interest rate: "Four interest-only payments of $700 shall be made on June 15th of each year, starting on June 15th, 2011, and the fifth annual payment shall be made on June 15th (2015), consisting of $700 in remaining accrued but unpaid interest plus the full amount of the unpaid principal of $10,000, for a total final payment of $10,700." For further examples of repayment options and terms, see "Sample Promissory Note Forms" in Chapter 14.

Supporting Documentation —Promissory Notes

We recommend that you prepare a promissory note for each loan transaction and attach it to the board of directors' resolution approving the loan. Doing this records the terms of the loan and, as discussed earlier, can be used to help convince the IRS and others that the loan was a bona fide business transaction between the corporation and its directors, officers, shareholders, employees, or other insiders.

With this book and in the samples below, we provide a variety of promissory notes that can be used to document the terms of corporate loans to insiders. These forms are similar to the promissory notes covered in Chapter 14 for loans to the corporation by insiders, except key wording, instructions, and commentary have been changed, since the underlying loan transaction is reversed here.

All promissory note forms in this section allow you to have the note prepared and signed by one or two borrowers. If a second borrower signs (typically a spouse), both borrowers are jointly liable for repayment of the note. This means the corporation may seek to collect against either borrower for the full amount owed under the note if the loan is defaulted on, meaning payments are missed. This is the best way to lend money to an insider who is married. By doing this, each spouse agrees to the repayment obligation—something that can avoid later legal complications should there be a default, a dissolution of marriage, or other change in the spouses' legal status. If the borrower is unmarried, that person may sign the note alone.

To select a promissory note, scan the promissory notes that follow and choose one that suits the lending arrangement you wish to use—most are self-explanatory, but we include additional information in the discussion accompanying each promissory note form below. For additional background information on the various loan repayment terms reflected in the notes below, see "Sample Promissory Note Forms" in Chapter 14.

Simple Versus Compound Interest

The promissory notes provided in this chapter call for simple, rather than compound, interest. With simple interest, interest is charged on the remaining unpaid principal due under the note, but not on any unpaid interest.

As a practical matter, compound interest should not be an issue for most insider loans. If the loan is paid off in installments, the borrower will usually pay off all accrued interest with each payment. For long-term loans that don't call for any payments for quite a while (perhaps a year or more), it's possible to compound the interest due, although most smaller corporations won't choose to do so. If you want to figure out compound interest, you may use a future value table; check with your tax person, bank, or real estate broker.

Promissory Note: Monthly Installment Payments of Principal and Interest (Amortized Loan)

Let's start with the most familiar note form, which provides for equal payments of principal plus interest over the term of the loan. Typically, payments are scheduled to be made monthly, but you can decide on any payment plan you wish.

CD-ROM

Fill in the note titled Promissory Note: Monthly Installment Payments of Principal and Interest (Amortized Loan) as you follow the sample and special instructions below. The tear-out version is contained in Appendix C.

Promissory Note:
Monthly Installment Payments of Principal and Interest
(Amortized Loan)

For Value Received, ___*[name(s) of director, officer, shareholder, or other borrower (also list name of spouse as*___
___*borrower here if previous person is married, and have spouse sign as borrower #2 at bottom of note)]*___ , the
borrower(s), promise(s) to pay to the order of ___*[name of corporation]*___ , the noteholder,
the principal amount of $___*[principal amount of loan]*___ , together with simple interest on the unpaid
principal balance from the date of this note until the date this note is paid in full, at the annual rate of
___*[annual rate of interest]*___ %. Payments shall be made at ___*[address of corporation]*___ .

Principal and interest shall be paid in equal installments of $ *[amount of each payment]* ❶, beginning
on ___*[date of first payment]*___ , 20___ and continuing on ___*[day for ongoing payments, for example,*___
___*"the fifteenth day of each month"]*___ until the principal and interest are paid in full. Each payment on
this note shall be applied first to accrued but unpaid interest, and the remainder shall be applied to unpaid
principal.

This note may be prepaid by the borrower(s) in whole or in part at any time without penalty. This note
is not assumable without the written consent of the noteholder, which consent shall not be unreasonably
withheld. This note is nontransferable by the noteholder. ❷

If any installment payment due under this note is not received by the noteholder within *[number of days]*
of its due date, the entire amount of unpaid principal and accrued but unpaid interest of the loan shall, at
the option of the noteholder, become immediately due and payable without prior notice by the noteholder
to the borrower(s). In the event of a default, the borrower(s) shall be responsible for the costs of collection,
including, in the event of a lawsuit to collect on this note, the noteholder's reasonable attorneys' fees as
determined by a court hearing the lawsuit. If two persons sign below, each shall be jointly and severally liable
for repayment of this note.

Signature of Borrower #1: _____ ❸

Name of Borrower #1: _____

Address: _____

City or County, State Where Signed: _____

Date of Signing: _____

Signature of Borrower #2: _____

Name of Borrower #2: _____

Address: _____

City or County, State Where Signed: _____

Date of Signing: _____

Special Instructions

❶ For instructions on computing the amount of installment payments due under your note, see "Promissory Note: Installment Payments of Principal and Interest (Amortized Loan)" in Chapter 14.

❷ This paragraph specifies that the loan may be repaid at any time without triggering a penalty (known in the loan trade as a prepayment penalty). This allows the borrower to pay off the loan at any time.

The loan is also made assumable with the permission of the noteholder (the corporation), but it is unlikely that another person will wish to assume payments under the loan. Finally, the note is made nontransferable—the corporation may not transfer the note to another company or person. This provision is normal for loans in a small corporation, but you can easily change this sentence to allow transfers if you wish (but no one is likely to want to buy this type of note, even at a discount).

❸ The borrower should complete and sign the first set of signature lines. If the shareholder is married, the spouse should complete and sign the second set; otherwise, it should be deleted.

Promissory Note: Installment Payments of Principal and Interest (Amortized Loan) Secured by Property

This promissory note is the same as the previous note form but adds a clause that secures the loan with the borrower's real estate or personal property. For a discussion of securing loans, see "Securing Loans with Interests in Corporate Property" in Chapter 14.

TIP

How to use the security clause in other note forms. You may copy the security clause—the last paragraph in the text of the promissory note—to any of the other promissory note forms covered in this chapter to pledge property as security for the repayment of a note.

CD-ROM

Fill in the note titled Promissory Note: Installment Payments of Principal and Interest (Amortized Loan) Secured by Property as you follow the sample and special instructions below. The tear-out version is contained in Appendix C.

Special Instructions

❶, ❷, and ❸. For instructions on filling in the blanks and an explanation of promissory note provisions, see Special Instructions ❶, ❷, and ❸ that follow the promissory note immediately above.

❹ This is the security clause. Specify the security agreement used to pledge the property as repayment of the loan, together with a description of the property. For real property, you will want to complete and record a mortgage deed or deed of trust with the county recorder. For personal property, under state law, you'll normally need to complete and file a security agreement to enforce the security clause in your note. A legal forms stationer may have these forms on hand, or you can contact a real estate broker or tax or legal advisor to obtain these forms and/or have them prepared for you. Attach a completed copy of the security document to the resolution.

Promissory Note:
Installment Payments of Principal and Interest
(Amortized Loan) Secured by Property

For Value Received, ___[name(s) of director, officer, shareholder, or other borrower (also list name of spouse as___

___borrower here if previous person is married, and have spouse sign as borrower #2 at bottom of note)]___, the

borrower(s), promise(s) to pay to the order of _____[name of corporation]_____, the noteholder,

the principal amount of $___[principal amount of loan]_____, together with simple interest on the unpaid

principal balance from the date of this note until the date this note is paid in full, at the annual rate of

___[annual rate of interest]_____%. Payments shall be made at ___[address of corporation]_____.

    Principal and interest shall be paid in equal installments of $_[amount of each payment]_ ❶, beginning

on ___[date of first payment]_____, 20___ and continuing on ___[day for ongoing payments, for example,

"the fifteenth day of each month"]_____ until the principal and interest are paid in full. Each payment on

this note shall be applied first to accrued but unpaid interest, and the remainder shall be applied to unpaid

principal.

    This note may be prepaid by the borrower(s) in whole or in part at any time without penalty. This note

is not assumable without the written consent of the noteholder, which consent shall not be unreasonably

withheld. This note is nontransferable by the noteholder. ❷

    If any installment payment due under this note is not received by the noteholder within _[number of days]_

of its due date, the entire amount of unpaid principal and accrued but unpaid interest of the loan shall, at

the option of the noteholder, become immediately due and payable without prior notice by the noteholder

to the borrower(s). In the event of a default, the borrower(s) shall be responsible for the costs of collection,

including, in the event of a lawsuit to collect on this note, the noteholder's reasonable attorneys' fees as

determined by a court hearing the lawsuit. If two persons sign below, each shall be jointly and severally liable

for repayment of this note. ❸

    Borrower(s) agree(s) that until such time as the principal and interest owed under this note are paid in full,

the note shall be secured by the following described mortgage, deed of trust, or security agreement:

_[describe security agreement or deed of trust or mortgage used to pledge security of the property, including a___

description of the property] ❹ _____.

Signature of Borrower #1: _____

Name of Borrower #1: _____

Address: _____

City or County, State Where Signed: _____

Date of Signing: _____

Signature of Borrower #2: _____

Name of Borrower #2: _____

Address: _____

City or County, State Where Signed: _____

Date of Signing: _____

EXAMPLE 1 (Real Property as Security):

"Deed of Trust to real property commonly known as ____[address]____, owned by ____[name of borrower(s)]____, executed on ____[date of signing of deed of trust]____, at ____[city/state where signed]____, and recorded at ____[place recorded]____, in the records of ____[name of recording office]____, ____[name of county and state]____."

EXAMPLE 2 (Automobile as Security):

"Security Agreement signed by ____[name of borrower(s)]____, on ____[date of signing]____, pledging title to ____[make and model and year of automobile with Vehicle ID #]____."

Promissory Note: Installment Payments of Principal and Interest (Amortized Loan) With Balloon Payment

This next promissory note differs from the previous form by specifying a balloon payment (large final payment), which consists of all remaining unpaid principal and interest due under the note. Use this note if you wish to schedule regular (amortized) payments of principal and interest for a period of time but wish to cut short the term of the note with a final payment of all remaining principal on a specific date. You will need to use a special amortization table that allows you to calculate the balloon payment.

CD-ROM

Fill in the note titled Promissory Note: Installment Payments of Principal and Interest (Amortized Loan) With Balloon Payment as you follow the sample and special instructions below. The tear-out version is contained in Appendix C.

Special Instructions

❶ For instructions on filling in the blanks and an explanation of the promissory note provisions, see the special instructions for Promissory Note: Monthly Installment Payments of Principal and Interest (Amortized Loan), above.

❷ See Special Instruction ❶ in "Promissory Note: Installment Payments of Principal and Interest (Amortized Loan) With Balloon Payment" in Chapter 14 for an explanation of how to figure out the payment schedule and balloon payment amount.

Promissory Note:
Installment Payments of Principal and Interest
(Amortized Loan) With Balloon Payment

For Value Received, _[name(s) of director, officer, shareholder, or other borrower (also list name of spouse as_ _borrower here if previous person is married, and have spouse sign as borrower #2 at bottom of note)]_ , the borrower(s), promise(s) to pay to the order of _____ _[name of corporation]_ _____ , the noteholder, the principal amount of $ _[principal amount of loan]_ _____ , together with simple interest on the unpaid principal balance from the date of this note until the date this note is paid in full, at the annual rate of __ _[annual rate of interest]_ ____%. Payments shall be made at ____ _[address of corporation]_ _____ .

Principal and interest shall be paid in equal installments of $ _[amount of each payment]_ ❶ , beginning on __ _[date of first payment]_ _____ , 20___ and continuing on ____ _[day for ongoing payments, for example,_ __ "the fifteenth day of each month"]_ ___ , except that a final payment of the remaining unpaid principal amount together with all accrued but unpaid interest shall be paid on __ _[date of balloon payment]_ ❷ ____ . Each payment on this note shall be applied first to accrued but unpaid interest, and the remainder shall be applied to unpaid principal.

This note may be prepaid by the borrower(s) in whole or in part at any time without penalty. This note is not assumable without the written consent of the noteholder, which consent shall not be unreasonably withheld. This note is nontransferable by the noteholder.

If any installment payment due under this note is not received by the noteholder within _[number of days]_ of its due date, the entire amount of unpaid principal and accrued but unpaid interest of the loan shall, at the option of the noteholder, become immediately due and payable without prior notice by the noteholder to the borrower(s). In the event of a default, the borrower(s) shall be responsible for the costs of collection, including, in the event of a lawsuit to collect on this note, the noteholder's reasonable attorneys' fees as determined by a court hearing the lawsuit. If two persons sign below, each shall be jointly and severally liable for repayment of this note.

Signature of Borrower #1: _____

Name of Borrower #1: _____

Address: _____

City or County, State Where Signed: _____

Date of Signing: _____

Signature of Borrower #2: _____

Name of Borrower #2: _____

Address: _____

City or County, State Where Signed: _____

Date of Signing: _____

Promissory Note: Periodic Payments of Interest With Lump Sum Principal Payment

This next promissory note provides for regular payments of interest for a designated period, at the end of which a lump sum payment of the entire principal amount of the loan is due. This form of note makes sense if the loan amount is not excessive and the borrower can come up with the entire principal amount of the loan at the end of the loan period.

 CD-ROM

Fill in the note titled Promissory Note: Periodic Payments of Interest With Lump Sum Principal Payment as you follow the sample and special instruction below. The tear-out version is contained in Appendix C.

Special Instructions

For instructions on filling in the blanks and an explanation of note provisions, see the special instructions for Promissory Note: Monthly Installment Payments of Principal and Interest (Amortized Loan), above.

Promissory Note:
Periodic Payments of Interest
With Lump Sum Principal Payment

For Value Received, __[name(s) of director, officer, shareholder, or other borrower (also list name of spouse as__ __borrower here if previous person is married, and have spouse sign as borrower #2 at bottom of note)]__ , the borrower(s), promise(s) to pay to the order of _____[name of corporation]_____ , the noteholder, the principal amount of $_[principal amount of loan]_____ , together with simple interest on the unpaid principal balance from the date of this note until the date this note is paid in full, at the annual rate of ___[annual rate of interest]_____%. Payments shall be made at ____[address of corporation]_____ .

Interest shall be paid in equal installments of $__[amount of each interest payment]____ , beginning on _[date of first payment]_____ , 20___ and continuing on _____[day for ongoing payments, for example,__ "the fifteenth day of each month"]_____ until ___[ending date of loan period]_____ , on which date the entire principal amount, together with total accrued but unpaid interest, shall be paid by borrower(s).

This note may be prepaid by the borrower(s) in whole or in part at any time without penalty. This note is not assumable without the written consent of the noteholder, which consent shall not be unreasonably withheld. This note is nontransferable by the noteholder.

If any installment payment due under this note is not received by the noteholder within [number of days] of its due date, the entire amount of unpaid principal and accrued but unpaid interest of the loan shall, at the option of the noteholder, become immediately due and payable without prior notice by the noteholder to the borrower(s). In the event of a default, the borrower(s) shall be responsible for the costs of collection, including, in the event of a lawsuit to collect on this note, the noteholder's reasonable attorneys' fees as determined by a court hearing the lawsuit. If two persons sign below, each shall be jointly and severally liable for repayment of this note.

Signature of Borrower #1: _____

Name of Borrower #1: _____

Address: _____

City or County, State Where Signed: _____

Date of Signing: _____

Signature of Borrower #2: _____

Name of Borrower #2: _____

Address: _____

City or County, State Where Signed: _____

Date of Signing: _____

Promissory Note: Lump Sum Payment of Principal and Interest at Specified Date

This promissory note is similar to the previous note in that the entire amount of principal is paid in one lump sum at the end of the loan period. However, unlike the previous note form (where interest payments are made in regular installments during the loan period), here the entire interest amount is paid along with the principal amount in one lump sum at the end of the loan term.

 CD-ROM

Fill in the note titled Promissory Note: Lump Sum Payment of Principal and Interest at Specified Date as you follow the sample and special instructions below. The tear-out version is contained in Appendix C.

Special Instructions

For instructions on filling in the blanks and an explanation of note provisions, see the special instructions for "Promissory Note: Monthly Installment Payments of Principal and Interest (Amortized Loan)," above.

Promissory Note:
Lump Sum Payment of Principal
and Interest at Specified Date

For Value Received, ___*[name(s) of director, officer, shareholder, or other borrower (also list name of spouse as*___ ___*borrower here if previous person is married, and have spouse sign as borrower #2 at bottom of note)]*___, the borrower(s), promise(s) to pay to the order of _____*[name of corporation]*_____, the noteholder, the principal amount of $_*[principal amount of loan]*_____, together with simple interest on the unpaid principal balance from the date of this note until the date this note is paid in full, at the annual rate of ___*[annual rate of interest]*_____%. Payments shall be made at _____*[address of corporation]*_____.

The entire principal amount of the loan, together with total accrued but unpaid interest, shall be paid by the borrower(s) on _*[due date for payment of all principal and interest]*_____. Any payment made under this note shall be applied first to accrued but unpaid interest, and the remainder shall be applied to unpaid principal.

This note may be prepaid by the borrower(s) in whole or in part at any time without penalty. This note is not assumable without the written consent of the noteholder, which consent shall not be unreasonably withheld. This note is nontransferable by the noteholder.

In the event of a default, the borrower(s) shall be responsible for the costs of collection, including, in the event of a lawsuit to collect on this note, the noteholder's reasonable attorneys' fees as determined by a court hearing the lawsuit. If two persons sign below, each shall be jointly and severally liable for repayment of this note.

Signature of Borrower #1: _____

Name of Borrower #1: _____

Address: _____

City or County, State Where Signed: _____

Date of Signing: _____

Signature of Borrower #2: _____

Name of Borrower #2: _____

Address: _____

City or County, State Where Signed: _____

Date of Signing: _____

Promissory Note: Lump Sum Payment of Principal and Interest on Demand by Noteholder

A demand note allows the noteholder (lender) to call the note due at any time. Rather than specifying a particular date in the future for repayment, the lender is given the power to call the loan due and payable by making a written demand for payment.

The promissory note specifies how much time the borrower has to pay off the loan after receiving the written demand by the noteholder. Thirty days is often specified as the period; up to three months or more may be allowed for repayment after receiving the demand.

Demand loans have certain technical advantages over term loans with respect to the IRS below-market loan rules. Generally, if the demand note is treated as a below-market note, the lender gets to spread recognition of interest income over the life of the loan. By contrast, with fixed-term loans, the lender must report and pay taxes on interest income imputed to him or her all at once, at the beginning of the loan term.

SEE AN EXPERT

Below-market demand notes. There are other technical differences that apply to how the corporation handles imputed interest under a below-market demand note. See your tax adviser if you plan to lend money to a corporate insider under a no-interest or low-interest promissory note.

CD-ROM

Fill in the note titled Promissory Note: Lump Sum Payment of Principal and Interest on Demand by Noteholder as you follow the sample and special instructions below. The tear-out version is contained in Appendix C.

Special Instructions

For an explanation of these note provisions, see the special instructions for "Promissory Note: Monthly Installment Payments of Principal and Interest (Amortized Loan)," above.

**Promissory Note:
Lump Sum Payment of Principal and Interest
on Demand by Noteholder**

For Value Received, ____[name(s) of director, officer, shareholder, or other borrower (also list name of spouse as____ borrower here if previous person is married, and have spouse sign as borrower #2 at bottom of note)]____, the borrower(s), promise(s) to pay to the order of _____[name of corporation]_____, the noteholder, the principal amount of $__[principal amount of loan]____, together with simple interest on the unpaid principal balance from the date of this note until the date this note is paid in full, at the annual rate of ____[annual rate of interest]____%. Payments shall be made at ____[address of corporation]_____.

The entire principal amount of the loan, together with total accrued but unpaid interest, shall be paid within [period, for example "30 days"]____ of receipt by the borrower(s) of demand for repayment by the noteholder. A demand for repayment by the noteholder shall be made in writing and delivered or mailed to the borrower(s) at the following address:[address of borrower and address of spouse if they are coborrowers]__. If demand for repayment is mailed, it shall be considered received by the borrower(s) on the third business day after the date when it was deposited in the U.S. mail as registered or certified mail.

Any payment made under this note shall be applied first to accrued but unpaid interest, and the remainder shall be applied to unpaid principal.

This note may be prepaid by the borrower(s) in whole or in part at any time without penalty. This note is not assumable without the written consent of the noteholder, which consent shall not be unreasonably withheld. This note is nontransferable by the noteholder.

In the event of a default, the borrower(s) shall be responsible for the costs of collection, including, in the event of a lawsuit to collect on this note, the noteholder's reasonable attorneys' fees as determined by a court hearing the lawsuit. If two persons sign below, each shall be jointly and severally liable for repayment of this note.

Signature of Borrower #1: _____

Name of Borrower #1: _____

Address: _____

City or County, State Where Signed: _____

Date of Signing: _____

Signature of Borrower #2: _____

Name of Borrower #2: _____

Address: _____

City or County, State Where Signed: _____

Date of Signing: _____

Promissory Note: Variable Schedule of Payments of Principal and Interest

This promissory note form allows you to specify a custom-made schedule for repayments of principal and interest under the loan. Typically, the schedule will require principal and/or interest payments of unequal amounts and irregular intervals during the life of the note, ending with a final payment of principal and all accrued and unpaid interest due under the note. Remember, we assume all loans will make provisions for the payment of interest on the borrowed funds, unless, of course, you are purposely setting up a below-market loan program.

The options here are unlimited; but here's one example.

EXAMPLE:

On July 1, Hamid's corporation lends him $10,000 for five years at 8% interest. They agree that Hamid will not make payments until the end of the second year. He'll then pay $1,600 in interest-only payments for the first two years of the loan ($10,000 x .08 x 2). Hamid will also make an interest-only payment of $800 at the end of the third year. At the end of the fourth year, he will make an $800 interest payment, along with a payment of $4,000 in principal, leaving a principal balance of $6,000. Finally, at the end of the fifth year, Hamid will make his last payment, which consists of the balance of $6,000 principal along with $480 in interest ($6,000 x .08). Here is the customized repayment schedule:

On June 30 of 2nd year:	$1,600	(interest)
On June 30 of 3rd year:	$800	(interest)
On June 30 of 4th year:	$4,800	($4,000 principal; $800 interest)
On June 30 of 5th year:	$6,480	($6,000 principal; $480 interest)
Total Payments:	$13,680	($10,000 principal; $3,680 interest)

 CD-ROM

Fill in the note titled Promissory Note: Variable Schedule of Payments of Principal and Interest as you follow the sample and special instructions below. The tear-out version is contained in Appendix C.

Special Instructions

For an explanation of these note provisions, see the special instructions for "Promissory Note: Monthly Installment Payments of Principal and Interest (Amortized Loan)," above.

**Promissory Note:
Variable Schedule of Payments
of Principal and Interest**

For Value Received, ___*[name(s) of director, officer, shareholder, or other borrower (also list name of spouse as*___

*borrower here if previous person is married, and have spouse sign as borrower #2 at bottom of note)]*___ , the

borrower(s), promise(s) to pay to the order of ___*[name of corporation]*___ , the noteholder,

the principal amount of $___*[principal amount of loan]*___ , together with simple interest on the unpaid

principal balance from the date of this note until the date this note is paid in full, at the annual rate of

___*[annual rate of interest]*___%. Payments shall be made at ___*[address of corporation]*___ .

Principal and interest shall be paid as follows:

___*[include schedule of payments here]*_____

_____ .

[*For last payment, you can insert the following:* "The borrower(s) shall make a final payment in the amount

of all remaining principal and all accrued but unpaid interest on __*(date)*__."]

This note may be prepaid by the borrower(s) in whole or in part at any time without penalty. This note

is not assumable without the written consent of the noteholder, which consent shall not be unreasonably

withheld. This note is nontransferable by the noteholder.

If any installment payment due under this note is not received by the noteholder within _____

of its due date, the entire amount of unpaid principal and accrued but unpaid interest of the loan shall, at

the option of the noteholder, become immediately due and payable without prior notice by the noteholder

to the borrower(s). In the event of a default, the borrower(s) shall be responsible for the costs of collection,

including, in the event of a lawsuit to collect on this note, the noteholder's reasonable attorneys' fees as

determined by a court hearing the lawsuit. If two persons sign below, each shall be jointly and severally liable

for repayment of this note.

Signature of Borrower #1: _____

Name of Borrower #1: _____

Address: _____

City or County, State Where Signed: _____

Date of Signing: _____

Signature of Borrower #2: _____

Name of Borrower #2: _____

Address: _____

City or County, State Where Signed: _____

Date of Signing: _____

Release of Promissory Note

This next form can be used to show that a promissory note has been paid in full. When this occurs, the noteholder should fill in and sign and date the form. The promissory note also should be marked "paid in full" by the noteholder and attached to the release form. Copies of both should be placed in the corporate records book. (You should also record whether the loan was secured by property and if a security interest document, such as a deed of trust, was recorded for the original loan transaction.)

CD-ROM

Fill in the form titled Release of Promissory Note as you follow the sample below. The tear-out version is contained in Appendix C.

Release of Promissory Note

The undersigned noteholder, __[name and address of noteholder]_____

_____, in consideration of full payment of the promissory

note dated ___[date of note]_____ in the principal amount of $_[principal amount of note]___, hereby

releases and discharges the borrower(s), _____[name of borrower(s)]_____

, _[address of borrower(s)]_____ from any claims or obligations on account

of the note.

Date: _____

Name of Noteholder: ____[name of noteholder]_____

By: _____[signature of treasurer]_____, Treasurer

Signature: _____

Fringe Benefit and Reimbursement Resolutions

This chapter covers resolutions that can be used by your board of directors to approve the most popular employee fringe benefits available to employees of small corporations, including the business owners themselves. It also includes a discussion about setting up employee reimbursement plans that have tax advantages for your corporation—after all, since you are now an employee of your own corporation, being able to pay yourself back for business meals, travel, and other employee expenses is one of the perks of doing business as a corporation. Finally, we briefly discuss the basic rules for reimbursing other employees of your corporation for business-related expenses (travel, meals, entertainment, and the like).

RELATED TOPIC

For special resolutions to grant authority to and approve compensation for directors and officers, see Chapter 12. In addition, tax information and resolutions related to the adoption of employee retirement plans are provided separately in Chapter 17.

TIP

Board, and sometimes shareholders, should approve resolutions. The corporate resolutions contained in this chapter need to be approved by the board of directors alone. We flag instances where shareholders should also approve them. Of course, you may choose to have shareholders approve or ratify any decision made by the board. Normally, you will not wish to take this extra step unless shareholder approval is legally required or the decision is important enough to warrant the extra time and effort.

How to Select and Use Corporate Resolutions

- Scan the table of contents at the beginning of the chapter to find resolutions of interest to you (for a full list of resolutions included with this book, see Appendix C).

- Read the background material that precedes each pertinent corporate resolution.

- Follow the instructions included with the sample resolution and complete a draft using your computer. (You'll have to fill in the tear-out resolution included in Appendix C if you don't have a computer.) If you need guidance on selecting and using the CD-ROM files, see Appendix A.

- Complete any needed attachment forms, such as account authorization forms or lease agreements.

- If a resolution involves complex issues that will benefit from expert analysis, have your legal or tax adviser review your paperwork and conclusions.

- Prepare minutes of a meeting or written consent forms as explained in Chapters 5 through 8, and insert the completed resolution(s) in the appropriate form. If you're seeking shareholder approval in addition to board approval, prepare two sets of minutes or written consent forms—one for your directors and one for your shareholders.

- Have the corporate secretary sign the printed minutes or have directors and/or shareholders sign any written consent forms and waivers. Then place the signed forms, together with any attachments, in your corporate records book.

Introduction to Employee Fringe Benefits

In general, the employment-related benefits and fringes covered in this chapter are popular because they are:

- tax-deductible by the corporation, in full or part, and

- neither included in, nor taxed as part of, the income of the employees.

We introduce the main tax points associated with each corporate fringe benefit as we cover the individual resolutions below. We don't, however, attempt to cover the ins and outs of each fringe benefit or provide a discussion of each perk as tailored to your specific business. See your tax adviser for additional information and the most current rules.

When to Use Resolutions

The information below can help you decide whether to approve and implement various employee fringe benefits. But remember that you do not always need to go to the extra time and trouble of preparing resolutions to make these decisions. Here's some guidance:

- First and foremost, prepare a resolution for approval by your board if your tax adviser recommends doing so.

- Prepare a resolution if you think your management, staff, or rank-and-file workers will benefit from having the nature and extent of the fringe benefit spelled out in a formal board resolution.

- If a fringe benefit is substantial in terms of corporate dollars (for example, a plan to reimburse corporate employees directly for

medical expenses), having your board meet to consider and approve the plan may help allay fears of reckless spending entertained by corporate principals or shareholders.

You may have other reasons to prepare some of the resolutions in this chapter—and, of course, it's okay to use them just because you think they will help fortify your corporate records by providing evidence that your board meets to discuss and approve important corporate tax decisions. But the main point is this: If you can't think of a good reason to prepare this extra paperwork, don't do so. Your time will be better spent taking care of other corporate business.

Antidiscrimination Rules

The Internal Revenue Code and regulations contain strict antidiscrimination rules that forbid businesses from providing medical insurance and other fringe benefits to the highly paid executives only. This is not a problem if you run a closely held corporation where your only employees are the main corporate shareholders; but once you start hiring other workers, these rules will apply to your employee benefit plans.

These antidiscrimination rules and the exceptions to them change often, so we do not cover them here. For the latest coverage rules for health insurance, medical reimbursement plans, and other fringe benefits discussed below, see IRS publications and other tax resources. And, of course, your adviser should know the latest rules and can tell you if your employee benefits are eligible for favorable tax treatment.

Other Resources on Employment Fringe Benefits

A wealth of tax materials can help guide you through current IRS employment fringe benefit requirements. Here are just a few:

- *Tax Savvy for Small Business,* by Frederick W. Daily (Nolo), is an informative and understandable guide for small incorporated and unincorporated businesses. It explains how to make the best tax decisions for your business and guides you through the tax issues associated with corporate fringe benefits.

- *Deduct It!* ,by Stephen Fishman (Nolo), is a comprehensive guide to tax deductions for small businesses.

- IRS Publication 334, *Tax Guide for Small Business,* does an excellent job of laying out the basic rules related to employee fringe benefits. This is, of course, a very straightforward treatment, not a user-friendly explanation of the ins and outs.

- IRS Publication 535, *Business Expenses,* Chapter 5, contains an excellent summary of the requirements for providing the tax-qualified employee benefit plans discussed below. You may also be interested in IRS Publication 463, *Travel, Entertainment, Gift, and Car Expenses,* and IRS Publication 1542, *Per Diem Rates.*

- For a specific treatment of employee auto and travel expense tax requirements, see *Business Auto & Travel,* by Crouch (Allyear Tax Guides).

Group Health, Accident, and Disability Insurance

Your corporation can deduct payments made to purchase insurance for employees, including owner-employees. Your tax or insurance person can fill you in on the various types of group health and accident policies available to your corporation and the current tax requirements and consequences. Let's look at the basic rules.

Health Insurance

Employees are not taxed on premiums paid by the corporation or on proceeds received by them under corporate-paid health insurance policies. (There is an exception: S corporation owners who own more than 2% of the corporation may not deduct the premiums paid for group health insurance coverage.)

CAUTION

Check for changes. Due to sweeping federal changes enacted in 2010, employer and employee health insurance rules, including the deductibility of premiums, may change. Check the IRS website (www.irs.gov) and ask your tax adviser for the latest rules.

TIP

Employees can pick their own health policies. Tax law also allows the corporation to reimburse individual employees who buy their own health insurance policies.

Accident and Disability Coverage

Premiums paid by the corporation for accident or disability coverage may be deducted by the corporation, and the premiums paid by the corporation for the insurance are not taxed as income to the employees.

However, wage continuation payments and other disability income received as benefits under these policies are generally taxed as income to the employee. An important exception applies if the policy pays for permanent injuries (permanent disfigurement, loss of a limb or function, and the like) with benefits determined by the nature of the injury rather than the period of disability. (Internal Revenue Code § 105(c).)

Resolution Authorizing Health, Accident, or Disability Insurance

The sample resolution below can be used to authorize the purchase of group health, accident, or disability insurance by the corporation for employees.

CD-ROM

Fill in the resolution titled Authorization of Group Health, Accident, or Disability Insurance for Employees as you follow the sample and special instructions below. The tear-out version is contained in Appendix C.

Special Instructions

Even if IRS rules allow your corporation to legally cover fewer than all employees, it is unusual for corporations not to include all full-time employees in their prepaid health, accident, or disability insurance program. In fact, one of the difficulties small corporations face is having a sufficient number of employees on the payroll to qualify for group plans and rates.

Authorization of Group Health, Accident, or Disability Insurance for Employees

After discussion of the importance of promoting employee-company relations by providing ___["health," "accident," *and/or* "disability"]___ insurance to employees, it was agreed that the corporation shall purchase ___["health," "accident," *and/or* "disability"]___ insurance policies as part of a group plan provided by ___[*name of insurance carrier*]_____.

The following employees shall be eligible to participate in and receive ___["health," "accident," *and/or* "disability"]___ insurance under the plan: ___[state "all full-time employees" *if all will be covered;* *otherwise, name the individuals who will be covered or specify the criteria an employee must meet to qualify, for example* "all employees with three months of consecutive, full-time employment with the corporation."]___.

Self-Insured Medical Reimbursement Plans

A special tax advantage of operating a corporation is that the corporation may pay and deduct all medical care costs of its employees and their families. Such a self-insured medical reimbursement plan differs from the normal arrangement where a business pays for employees' health insurance premiums and the insurance company foots the bill (minus deductions and exclusions under the policy). Here, the corporation pays the entire bill for medical costs directly, without the use of health insurance provided by a commercial insurance company.

Self-insured medical reimbursement plans of this type are more common for one-person or small closely held corporations than for larger corporations with a more extensive payroll. When a corporation starts to hire additional nonowner employees, instead of footing the bill directly for their often substantial medical expenses, the corporation usually purchases health insurance for all employees to cover medical costs.

Under Section 105 of the Internal Revenue Code (IRC), amounts paid by the corporation to reimburse employees and their dependents for medical care that is not covered by health or accident insurance is deductible by the corporation and is not included in the gross income of the employees.

SEE AN EXPERT

S corporation strategy. For S corporation shareholder-employees, the IRS has informally taken the position that the full cost of medical reimbursement benefits paid to a shareholder who owns 2% or more of the corporation's shares is reportable by the shareholder-employee as income (in other words, these shareholders must pay taxes on these benefits). Some aggressive tax advisers suggest only including as income the amount of medical reimbursement equal to the costs of commercial health insurance. If you have an S corporation, check with your tax adviser for more information on this point.

Problems With These Plans

As mentioned, not all corporations wish to, or can, provide employees with the lavish benefits of a medical reimbursement plan. The reason is obvious: In the event of a major medical illness or injury requiring hospitalization, the corporation may be required to pay substantial medical care costs. To protect itself, the corporation can, however, specify a limit for annual medical payments under the plan.

Especially if the plan limits coverage, larger corporations may opt to use it in conjunction with health insurance paid for by the corporation. Under this combined plan approach, the corporation reimburses employees only for medical costs not covered by the medical insurance plan. Under many medical insurance policies, the corporation will end up paying the annual deductible amount under the medical insurance plan, plus 20% of all medical bills. However, even here, costs can go through the ceiling if an employee is hospitalized, as uncovered hospital bills may amount to a hefty sum. Also, a prolonged illness or one that is not covered under the terms of the health insurance policy—such as a preexisting condition—can severely strain the business's cash flow if the corporation picks up the tab.

Resolution for Adoption of Self-Insured Medical Reimbursement Plan

The following resolution can be used to show board approval of a medical reimbursement plan. Note that the terms of the resolution allow the corporation to adopt a medical reimbursement plan either alone or in conjunction with the adoption of an employee health insurance plan. In either case, the corporation is only obligated to pay costs not covered by any health or accident insurance.

TIP

Coverage must comply with tax laws.
Remember to check with your tax adviser prior to approving this resolution to make sure your planned coverage meets current IRS antidiscrimination rules and other tax requirements.

CD-ROM

Fill in the resolution titled Adoption of Self-Insured Medical Reimbursement Plan as you follow the sample and special instructions below. The tear-out version is contained in Appendix C.

Special Instructions

❶ Currently, IRC Section 105 allows medical reimbursement plans to exclude employees who have not completed three years of service, employees under the age of 25, and part-time or seasonal employees. Generally, benefits must be the same for highly paid and rank-and-file employees. Again, your tax person can fill you in on the latest coverage requirements.

❷ To keep costs from getting out of hand, it may make sense to set a limit on reimbursements, even if the reimbursement program supplements basic medical health insurance coverage. Of course, if you set a limit on reimbursements without health insurance coverage, an employee will be personally liable for any nonreimbursed medical bills—it goes without saying that even one uncovered illness or hospitalization could prove financially disastrous to an employee without basic health care coverage. If you do not wish to set a reimbursement spending limit, delete this paragraph from the resolution.

Adoption of Self-Insured Medical Reimbursement Plan

After discussion, it was decided that it would be in the best interests of the corporation to reimburse all eligible employees for expenses incurred by themselves and their dependents for medical care expenses that are not covered by health or accident insurance, subject to specific exceptions as further discussed by the board. With the intention that the benefits payable under this plan shall be excluded from the employees' gross income under Internal Revenue Code Section 105, it was decided:

Following are the eligibility requirements for participation in the medical reimbursement plan: _____ *[list years of service and other requirements for participation; generally, you cannot* *discriminate in favor of highly compensated employees]* ❶ _____

The corporation shall reimburse any eligible employee no more than $ __*[if appropriate, specify annual dollar* *limit for reimbursements to an employee]*__ in any fiscal year for medical care expenses. ❷

Reimbursement under this plan shall only be made by the corporation to the extent that such reimbursement or payment is not provided under a medical, health, or other type of insurance policy, whether owned by the corporation or another person or entity, or under any health or accident wage continuation plan. If there is such an insurance policy or wage continuation plan in effect, the corporation shall be relieved of liability for reimbursement to the extent of coverage under such policy or wage continuation plan.

Any eligible employee who wishes to receive benefits under this plan shall submit to the secretary of the corporation, at least monthly, all bills for medical care for verification by the corporation prior to payment. If the employee fails to supply such medical bills in a timely manner, the corporation may, at its option, decide not to pay the bills in question.

This plan may be discontinued at any time by vote of the board of directors, provided that the corporation shall be obligated to pay any qualifying medical bills for services provided to an employee prior to the date of discontinuation of the plan.

The _____*[title of officer]*_____ shall determine and resolve questions regarding coverage under this plan, except that reimbursement claimed by this officer shall be administered and decided by _____*[title of officer]*_____.

Resolution Authorizing Group Term Life Insurance

Corporations may provide a tax-deductible fringe benefit of up to $50,000 of group term life insurance for each employee. Under this arrangement, the corporation pays premiums, and the employees' beneficiaries receive the proceeds. Premiums paid under these policies are not included in the income of employees, and insurance payouts to beneficiaries are received as tax-free income. Because term life insurance simply provides insurance coverage for a rate that is guaranteed for a term of years, it is relatively cheap to buy for all but the oldest employees.

TIP

Opting for policies over $50,000. Some corporations decide to buy each employee more than $50,000 worth of life insurance coverage. The Internal Revenue Code lets corporations do this as long as the extra coverage is not substantially disproportionate between different classes of employees—for example, with a person making twice the salary of others getting four times the amount of life insurance coverage. Under the Internal Revenue Code, the employee will be taxed on the cost attributed for coverage exceeding $50,000. This is still an advantage to the employee and the corporation because the cost for this extra coverage is determined from IRS tables—this means the imputed cost is normally significantly lower than the actual cost of the extra insurance.

The Difference Between Term and Whole Life Policies

Unlike term policies, whole life insurance accumulates cash values—a portion of the premiums and earnings under the policy are credited to the account of and can be cashed in by the policy owner (in this context, the employee). For a good, basic overview of the differences between term and whole life insurance from a personal investment perspective, see *Your Life Insurance Options*, by Alan Lavine (John Wiley & Sons).

RESOURCE

Estate planning resource. For more information on estate planning, see *Plan Your Estate*, by Denis Clifford (Nolo).

CD-ROM

Fill in the resolution titled Purchase of Group Term Life Insurance as you follow the sample and special instructions below. The tear-out version is contained in Appendix C.

Special Instructions

❶ Remember, antidiscrimination rules apply, but, generally, you can exclude part-time employees or those with less than three years of service; check with your tax person for the latest rules.

❷ Usually, $50,000 worth of coverage is obtained to take full advantage of this tax break.

Purchase of Group Term Life Insurance

The board discussed the advisability of providing corporate employees with the benefit of group term life insurance. After discussion, it was decided that all full-time employees with a minimum of ___[number of years]___ ❶ year(s) of service with the corporation shall receive life insurance coverage in the amount of $___[amount]___ ❷ ___.

Authorization of Death Benefit Contract

Sometimes corporations choose to pay a small cash death benefit to the family or other beneficiary designated by an employee when the employee dies. As long as a corporation authorizes the payment of a death benefit before an employee dies, the corporation may deduct the actual payment as an ordinary and necessary business expense. The beneficiary may exclude up to $5,000 of death benefits in figuring his or her income taxes.

EXAMPLE:

Silver Lining Rain Gear, Inc., a one-person corporation owned and operated by Karen, its sole director-employee-shareholder, opts to pay a $5,000 death benefit to Karen's designated beneficiary. Karen does not pay income taxes on this benefit when it is approved. Likewise, her beneficiary will not pay taxes on the death benefit when it is paid.

SEE AN EXPERT

Death benefits and taxes can be complicated. There are additional, collateral tax considerations and benefits associated with the payment of a cash death benefit to owner-employees of a closely held corporation. For example, the payment of a sizable death benefit may reduce the estate tax value of the owner's shares (because the death benefit is taken from corporate cash prior to a valuation of the business). In addition, death benefits qualify for an exclusion from the taxable estate of the deceased owner-employee for estate tax purposes. Ask your tax adviser for additional information on these technical rules before approving a death benefit plan for employees.

Resolution Authorizing Employee Death Benefit

The board can approve the payment of the death benefit by passing the resolution shown below.

CD-ROM

Fill in the resolution titled Authorization of Employee Death Benefit as you follow the sample and special instructions below. The tear-out version is contained in Appendix C.

Special Instructions

❶ Note that we have included wording you can use to require the corporation to pay the benefit under one or both of the following conditions: (1) when the employee dies if he or she is still working for the corporation at the time of death, and/or (2) when the employee retires and is eligible for benefits under the company's retirement plan.

❷ This resolution refers to an attached death benefit contract. We cover this agreement just below.

Authorization of Employee Death Benefit

It was agreed that the corporation shall contractually commit itself to pay to the named beneficiary(ies) of

_____[name(s) of employee(s)]_____, who is/are employees of the corporation, the sum of

$_____[specify amount up to $5,000]_____ if the employee(s) ["is/are still employed by the corporation at the

time of his/her/their death(s)" _and/or_ "has(have) retired from the employ of the corporation in accordance

with the corporation's retirement plan"]. ❶ A copy of the agreement regarding death benefits is attached

to this resolution. ❷

Supporting Documentation— Death Benefit Agreement

To back up the board resolution approving death benefits for employees, you should prepare a death benefit agreement that obligates the corporation to pay the benefit. Again, this agreement must be prepared prior to the employee's death (and checked by your tax adviser).

There are two ways to prepare this agreement:

- as part of an employment contract that includes a death benefit provision for the employee, or

- as part of a separate death benefit agreement between each employee and the corporation.

To prepare a separate death benefit agreement, use the form shown below. Prepare a separate form for each employee who is eligible for the death benefit.

CD-ROM

Fill in the agreement titled Agreement Regarding Death Benefits as you follow the sample and special instructions below. The tear-out version is contained in Appendix C.

Special Instructions

To avoid complications when funds are disbursed, we assume the employee will designate only adults, not minors, as beneficiaries in this agreement.

Agreement Regarding Death Benefits

This is an agreement between _____ [name of corporation] _____, referred to below as the corporation, and _____ [name of employee] _____, referred to below as the employee. In consideration of valuable services performed and to be performed by the employee, the corporation hereby agrees to pay a death benefit of $_ [specify amount of $5,000 or less] _ to [name of beneficiary or beneficiaries selected by employee] _, hereafter referred to as the beneficiary, if the beneficiary survives the employee, in the event the employee dies _ ["while in the employ of the corporation" and/or "while retired from the employ of the corporation in accordance with the retirement plan of the corporation"] _____.

The foregoing death benefit shall be paid by the corporation to the beneficiary according to the following schedule: [specify in "one lump sum payment" or describe the periodic payment schedule] _.

The employee may change the designation of a beneficiary named in this agreement by submitting a written statement to the secretary of the corporation naming the new beneficiary.

Date: _____

Signature of employee: ____ [signature of employee] _____

Name of employee: _____ [typed or printed name of employee] _____

Date: _____

Name of corporation: ____ [name of corporation] _____

By: ____ [signature of corporate officer] _____

Name/Title of officer: ____ [typed or printed name and title of corporate officer] _____

Payment of Employee Automobile Expenses

Some corporations pick up the entire tab for the purchase or lease of an employee's company car. If the corporation can afford it, this is a great deal for an employee-owner of a small corporation.

This is particularly common in closely held corporations, where the corporation buys or leases a car for a shareholder-employee to use to commute to and from work, for business purposes during the day, and for personal use in the evenings and on weekends.

Even though the employee must report as income the portion of the value of the car used for personal purposes, it is far less expensive for the employee to do this than to pay the entire price for an automobile with after-tax dollars.

Sometimes corporations take a more modest approach by paying employees for the cost of the business use of an automobile. Of course, a corporation can mix and match—for example, purchasing a car for key corporate personnel and paying car expenses for other employees.

Resolution Authorizing Purchase or Lease of Company Car for Employees

The following board resolution authorizes the purchase or lease of a company car.

RESOURCE

Technical valuation rules. IRS regulations provide several valuation formulas that can be used to value the personal benefit portion of the use of a company car—the amount that must be included on the employee's individual tax return as income. IRS publications and your tax advisor can help you do the math if you use a company car for both business and personal purposes. See IRS Publication 525, *Taxable and Nontaxable Income*, "Employee Compensation, Fringe Benefits, Employer-Provided Vehicles," for more information.

CD-ROM

Fill in the resolution titled Purchase or Lease of Company Car as you follow the sample and special instructions below. The tear-out version is contained in Appendix C.

Special Instructions

If you wish to set time, use, or other conditions or procedures for use of the cars by one or more employees, specify them. For example, "The car shall be used only on company business, including travel and commuting to and from work. The car must be left with the corporation for use by other employees while the employee is on vacation."

Purchase or Lease of Company Car

After discussion, the board decided that it would be in the best interests of the corporation for it to _["purchase" or "lease"]_ a total of _[number]_ car(s) for use by the following corporate employees:

_____

_____.

The board further agreed that the amount spent to _["purchase" or "lease"]_ car(s) for the above employee(s) would be limited to the following maximum amounts: $_[if appropriate, show maximum purchase price or maximum yearly lease rate to be spent for one or more cars for the above employees]_____.

It was further agreed that the use of the cars by employees would be subject to the following terms: _[include any conditions of use of automobiles by employees]_____.

The treasurer was authorized to spend corporate funds for the _["purchase" or "lease"]_ of vehicles after verifying that the amounts expended do not exceed the monetary limits set by the board. The treasurer is directed to see that procedures are established to ensure that use of the car(s) by employee(s) meets any additional terms set by the board.

Resolution Authorizing Reimbursement of Employee Automobile Expenses

Instead of picking up the entire tab for an employee to purchase or lease a company car, many corporations reimburse employees—particularly those who are not owner-employees—for the cost of business use of an automobile. This can be an important benefit for employees who must drive a significant number of miles while working for the corporation, such as sales representatives, on-site customer service personnel, traveling executives, and others.

Under this arrangement, the corporation gets to deduct the reimbursed expenses. Generally, the reimbursements are not treated as income to the employee. If, however, reimbursements are based on mileage rates, the employee must report as income any reimbursements made that exceed the IRS standard mileage rate.

Federal tax rules allow an employer to reimburse an employee's auto expenses by paying one of the following:

- a standard mileage allowance provided for under IRS rules
- the actual operating costs associated with the business use of the car, or
- a mileage reimbursement rate of pay established by the corporation, using a special formula fixed and variable rate allowance (FAVR) that pays a cents-per-mile rate plus a flat amount for fixed costs.

To avoid excessive record keeping, employers typically reimburse employees under the standard IRS mileage rate. With this method, only the dates, places, business purpose, and number of miles an employee's car is used on business need be substantiated; actual operating costs are ignored.

CD-ROM

Fill in the resolution titled Authorization of Payment of Standard Mileage Allowance to Employees as you follow the sample below. The tear-out version is contained in Appendix C.

Authorization of Payment of Standard Mileage Allowance to Employees

After discussion, it was agreed that the corporation shall pay the current federal standard mileage rate to the following employees of the corporation for their business use of their automobiles while working for the corporation:

_____

_____.

It was agreed, and the treasurer of the corporation was instructed, to reimburse any of the above employees on a _[state period; "monthly" usually works best]_ basis according to the above rate, after receiving a statement from the employee showing the dates, places, business purpose, and mileage accumulated on the employee's automobile during the period.

Payment of Meals and Lodging

Corporations sometimes wish to pick up the tab for business meals and lodging. In fact, in today's travel-ridden business world, not to do so would be considered unfair by most employees—after all, they should not be made to pay personally for the cost of these necessary business expenses.

The flip side of the coin is that the IRS is a little leery of letting business owners, particularly corporate shareholder-employees who work for their own company, deduct the cost of meals or other expenses without proving that business is a bona fide purpose of the expense.

 RESOURCE

Tax rules for deducting meals and lodging. Again, we are just scratching the surface of the tax rules for these business deductions, and cover this material primarily to provide a resolution that can be used to approve the payment of these expenses by the corporation. See IRS Publication 535, *Business Expenses*, and Publication 463, *Travel, Entertainment, Gift, and Car Expenses*, or your tax adviser for a more thorough treatment.

Resolution to Pay Off-Premises Meals for Employees and Business Clients

A corporation may deduct 50% of meal costs, including sales tax and tips, incurred by employees while they are promoting the business in the local area (travel-related meal expenses are discussed separately, in "Reimbursement of Employee Business Expenses," below). A corporate deduction is not allowed, however, if the meals are extravagant under the circumstances or if a corporate employee is not present at the meal. In addition, a client, customer, or other outsider also must be present for the meal to be 50% deductible. For example, this deduction would not be allowed if several employees discussed business over lunch, although the business could certainly pay for the lunch.

To keep a handle on expenses, the following specific resolution authorizes a maximum monthly allotment to one or more employees to spend corporate funds to pay for meals of the employees and their business clients.

CD-ROM

Fill in the resolution titled Business Meal Expense Allotment for Employees as you follow the sample and special instructions below. The tear-out version is contained in Appendix C.

Special Instructions

This resolution authorizes monthly amounts to cover meal expenses. You may change the period for the allotment to "weekly," "semi-weekly," "semiannually," or any other period you wish. Remember to make appropriate changes to the resolution to reflect this new time period.

Business Meal Expense Allotment for Employees

After a discussion of the business necessity for the corporation to pay for the meals of its employees while meeting with present or prospective clients and customers of the corporation or others with whom employees wish to discuss corporate business, it was agreed that the following employees of the corporation are authorized to spend up to the following monthly amounts to cover expense of meals while dining away from the premises of the corporation and discussing corporate business:

Name   Allotment

_____ $_____

_____ $_____

The treasurer was instructed to communicate these spending limits to the above employees and to instruct them to submit monthly receipts for reimbursement to the treasurer when they wish to be reimbursed for off-premises business meals. The treasurer was further instructed to reimburse employees for these expenditures after verifying that they do not exceed the employee's monthly allotment and that the expenses were reasonable and directly related to the business purposes of the corporation.

Copies of all reimbursed receipts for employee and client or customer meals shall be kept by the treasurer and placed with the financial records of the corporation.

Resolution to Furnish On-Premises Meals and Lodging to Employees

Depending on a corporation's needs, employees may be required to stay on the premises around the clock. This might be the case, for example, if they work for a business that is open unusually long hours, such as a motel, hotel, storage locker rental facility, 24-hour restaurant, minimarket, or other business. A corporation is allowed to deduct the full cost of providing employee meals and lodging as long as:

- meals and/or lodging are provided for the "convenience of the employer's business" (not simply for the convenience of the employee)
- meals and/or lodging are furnished to the employee on the business premises, and

- if lodging is provided, use of the lodging by the employee is a condition of employment.

If the above requirements are met, the corporation may deduct the cost of providing these fringe benefits. In turn, the employee does not include the value of these perks as income on his or her individual tax return.

The board resolution approving this fringe benefit should state that the continuous presence of the employee is a required condition of employment.

CD-ROM

Fill in the resolution titled On-Premises Meals and Lodging for Employees as you follow the sample and special instructions below. The tear-out version is contained in Appendix C.

Special Instructions

❶ Tax-free meals can be provided to employees even if they do not sleep or live on the business premises. Meals must, however, be provided for the convenience of the corporation to have the employees on the business premises during working hours. In other words, the corporation must require the person to stay on the premises—rather than go out to eat—to handle customers, clients, shoppers, order-taking, and the like.

❷ Instead of listing the name of each eligible employee, you may use this space to specify the class or types of employees who will receive these perks, such as "security personnel," "customer service representatives," and the like.

On-Premises Meals and Lodging for Employees

After discussion, it was decided that the corporation will provide on-premises _____ ["meals" ❶ _____

and/or "lodging"] _____ to the following employees of the corporation:

_____

_____. ❷

    It was agreed that the furnishing of these benefits was for the convenience of the corporation's

business and that the continued presence of the above employee(s) on the premises of the corporation

was indispensable to the corporation's business and was a required condition of employment for the

above employee(s).

Resolution Authorizing Business Expenses With Corporate Credit or Charge Card

Instead of reimbursing employees for business expenses incurred both at home and on the road, corporations often pick up the tab for employees by issuing a corporate credit or charge card.

With this arrangement, the corporation receives the bill and pays the employee's business expenses directly, rather than reimbursing the employee. The corporation gets to deduct the expenses (subject to any applicable limits for particular types of expenses). The employee neither reports extra income nor deducts any of the charges from his or her income.

CD-ROM

Fill in the resolution titled Authorization of Corporate Credit and Charge Cards for Employees as you follow the sample and special instructions below. The tear-out version is contained in Appendix C.

Special Instructions

Fill in the names of employees and the account numbers or names of the accounts each is authorized to use. If you wish to specify a maximum monthly spending limit, fill in the amount. Otherwise indicate "not applicable" in the rightmost column.

Authorization of Corporate Credit and Charge Cards for Employees

After discussion, it was agreed that to facilitate the transaction of business necessary to the corporation, the treasurer of the corporation is authorized and instructed to issue credit cards and/or charge cards for the following corporate accounts for use by the following corporate employees.

   [If appropriate, add the following paragraph and fill in the maximum expenditures column at right: "It was further agreed that employees shall not exceed the spending allocation limits shown next to their names below:"]

Name	Acc't. No./Name	Maximum Amount
_____	_____	$_____
_____	_____	$_____

Such credit cards and/or charge cards shall be used solely by employees to incur expenses that are reasonable and necessary to the business of the corporation.

The treasurer was further instructed to monitor credit card and/or charge card purchases and receipts incidental to the card privileges hereby authorized, and, if appropriate, to revoke the card privileges of any employee who exceeds any spending limits imposed by the board or uses the card for personal expenses or expenses that are not reasonable or necessary for the accomplishment of the ongoing business of the corporation.

Reimbursement of Employee Business Expenses

Large and small corporations authorize expense reimbursements for their business owners and other key employees. These expense accounts are used to reimburse employees for business-related expenses incurred at home and working while traveling on business for the corporation.

> **TIP**
>
> **Prepare paperwork only if it makes sense.** Again, you do not always need to pass a formal board resolution to implement these reimbursement arrangements. Do the paperwork only if you think your executives, other employees, or shareholders will benefit from the passage of a formal resolution that will spell out the details of your employee reimbursement arrangement. Small corporations sometimes ignore extra paperwork of this sort, while larger corporations decide that having the board approve a formal corporate employee reimbursement plan is helpful to get directors to focus on the details of the arrangement and to provide a record of the limits of the reimbursement plan.

Employee Business Expense Tax Rules

Some corporations reimburse employees for actual business expenses incurred; others issue employees a corporate credit card to use for business purposes. Of course, other arrangements are possible, particularly for travel-related expenses, such as providing a per diem expense account to an employee while he or she is out of town on business regardless of actual expenses. Before presenting the resolutions to use to approve these employee reimbursement perks, let's take a glance at some of the tax rules.

Which Business Expenses Are Deductible

The tax rules for deductible employee business expenses can be a bit involved. Generally, if an expense is deductible, either the corporation or the employee can deduct it, but not both. The corporation gets the deduction if it reimburses the employee for the expense. An employee who pays a business expense and is not reimbursed may deduct the expense by itemizing it on Schedule A of his or her Form 1040 tax return. Only those expenses that exceed 2% of the employee's adjusted gross income are deductible.

The most common types of deductible business-related expenses include the following:

- **Car.** Costs of operating and maintaining a car when traveling away from your company on business. Reimbursement may be based on actual expenses or the standard mileage rate, including tolls and parking charges. If a car is leased while traveling on business, only the business-related portion of leased vehicle expenses may be deducted.

- **Transportation.** Costs of travel by airplane, train, or bus between home and your business destination. Commuting from work to a customer's workplace is deductible, but commuting from home to work isn't.

- **Taxi, commuter bus, and limousine.** Fares paid for transportation between an airport or bus or train station and your hotel, or between the hotel and an out-of-town work site, when traveling on business.

- **Baggage and shipping.** Expenses of sending baggage and sample or display material between your company or home and out-of-town work locations.

- **Lodging and meals.** If you must stay at a hotel or other lodging to get substantial rest to perform business duties, amounts spent for food, beverages, taxes, and related tips are deductible. Reimbursement may be based on actual costs of meals or the standard meal allowance (the latter is not available to certain employees who are "related" to the employer, including employees who own more than 10% of the corporation's stock).

- **Business entertainment expenses.** Picking up the tab for a nontravel-related business meal attended by the employee and one or more business clients (see "Payment of Meals and Lodging," above, for a specific resolution to use for this purpose).

- **Cleaning.** Cleaning and laundry expenses while away on business overnight.

- **Telephone.** Cost of business calls during a business trip, including fax, cellular, or other telecommunication transmissions.

- **Tips.** Any tips associated with other deductible business expenses while traveling.

- **Other expenses.** Other ordinary and necessary expenses related to business travel, for example, renting a computer or audiovisual presentation equipment.

The type and amount of the allowable deduction that a corporation can take for business expenses that it reimburses to employees depends on the type of employee business expense reimbursement plan set up by the business. There are two types of plans, which are treated differently under IRS tax rules: accountable and nonaccountable reimbursement plans. We briefly review each of these below.

TIP

Closely held corporations may benefit from either type of employee reimbursement plan. You'll see below that some reimbursement plans have more favorable tax results for employers, and others for employees. In closely held corporations where the main employees are also the primary shareholders, these different tax treatments have less significance, because the employee-owners stand to benefit either way.

Accountable Reimbursement Plan

Under an accountable employee business expense reimbursement plan, the employer must require workers to follow these rules for their expenses to be reimbursable:

- The expenses must be business related. That is, the employee must have incurred them while performing services for the corporation.

- The employee must substantiate the expenses within a reasonable amount of time. What kinds of receipts and records are required depends on the type of expense— whether related to travel or meals and entertainment.

- Any reimbursement paid for expenses not properly accounted for must be returned to the corporation within a reasonable period of time. Reimbursement within 120 days is usually considered reasonable.

If an employee must account for expenses according to the above rules, the corporation may deduct the reimbursement, subject to any deduction limitations that apply to particular employee business expenses—for example, generally only 50% of business meal or entertainment expenses are deductible. The employee does not have to report the reimbursement made by the corporation as income on his or her tax return.

EXAMPLE:

Bob works for KnickKnacks Supply Corp. He is required to report and provide receipts for business expenses shortly after the end of each month. KnickKnacks' accountable reimbursement expense plan also requires he pay back any expenses that have been reimbursed but not properly substantiated. Bob is reimbursed $500 for business meal and entertainment expenses while away on assignment for the corporation. The corporation can deduct $250 (generally only 50% of business meal and entertainment expenses can be deducted). Bob does not report the $500 as income on his tax return—of course, he cannot list these reimbursed expenses as deductions on his tax return either.

Nonaccountable Reimbursement Plan

If an employee expense reimbursement plan does not meet the requirements listed in "Accountable Reimbursement Plan" just above, reimbursements made by the corporation are treated as compensation-related payments paid as part of a nonaccountable plan. This means that reimbursement is considered to be compensation (pay) to the employee, and the corporation can take a full (100%) deduction for the reimbursement of these expenses.

The employer treats the compensation amounts as payroll. The employee must report the entire amount of the reimbursement as income. The employee is allowed to take deductions for business-related expenses on his or her tax returns, but there are limits on the deductibility of these payments as mentioned earlier. The bottom line: The employee pays more taxes when expenses are reimbursed as part of a nonaccountable plan.

EXAMPLE:

Marsha incurs $325 in deductible employee expenses while traveling on a work assignment for her corporation. She pays these expenses with her personal credit card and obtains reimbursement from her corporation as part of its nonaccountable expense account plan. She must report and pay taxes on the extra $325 income from her corporation, but she gets to list and deduct her travel expenses on her tax return at the end of the year.

RESOURCE

Information on deductible business expenses. For a list and explanation of the various types and amounts of deductible business expenses and the rules for accountable and nonaccountable employer reimbursement plans, see the following IRS publications: IRS Publication 334, *Tax Guide for Small Business*, and IRS Publication 463, *Travel, Entertainment, Gift, and Car Expenses*. For more information on tax deductions for small businesses, see *Deduct It!*, by Stephen Fishman (Nolo).

Which Reimbursement Plan Is Best?

Corporations sometimes favor nonaccountable reimbursement plans for the reimbursement of business-related expenses of employees, because this type of plan allows full deductions for payments of bona fide business expenses. One downside is that the corporation must go to the trouble of including the value of these compensation-related payments in its payroll reporting and withholding process (but, as mentioned above, the employee is allowed to deduct the expense directly on his or her income tax return). All this paperwork (plus the fact that employee business expenses are subject to the 2% adjusted gross income floor as explained earlier) is a nuisance all around.

Employees, on the other hand, usually prefer accountable plans, because they do not have to report reimbursements as income and pay taxes on reimbursements received under this type of plan.

Again we repeat the point that in closely held corporations where the owners are the only employees of the corporation, the owners benefit either way. Your tax adviser can help you decide whether to establish an accountable or nonaccountable expense account plan for your corporation; you can't pick both.

Documentation Requirements for Reimbursements

The corporation must keep receipts and other records for deductible employee business expense reimbursements. The main requirement is that the date, amount, location, and business purpose of each expense must be documented. If an entertainment expense is a business meal, the names and occupations of those attending should be listed, and the presence of a corporate employee at the meal and the business purpose of the meal should be noted in the records.

Per Diem Allowance

Regardless of the type of reimbursement plan a corporation has adopted, it may pay employees a per diem (daily) allowance instead of reimbursing them for actual travel, lodging, meal, and incidental expenses while spending time away from home on business for the corporation. Employers usually set a per diem rate that is equal to the federal per diem rate. (See IRS Publication 1542 for current federal per diem rates for different localities throughout the United States.)

How the per diem rate is treated depends on how it compares to the allowable federal per diem rate for the locality where the employee is located:

- **Rate equal to or less than the allowable federal per diem rate.** Per diem payments are considered paid as part of an accountable plan. In other words, the corporation gets to deduct the payment, subject to any special deductibility limits for particular expenses, and the payment is not included in the employee's income on his or her individual tax return.

- **Rate greater than the applicable federal per diem rate.** The employee is not required to pay the excess amount back to the corporation, but this extra amount will be treated as having been paid under a nonaccountable plan. In other words, the excess payment is included in the employee's income and reported and taxed on his or her individual tax return. In this case, the corporation may deduct 100% of this excess amount as a compensation-related expense. The corporation is also obliged to keep track of the amounts in its payroll.

Resolutions Authorizing Reimbursement of Employee Travel-Related Expenses

Most employee expense account plans provide for the reimbursement of business-related expenses paid by employees while traveling away from home on corporate business. We cover these travel-expense plan resolutions first. After these resolutions, we look at other resolutions that can be used to reimburse employees for their expenses, either on a per diem rate or under special plans.

Resolution Authorizing Reimbursement of Travel Expenses Under Accountable Reimbursement Plan

The resolution below can be used to authorize the reimbursement of actual business-related travel expenses paid by an employee under an accountable reimbursement plan.

CD-ROM

Fill in the resolution titled Reimbursement of Actual Travel and Entertainment Expenses to Employees Under Accountable Reimbursement Plan as you follow the sample and special instructions below. The tear-out version is contained in Appendix C.

Special Instructions

Under Treasury regulations, if an employee is required to substantiate an expense within 60 days of incurring or paying a business expense, that's considered a reasonable amount of time. Similarly, if an excess (unsubstantiated) reimbursement must be returned to the corporation within 120 days after an expense is incurred or paid, this too is reasonable. An employer may send quarterly or more frequent statements to employees listing unsubstantiated payments and requiring substantiation or payback of the listed amounts within 120 days of the statement.

Reimbursement of Actual Travel and Entertainment Expenses to Employees Under Accountable Reimbursement Plan

After discussion, it was agreed that the corporation shall adopt an accountable plan for the reimbursement of business-related travel and entertainment expenses paid by corporate employees while traveling away from home on business of the corporation. It was agreed that the treasurer of the corporation be instructed to reimburse the following corporate employees for their reasonable and necessary travel and entertainment expenses while performing services for the corporation on the terms noted below:

Name   Title

_____   _____

_____   _____

It was further agreed that, prior to any reimbursement, the employee be required to substantiate by receipts or other records, within a reasonable amount of time as set by the treasurer in accordance with IRS regulations, the date, type, amount, and business purpose of each expense, and any other information required for the expenses to be deductible by the corporation under Sections 162 and 247 of the Internal Revenue Code.

Upon providing proper substantiation, an employee shall be reimbursed for these expenses within [*specify period, or state "a reasonable amount of time under IRS rules"*] . If the treasurer determines that an employee has been reimbursed for expenses that have not been properly substantiated, the treasurer shall see to it that the employee pays back the amount of unsubstantiated reimbursement within [*specify number of days, or state* "a reasonable amount of time as set by the treasurer in accordance with IRS regulations"] of the treasurer's determination.

It was further agreed that reimbursement of the above expenses to the above employees shall be subject to the following additional terms:

[*you may wish to limit the amount of monthly reimbursements or set other conditions for repayment*]

_____ .

Resolution Authorizing Reimbursement of Travel Expenses Under Nonaccountable Reimbursement Plan

The next resolution may be used to authorize the reimbursement of actual travel-related business expenses incurred by an employee under a nonaccountable plan.

CD-ROM

Fill in the resolution titled Reimbursement of Actual Travel and Entertainment Expenses to Employees Under Nonaccountable Reimbursement Plan as you follow the sample below. The tear-out version is contained in Appendix C.

Reimbursement of Actual Travel and Entertainment Expenses to Employees Under Nonaccountable Reimbursement Plan

After discussion, it was agreed that employees of the corporation should be reimbursed by the treasurer of the corporation for reasonable and necessary travel and entertainment expenses incurred and paid by employees while performing their duties for the corporation away from home.

It was agreed that the amounts so reimbursed shall be paid to employees by way of compensation such that the employees would be required to report such reimbursements as income on their individual tax returns.

The board agreed that any reimbursement by the treasurer shall be subject to the following terms, conditions, and limitations:

[specify any terms or conditions on the types, amounts, or persons for which or to whom reimbursements may be made—for example, you may wish to limit reimbursements to $500 or less per employee per month, or specify that the reimbursement plan shall only apply to executive-level managers, vice-presidents, and the like]   .

The treasurer was instructed to communicate to employees the terms and conditions of this resolution and the requirement that they report as income and pay taxes on any reimbursements made under this nonaccountable employee business expense reimbursement plan.

Resolution Authorizing Per Diem Travel Allowance for Employees

This resolution allows a corporation to pay employees a per diem rate for business expenses incurred while away on business instead of tying payments to the reimbursement of actual expenses. (See "Per Diem Allowance," above, for a brief look at how per diem allowances differ from reimbursements of actual expenses under the tax rules.)

CD-ROM

Fill in the resolution titled Authorization of Per Diem Travel Allowance for Employees as you follow the sample and special instructions below. The tear-out version is contained in Appendix C.

Special Instructions

You can insert an exact amount in the blank, or you can tie the allowance to the allowable federal per diem rate for each particular location by using the language included within the brackets.

There are a few methods you can use to figure the allowable federal rate, as explained more fully in IRS Publication 334, *Tax Guide for Small Business*, and IRS Publication 1542, *Per Diem Rates*.

Authorization of Per Diem Travel Allowance for Employees

After discussion, the board agreed that the corporation shall pay its employees a per diem allowance of $ [*per diem amount or* "the allowable federal per diem rate for each particular locality where the employee stops or stays over"] in addition to their regular salary and other compensation while traveling away from home on business for the corporation.

It was further agreed that any part of the allowance paid in excess of the allowable federal per diem rate for the locality where the employee stops or stays over would be required to be included in the employee's income for tax purposes.

Resolution Approving Stock Bonus or Stock Option Plan

The resolution shown below can be used by the board to approve the adoption of a corporate stock bonus plan or stock option plan. Many high-tech companies find a plan of this sort the best way to attract key employees and reward them for their work by giving them shares of the company's stock—or by allowing them to purchase the shares at a low price after a specified number of years' service with the corporation. The ability to give employees an ownership stake in the company by issuing shares of stock to employees is a unique perk of doing business as a corporation.

 **CD-ROM**

Fill in the resolution titled Board Approval of Stock Bonus or Stock Option Plan as you follow the sample and special instructions below. The tear-out version is contained in Appendix C.

Special Instructions

If you feel it is not necessary to obtain shareholder ratification of the retirement plan, delete the optional language that refers to approval of shareholders and have the resolution approved by the board alone.

Board Approval of Stock Bonus or Stock Option Plan

The corporate treasurer presented to the board a stock _____ ["bonus" *or* "option"] _____ plan for the benefit of employees of the corporation. After a discussion of the importance of rewarding employee loyalty and encouraging employee loyalty and productivity through the maintenance of such a plan, the stock _____ ["bonus" *or* "option"] _____ plan was approved by the board and a copy of the plan was attached to this resolution by the secretary of the corporation.

   [*OPTIONAL:* "The secretary was instructed to submit a copy of the plan to the shareholders for approval."]

   After shareholder consent to the plan is obtained, the treasurer is instructed to implement the stock _____ ["bonus" *or* "option"] _____ plan and to take any and all actions necessary to the establishment and maintenance of the plan.

Retirement Plan Resolutions

Many small corporations adopt corporate retirement plans that help provide additional compensation to shareholder-employees and their families after they leave the employ of the corporation. The opportunity to set up and use a qualified tax-advantaged retirement plan is among the biggest perks that go along with incorporating your business.

There are a number of practical and tax advantages involved in adopting a retirement plan. Money paid into a plan, as well as earnings from investments made by the plan, are not taxed to the employee until retirement when the individual's tax brackets (and therefore taxes) will presumably be lower. In addition, money paid into a qualified retirement plan by the corporation is also deductible by the corporation.

Before you glance through this material, we want to underscore one important point. Traditional corporate pension and profit-sharing retirement plans are normally adopted by only two types of corporations:

- the smallest closely held corporations, whose employees consist of the principal shareholders of the corporation (with possibly a few additional people on payroll), and

- large corporations with hefty cash flow and reserves (who probably are not using this book).

Here's why other corporations don't usually provide these plans. Tax laws generally require that qualified (tax-favored) retirement plans must provide coverage for all full-time employees, whether principal shareholder-employees or regular rank and file. Also, under many types of corporate retirement plans,

contributions by the corporation must be made each year, regardless of corporate profits. As a result, providing a retirement plan is often prohibitively expensive for small to midsized corporations, even those with a modest payroll (ten or more employees).

Fortunately, another retirement plan, which is often more advantageous, is available for small to midsized corporations. These corporations may wish to adopt a far more cost-effective 401(k) retirement plan. This type of profit-sharing plan can be set up with employee contributions only (with the corporation limiting its expenses to administrative costs and fees) or the corporation can agree to match what the employee contributes, up to certain levels. We discuss these plans in more detail in "401(k) Plans," later in this chapter.

Helpful Retirement Plan Publications

The following free IRS publications provide additional detail on the requirements and benefits of various corporate, noncorporate, qualified, and nonqualified retirement plans (go to www.irs.gov to download these forms directly from the Web or call 800-TAX-FORM to order):

IRS Publication Number and Title

334 *Tax Guide for Small Business*

560 *Retirement Plans for Small Business*

575 *Pension and Annuity Income*

590 *Individual Retirement Arrangements*

To learn more about the advantages, disadvantages, requirements, and benefits associated with different types of retirement plans, we recommend *Pensions and Profit Sharing*, published by Dearborn R&R Newkirk, an excellent resource for additional information in this technical area.

How to Use This Chapter

Learning the ins and outs of adopting a corporate retirement plan is complicated. Understand up front that to make truly informed decisions, you will need to do research in addition to what you read here. You'll probably need to consult a tax specialist or retirement plan adviser. To give you a head start with the task, we provide basic background information on the legal and tax advantages and requirements of various tax-deductible corporate retirement plans. And, of course, our primary purpose is not to plumb the depths of this material but to give you a handy set of corporate resolutions your board can use to approve a corporate retirement plan once you've picked one out.

Here are some suggestions as to how best to proceed.

- **Step 1:** Skim the material in this chapter, then go back and spend a few more minutes with areas of interest to you, delving into the discussion to get a basic idea of the most important tax or legal considerations associated with each type of plan.

- **Step 2:** For further information on a given topic, see the IRS tax publications listed as resources in "Helpful Retirement Plan Publications," above, and consult with your tax or benefit plan advisor.

- **Step 3:** Before you implement a retirement plan, have your tentative conclusions checked by a tax adviser versed in the intricacies of corporate retirement and employee fringe benefit plans. By taking this cautious approach, you can feel confident that the retirement plan(s) you've selected will work for you when you (and other employees) stop working for the corporation.

- **Step 4:** Prepare the resolution(s) that must be approved by the board, and perhaps your shareholders, as discussed below. These may be inserted into the minutes of regular or special board meetings, or adopted using written consent forms. (See Chapters 5, 6, and 8 for instructions and forms to use to prepare minutes of meetings and written consent forms.) Remember to attach copies of all appropriate documents, such as retirement plan agreements and trust agreements.

TIP

Consider having shareholders approve resolutions for the adoption of retirement plans. Normally, only the board of directors needs to approve the adoption of corporate retirement benefit plans. But if you have nonemployee shareholders and wish to ensure a complete corporate consensus on the adoption of a plan, it can make sense to have all of your shareholders adopt a resolution approving your plan. While not legally necessary, this precaution can help avoid later griping by nonemployee shareholders, who may find fault with the amount or type of benefits provided under your plan to yourself and other corporate insiders.

How to Select and Use Corporate Resolutions

- Scan the table of contents at the beginning of the chapter to find resolutions of interest to you (for a full list of resolutions included with this book, see Appendix C).

- Read the background material that precedes each pertinent corporate resolution.

- Follow the instructions included with the sample resolution and complete a draft using your computer. (You'll have to fill in the tear-out resolution included in Appendix C if you don't have a computer.) If you need guidance on selecting and using the CD-ROM files, see Appendix A.

- Complete any needed attachment forms, such as account authorization forms or lease agreements.

- If a resolution involves complex issues that will benefit from expert analysis, have your legal or tax adviser review your paperwork and conclusions.

- Prepare minutes of a meeting or written consent forms as explained in Chapters 5 through 8, and insert the completed resolution(s) in the appropriate form. If you're seeking shareholder approval in addition to board approval, prepare two sets of minutes or written consent forms—one for your directors and one for your shareholders.

- Have the corporate secretary sign the printed minutes or have directors and/or shareholders sign any written consent forms and waivers. Then place the signed forms, together with any attachments, in your corporate records book.

Overview of Corporate Retirement Plans

This chapter provides a very basic overview of the different types of retirement plans available to corporations. Our primary intent is to introduce the alternatives available and the essential elements of each type of plan, not to cover all the fine print and technicalities.

We use the term retirement plan to describe any one of the several types of corporate pension and profit-sharing plans that can be used to provide income to business owners or other employees after they retire from the business. By pension plan, we generally mean one where the corporation sets aside a guaranteed amount each year to fund the retirement benefits of an employee or guarantees a set benefit for employees upon retirement.

To understand the available options for corporate retirement plans, you'll need to understand the basic features of different types of plans, including:

- qualified plans
- nonqualified plans
- defined benefit plans, and
- defined contribution plans.

Qualified Plans

There are two broad categories of corporate retirement plans: qualified and nonqualified plans. Most small corporations set up qualified plans, so let's look at those first.

Qualified plans meet requirements imposed under the federal Employee Retirement Income Security Act (ERISA) and have been approved by the Internal Revenue Service (IRS) or Department of Labor (DOL). As mentioned earlier, if a plan is qualified, it gives the corpo-

The Best Time to Set Up a Retirement Plan

The directors of most smaller corporations do not incorporate one day and adopt a retirement plan the next. Rather, they usually wait a few years until the company starts turning a large enough profit that they can reasonably predict continued profits and a positive cash flow in the coming years.

There are exceptions, however. One typical case is high-tech or biotech start-up companies that hope to offer a competitive job benefits package to induce key employees away from competing companies. In competitive industries dependent on highly skilled employees, the establishment of various pension and profit-sharing plans, as well as stock option and bonus packages, has become de rigueur, even from the outset of corporate operations.

If your corporation is in a slightly slower lane, but is nevertheless determined to adopt a retirement plan from the start, two types of qualified plans may be particularly suited, especially if you aren't sure that you'll immediately be earning substantial profits. These are profit-sharing plans and 401(k) plans, discussed in more detail below. Each of these options gives your corporation the discretion to decide on the amount and level of contribution it wishes to make.

ration and plan participants substantial tax breaks, the most significant of which include:

- The corporation gets to write off contributions made to fund the plan as current deductions on its annual corporate income tax return.
- Contributions that the corporation makes—as well as interest income, dividends, and asset appreciation earned and allocated to participants under the plan—are not passed along to the participants each year as taxable income.
- Individual tax payments on contributions to and earnings from the plan are deferred until the participant retires and begins receiving retirement benefits from the plan (presumably when the participant is in a lower income tax bracket).
- Retirement plan funds do not go through probate when a plan participant dies with a balance in his or her retirement plan account. Instead, the funds are distributed to the participant's designated beneficiaries. This avoids time-consuming delays and probate fees. Of course, the death of a plan participant may have estate tax and income tax consequences.

RESOURCE

Other estate planning resources. For further information on estate planning and taxes, see *Plan Your Estate*, by Denis Clifford (Nolo). For a discussion of the interplay among the various income and estate tax consequences of retirement plans, see *Estate Planning Made Easy*, by Philips and Wolfkiel (Dearborn).

Adopting a Prototype Plan

To avoid piles of paperwork and the time and expense involved with getting a retirement plan qualified, most smaller companies adopt a master or prototype retirement plan that has been qualified ahead of time by the IRS or DOL. Qualified master or prototype plans are sold by pension plan specialists or other retirement plan providers, such as insurance companies, brokerage houses, professional associations, mutual funds, and banks. (There is another alternative: You can set up a plan that attempts to meet all of the retirement plan rules, but not go to the trouble to get it approved by the IRS or DOL. This type of unapproved "qualified" plan is risky and not recommended for employers who wish to provide employees with a guarantee of favorable tax treatment by the IRS.)

TIP

Choosing a plan sponsor. Chances are your business has already been approached by several plan sponsors. But before you sign up for a plan, we recommend that you canvass older incorporated businesses in your industry or community to see what their experience has been. Finding a plan sponsor who is easy to work with, doesn't make mistakes, and charges a reasonable fee isn't always easy. Once you have located several likely candidates, establish an employee committee and invite the candidates to make presentations. Pay attention to what your employees think. After all, the plan is for their benefit, and if they feel excluded, you'll surely be blamed if it works out less than perfectly.

When adopting a master or prototype plan, the corporation selects various contribution and benefit options preapproved as part of the plan. Service fees are charged by the provider for setting up and administering the plan for the corporation each year. Typically, a flat annual fee plus a per-employee or asset fee will be charged (with extra actuary fees to set contributions each year under a defined benefit plan), such as $1,500 plus $50 per employee or $5,000 plus $20 per employee each year.

Qualified Plans Can't Discriminate

To qualify for favorable tax treatment, qualified retirement plans cannot be set up just to benefit highly compensated employees of the corporation. Highly compensated employees include those owning 5% or more of the company and those among the top 20% in salary whose pay is above a certain threshold amount.

As a practical matter, who is and who isn't highly compensated won't be a consideration for a small, closely held corporation whose only employees are the founders (the highly paid officers-directors-shareholders). If, however, you have a few full-time workers in addition to the closely held corporate execs, you will need to abide by these rules. In other words, you must include regular employees in your plan. Be aware that for many small corporations, the extra cost of covering these workers may be more than your corporation can handle.

A number of qualified retirement plan rules are designed to create a level playing field among all plan participants. These plans include a set of provisions known as top-heavy rules, which seek to prevent plans from serving mostly as a tax shelter device or retirement funding vehicle only for those in control of a business.

A plan is considered top-heavy if the value of accumulated benefits in the plan for key employees exceeds 60% of the value for all plan participants. Because a key employee includes any 5% owner of the business, as well as even moderately paid officers, plans set up by closely held corporations will normally be considered top-heavy plans. As such, they will have to abide by these top-heavy rules for any non-key employees. Top-heavy rules provide for quicker vesting of employee benefits (vesting occurs when a participant has legal ownership of benefits under a plan), as well as special contribution formulas that ensure that lower-paid employees get a fair share of contributions made by the employer under the plan. Again, the cost of complying with these extra coverage rules may be prohibitive for small corporations with a payroll that extends beyond the original shareholder-employees of the corporation.

Nonqualified Plans

Even though there is significant leeway allowed under the retirement plan qualification requirements, some corporations opt for a nonqualified plan—one that is not approved by the IRS or Department of Labor (DOL). Two important issues usually factor against nonqualified plans:

- employees must report and pay taxes on contributions the business makes on their behalf each year, and

- some of the key tax advantages to the corporation and employees associated with qualified plans are not available.

Still, if a corporation and the participants are prepared to accept these extra tax costs, a nonqualified plan can be used by a corporation as an additional perk to help keep key employees happy (by paying extra benefits to top execs). By the way, corporations often pick up the personal income tax tab charged to participants under a nonqualified plan as a way of making the plan more attractive to key employees who participate in the nonqualified plan.

Here are some of the main reasons why a corporation might spring for a nonqualified plan:

- to provide extra plan benefits to a select few corporate employees and not to others (who would have to be included under a qualified plan)

- to exceed the qualified retirement plan contribution limits for funding a plan

- because setting up a qualified plan takes too much time, trouble, and money (although prequalified master or prototype plans can mitigate much of this disadvantage), or

- to set its own rules rather than choosing among a limited list of options available through a qualified plan.

EXAMPLE:

A small coffee bean importer and distributor is owned and managed by three long-time business associates. They have a minimum payroll, consisting of two full-time workers who handle phone calls, ordering, and invoicing. The remainder of the business is accomplished by arrangement with other companies or outside contractors. Business has been brisk, despite seasonal fluctuations in coffee prices, and the owners decide to reward themselves by setting up a nonqualified profit-sharing plan. This plan provides that a specified percentage of the corporation's net profits will accrue to the three principal corporate employee-shareholders (nonshareholder employees cannot participate in the plan). The funds are to be paid into three special corporate accounts, with each participant eligible to withdraw funds upon retirement. The corporation will pay, as extra compensation each year, an amount sufficient to cover the additional individual income tax liability incurred by each plan participant each year. The paperwork for implementing the plan is minimal—just the forms necessary to set up the accounts at the corporation's bank. (The bank invests funds in mutual stock funds and other investments just like any other plan administrator.) Even though all of the tax breaks of a qualified plan are not available, the corporation and its corporate principals feel the tax cost associated with the plan is more than offset by the benefit of rewarding key corporate personnel with additional profits they have helped earn for the corporation.

Qualified Plans: Defined Benefit Versus Defined Contribution

Qualified retirement plans are generally classified under law as defined benefit or defined contribution plans. Not surprisingly, retirement plan lawyers, accountants, and other specialists are an aggressive lot who delight in cutting across boundaries if they can obtain a tax advantage. As a result, plan specialists have mixed and matched these two basic types of plans into a multiplicity of hybrid forms. Nonetheless, if you keep these two terms in mind, you will quickly get a good mental grip on the major differences between various types of retirement plan alternatives offered to business owners and employees.

Defined Benefit Plans

A defined benefit plan sets a preestablished (or defined) benefit that will be paid to retiring employees when they leave the company. Plans of this sort are often informally called *pension plans*. The actual amount the corporation contributes to the plan for each employee varies from year to year, depending upon the investment results of funds previously contributed to the plan and the age of each participant. With a defined benefit plan, each participant can enjoy the security of knowing exactly how much money he or she will be paid upon retirement.

The big plus for defined benefit plans is that the corporation has the flexibility to pay large amounts into the retirement plan quickly. Especially if the corporation has older business owners and other employees and is making lots of money, this option to put lots of money in fast can be extremely important.

EXAMPLE:

Tasty Pastries, Pudding & Pies, Incorporated, is a closely held corporation formed by three shareholders who have decided to escape the workaday world of big corporate bakeries to set up their own bakery shop. There are no other full-time employees (part-time student workers don't need to be covered under qualified plans), and the owners want to fund their retirement plans as quickly as possible. They decide to establish a defined benefit plan that will guarantee each 80% of their top salary upon retirement. Of course, they don't set up the plan until they can count on corporate profits being sufficient to fund the annual contribution requirements under the plan (which will be substantial even in early years, since all participants are in the middle of their baking careers).

The sky is not the limit, however, when it comes to funding a qualified defined benefit plan. Maximum annual pension benefits are restricted to the lesser of a maximum dollar amount (which can change from year to year) or the employee's highest pay. (See the IRS publications listed in the beginning of the chapter.)

As an added limitation, the benefit cannot exceed a maximum statutory amount under federal rules, which is scheduled to be adjusted annually for inflation.

Defined benefit plans are not for everyone. Particularly problematic is the fact that a defined benefit plan must maintain a balance sufficient to fund the specified retirement benefit for its participants. Although funding rules take into account expected fluctuations in the age and numbers of the corporation's workforce, as well as changes in interest rates and investment results, this may not be sufficient to cover dramatic shifts in market conditions that severely affect the performance of the invested funds.

If, at the end of a plan year, the overall balance in the pension fund dips below the amount then considered necessary to fund the corporation's current workforce, the business is legally required to make up the deficiency on the spot. In other words, if your corporation adopts a defined benefit plan, it may be required to pay in a substantial chunk of cash in years when it can least afford to—for example, when fund balances under a retirement plan heavily invested in mutual stock funds plummet due to a downturn in the stock market.

We don't want to overemphasize this point, however—most pension plan prognosticators (plan actuaries who use mathematical models to predict fund balances in the future) are conservative in projecting future interest and other investment returns and try to stay ahead of any major downturns or shifts in corporate personnel. Just keep in mind that the required level of contributions to defined benefit plans can change from year to year and may not always correspond to the corporation's cash on hand (you may need to borrow funds from a bank to fund your plan in particularly lean years).

 CAUTION

Defined benefit plans can be costly. Defined benefit plans are relatively complicated and expensive to maintain. For example, the cash value of assets held in the plan must be valued and certified by an actuary (a statistician who computes insurance risks and premiums). Expect to pay more to set up and maintain this type of plan than you would for a defined contribution plan, discussed just below.

Defined Contribution Plans

Most start-up companies wait a while before setting up any type of retirement plan for employees, and, when they do, they often choose to establish a defined contribution plan instead of guaranteeing a total retirement benefit (payout) to employees, as with a defined benefit plan.

A defined contribution plan simply specifies the amount the corporation will pay into the plan each year on behalf of plan participants; the corporation doesn't guarantee employees a certain amount at retirement. In other words, if the plan does not obtain a favorable return on contributions made to the plan, the amount each employee receives upon retirement will be reduced accordingly—the corporation is not required to make up for poor investment returns.

Usually, the amount paid in by the corporation is a percentage of each employee's annual compensation. This allows the business to budget an easily predictable annual amount to fund the plan. For example, a small corporation might choose to set up a retirement plan that requires it to contribute 10% of each employee's annual compensation to the plan each year.

Advantages associated with defined contribution plans include the following:

- Funds can generally be invested aggressively in an attempt to obtain higher investment returns. (By contrast, plan administrators of defined benefit plans must act more cautiously to ensure that the plan will be able to fund the specified benefits for all participants when they retire.)

- Employees are usually allowed some degree of control as to where their funds are invested.

- Loan provisions associated with this type of plan are generally more flexible than those offered under a defined benefit plan, and typically allow participants to borrow a portion of the funds accumulated in their account to buy a house, fund college, or meet other expenses.

Because of contribution limits for defined contribution plans, these plans are often best for younger owner-employees of a small corporation, who anticipate a longer employment history during which they can gradually contribute and accumulate retirement benefits in the plan. Unlike older owner-employees, they are less likely to be concerned with quickly funding a retirement plan (a feature offered by defined benefit plans).

Common Types of Qualified Defined Contribution Plans

The basic limit on the amount of tax-deductible contributions that may be made by the business each year for a participant in a qualified defined contribution plan is usually an amount equal to 100% of an employee's pay or $40,000, whichever is less. This number is indexed for inflation and may change each year. Check the IRS website (www.irs.gov) for the latest contribution limit amounts.

Let's look at the most common types of defined contribution plans.

Money Purchase Plans

Under a defined contribution money purchase plan, employer contributions are made for each employee according to a set formula, usually based upon a percentage of annual compensation—for example, 15% of salary per year. Upon retirement, each employee receives the amount of money that has been paid into his or her account plus interest and investment earnings on this money.

Although a money purchase plan is a defined contribution retirement plan under the tax rules, it is formally referred to as a money purchase pension plan. This is strange since, in almost every other context, a pension plan refers to a defined benefit that is *guaranteed* upon retirement. Apparently, the idea behind this nomenclature is that a money purchase plan, while not guaranteeing the amount of benefits each participant will ultimately receive, at least guarantees the amount that will be paid into the fund each year. So don't be thrown off the track if your retirement plan adviser starts calling this type of plan a pension plan. We both know that it does *not* guarantee a fixed pension amount upon retirement.

Profit-Sharing Plans

A profit-sharing plan is another popular type of defined contribution plan, often set up by start-up and small companies that need flexibility when funding their employees' retirement benefits. As the name implies, contributions are funded from the profits of the business (typically as a percentage of the company's annual profits).

The percentage of profits that will be paid into the plan each year does not, however, have to be determined ahead of time—meaning the board has significant discretion and flexibility in funding decisions each year. For instance, in a cash-crunch corporate year, the board may decide to let the plan go unfunded for that year—an option unavailable to plans that require yearly contributions regardless of the corporation's profitability. (Note, however, that this flexibility is not open-ended. Although you are allowed to skip contributions entirely in some years, the IRS says that contributions made to the plan generally must be "recurring and substantial." If you make a habit of not paying into the plan, the IRS may consider the plan terminated, with a consequent loss of tax benefits.)

Profit-sharing plans differ from other defined contribution plans in one other important respect. The corporation only gets to deduct contributions made to the plan on behalf of employees up to a maximum of 25% of its entire annual payroll. For this reason, profit-sharing plans often establish lower annual contribution formulas for employees than other types of defined contribution plans.

Companies that want to go beyond this limit on deductible contributions sometimes set up a profit-sharing plan on top of a money purchase plan, thus effectively beefing up the amount of tax-deductible contributions that the business can pay into the plan each year.

TIP

Combining plan options. IRS rules antici-pate the creative use of retirement plan options and combinations. When two types of plans are combined, there is an annual limit on the dollar amount of contributions that may be made on behalf of any employee. Further, if you decide to combine a defined contribution plan with a defined benefit plan (another tactic for increasing the amount of tax-deductible contributions that may be made under a plan) the maximum amount that may be put into the combined plan in any year can be no more than 125% of the funds that could be placed into either plan individually. Ask your plan adviser about these additional contribution limitations if you are thinking about setting up a combination or hybrid retirement plan.

Targeted Benefit Plans

A targeted benefit plan combines features of defined benefit and defined contribution plans. More specifically, it targets a retirement benefit but does not require that it be achieved. Even though a corporation sets up the plan with a targeted benefit, the actual amount an employee will receive upon retirement is unknown, because it is contingent on how well or poorly the funds do while invested in the plan. The corporation does not have to decrease or increase its contribution to the plan if earnings of the fund are not in line with expectations.

Pension plan specialists like targeted benefit plans for the following reasons:

- Substantial contributions can be made quickly to fund a targeted benefit for older employees (because a corporation can contribute the amount necessary to meet the minimum funding standard for the targeted benefit).

- The corporation is not liable if the funds fail to bring the expected return and are insufficient to fund the targeted benefit for an employee.

- These plans are easier to set up and maintain than defined benefit plans, as they don't require actuarial certification (an annual endorsement by a statistician that the funds paid into the plan will be sufficient at the time of employee retirement to pay the targeted benefit).

- The plan trustee can seek higher returns by making higher-risk investments.

401(k) Plans

A 401(k) plan is a form of profit-sharing plan that is enjoying a wide degree of popularity among small and midsize corporations. For most small corporations that have more than a very few employee-shareholders, 401(k) plans are the only affordable retirement plan option, because most (or all) of the money is contributed by the employees, not the business.

Here's how 401(k) plans work: Employees have the opportunity to instruct their employer to contribute a portion of the employee's pre-tax salary to the plan, and funds are invested in a list of investments preselected by the plan sponsor—tax-free. The employer also can decide to make matching or proportionate contributions, for example, paying in 25 cents for each dollar contributed by employees.

Because employee contributions are made before taxes are withheld on the money funneled into the plan, 401(k) plans are sometimes called *salary reduction plans*. Of course, an employee can decide not to make any contribution in a given year, and thus not have any tax reduction.

One big benefit for many companies that are not highly profitable is that the 401(k) may be funded solely from employee contributions. Later, should the business become more predictably profitable, the corporation can commit to make matching tax-deductible contributions for each participating employee.

Employee contributions to a 401(k) are limited to a maximum amount each year, with annual adjustments for inflation. Also, the total combined employer and employee contributions in a given year cannot exceed specified amounts. Amounts contributed by the employee above the annual limits are taxed to the employee as income.

> **TIP**
>
> **401(k) money is still subject to Social Security taxes.** Although salary amounts diverted into a 401(k) escape income taxes, they do not avoid Social Security (FICA) taxes. So, for example, if Geoffrey decides to make a $5,000 annual contribution from his $55,000 salary to his company's 401(k), only $50,000 of his salary will be subject to income tax withholding, but the full $55,000 will be subject to Social Security taxes.

Resolutions to Adopt Retirement Plans

The resolutions below show board approval of employee retirement plans presented to the board by the corporation's treasurer. Normally, you will not feel it necessary to obtain shareholder approval of a retirement plan, but we provide an additional shareholder resolution for this purpose if you wish to do so.

If your retirement plan administrator does not ask for copies of a board and/or shareholder resolution approving your retirement plan, there is no absolute need to prepare this extra paperwork. As always, use your own common sense and comfort level in deciding whether to prepare retirement plan resolutions. If you run a small corporation with outside shareholders, this extra paperwork may make sense to show that the plan was considered and approved by the board (you may even want to take the extra step of having the plan ratified by the shareholders).

A corporation often adopts a master or prototype retirement plan that has already been qualified and approved by the IRS. Typically, the plan will be available through the corporation's accountant or a bank, trust company, or other financial institution. Most retirement plans are overseen by a plan trustee: the financial institution or company that receives the money, invests it, makes reports to plan participants, and distributes benefits to participants upon retirement.

Two documents are normally presented to the board for approval:

- **a retirement plan agreement,** which describes the age and years-of-service requirements for employee participation in the plan, plan contribution requirements and limits, and a benefits vesting schedule, as well as other plan features, and

- **a trust agreement,** which appoints the trustee and defines the scope of the trustee's powers and responsibilities.

In a small company retirement plan, principals of the corporation such as the company president and treasurer are often appointed as trustees of the plan. These individuals are responsible for distributing plan documents to participants. Typically, as with 401(k) plans, the employees themselves direct the investment of their contributions into funds listed with the plan, but the trustees may make the initial decision as to the particular funds that are available for investment by employees under the plan. The financial institution or company that provides the master or prototype plan is called the "plan sponsor" and handles all the complicated reporting and actual investment of funds.

General Resolution for Adoption of Retirement Plan

Below is a sample of the general-purpose resolution you can use to show board approval of the adoption of any type of retirement plan.

RELATED TOPIC

You can use different resolutions for employee profit-sharing or stock bonus/stock option plans. If you want to use a resolution that has been drafted specifically for the adoption of an employee profit-sharing or stock bonus/stock option plan, see the alternative resolutions covered below in "Resolution for Adoption of Profit-Sharing Plan." To obtain shareholder approval, see "Resolution by Shareholders Approving Retirement Plan," below.

CD-ROM

Fill in the resolution titled Board of Directors' Adoption of Retirement Plan as you follow the sample and special instructions below. The tear-out version is contained in Appendix C.

Special Instructions

If you are adopting a hefty retirement plan package for the principals of a closely held corporation, you may want to get the nod from any outside shareholders who do not also work for the corporation. If so, include the optional paragraph regarding shareholder approval. Delete this paragraph if you feel shareholder approval of your plan is unnecessary.

Board of Directors' Adoption of Retirement Plan

The board of directors discussed the importance of fostering employee incentive and loyalty and the desirability of assisting employees in setting aside funds for their retirement. The corporate treasurer gave an oral presentation of the favorable tax benefits that could accrue to employees in establishing and maintaining a qualified retirement plan and presented an outline of provisions of the qualified master or prototype retirement plan being presented to the board for approval.

Copies of the following documents were distributed to each director for review and approval:

[list documents submitted to the board for review and approval, such as "retirement plan application and agreement," "trust agreement," "copy of IRS approval of prototype plan," *and any other documents]* .

After a review of these documents and additional discussion by the board, it was resolved that the *[insert name and type of plan, for example* "Tri-State Mutual defined contribution," "defined benefit," "targeted benefit," "401(k) profit-sharing"]* plan submitted at this meeting is approved for adoption by this corporation, per the terms of the plan agreement and other documents attached to this resolution.

[OPTIONAL: "It was further resolved that, because the adoption of this plan was a significant corporate decision involving the long-term expenditure of corporate funds, the attached plan documents shall be submitted for ratification by the shareholders of the corporation."]

The appropriate officers of the corporation are directed to sign all documents and perform other acts necessary to establish and implement the retirement plan, and the corporate treasurer is instructed to make contributions on behalf of employees, file tax reports and returns, and distribute employee notice forms as may be required under the plan in a timely manner.

Resolution for Adoption of Profit-Sharing Plan

The following resolution can be used by the board to approve the terms of a profit-sharing retirement plan. Remember that this type of plan is often appropriate for newly formed smaller corporations that wish to have the discretion to fund a retirement plan for the owner-employees with the profits of the business. (See "Profit-Sharing Plans," above, for more information.)

CD-ROM

Fill in the resolution titled Board of Directors' Adoption of Profit-Sharing Plan as you follow the sample and special instructions below. The tear-out version is contained in Appendix C.

Special Instructions

If you feel it is not necessary to obtain shareholder ratification of the profit-sharing plan—for example, if you own and operate a one-person corporation—delete the language in this and the following paragraph that refers to approval of shareholders and have the resolution approved by the board alone. (If you want shareholder approval, include the optional paragraph and see "Resolution by Shareholders Approving Retirement Plan," below.)

Board of Directors' Adoption of Profit-Sharing Plan

After a discussion of the importance of allowing employees to share in the profits of the corporation and a review of the provisions of a profit-sharing plan presented to the board by the corporate treasurer, it was agreed that the profit-sharing plan presented to the board, a copy of which is attached to this resolution, is approved.

It was further agreed that the trust agreement with _____[*trust company*]_____ provided for in the plan, a copy of which is also attached to this resolution, is also approved.

[OPTIONAL: "It was further agreed that copies of the above-referenced profit-sharing plan and trust agreement be submitted for shareholder approval."]

The treasurer of the corporation is authorized to execute the trust agreement on behalf of the corporation and to take any additional steps necessary to effectuate and implement the profit-sharing plan approved by the board [and shareholders], including certifying to the trust company as to the effectiveness of all board [and shareholder] resolutions relating to the plan and trust agreement.

Resolution by Shareholders Approving Retirement Plan

To obtain shareholder approval of a retirement plan, hold a shareholders' meeting or obtain shareholder written consents that ratify the resolution and plan documents approved by the board. (See Chapters 5 and 8.) Insert this shareholders' resolution into your minutes of shareholders' meeting or shareholder consent form.

 **CD-ROM**

Fill in the resolution titled Shareholder Ratification of Retirement Plan as you follow the sample below. The tear-out version is contained in Appendix C.

Shareholder Ratification of Retirement Plan

After discussion, the shares _____ *[if the resolution is approved by written consent, insert:* "owned or held by the shareholders whose names appear below" *or, if the resolution is approved at a shareholders' meeting, insert:* "constituting a majority of the shares present or represented at the meeting of shareholders"] _____ ratified the board resolution and plan documents attached to this resolution that establish and implement a

_____ *[state type of plan, such as* "defined benefit retirement," "profit-sharing," "stock option"] _____ plan on behalf of the employees of the corporation.

Name of Shareholder   Shares Owned

_____   _____

_____   _____

Stock Dividend Resolutions

This chapter provides sample forms and instructions for corporate resolutions you can use to approve the payment of dividends to shareholders of your corporation.

RELATED TOPIC

Use different resolutions if you want to issue stock or adopt a stock bonus/stock option plan. For additional stock-related resolutions, see Chapter 19, where we cover the issuance of shares to shareholders, and Chapter 16, which contains a resolution for the approval of a stock bonus or stock option plan.

TIP

Board should approve resolutions. The corporate resolutions contained in this chapter need to be approved by the board of directors alone. Of course, you may choose to have shareholders approve or ratify any decision made by the board.

Normally, you will not wish to take this extra step unless shareholder approval is legally required or the decision is important enough to warrant the extra time and effort.

Stock Dividend Rules

Most smaller, closely held corporations do not declare and pay dividends because dividends are not deductible by the corporation and shareholders must pay individual taxes on them. In other words, dividends are taxed twice— once at the corporate level and again at the shareholder level (at special dividend tax rates).

Smaller corporations without outside shareholders often prefer to pay their shareholder-employees a salary instead of dividends. Under this arrangement, the shareholders must report the salary as income and pay taxes on it, but the corporation gets to sidestep corporate taxes and deduct salaries paid to the owners.

How to Select and Use Corporate Resolutions

- Scan the table of contents at the beginning of the chapter to find resolutions of interest to you (for a full list of resolutions included with this book, see Appendix C).

- Read the background material that precedes each pertinent corporate resolution.

- Follow the instructions included with the sample resolution and complete a draft using your computer. (You'll have to fill in the tear-out resolution included in Appendix C if you don't have a computer.) If you need guidance on selecting and using the CD-ROM files, see Appendix A.

- Complete any needed attachment forms, such as account authorization forms or lease agreements.

- If a resolution involves complex issues that will benefit from expert analysis, have your legal or tax advisor review your paperwork and conclusions.

- Prepare minutes of a meeting or written consent forms as explained in Chapters 5 through 8, and insert the completed resolution(s) in the appropriate form. If you're seeking shareholder approval in addition to board approval, prepare two sets of minutes or written consent forms—one for your directors and one for your shareholders.

- Have the corporate secretary sign the printed minutes or have directors and/or shareholders sign any written consent forms and waivers. Then place the signed forms, together with any attachments, in your corporate records book.

In some circumstances, even smaller corporations pay dividends. Why? In order to attract outside investors—who do not work for the corporation and, therefore, do not receive a salary—they must promise to pay them a dividend on their shares.

Dividends fall into two categories:

- **Regular dividends.** In corporations with outside investors, a regular dividend may be required under corporate bylaws. This type of dividend is automatically declared and paid by the corporation to shareholders at regular intervals, often yearly, unless the board decides to rescind the regular dividend in a given year. In other words, once the directors approve the initial bylaw that provides for regular dividends, they do not need to approve each regular dividend payment.

- **Extraordinary dividends.** The board may also authorize the payment of extraordinary dividends—dividends declared and paid during or at the end of the year in addition to regular dividends. For example, your corporation may pay a regular dividend of $100 to shareholders each year, and pay an additional $200 extraordinary dividend—which is approved by the board—if earnings are sufficient at the end of the fiscal year.

In most instances, dividends are payable to all holders of issued shares of the corporation. However, if a corporation has two or more classes or series of shares, the dividend may be limited to only one class, such as Class A preferred shareholders.

Financial Test for Dividend Payments

Under state laws, the board must pass a formal resolution approving the payment of a dividend. These laws also require that a corporation meet specific financial tests before a dividend may be approved by the board. State laws normally mandate that corporate assets exceed liabilities by a specified ratio and/or that the corporation will still be solvent (able to pay its debts) after the dividend is paid.

Your bylaws should reiterate the financial tests that must be met in your state prior to the declaration of a dividend by your board. Your business corporation laws will also contain these requirements if you wish to look them up yourself. Or you may wish to ask your lawyer or tax person. (See Chapter 20 for information on doing your own legal research and guidelines on finding and using legal and tax advisers.)

Personal Liability for Dividend Payments

If the board of directors authorizes a dividend in violation of state law, each director can be held personally liable for the amount of the dividend. While lawsuits of this sort don't occur frequently in the context of smaller, privately held corporations, you need to be careful any time you decide to pay dividends. If the dividend places a financially troubled business on even shakier ground, creditors may sue—and directors may have to pay back unwarranted dividend payments that violated the statutory rules.

Fortunately, most states relieve directors from personal liability if they relied on financial statements prepared or reported by a corporate officer or an accountant when authorizing the distribution of dividends. This is another good reason to check with your accountant before approving a dividend. As an added measure of safety, you may wish to attach to your stock dividend resolution a statement or report from your treasurer or accountant that your corporation met the dividend financial tests required in your state when the board approved the dividend decision. The Declaration of Cash Dividend resolution and Declaration of Year-End Dividend resolution, below, contain a statement to this effect.

Record Date for Share Ownership

Corporation laws allow the directors to set a record date for shares. This is the date by which a shareholder must be listed as a record holder of corporate shares in order to qualify for a dividend payment.

The boards of smaller corporations often don't bother to set record dates because stock is owned by a very few people, all of whom will receive dividends. In this case, state law normally says that all shareholders listed on the books as of the date of the board meeting (or the written consent) declaring the dividend are entitled to receive a dividend payment.

Even if your directors decide to specify a record date for a dividend, state law limits how far they can go back to include shareholders of the corporation. Typically, any record date specified cannot be more than 60 to 90 days prior to the declaration date for the dividend. The idea behind these corporate laws is that directors should only pay out profits to current and recent shareholders.

EXAMPLE:

On January 15th, the board of Super Tubes & Sprockets, Inc., declares a dividend that is payable to all shareholders listed on the books of the corporation as of the first of the year (15 days earlier).

Different Types of Dividend-Receiving Shares

Most corporations have only one class of stock. In these corporations, if a dividend is declared, all shareholders are entitled to receive it (as long as they own shares on the record date for the dividend—see "Record Date for Share Ownership," above).

However, some corporations split their shares into different classes or series of shares. If different classes of shares are authorized in the articles of incorporation, it is customary for one class to be designated Class "A," another Class "B," and so on, with Class A given full voting rights, and the other classes given full voting rights and/or any special preferences with respect to dividends or liquidation proceeds—for example, "Class B preferred."

Your articles must state whether your corporation has more than one class of stock and, if so, the different privileges and restrictions associated with each. Here's how to proceed:

- **If your corporation has only one class of shares.** You don't need to be concerned with the rest of this discussion. All shareholders will have the same rights to receive dividends.

- **If your corporation has more than one class of shares.** The board must follow the rules for dividend payment spelled out in your articles if they wish to pay dividends selectively to one or more classes of shares. The board can declare a dividend for one or more classes only, or state that one class gets the dividend first and, if profits are sufficient, then the remaining classes receive a dividend, too.

If your corporation has set up special classes or shares with special dividend rights, they mostly likely will be called preferred shares (as opposed to common shares, where all shares have the same voting, dividend, and other rights). Preferred shares are generally given the first right to receive a dividend declared by the board. Special types of preferred shares also can be created. For example, a class of cumulative preferred shares may be entitled to accumulate dividends—if the board does not distribute a dividend in a given year, the dividends accumulate and must be paid to the preferred shareholders in later years before any other shareholders are entitled to receive a dividend.

> ⚠ **CAUTION**
>
> **Check your articles and bylaws.** Check your articles to see if your corporation has special classes of shares with special dividend rights. Also check your bylaws to see if dividends must be paid yearly, are required to accumulate, or have other conditions or terms.

Stock Dividend Resolutions

Below, we present resolutions that can be used by your board to approve the payment of a dividend to shareholders. Again, your board should always pass a resolution to approve (declare) a dividend. The approval and payment of dividends are important legal matters that require formal board approval.

We start with a basic cash dividend resolution, followed by resolutions with different dividend declaration and payment options. Pick the resolution form that best fits the terms of your upcoming dividend, making any changes necessary to reflect your board's dividend decision.

Resolution Declaring Cash Stock Dividend

The following resolution contains the basic information necessary to approve the payment of a cash dividend on corporate shares.

> 💿 **CD-ROM**
>
> Fill out the resolution titled Declaration of Cash Dividend as you follow the sample and special instructions below. The tear-out version is contained in Appendix C.

Special Instructions

❶ Specify the type of shares eligible for the dividend. In the typical smaller corporation with one class of shares, all shares will be eligible to receive the dividend, and the word "common" should be inserted here. In larger corporations with multiple classes of shares, dividends may be limited to special classes or series of shares, such as "Class A preferred" shares only.

❷ Fill in the record date by which a shareholder must own shares in order to be eligible for the dividend. (See "Record Date for Share Ownership," above, for more on record dates.) In most cases, you will wish to pay a dividend to all current shareholders as of the date the dividend is declared, so you'll simply list the date of your board of directors' decision.

❸ This resolution states that you have checked with your accountant ahead of time to make sure your corporation is in good enough financial shape—meets the applicable insolvency and balance sheet tests under state law—for the payment of dividends. If you wish, attach corporate financial statements (a balance sheet) and any written report prepared by the treasurer or accountant that the directors relied upon to authorize the dividend. (See the discussion in "Stock Dividend Rules," above.)

❹ The dividend distribution date should be shortly after the date of the board decision, usually within one or two weeks. If you wait too long—say, more than one month—the financial condition of your corporation may have changed and you will need to analyze whether your corporation still meets the financial tests for paying the dividend.

Declaration of Cash Dividend

The board of directors resolves that the corporation shall pay a dividend to persons who are listed as

owners of its ___[type of shares]___ ❶ ___ shares on its books as of ___[record date for share ownership]___ ❷ ___

in the amount of $___[amount]___ per share.

The treasurer announced that he/she had consulted the corporation's accountant ❸ and the

corporation would, after giving effect to the dividend, meet all applicable financial and legal tests under

state law for the payment of dividends to shareholders.

The treasurer of the corporation is instructed to mail a corporate check drawn in the appropriate

amount to each shareholder entitled to the dividend no later than ___[date of dividend payment]___ ❹ ,

addressed to each shareholder at the last address shown for the shareholder on the books of the

corporation.

Resolution Authorizing Cash Dividend Payable in Installments

Sometimes a corporation wishes to declare (approve) and pay a dividend, but the corporation either cannot meet the financial tests under state law for paying the full dividend all at once or, even if legal rules can be met, the board wishes to pay out the dividend in installments so as not to excessively burden corporate cash flow. In either case, the board may decide to declare the dividend but pay it to shareholders in manageable installments. The resolution below can be used for this purpose.

CD-ROM

Fill out the resolution titled Authorization of Cash Dividend Payable in Installments as you follow the sample and special instructions below. The tear-out version is contained in Appendix C.

Special Instructions

❶ See Special Instructions ❶ and ❷ in "Resolution Declaring Cash Stock Dividend," above, for instructions on picking record and payment dates for your dividend.

❷ Specify the dates installments will be paid and the amount of each. If dividends will be paid to different classes of shares at different times or in different amounts, specify the class of shares for each payment date.

Authorization of Cash Dividend Payable in Installments

After a report by the treasurer of the corporation that the retained earnings and profits of the corporation as of ____*[date of financial statement]*____ totaled $____*[amount]*____, the board agreed that a dividend of $____*[amount]*____ per share on the outstanding ____*[class of shares, such as "common"]*____ shares of the corporation is declared for all shareholders of record as of ____*[record date]* ❶____.

The board further agreed that the above dividend be paid on the following dates in the following installments: ❷

Date	Installment Amount
_____	$_____
_____	$_____
_____	$_____

Resolution Authorizing Annual Year-End Stock Dividend

Below is a year-end dividend resolution you can use if your corporation wishes to declare and pay a dividend at the end of the tax year, shortly after the preparation of the corporation's annual balance sheet. This is normally a good time to declare a dividend, since the financial figures have just been prepared and dividends will be paid out of profits on hand that were earned during the prior year.

 **CD-ROM**

Fill out the resolution titled Declaration of Year-End Dividend as you follow the sample and special instructions below. The tear-out version is contained in Appendix C.

Special Instructions

See Special Instructions ❶ and ❷ in "Resolution Declaring Cash Stock Dividend," above, for instructions on picking record and payment dates for your dividend.

Declaration of Year-End Dividend

The treasurer of the corporation presented a balance sheet of the corporation as of the last day of the fiscal year ending __[date]__ that shows the corporation has retained earnings of $__[amount]__. The treasurer reported that the corporation's accountant has certified that the balance sheet fairly reflects the financial condition and assets and liabilities of the corporation.

After examining the balance sheet and determining that the corporation could pay the dividend noted below and still be able to pay its bills as they become due in the normal course of business, as well as meet other legal requirements necessary for the declaration and payment of dividends under state law as reported by the treasurer, the board agreed to pay a dividend of $__[dollar amount]__. This dividend is to be paid out of the net earnings of the corporation on __[date]__ to shareholders of record on the books of the corporation as of the close of business on __[record date]__.

Resolution Declaring Regular and Extraordinary Dividends

The following resolution is appropriate for use by corporations that wish to declare regular and extraordinary dividends at the same time. As discussed earlier, a regular dividend is one that is routinely declared and paid at one or more periods during the fiscal year of the corporation. An extraordinary dividend is one that is declared at any other time.

 CD-ROM

Fill out the resolution titled Declaration of Regular and Extra Dividend as you follow the sample and special instructions below. The tear-out version is contained in Appendix C.

Special Instructions

See Special Instructions ❶ and ❷ in "Resolution Declaring Cash Stock Dividend," above, for instructions on picking record and payment dates for your dividend.

Declaration of Regular and Extra Dividend

After discussion and a report from the treasurer that the earnings and profits of the corporation were sufficient, it was agreed that a regular _____ [*state period, such as "quarterly," "semiannual," or "annual"*] _____ dividend be declared and paid on or by ___ [*date of payment of dividend*] ___ to the holders of shares as shown on the records of the corporation as of the close of business on _____ [*date*] _____, as follows: _ [*state amount and type of dividend, for example:* "a dividend of (*percent*)% on outstanding _____ preferred shares and a $ (*amount*) dividend on outstanding common shares without par value"] _____ .

It was further agreed that surplus of earnings and profits warranted the declaration and payment of an additional dividend. After discussion, the following additional dividend was approved by the board:

_ [*state type and amount of additional dividend and class of shares eligible for the extra amount, for_ _____ *example:* "an extra dividend of $ (*amount*) upon the outstanding common shares of the corporation _____ as shown on the corporate records on (*record date*) to be paid on (*payment date*)"] _____ .

Resolution Declaring Accumulated Dividend to Preferred Shareholders

As mentioned earlier, a few corporations issue cumulative preferred shares, where dividends declared on these special shares accumulate and must be paid before any other shareholders receive a dividend. In this situation, dividends can accumulate for a number of reasons— simply because the board decides not to pay a dividend in a given year, or because the corporation is not financially sound enough (unable to meet the legal tests) necessary to pay a particular dividend in a certain year.

When the board decides to pay up these outstanding dividends, it can use the following resolution, which authorizes payment of accumulated dividends to the preferred shareholders to whom they are owed.

 CD-ROM

Fill out the resolution titled Declaration of Accumulated Dividend to Preferred Shareholders as you follow the sample and special instructions below. The tear-out version is contained in Appendix C.

Special Instructions

See Special Instructions ❶ and ❷ in "Resolution Declaring Cash Stock Dividend," above, for instructions on picking record and payment dates for your dividend.

**Declaration of Accumulated Dividend
to Preferred Shareholders**

The board of directors, after examining a balance sheet for the fiscal year ended _____[date]_____

presented by the treasurer of the corporation, determined that earnings were sufficient for the payment

of a dividend to holders of cumulative preferred stock of the corporation of record as of the close of

business on __[record date]__, in the amount of $__[dollar amount]__ per share, which dividend

represents the payment of unpaid dividends that have accumulated on these shares since __[date]__.

Resolution Authorizing Payment of Property Dividend to Shareholders

Although it's somewhat unusual, if your corporation has excess assets, your board may decide to pay a property—rather than a cash—dividend to shareholders. One way is to transfer title to the property to shareholders jointly so that each receives a proportionate, undivided interest in the transferred property. The resolution below authorizes a property dividend and recites the facts that form the basis of this transaction: that ownership of the property being distributed is no longer necessary for the business of the corporation.

CAUTION

Beware of tax consequences of property dividends. A property dividend can have complex tax consequences and other special considerations. For example, it may be complicated to assess the fair market value of the property or to determine the income tax effect of the transfer (the effect on the income tax basis in the property in the hands of the shareholders). Check with your small business tax or legal adviser before approving a property dividend for shareholders.

CD-ROM

Fill in the resolution titled Authorization of Property Dividend to Shareholders as you follow the sample and special instructions below. The tear-out version is contained in Appendix C.

Special Instructions

Check with your tax or legal adviser for the best way for the shareholders to take title to property, and whether there are any restrictions on the breakdown of percentages owned—for example, joint tenancy property must be owned equally by all owners. A new title document to the property, such as a deed, should be prepared and recorded for the property. (Californians transferring real property may be interested in *Deeds for California Real Estate*, by Mary Randolph (Nolo).)

Authorization of Property Dividend to Shareholders

The board discussed and agreed to the following facts:

1. Corporate profits of $_____[amount]_____ are currently invested and represented in the following pieces of property owned by the corporation:

____[describe property to be distributed]____ ["with a fair market value of $ (amount)"]____

____[market value of property determined with help of tax adviser]_____.

2. Ownership and use by the corporation of the above property is no longer necessary to the business and purposes of the corporation.

3. The shareholders of the corporation have expressed to the appropriate corporate officers a willingness to accept their proportionate shares of the property in a joint conveyance from the corporation to the shareholders, rather than having their interests reduced to money through a sale of the property to others before being distributed to them.

The board further agreed that the president and treasurer of the corporation are authorized and instructed to convey the above property jointly to the following shareholders, in the proportions set forth below, as ___[state how the shareholders will hold joint title, for example, "tenants in common" or "joint ____tenants"]_____ :

Name	Percentage
_____	_____%
_____	_____%

Stock Issuance Resolutions

This chapter presents many of the key issues involved in the approval of the issuance of shares by a corporation's board of directors. If you decide to issue shares, you'll find several resolutions useful for this purpose.

RELATED TOPIC

Use different resolutions if you want to pay dividends to shareholders or adopt a stock bonus/stock option plan. Chapter 18 covers resolutions that can be used to approve the payment of cash, stock, and property dividends to shareholders. Chapter 16 contains a resolution for the approval of a stock bonus or stock option plan.

TIP

Resolutions require board, and sometimes shareholder, approval. Stock issuance resolutions must be approved by your board. In instances where the rights of existing shareholders are affected, the resolutions also must be approved by shareholders—for example, if a new class of shares is given rights that supersede rights attached to current shares. We flag these situations later in the chapter.

Legal and Tax Issues Affecting Stock Issuance

Below are several issues to keep in mind when deciding whether to approve the issuance of shares. The intent is not to stop you in your tracks when issuing new shares but simply to alert you to potential legal and tax consequences. If any of these issues apply to you, check it further with your legal or tax adviser.

How to Select and Use Corporate Resolutions

- Scan the table of contents at the beginning of the chapter to find resolutions of interest to you (for a full list of resolutions included with this book, see Appendix C).
- Read the background material that precedes each pertinent corporate resolution.
- Follow the instructions included with the sample resolution and complete a draft using your computer. (You'll have to fill in the tear-out resolution included in Appendix C if you don't have a computer.) If you need guidance on selecting and using the CD-ROM files, see Appendix A.
- Complete any needed attachment forms, such as account authorization forms or lease agreements.

- If a resolution involves complex issues that will benefit from expert analysis, have your legal or tax adviser review your paperwork and conclusions.
- Prepare minutes of a meeting or written consent forms as explained in Chapters 5 through 8, and insert the completed resolution(s) in the appropriate form. If you're seeking shareholder approval in addition to board approval, prepare two sets of minutes or written consent forms—one for your directors and one for your shareholders.
- Have the corporate secretary sign the printed minutes or have directors and/or shareholders sign any written consent forms and waivers. Then place the signed forms, together with any attachments, in your corporate records book.

- **Shares must be authorized in the articles.** Before shares can be issued to shareholders, the shares must be authorized—that is, the corporation's articles of incorporation must include a statement permitting the issuance of a certain number and type of shares. Once shares have been authorized in the articles, the board may approve the issuance of some or all of those shares. The board cannot, however, approve the issuance of more than the number of shares authorized in the corporation's articles. If you need to issue more shares, you must amend your articles to increase the existing number of authorized shares and/or to create a new class or series of shares. (Instructions on how to do this are contained in "Amending Your Articles of Incorporation" in Chapter 11.)

- **Shares in exchange for future payment may not be allowed.** Many states limit the issuance of shares for future services or in return for a promise to pay for the shares later (such as a promissory note), and instead require that shares be purchased with cash or property. Check your bylaws or state business corporation laws to be sure future payments are allowed. (In Chapter 20, we discuss how to do your own legal research.)

- **Value payment for shares at fair market value.** To avoid unfairness to existing shareholders, the board should scrupulously value any noncash consideration (property) paid for shares at its fair market value. For example, if shares are purchased with a truck owned by the shareholder, place a middle *Blue Book* value on the truck, not an overpriced figure that results in the shareholder's getting more shares than he or she deserves. If shares are paid for in exchange for future services, you will not want to inflate the value of these services—set a value on the services

that reflects what the shareholder would normally be paid for these services.

- **Comply with securities laws.** Whenever shares are issued, state and federal securities laws must be examined to make sure the sale is exempt from registration under state and federal rules.

TIP

Small stock issuances may be exempt from securities registration. Fortunately, most states, as well as the federal Securities and Exchange Commission (SEC), exempt from registration small, private issuances of shares to a limited number of related or sophisticated investors (usually 35 or fewer). If your corporation involves a relatively small number of shareholders and does not intend to sell shares to the public, chances are the issuance of shares will be exempt. (For a discussion of securities rules and exemptions, see *Incorporate Your Business*, by Anthony Mancuso (Nolo).)

- **Effect on S corporation tax status.** If you decide to add a second class of shares— perhaps to issue shares to investors with special dividend rights—and you have elected S corporation tax status, you may have trouble, because the creation of a second class of shares may make the corporation ineligible for S corporation tax status. (See "S Corporation Tax Election" in Chapter 10 for a discussion.)

TIP

S corporation shares may have different voting rights. S corporations may have voting and nonvoting shares, but if the shares differ in other respects—such as with respect to participating in dividends or liquidation proceeds—the IRS will decide that the corporation has two classes of shares, which is not permitted under current S corporation tax rules.

Par Value Shares

Under many state corporate laws, shares may be authorized and issued with a stated par value—a nominal dollar or cent amount attached to each share. Corporations often use a par value when allowed, since incorporation filing fees (the fees you pay to incorporate when you file your original articles with the corporate filing office) are usually less for par value shares than for shares without par value—also known as no-par shares.

You can tell whether your shares have a stated par value by reading your articles—for example, your articles may provide: "This corporation is authorized to issue 100,000 shares of common stock having a par value of $1.00 each." If you see an article that contains par value language, you'll need to authorize and issue par value shares when increasing the number of corporate shares in the future.

Legally, par value shares must be sold for an amount that is at least equal to their stated par value; this par value amount is normally a nominal amount that is but a fraction of the amount for which the shares are sold.

EXAMPLE: The articles of DuraTech Computer Peripherals, Inc., authorize the issuance of 100,000 shares with a stated par value of $1. An initial sale of 10,000 shares is made to the founders of the corporation, and each share is sold for $5. Only $1 received for each share is applied to the corporation's par value account (called the stated capital account) on the corporate books.

- **Shares in exchange for services are ineligible for Internal Revenue Code Section 1244 benefits.** Shares issued in return for services are not eligible for the tax benefits of Internal Revenue Code Section 1244, which allows small corporation shareholders to deduct an extra share of losses on their individual tax returns if their corporation should go under and their stock become worthless. (See "Section 1244 Stock Plan" in Chapter 10.)

- **Par value shares.** If your articles authorize par value shares, any new shares will need to be par value shares as well. (See "Par Value Shares" above, for more information.)

Stock Issuance Resolutions

The following resolutions can be used by the board to approve the issuance of shares. Special instructions have been added after each resolution as needed.

You may use the basic stock issuance resolution, just below, to issue shares for different types of payment—such as cash and property. Or, if you prefer, you may select one of the specific resolutions in the remainder of the sections to issue shares in return for the payment of a particular type of property. Choosing whether to use a general resolution or one of the more specific ones is a matter of personal preference.

Basic Stock Issuance Resolution

This basic resolution may be used by the board of directors to approve the issuance of shares to one or more shareholders for different types of payment.

CD-ROM

Fill out the resolution titled Approval of the Issuance of Shares as you follow the sample and special instructions below. The tear-out version is contained in Appendix C.

Special Instructions

❶ Describe the type of shares you are issuing. As mentioned earlier, most corporations have one class of shares only, and will show "common" shares in this blank—this means shares without any preferences or special voting rights or restrictions.

If you are issuing a special class of shares that are provided for in your articles, specify their designation here—for example, "Class A preferred" or "Class B nonvoting." Simply copy the designation of the class of shares from the language in your articles. If you wish to issue more than one class of shares, show both in the blank, and specify how many of each type each shareholder will receive in the list following this paragraph.

EXAMPLE (to issue 100 Class A and 20 Class B shares to separate shareholders):

"After discussion, it was agreed that the corporation shall issue the following number of Class A voting and Class B nonvoting shares to the following persons in exchange for payment of the following:

Name	Number of Shares	Payment	Value
Janice Freelander	100 Class A	$1,000	Cash
Stephan Mingus	200 Class B	$2,000	Cash

❷ Your articles of incorporation will tell you whether you must issue par shares—and, if so, the par value of each share. If your articles authorize shares that are without par value, simply show that the shares are "without par value" in this blank. (See "Par Value Shares," above, for more on par value shares and state law requirements.)

If your articles authorize shares with par value, state the par value amount here. If you issue par value shares, your stock certificates must indicate the stated par value of each share.

❸ Show the type of payment to be made by each shareholder. Legally, in all states payments may be for cash, property, past services, and the cancellation of indebtedness owed by the corporation to the prospective shareholder.

Some states also allow shares to be issued in return for a promise to pay for the shares later (in return for a promissory note signed by the shareholder) or in return for future services (a signed agreement by the shareholder, such as an employment contract, binding him or her to perform future services for the corporation to pay off the shares). Your bylaws should tell you what types of payment for shares are legal in your state.

❹ Typically, state corporate laws require the board to specify the fair value to the corporation of any noncash payment for the shares. Indicate the fair market value of any property or service exchanged for shares in this column. If the shareholder is making a cash payment, fill in the word "cash."

TIP

Future payment for stock. Below we have a specific resolution you can use if a shareholder will pay part of the purchase price for shares in cash, signing a promissory note to pay the balance in future installments (not all states allow this—check your bylaws and state business corporation laws if you have doubts). Also see Chapter 15, which contains several examples of promissory note forms that may be of use here. Finally, if a person is issued shares in return for future services, it's wise to document the nature and extent of these services by having the shareholder-employee sign an employment contract. Warning: The issuance of stock for services is usually taxable—check with your tax adviser.

Approval of the Issuance of Shares

After discussion, it was agreed that the corporation shall issue the following number of __[type of shares]__ ❶

shares ___["without par value" *or, if shares have par value,* "with a stated par value of $ (*amount*)"]__ ❷

to the following persons in exchange for payment of the following:

Name	Number of Shares	Payment ❸	Value ❹
_____	_____	$_____	$_____
_____	_____	$_____	$_____

The president and treasurer are instructed to issue share certificates to each of the persons in accordance with the above terms upon receipt by the corporation of the payment for the shares and after preparing all papers necessary to complete and document the transfer of the payment to the corporation.

Resolution to Issue Stock in Exchange for Property

This resolution approves the issuance of shares for items of property or real property transferred to the corporation. If you plan to issue shares in return for the assets of a business, use the Sale and Issuance of Shares for Property resolution (below).

CD-ROM

Fill out the resolution titled Sale and Issuance of Shares for Property as you follow the sample and special instructions below. The tear-out version is contained in Appendix C.

Special Instructions

❶ See special instructions ❶ and ❷ to the basic stock issuance resolution, above, for help in filling in these par/no-par blanks.

❷ In describing any property transferred, be as specific as you can. For example, give the year, make, and vehicle ID number for a truck or the make, model, and serial number of a computer. As an alternative, you can attach a receipt or other description of the property to the resolution and refer to this paperwork in the resolution, such as "computer equipment listed in attached Schedule 1."

❸ Additional legal paperwork is needed to transfer assets with title or ownership certificates to a corporation. For example, to transfer a car to a corporation, you will need to sign over a title slip and send it to the department or registrar of motor vehicles. For transfers of real estate, new deeds should be prepared transferring the property to the corporation and recorded at your county recorder or deeds office. Check with a broker or office supply store for copies of standard deed or transfer forms. (An excellent source of deeds forms and legal information on transferring real property interests in California is *Deeds for California Real Estate*, by Mary Randolph (Nolo).)

Resolution to Issue Stock in

Sale and Issuance of Shares for Property

After discussion by the board of directors, it was

RESOLVED, that this corporation shall sell and issue shares of its stock ___[if appropriate, add___ "without par value" *or* "with a stated par value of $ *(amount)*"] ___❶___ to the following persons in consideration of property actually received, as follows:

Name	No. Shares	Description of Property ❷	Value of Property
_____	_____	_____	$_____
_____	_____	_____	$_____

RESOLVED FURTHER, that the board of directors of this corporation determines that the fair value of such property to this corporation in monetary terms is the value shown above.

RESOLVED FURTHER, that the appropriate officers of this corporation are directed to take such actions and execute such documents as are necessary to sell and issue the shares listed above. ❸

Exchange for Indebtedness Canceled

A common way to pay for shares in a closely held corporation is for a shareholder to give up the right to be repaid for outstanding loans or advances he or she made to the corporation.

EXAMPLE:

Dan lends his corporation $1,000 at a rate of 9% interest per year, due in one year. At the end of the year, the corporation owes him $1,090. Instead of paying him cash, his corporation issues him 109 shares at a selling price of $10 per share. Dan cancels the debt owed to him by his corporation in return for these shares.

CD-ROM

Fill out the resolution titled Sale and Issuance of Shares for Indebtedness Canceled as you follow the sample and special instructions below. The tear-out version is contained in Appendix C.

Special Instructions

❶ See special instruction ❷ to the basic stock issuance resolution, above, for help in filling in these par/no-par blanks.

❷ Describe the specifics of the debt here—for example, "loan to corporation on 12/1/2010." Or, if the loan was previously documented with a promissory note, you can refer to it here instead—for example, "see attached promissory note dated 12/1/2010." Make sure the shareholder (former lender) marks the promissory note "paid in full," signs and dates the note, and attaches a copy of the canceled note to the minutes or written consent form used to approve the resolution. (For instructions on preparing promissory notes to document loans made by shareholders, see Chapter 15. A Release of Promissory Note form is in Chapter 15.)

❸ List the amount of principal and interest currently owed on the loan or cash advance in

---

Sale and Issuance of Shares for Indebtedness Canceled

After discussion by the board of directors, it was

    RESOLVED, that this corporation shall sell and issue shares of its stock ___[if appropriate, add___

"without par value" *or* "with a stated par value of $ (*amount*)"] ❶ _____ in consideration of indebtedness

cancelled, as follows:

Name	No. Shares	Description of Indebtedness Cancelled ❷	Amount of Indebtedness Cancelled ❸
_____	_____	_____	$_____
_____	_____	_____	$_____

    RESOLVED FURTHER, that the board of directors determines that the fair value of the indebtedness to this corporation canceled in return for the issuance of the above shares in monetary terms is the dollar amounts shown above.

    RESOLVED FURTHER, that the officers of this corporation are authorized to sign documents on behalf of the corporation and take any other action necessary to sell and issue the shares listed above.

your description, taking into account interest that accrues up to and including the date of cancellation of the note (normally the date when the share certificates are issued).

Resolution to Issue Stock in Exchange for Services

Sometimes, particularly in closely held corporations, one of the principals of the business receives shares in return for services performed for the corporation.

EXAMPLE:

Allison and Raymond incorporate Two-Reel, Inc., an audio recording studio. Raymond antes up cash for his shares, but Allison is unable to come up with the cash for hers. Instead, she receives shares in return for her work for the studio (she agrees to forgo payment of a portion of her salary). Allison enters into an employment agreement with her corporation, agreeing to receive shares, instead of salary, for services to be performed for the corporation.

Warning: The issuance of stock for services is taxable. Check with your tax adviser.

CAUTION

Issuing shares for future services may not be allowed. As we mentioned earlier, all states allow the issuance of shares for past services, but some states prohibit the issuance of shares for the performance of future services. Check your bylaws—they will usually tell you the types of legal payment acceptable for shares in your state. If your bylaws are silent on this point and you wish to issue shares in return for the performance of future services for the corporation, check your state's business corporation laws or ask a lawyer or accountant.

CD-ROM

Fill out the resolution titled Sale and Issuance of Shares for Services as you follow the sample and special instructions below. The tear-out version is contained in Appendix C.

Special Instructions

❶ See special instruction ❷ to the basic stock issuance resolution, above, for help in filling in these par/no-par blanks.

❷ Select the appropriate wording ("done" or "to be done") to indicate whether shares will be issued in return for the performance of past or future services.

❸ Describe the past or future services, giving dates, periods of employment, and/or the nature of the work.

❹ Place a reasonable, fair value for the past or future services. If, for example, you issue $5,000 in shares for two hours of work, other shareholders are most likely being cheated and may well have good cause to file a lawsuit. To avoid this possibility, the invoice or bill for past services should reflect a transparently fair hourly or project cost.

To value future services (assuming they constitute legal payment for the issuance of shares in your state), it's a good idea to use an employment agreement.

TIP

Attach invoices or bills if available. It can be a good idea to attach to this resolution invoices or bills for past services. This detail can prevent future problems should other shareholders later question the nature, extent, and worth of the property transferred as payment for shares. If this eventuality is highly unlikely (as with very small corporations where everyone knows one another well), you can safely skip it.

Sale and Issuance of Shares for Services

After discussion by the board of directors, it was

     RESOLVED, that this corporation shall sell and issue shares of its stock ___*[if appropriate, add*___

"*without par value*" *or* "*with a stated par value of $ (amount)*"] ❶ _____ in payment of services or labor

["*done*" *or* "*to be done*"] ❷ _____ for the corporation, as follows:

Name	No. Shares	Description of Services ❸	Value of Services ❹
_____	_____	_____	$_____
_____	_____	_____	$_____

     RESOLVED FURTHER, that the board of directors determines that the fair value of such services or labor

["*done*" *or* "*to be done*"] _____ for this corporation in monetary terms is the amount(s) shown above.

     RESOLVED FURTHER, that the officers of this corporation are directed to execute documents and take other actions necessary to sell and issue the shares listed above.

Resolution to Issue Stock in Exchange for Assets of a Business

Often, when business owners incorporate an existing business, they transfer the assets and liabilities of their unincorporated business (partnership or sole proprietorship) to their corporation in return for shares. Normally, the shareholders of the new corporation get a portion of the initial shares that equals their percentage interest in the unincorporated business.

CD-ROM

Fill out the resolution titled Sale and Issuance of Capital Stock for Assets and Liabilities of a Business as you follow the sample and special instructions below. The tear-out version is contained in Appendix C.

Special Instructions

❶ Attach a schedule of assets and liabilities to be transferred to the corporation (a balance sheet) to the resolution. Your tax adviser can help you prepare this statement. You also may wish to consult your adviser to place a value on the business as discussed in special instruction ❸, below.

❷ See special instruction ❷ to the basic stock issuance resolution presented in "Basic Stock Issuance Resolution," above, for help in filling in these par/no-par blanks.

❸ This valuation figure should equal the total of the separate values listed for each shareholder in this resolution. If, for example, you issue $75,000 worth of shares to all shareholders, the total value of the business should equal this amount.

Valuation of private businesses can involve complicated and subjective computations and estimates. Your accountant can help you determine the best formula (book value, net asset value, fair market value) to use for valuing business assets.

RESOURCE

Resource for valuing a business. An excellent resource in this area is *The Small Business Valuation Book*, by Tuller (Bob Adams, Inc.). It provides discussions and examples of various valuation methods, as well as sound, realistic advice.

Don't worry too much over a valuation figure if you don't have outside shareholders. The absolute amount of this valuation figure is not critical if the only corporate shareholders after the transfer are the prior business owners. Regardless of the value arrived at, each will receive a portion of the shares that equals his or her ownership interest in the business. It is the percentage of share ownership that matters in this instance, not the absolute dollar amount used to value the unincorporated business.

EXAMPLE:

Gregory and Miya transfer the assets of their equally owned unincorporated pet shop, Hamster Haven, to their new corporation, Hamster Haven, Inc. Each receives 50% of the shares in the corporation, regardless of the value placed on the assets of the prior business.

Of course, the determination of value of transferred business assets takes on importance if the corporation has other shareholders who will not receive a proportionate amount of the shares issued in exchange for the business to the corporation.

EXAMPLE:

If Gregory and Miya add a third owner, who pays $50,000 for shares, the third shareholder will have a stake in the outcome of the business valuation. Now, if George and Miya inflate the value of their business, they will receive a disproportionate number of shares relative to the third shareholder's cash investment, which would risk future arguments and possibly a lawsuit.

❹ Many states have enacted bulk sales laws that require the publication and filing of a notice of sale when the bulk of the assets of a business are sold to another person or entity. This filing, intended to protect creditors of a business that is sold to others, is normally a formality when a sole proprietor or partners transfer the assets of an existing business to a corporation. This is so because the existing creditors can still easily find and go after the previous business owners, who are still personally liable for the prior business's debts. Your local legal newspaper (or any newspaper that prints legal notices) should have information on bulk sale publication requirements and be able to perform this standard formality for your corporation for a small fee if it is required.

TIP

Another approach is to use a bill of sale. Below, we present a bill of sale form that you can use to document the terms of a sale of an existing business to your new corporation. If you prepare a bill of sale, you can avoid preparing a separate statement of assets and liabilities now—you will prepare one later and attach it to your bill of sale. If you decide to prepare a bill of sale, simply change the language of the first paragraph in the resolution as follows—the changed text is italicized:

"The chairperson announced that the following persons have offered to transfer to this corporation the assets and liabilities of a business, *according to the terms of the bill of sale to be entered into by the corporation and the prior business owners and attached to this resolution at the time of sale,* in return for the number of shares..."

Sale and Issuance of Capital Stock for Assets and Liabilities of a Business

The chairperson announced that the following persons have offered to transfer to this corporation the assets and liabilities of a business, listed in Schedule A attached to this resolution, ❶ in return for the number of shares _[if appropriate, add_ "without par value" _or_ "with a stated par value of $ (_amount_)"] ❷ _____ listed opposite each of their names:

Name	No. Shares	Description of Business Interest	Value of Business Interest
_____	_____	_____	$_____
_____	_____	_____	$_____

After discussion, it was

RESOLVED, that in the judgment of the board of directors of this corporation, the value of the business offered is $ _[fair value of business transferred]_ ❸ .

RESOLVED, that the officers of the corporation are authorized to accept the offer on behalf of this corporation, and it was further

RESOLVED, that the officers execute and deliver to each offerer a certificate representing the number of shares of stock listed opposite each of their names above, and take all other action necessary to purchase the business and transfer title of the business to this corporation. The officers are further directed to sell and issue shares to the offerers in return for the transfer of the business according to the terms of this resolution. ❹

Supporting Documentation—Bill of Sale

You can use this basic bill of sale form to document the terms of a sale of the assets and liabilities of an unincorporated business to your corporation. As mentioned, documentation of this sort can come in handy in case a shareholder later questions the terms or fairness of the sale.

CD-ROM

Fill out the form titled Bill of Sale and Agreement as you follow the sample and special instructions below. The tear-out version is contained in Appendix C.

Special Instructions

❶ Insert the names of the unincorporated business owner(s).

❷ Show the name of your corporation.

❸ Enter the total number of shares to be issued to the owners of the unincorporated business in return for their transfer of the business to the corporation. If a one-person business is being incorporated, all shares will be issued to the prior business owner. If multiple owners are involved, each will normally receive a percentage of the shares that equals his or her percentage interest in the unincorporated business—for example, a 10% partner will receive 100 of 1,000 newly issued shares; a 90% partner will receive 900.

EXAMPLE:

If Patricia and Kathleen will each receive 2,000 shares in return for their respective half-interests in their preexisting 50/50 partnership (which they are now transferring to their corporation), they would indicate 4,000 shares as the total here.

❹ Attach a balance sheet showing the assets and liabilities of the prior business to be transferred to the corporation.

❺ List any assets of the prior business that are not being transferred to the corporation. For example, the transferors may wish to continue to own real property used by the unincorporated business, leasing rather than selling it to the corporation.

❻ Indicate the name and address of the unincorporated business being transferred to the corporation.

❼ This paragraph indicates that your corporation will assume the liabilities of the prior business. In the blank, list any liabilities of the prior business that will not be assumed by your corporation. A complete list of the current liabilities of the business should be reflected on the balance sheet attached to your bill of sale.

❽ This paragraph states that your corporation is appointed to collect for itself any debts and obligations (accounts receivable) owed to the prior business that are being transferred to the corporation.

❾ The business owners of the unincorporated business and the corporate officers should date and sign the bill of sale on the date the assets are formally transferred to the corporation in return for shares.

Place a copy of the bill of sale, balance sheet, and minutes of meeting or written consent form showing the board's approval of the issuance of shares in your corporate records book.

Bill of Sale and Agreement

This is an agreement between _[name(s) of prior business owner(s)]_ ❶ , referred to below as "transferor(s),"

and _____ [name of corporation] ❷ _____ , referred to below as "the corporation."

In return for the issuance of _[number of shares]_ ❸ shares of stock of the corporation, transferor(s)

sell(s), assign(s), and transfer(s) to the corporation all right, title, and interest in the following property:

All the tangible assets listed on the balance sheet attached to this Bill of Sale, ❹ and all stock in trade,

goodwill, leasehold interests, trade names, and other intangible assets except _[list any nontransferred assets]_ ❺

of _____ [name and address of unincorporated business] ❻ _____ .

In return for the transfer of the above property to the corporation, the corporation agrees to assume, pay, and

discharge all debts, duties, and obligations that appear on the date of this agreement on the books and owed on

account of said business and as reflected on the attached balance sheet except _[list any unassumed liabilities]_ ❼ .

The corporation agrees to indemnify and hold the transferor(s) of said business and their property free from any

liability for any such debt, duty, or obligation, and from any suits, actions, or legal proceedings brought to enforce or

collect any such debt, duty, or obligation.

The transferor(s) hereby appoint(s) the corporation as representative to demand, receive, and collect for

itself any and all debts and obligations now owing to said business and hereby assumed by the corporation. The

transferor(s) further authorize(s) the corporation to do all things allowed by law to recover and collect any such

debts and obligations and to use the name(s) of the transferor(s) in such manner as it considers necessary for the

collection and recovery of such debts and obligations. ❽

Date: _____ ❾

Signature(s) of prior business owner(s):

_____ [signature of prior business owner] _____

_____ [typed or printed name] _____ , Transferor

_____ [signature of prior business owner] _____

_____ [typed or printed name] _____ , Transferor

Date: _____

_____ [name of corporation] _____ , Corporation

_____ [signature of corporate officer] _____

_____ [typed or printed name] _____ , President

_____ [signature of corporate officer] _____

_____ [typed or printed name] _____ , Treasurer

Resolution for Stock Issuance in Exchange for Assignment of Trademark, Service Mark, Patent, or Copyright

If a business was in operation before incorporation, the owners may have established and registered a copyright, patent, trademark, or service mark in connection with the sale of products or services of the business. For some small businesses, particularly those in the software or technical development business, a copyright or patent may be their only significant asset. When the owners of the prior business incorporate, they sometimes transfer the copyright or patent to the new corporation in exchange for shares.

RESOURCE

Intellectual property resources. See the following Nolo titles for additional information on each of these specialized areas of intellectual property law:

- *Trademark: Legal Care for Your Business & Product Name,* by Steve Elias and Richard Stim

- *Patent It Yourself,* by David Pressman

- *The Copyright Handbook,* by Stephen Fishman

- *Legal Guide to Web & Software Development,* by Stephen Fishman, and

- *Patent, Copyright & Trademark,* by Richard Stim.

Assets of this sort are intangible (a legal term for nonphysical assets), and their value is often speculative at best. Nonetheless, it is legal and appropriate to issue shares to the programmer of a software product, the creator of an invention, or the owner of a trademark or service mark if the rights to these assets are assigned (transferred) to the corporation.

CD-ROM

Fill out the resolution titled Issuance of Shares in Exchange for Assignment of Trademark, Service Mark, Patent, or Copyright as you follow the sample and special instructions below. The tear-out version is contained in Appendix C.

Special Instructions

❶ See special instruction ❷ to the basic stock issuance resolution, above, for help in filling in these par/no-par blanks.

❷ Identify the patent, trademark, service mark, or copyright by reference to the number assigned by the federal U.S. Copyright Office or U.S. Patent and Trademark Office, for example, "U.S. Copyright # ___[number]___, issued ___[date]___."

❸ To avoid shortchanging other shareholders who contribute cash or other types of tangible property, pick a fair (conservative) value for the copyright, patent, trademark, or service mark being transferred to the corporation. You may think the property worth a lot, but other shareholders may not agree.

One way to avoid conflict, particularly if you think a patent or other intellectual property is valuable, is to obtain an appraisal from a reputable, knowledgeable source—someone who has experience with valuing products and property in your field of operation (software, manufacturing processes, solar energy, or other area). Another way is to have your shareholders expressly consent to this resolution.

Issuance of Shares in Exchange for Assignment of Trademark, Service Mark, Patent, or Copyright

The chairperson announced that _[name(s) of patent, trademark, or copyright holder(s)]_ offered to assign

to the corporation all of his/her/their rights to a ___ ["patent," "trademark," "service mark," _or_ "copyright"] ___

related to the following invention, trademark, service mark, or original work: _[describe the general_

subject matter of the patent or copyright or the name and nature of the trademark or service mark]

in return for the issuance of the following number of ___ [type of shares] ___ shares

[if appropriate, add "without par value" _or_ "with a stated par value of $ (amount)"] ❶ as follows:

Name	No. Shares	Identification of Patent, Trademark, Service Mark, or Copyright (date and reference number) ❷
_____	_____	_____
_____	_____	_____
_____	_____	_____

The board agreed that the acquisition of the above patent, trademark, service mark, or copyright was

in the best business interests of the corporation and that the fair value of these rights to the corporation is

$ _[fair market value of assigned patent, trademark, service mark, or copyright]_ ❸ .

The secretary is directed to see that the shares listed above are issued to ___ [names(s) of patent,

trademark, service mark, or copyright holder(s)] ___ after he/she/they execute(s) and deliver(s) to the

corporation all legal documents necessary to assign his/her/their rights in the above ___ ["patent"/

"copyright"/"trademark"/"service mark"] ___ to the corporation. The secretary also shall see to it that

a copy of a properly executed assignment of rights in the patent, trademark, service mark, or copyright

is forwarded for filing to the U.S. Patent and Trademark Office or the U.S. Copyright Office and to any

appropriate state offices or agencies.

Supporting Documentation—Assignment of Rights

Below is a simple, no-frills assignment form that may be used to transfer a person's full interest in a copyright, trademark, service mark, or patent to the corporation. A copy of this form should be filed with the U.S. Patent and Trademark Office or U.S. Copyright Office and with any state office where the trademark, service mark, copyright, or patent is also registered.

There is no need to mention the number of shares issued to the assignor (the person transferring the patent, trademark, service mark, or copyright) in this stand-alone assignment form.

CD-ROM

Fill out the form titled Assignment as you follow the sample and special instructions below. The tear-out version is contained in Appendix C.

Special Instructions

❶ This form should be dated and signed by the seller in the presence of a notary. Wait to sign this form when it is presented to a notary.

❷ We provide a general notary form, but technical language varies from state to state. It may be best to omit the notarization section and obtain a copy of your state's approved notarization language from a local notary.

Assignment

___[Name(s) and address(es) of patent, copyright, trademark, or service mark owner(s)]___, for consideration received, hereby assign(s) all right, title, and interest in [*"Patent," "Trademark," "Service Mark," or "Copyright"*]

No. ___[*registration number with U.S. Patent and Trademark Office or U.S Copyright Office*]___ dated ___[*date of registration*]___ to ___[*name and address of corporation*]___.

Date: _____ ❶

Signature(s) of assignor(s):

___[*signature(s) of assignor(s)*]_____

Name: ___[*typed or printed name(s)*]___, Assignor

Notarization ❷

State of _____)

County of _____)

On ___[*date*]___, 20___ before me personally appeared

___[*name(s) of assignor(s)*]___, the person(s) who signed this instrument and acknowledged that he/she/they is/are the person(s) who signed the instrument on his/her/their own behalf.

_____, Notary Public

NOTARY SEAL

Resolution to Issue Stock in Exchange for Cash and Promissory Note

The board may decide to approve the issuance of shares in return for part cash and a promise by the shareholder to pay the balance of the share purchase price over a period of time. To do this, your state must allow the issuance of shares in return for a promissory note; check your bylaws or state business corporation laws to be sure.

EXAMPLE:

Florence wants to purchase an additional 1,000 shares in her corporation. The shares have a current book value of $6 per share, but Florence only has $2,000 cash on hand. Her state's (Texas) business corporation laws allow shares to be issued in return for promissory notes, so she decides to buy the shares with a $2,000 cash payment and execute a promissory note for the balance of $4,000. The note may have any commercially reasonable terms; Florence and the board decide that a demand loan carrying a competitive interest rate of 8% is the best way to go.

TIP

Using promissory notes. Some states allow for stock to be issued in return for a promissory note; but other requirements may apply. For example, in California, a promissory note to pay for shares must be secured by property (collateral) other than the shares themselves. Check your bylaws to find out the requirements.

CD-ROM

Fill out the resolution titled Issuance of Shares in Return for Cash and Promissory Note as you follow the sample and special instructions provided. The tear-out version is contained in Appendix C.

Special Instructions

❶ See special instruction ❷ to the basic stock issuance resolution presented above for help in filling in these par/no-par blanks.

❷ This resolution provides for an up-front cash payment, with the balance financed by a promissory note signed by the shareholder.

❸ This resolution provides for the issuance of shares partially in exchange for a promissory note that is secured by the shares themselves. If the shareholder defaults on the note, the shares can be attached and seized in partial satisfaction of the debt. Some states that allow the issuance of shares in exchange for promissory notes say that the note must be secured by the pledge of assets other than the shares themselves. Again, check your bylaws or business corporation laws to see if this transaction is allowable in your state before using this resolution. (See our discussion of legal research in Chapter 20.)

❹ Make sure you attach the completed promissory note to the resolution. For samples, as well as instruction on selecting and using the shareholder promissory notes included with this book, see Chapter 15.

Issuance of Shares in Return for Cash
and Promissory Note

After discussion, it was agreed that the treasurer of the corporation is instructed to sell and issue
_____[number]_____ of _____[type of shares]_____ shares _____[if appropriate, add "without par value"_____
_or_ "with a stated par value of $ (amount)" ❶ to _____[name of shareholder]_____ for a purchase price of
$_____[total purchase price for shares]_____ , to be paid as follows: a cash payment of $____[cash payment]_ ❷
prior to the issuance of the shares, with the remaining balance of $ [balance of purchase price to be financed]
to be paid according to the terms of a promissory note executed by _____[name of shareholder]_____ ,
secured by a pledge of the stock purchased, ❸ with interest at [interest rate charged]_____ % per annum. ❹

Lawyers, Tax Specialists, and Legal Research

Much of the work in holding corporate meetings and documenting decisions is routine. Any knowledgeable and motivated businessperson can competently do the work himself or herself. But there's no way around it—from time to time you are bound to need help from outside sources. Some corporate decisions involve complex areas of law or taxation. Others involve a mix of business and legal savvy and are likely to be best made with the input of an experienced small business lawyer.

As we have discussed earlier, you may wish to turn to a lawyer for help in drafting resolutions to approve special items of business approved at meetings or with written consents of your directors and shareholders. And, of course, there will be important legal consequences associated with ongoing corporate decisions that may require input from an experienced legal professional (our instructions to the resolutions included with this book include discussions of the basic legal and tax effect of many items of ongoing corporate business— but you may want or need more information anyway). Obviously, one good way to learn more about any legal decision or form is to read up on these areas on the Internet or in a law or business library. Or you can decide, as many busy businesspeople do, to pay a lawyer, accountant, or financial adviser (such as a pension plan specialist, bank loan officer, or financial investment adviser) to check your conclusions about tricky legal areas and the completion of legal forms. In the sections below, we provide a few tips to help you in your search for competent expert information, assistance, and advice.

How to Find the Right Lawyer

Most small businesses can't afford to put a lawyer on retainer. Even when consulted on an issue-by-issue basis, lawyers' fees mount up fast—way too fast in most instances for legal advice to be affordable except for the most pressing problems. Just as with individuals, more and more small businesses are trying to at least partially close this legal affordability gap by doing as much of their own legal form preparation as possible. Often a knowledgeable self-helper can sensibly accomplish the whole task. Other times, it makes sense to briefly consult with a lawyer at an interim stage, or have the paperwork reviewed upon completion.

You already have taken one positive step in the direction of making your legal life affordable by deciding to use the forms in this book to prepare standard corporate minutes and written consent forms. Depending on the size of your business and the complexity of your legal needs, your next step is likely to be to find a cooperative lawyer who will help you consider important legal decisions—such as the approval of stock buy-back provisions, employment contracts, or pension plan and fringe benefit packages—and review or draft specific resolutions you will insert in your minutes to approve them.

You obviously don't want a lawyer who is programmed to try and take over all your legal decision making and form drafting while running up billable hours as fast as possible. Instead, you need what we call a *legal coach,* someone who is willing to work with you—not just *for* you. Under this model, the lawyer works to help you take care of many routine legal matters yourself, also being available to consult on more complicated legal issues as the need arises. Over time, your legal coach makes a decent, but not extravagant, living helping you—and others—help themselves.

TIP

You don't need a big-time corporate lawyer. There is a big lawyer surplus these days, and many newer lawyers, especially, are open to nontraditional business arrangements. Look for a lawyer with some small business experience, preferably in your field or area of operations. For the most part, you don't want a lawyer who works with big corporations. Not only will this person deal with issues that are far from your concerns, but he or she is almost sure to charge too much.

Don't Ask a Business Lawyer for Tax Advice

When it comes to corporate decisions that have tax implications, such as the type and number of shares to issue, the best share buy-sell provisions to adopt, or the most advantageous employee benefit plan to consider, accountants often have a better grasp of the issues than lawyers. And an added bonus is that although tax advice doesn't come cheap, accountants often charge less than lawyers.

Look and Ask Around

When you go looking for a lawyer, talk to people in your community who own or operate businesses you respect. Ask them about their lawyer and what they think of that person's work. If you talk to half a dozen business people, chances are you'll come away with several good leads. Other people, such as your banker, accountant, insurance agent, or real estate broker, may be able to provide the names of lawyers they trust to help them with business matters. Friends, relatives, and business associates within your own company may also have names of possible lawyers.

Lawyer referral services operated by bar associations are usually not that helpful. Often, these simply provide the names of lawyers who have signed on to the service, without independently researching the skills or expertise the lawyer claims to have. What about looking for a lawyer online? Obviously, many lawyers have their own websites, and there are a number of online lawyer directories. Look for sites that do two things:

- **Provide in-depth biographical information about a lawyer.** You want to know where the lawyer went to school, how long he or she has been in practice, the lawyer's specialties, and whether the lawyer has published articles or books on small business law or is a member of relevant trade organizations.

- **Provide helpful information about how a lawyer likes to practice.** For example, if a lawyer's biographical information states that he or she enjoys helping small business people understand the legal information they need to actively participate in solving their own legal problems, you may wish to set up an appointment.

RESOURCE

Check out Nolo's lawyer directory. Nolo maintains a lawyer directory on its website, www. nolo.com, which provides quite detailed profiles of listed lawyers. Although the directory doesn't yet cover the whole country, you can check whether there are lawyers listed in your area.

TIP

Let your legal coach refer you to experts when necessary. What if you have a very technical legal question? Should you start by seeking out a legal specialist? For starters, the answer is probably no. First, find a good business lawyer to act as your coach. Then rely on this person to suggest specialized materials or experts as the need arises.

Talk to the Lawyer Ahead of Time

After you get the names of several good prospects, don't wait until two days before an important corporate meeting or until a legal problem arises before contacting a lawyer. Once enmeshed in a crisis, you may not have time to find a lawyer who will work with you at affordable rates. Chances are you'll wind up settling for the first person available at a moment's notice—almost a guarantee you'll pay too much for poor service.

When you call a lawyer, announce your intentions in advance—that you are looking for someone who is willing to review your papers from time to time, point you in the right direction as the need arises, serve as a legal advisor as circumstances dictate, and tackle particular legal problems if necessary. In exchange for this, let the lawyer know you are willing to pay promptly and fairly. If the lawyer seems agreeable to this arrangement, ask to come in to meet for a half hour or so. Although many lawyers will not charge you for this introductory appointment, it's often a good idea to offer to pay for it. You want to establish that while you are looking for someone to help you help yourself, you are not looking for a free ride.

At the interview, reemphasize that you are looking for a nontraditional legal coach relationship. Many lawyers will find this unappealing—for example, saying they don't feel comfortable reviewing documents you have drafted using self-help materials. If so, thank the person for being frank and keep interviewing other lawyers. You'll also want to discuss other important issues in this initial interview, such as the lawyer's customary charges for services, as explained further below.

Pay particular attention to the rapport between you and your lawyer. Remember—you are looking for a legal coach who will work with you. Trust your instincts and seek a lawyer whose personality and business sense are compatible with your own.

Set the Extent and Cost of Services in Advance

When you hire a lawyer, get a clear understanding about how fees will be computed. For example, if you call the lawyer from time to time for general advice or to be steered to a good information source, how will you be billed? Some lawyers bill a flat amount for a call or a conference; others bill to the nearest six-, ten-, or twenty-minute interval. Whatever the lawyer's system, you need to understand it.

Especially at the beginning of your relationship, when you bring a big job to a lawyer, ask specifically about what it will cost. If you feel it's too much, don't hesitate to negotiate; perhaps you can do some of the routine work yourself, thus reducing the fee.

It's a good idea to get all fee arrangements—especially those for good-sized jobs—in writing. In several states, fee agreements between lawyers and clients must be in writing if the expected fee is $1,000 or more, or is contingent on the outcome of a lawsuit. But whether required or not, it's a good idea to get it in writing.

 TIP

Use nonlawyer professionals to cut down on legal costs. Often, nonlawyer professionals perform some tasks better and at less cost than lawyers. For example, look to management consultants for strategic business planning, real estate brokers or appraisers for valuation of properties, brokerage houses for small public or private placements of shares, financial planners for investment advice, accountants for preparation of financial proposals, insurance agents for advice on insurance protection, independent paralegals for routine corporate resolution or form drafting, and CPAs

How Lawyers Charge for Legal Services

There are no across-the-board arrangements on how lawyers' fees are to be charged. Expect to be charged by one of the following methods:

- **By the hour.** In most parts of the United States, you can get competent services for your small business for $150 to $250 an hour. Newer attorneys still in the process of building a practice may be available for paperwork review, legal research, and other types of legal work at lower rates.

- **Flat fee for a specific job.** Under this arrangement, you pay the agreed-upon amount for a given project, regardless of how much or how little time the lawyer spends. Particularly when you first begin working with a lawyer and are worried about hourly costs getting out of control, negotiating a flat fee for a specific job can make sense. For example, the lawyer may draw a real estate purchase agreement for $300, or review and finalize your share buy-sell provisions for $500.

- **Contingent fee based upon settlement amounts or winnings.** This type of fee typically occurs in personal injury, product liability, fraud, and discrimination type cases, where a lawsuit will likely be filed. The lawyer gets a percentage of the recovery (often 33%–40%) if you win and nothing if you lose. Since most small business legal needs involve advice and help with drafting paperwork, a contingency fee approach doesn't normally make sense. However, if your business becomes involved in a personal injury claim or lawsuit involving fraud, unfair competition, or the infringement of a patent or copyright, you may want to explore the possibility of a contingency fee approach.

- **Retainer.** Some corporations can afford to pay relatively modest amounts, perhaps $1,000 to $2,000 a year, to keep a business lawyer on retainer for ongoing phone or in-person consultations, routine premeeting minutes review, or resolution preparation and other business matters during the year. Of course, your retainer won't cover a full-blown legal crisis, but it can help you take care of ongoing minutes and other legal paperwork (for example, contract or special real estate paperwork) when you need a hand.

for the preparation of tax returns. Each of these matters is likely to have a legal aspect, and you may eventually want to consult your lawyer; but normally you won't need to until you've gathered information on your own.

Confront Any Problems Head-On

If you have any questions about a lawyer's bill or the quality of his or her services, speak up. Buying legal help should be just like purchasing any other consumer service—if you are dissatisfied, seek a reduction in your bill or make it clear that the work needs to be redone properly (a better buy-sell agreement, a more comprehensive lease, and so on). If the lawyer runs a decent business, he or she will promptly and positively deal with your concerns. If you don't get an acceptable response, find another lawyer pronto. If you switch lawyers, you are entitled to get your important documents back from the first lawyer.

Even if you fire your lawyer, you may still feel wronged. If you can't get satisfaction from the lawyer, write to the client grievance office of your state bar association (with a copy to the lawyer, of course). Often, a phone call from this office to your lawyer will bring the desired results.

Finding the Right Tax Adviser

Many corporate resolutions and ongoing corporate decisions involve tax issues and advice (such as selecting a corporate tax year, approving tax-deductible fringe benefits, or charging an IRS-approved rate of interest on corporate loans). To make good decisions in these and other complicated areas may require the expert advice of a tax adviser. Depending on the issue before you, this adviser may be a certified public accountant, financial or investment advisor, corporate loan officer at a bank, pension plan specialist, or inside or outside bookkeeper trained in employment and corporate tax reporting and return requirements.

Whatever your arrangement, consider the same issues for finding, choosing, using, and resolving problems with a tax professional as those discussed above, for legal services. Shop around for someone recommended by small business owners you respect, or who is otherwise known to you as qualified for the task. Again, you may be able to take advantage of the lower rates offered by newer local practitioners or firms. Your tax person should be available over the phone to answer routine questions, or by mail or fax to handle paperwork and correspondence, with a minimum of formality or ritual. It is likely that you will spend much more time dealing with your tax adviser than your legal adviser, so be particularly attentive to the personal side of this relationship.

Tax issues are often cloudy and subject to a range of interpretations and strategies, so it is absolutely essential that you discuss and agree to the level of tax aggressiveness you expect from your adviser. Some small business owners want to live on the edge, saving every possible tax dollar, even at the risk that deductions and other tax practices will be challenged by the IRS or state tax agents. Others are willing to pay a bit more in taxes to gain an extra measure of peace of mind. Whatever your tax strategy, make sure you find a tax adviser who feels the same way you do, or is willing to defer to your more liberal or conservative tax tendencies.

As with legal issues that affect your business, it pays to learn as much as you can about corporate and employment taxation. Not only will you have to buy less help from professionals, but you'll be in a good position to make good financial and tax-planning decisions. IRS forms, business and law library publications, trade groups, and countless other sources provide accessible information on corporate tax issues. Your accountant or other tax adviser should be able to help you put your hands on good materials. Banks are an excellent source of financial advice, particularly if they will be corporate creditors—after all, they will have a stake in the success of your corporation. Further, the federal Small Business Administration (SBA) can prove to be an ideal source of financial and tax information and resources (as well as financing in some cases).

RESOURCE

Resources for tax and financial information. Following are just a few suggestions for finding additional tax and financial information relevant to running your corporation. If you want free copies of IRS publications, you can usually download them directly from the IRS website, www.irs.gov, but you can also pick them up at your local IRS office or order by phone; call the toll-free IRS forms and publications request telephone number, 800-TAX-FORM.

- Start by obtaining IRS Publication 509, *Tax Calendars*, prior to the beginning of each year. This pamphlet contains tax calendars showing the dates for corporate and employer filings during the year.

- You can find further information on withholding, depositing, reporting, and paying federal employment taxes in IRS Publication 15, Circular E, *Employer's Tax Guide*, and the Publication 15 Supplement. Also helpful are IRS Publication 542, *Tax Information on Corporations*, and IRS Publication 334, *Tax Guide for Small Business*.

- You'll find helpful information on accounting methods and bookkeeping procedures in IRS Publication 538, *Accounting Periods and Methods*, and IRS Publication 583, *Starting a Business and Keeping Records*.

- Other helpful sources of tax information include *Small-Time Operator*, by Bernard Kamaroff (Bell Springs Publishing), an excellent primer on business bookkeeping practices that contains ledgers and worksheets, as well as *Starting Your Business*, by Crouch (Allyear Tax Guides), an investor and business tax guide.

How to Do Your Own Legal Research

Law is information, not magic. If you can look up necessary information yourself, you need not purchase it from a lawyer—although if it involves important issues, you may wish to check your conclusions with a lawyer, or use one as a sounding board for your intended course of action.

Much of the research necessary to understand your state's business corporation law can be done without a lawyer by spending a few minutes in a local law or business library or on the Internet. We explain the few simple steps necessary to go online to find your state's business corporation law in Chapter 1. Even if you need to go to a lawyer for help in preparing a corporate resolution to insert in your corporate minutes or to discuss the legal ramifications of a proposed corporate transaction, you can give yourself a leg up on understanding the legal issues surrounding your paperwork by reading practice manuals prepared for lawyers and law students at law and business libraries.

How do you find a law library open to the public where you can read lawyer materials? In many states, you need to look only as far as your county courthouse or, failing that, your state capitol. In addition, publicly funded law schools generally permit the public to use their libraries, and some private law schools grant limited access to their libraries—sometimes for a modest user's fee. If you're lucky enough to have access to several law libraries, select one that has a reference librarian to assist you. Also look through the business or reference department of a major city or county public library. These often carry corporate statutes as well as books on corporate law and taxation useful to the small business owner.

In doing legal research for a corporation or other type of business, there are a number of sources for legal rules, procedures, and issues that you may wish to examine. Here are a few:

- **Business corporation act.** These state statutes should be your primary focus for finding the rules for operating your corporation, including holding meetings and obtaining the approval of directors and shareholders to ongoing legal, tax, business, and financial decisions. (See Chapter 1 and Appendix B for information on how to find your state's business corporation act and your state's corporate filing office website.)

- **Other state laws, such as securities, commercial, civil, labor, and revenue laws.** These and other laws govern the issuance and transfer of corporate shares; the content, approval, and enforcement of commercial

contracts; employment practices and procedures; corporate and employment tax
requirements; and other aspects of doing
business in your state. Depending on the
type of business you have, you may also
want to research statutes and regulations
dealing with other legal topics such as
environmental law, product liability, real
estate, copyrights, and so on.

- **Federal laws.** These include the tax laws and
procedures found in the Internal Revenue
Code and Treasury Regulations implementing these code sections; regulations dealing
with advertising, warranties, and other
consumer matters adopted by the Federal
Trade Commission; and equal opportunity
statutes such as Title VII of the Civil Rights
Act administered by the Justice Department
and Equal Employment Opportunities
Commission.

- **Administrative rules and regulations.** Issued
by federal and state administrative agencies
charged with implementing statutes, state
and federal statutes are often supplemented
with regulations that clarify the statute and
contain rules for an agency to follow in
implementing and enforcing the statute.
For example, most states have enacted
special administrative regulations under
their securities statutes that provide exemptions to stock issuance registration for
small corporations and contain rules for
corporations to follow and forms to file
to rely on these exemptions. These rules
allow corporations with a limited number

of shareholders to issues shares without
going to the time and expense of obtaining
a permit to issue shares from their state's
securities board.

- **Case law.** These are decisions of federal and
state courts interpreting statutes—and
sometimes making law, known as common
law, if the subject isn't covered by a statute.
As we mention in Chapter 1, annotated
state corporation codes contain not only the
statute itself but also invaluable references to
court cases interpreting and implementing
specific provisions of the state's business
corporation law.

- **Secondary sources.** Also important in
researching corporate and business law
are sources that provide background information on particular areas of law. One
example is this book. Others are commonly
found in the business, legal, or reference
section of your local bookstore.

TIP

Consider joining a trade group. As a
final recommendation to finding your own legal
information, we suggest joining and participating in
one or more trade groups related to your business.
These groups often track legislation in particular
areas of business and provide sample contracts and
other useful legal forms. Some also retain law firms
for trade association purposes that may be able to
refer you to competent local lawyers.

Resources From Nolo

Below are a few titles published by Nolo that we believe offer valuable information to the small business owner:

- *LLC or Corporation?*, by Anthony Mancuso. A thorough comparison of the legal and tax benefits of each type of business entity. If you're wondering whether to form an LLC or a corporation, this book is for you.

- *Form Your Own Limited Liability Company*, by Anthony Mancuso. This national title shows you how to form this business entity under each state's LLC law and the federal rules. If you don't need the formality of the corporate form but would like to have limited personal liability for business debts, this book is for you.

- *Deduct It!*, by Stephen Fishman. An invaluable resource for small business owners to make sure they take full advantage of the many tax deductions available to them.

- *Legal Guide for Starting and Running a Small Business*, by Fred S. Steingold. This book is an essential resource for every small business owner, whether you are starting out or established. Find out how to form a sole proprietorship, partnership, or corporation; negotiate a favorable lease; hire and fire employees; write contracts; and resolve business disputes.

- *The Employer's Legal Handbook*, by Fred S. Steingold. Employers need legal advice daily. Here's a comprehensive resource they can refer to over and over again for questions about hiring, firing, and everything in between. The only book that compiles all the basics of employment law in one place, it covers safe hiring practices, wages, hours, tips and commissions, employee benefits, taxes and liability, insurance, discrimination, sexual harassment, and termination.

- *Tax Savvy for Small Business*, by Frederick W. Daily. Gives business owners information they need about federal taxes and shows them how to make the best tax decisions for their business, maximize their profits, and stay out of trouble with the IRS.

- *How to Write a Business Plan*, by Mike McKeever. If you're thinking of starting a business or raising money to expand an existing one, this book will show you how to write the business plan and loan package necessary to finance your business and make it work. Includes up-to-date sources of financing.

- *Patent It Yourself*, by David Pressman. This state-of-the-art guide is a must for any inventor who wants a patent—from the patent search to the application. Patent attorney and former patent examiner Pressman covers use and licensing, successful marketing, and infringement.

- *A Legal Guide to Web & Software Development* (book with disk: dual PC/Mac format), by Stephen Fishman. A reference bible for people in the software industry, this book explores copyright, trade secrets and patent protection, employment agreements, working with independent contractors and employees, development and publishing agreements, and multimedia developments. Sample agreements and contracts are included on the disk.

How to Use the CD-ROM

The CD-ROM included with this book can be used with Windows computers. It installs files that use software programs that need to be on your computer already. It is not a stand-alone software program.

In accordance with U.S. copyright laws, the CD-ROM and its files are for your personal use only.

Please read this appendix and the Readme. htm file included on the CD-ROM for instructions on using the CD-ROM. For a list of files and their file names, see the end of this appendix.

Note to Macintosh users: This CD-ROM and its files should also work on Macintosh computers. Please note, however, that Nolo cannot provide technical support for non-Windows users.

Note to eBook users: You can access the CD-ROM files mentioned here from the bookmarked section of the eBook, located on the left-hand side.

How to View the README File

To view the "Readme.htm" file, insert the CD-ROM into your computer's CD-ROM drive and follow these instructions:

Windows XP and Vista

1. On your PC's desktop, double-click the **My Computer** icon.

2. Double-click the icon for the CD-ROM drive into which the CD-ROM was inserted.

3. Double-click the file "Readme.htm."

Macintosh

1. On your Mac desktop, double-click the icon for the CD-ROM that you inserted.

2. Double-click the file "Readme.htm."

Installing the Files Onto Your Computer

To work with the files on the CD-ROM, you first need to install them onto your hard disk. Here's how:

Windows XP and Vista

Follow the CD-ROM's instructions that appear on the screen.

If nothing happens when you insert the CD-ROM, then:

1. Double-click the **My Computer** icon.

2. Double-click the icon for the CD-ROM drive into which the CD-ROM was inserted.

3. Double-click the file "Setup.exe."

Macintosh

If the Corporate Records Forms CD window is not open, double-click the Corporate Records Forms CD icon. Then:

1. Select the Corporate Records Forms folder icon.

2. Drag and drop the folder icon onto your computer.

Where Are the Files Installed?

Windows

By default, all the files are installed to the Corporate Records Forms folder in the **Program Files** folder of your computer. A folder called Corporate Records Forms is added to the **Programs** folder of the **Start** menu.

Macintosh

All the files are located in the Corporate Records Forms folder.

Using the Word Processing Files to Create Documents

The CD-ROM includes word processing files that you can open, complete, print, and save with your word processing program. All word processing files come in rich text format and have the extension ".rtf." For example, the file for the Notice of Meeting discussed in Chapter 3 is on the file "Notice.rtf." RTF files can be read by most recent word processing programs including MS Word, Windows WordPad, and recent versions of WordPerfect.

The following are general instructions. Because each word processor uses different commands to open, format, save, and print documents, refer to your word processor's help file for specific instructions.

Do not call Nolo's technical support if you have questions on how to use your word processor or your computer.

Opening a File

You can open word processing files in any of the three following ways:

- Windows users can open a file by selecting its "shortcut."
  1. Click the Windows **Start** button.
  2. Open the **Programs** folder.
  3. Open the **Corporate Records Forms** folder.
  4. Open the RTF subfolder.
  5. Click the shortcut to the file you want to work with.

- Both Windows and Macintosh users can open a file by double-clicking it.
  1. Use **My Computer** or **Windows Explorer** (Windows XP or Vista) or the **Finder** (Macintosh) to go to the **Corporate Records Forms** folder.
  2. Double-click the file you want to open.

- Windows and Macintosh users can open a file from within their word processor.
  1. Open your word processor.
  2. Go to the **File** menu and choose the **Open** command. This opens a dialog box.
  3. Select the location and name of the file. (You will navigate to the version of the **Corporate Records Forms** folder that you've installed on your computer.)

Editing Your Document

Here are tips for working on your document.

Refer to the book's instructions and sample agreements for help.

Underlines indicate where to enter information, frequently including bracketed instructions. Delete the underlines and instructions before finishing your document.

Signature lines should appear on a page with at least some text from the document itself.

Editing Forms That Have Optional or Alternative Text

Some files have check boxes that appear before text. Check boxes indicate:

- Optional text that you can choose to include or exclude.
- Alternative text that you select to include, excluding the other alternatives.

If you are using the tear-out files in Appendix C, mark the appropriate box to make your choice.

When you are using the CD-ROM, we recommend doing the following:

Optional text

Delete optional text you do not want to include and keep that which you do. In either case, delete the check box and the italicized instructions. If you choose to delete an optional numbered clause, renumber the subsequent clauses after deleting it.

Alternative text

Delete the alternatives that you do not want to include first. Then delete the remaining check boxes, as well as the italicized instructions that you need to select one of the alternatives provided.

Printing Out the Document

Use your word processor's or text editor's **Print** command to print out your document.

Saving Your Document

Use the "Save As" command to save and rename your document. You will be unable to use the "Save" command because the files are "read-only." If you save the file without renaming it, the underlines that indicate where you need to enter your information will be lost, and you will be unable to create a new document with this file without recopying the original file from the CD-ROM.

Files on the CD-ROM

The following files are in rich text format (RTF):

File Name	Form Title
Notice and Minutes Forms	
MEETSUM.RTF	Meeting Summary Sheet
CALL.RTF	Call of Meeting
MEETLIST.RTF	Meeting Participant List
NOTICE.RTF	Notice of Meeting
ACKREC.RTF	Acknowledgment of Receipt of Notice of Meeting
PROXY.RTF	Proxy
MAILCERT.RTF	Certification of Mailing
SHARANNL.RTF	Minutes of the Annual Meeting of Shareholders
SHARSPCL.RTF	Minutes of Special Meeting of Shareholders
DIRANNL.RTF	Minutes of the Annual Meeting of Directors
DIRSPCL.RTF	Minutes of Special Meeting of Directors
WAIVER.RTF	Waiver of Notice of Meeting
APPROVE.RTF	Approval of Corporate Minutes
PAPERLET.RTF	Cover Letter for Approval of Minutes of Paper Meeting
CONSENT.RTF	Written Consent to Action Without Meeting
Chapter 9	**Standard Corporate Business Resolutions**
CH09.RTF	Authorization of Treasurer to Open and Use Accounts
	Authorization of Treasurer to Open and Use Specific Corporate Account(s)
	Authorization of Corporate Account and Designation of Authorized Signers
	Authorization of Rental of Safe Deposit Box
	Adoption of Assumed Name
	Board Approval of Proposed Contract
	Approval of Lease
	Purchase of Real Property
	Authorization of Sale of Real Property
	Delegation of Authority to Corporate Employee
	Director Ratification of Employee's Acts
	Board Ratification of Contract
	Rescission of Authority of Employee
	Shareholder Ratification of Decisions or Acts
	Certification of Board or Shareholder Action
	Affidavit of Corporate Decision Making
	Acknowledgment

Chapter 10	**Corporate Tax Resolutions**
CH10.RTF	S Corporation Tax Election
	S Corporation Shareholders' Agreement
	Accumulation of Corporate Earnings
	Qualification of Shares Under Internal Revenue Code Section 1244
	Approval of Independent Audit of Corporate Financial Records
	Approval of Corporate Tax Year
	Payment and Deduction of Organizational Expenses
Chapter 11	**Resolutions to Amend Corporate Articles and Bylaws**
CH11.RTF	Approval of Amendment to Articles of Incorporation
	Approval of Restatement of Articles of Incorporation
	Amendment of Articles Form
	Approval of Amendment of Bylaws
Chapter 12	**Corporate Hiring and Appointment Resolutions**
CH12.RTF	Approval of Hiring of Corporate Employee
	Approval of Bonuses and Salary Increases
	Shareholder Ratification of Employee Pay
	Approval of Independent Contractor Services
	Appointment of Corporate Officers
	Authorization of Payment for Attending Meetings
	Annual Director or Officer Stipend for Attendance at Meetings
	No Compensation for Attending Corporate Meetings
	Indemnification and Insurance for Directors and Officers
Chapter 13	**Director Conflict of Interest Resolutions**
CH13.RTF	Board Approval of Transaction Benefiting a Director
	Directors' Written Consent to Transaction Benefiting a Director
	Shareholder Approval of Transaction Benefiting a Director
	Shareholder Written Consent to Transaction Involving a Director
Chapter 14	**Resolutions for Loans to the Corporation**
CH14.RTF	Authorization of Loan at Specific Terms
	Authorization of Maximum Loan on General Terms
	Unlimited Authorization of Loans for Business Needs
	Authorization of Line of Credit
	Authorization of Line of Credit With Cap on Each Transaction
	Authorization of Loan Terms Secured by Corporate Property
	Resolution Approving Loan to Corporation
	Promissory Note: Installment Payments of Principal and Interest (Amortized Loan)
	Promissory Note: Installment Payments of Principal and Interest (Amortized Loan) Secured by Corporate Property

		Promissory Note: Installment Payments of Principal and Interest (Amortized Loan) With Balloon Payment
		Promissory Note: Periodic Payments of Interest With Lump Sum Principal Payment
		Promissory Note: Lump Sum Payment of Principal and Interest at Specified Date
		Promissory Note: Lump Sum Payment of Principal and Interest on Demand by Noteholder
		Promissory Note: Variable Schedule of Payments of Principal and Interest
Chapter 15		**Resolutions for Loans by the Corporation to Insiders**
CH15.RTF		Approval of Corporate Loan to Insider
		Promissory Note: Monthly Installment Payments of Principal and Interest (Amortized Loan)
		Promissory Note: Installment Payments of Principal and Interest (Amortized Loan) Secured by Property
		Promissory Note: Installment Payments of Principal and Interest (Amortized Loan) With Balloon Payment
		Promissory Note: Periodic Payments of Interest With Lump Sum Principal Payment
		Promissory Note: Lump Sum Payment of Principal and Interest at Specified Date
		Promissory Note: Lump Sum Payment of Principal and Interest on Demand by Noteholder
		Promissory Note: Variable Schedule of Payments of Principal and Interest
		Release of Promissory Note
Chapter 16		**Employee Fringe Benefits and Business Expense Reimbursement Resolutions**
CH16.RTF		Authorization of Group Health, Accident, or Disability Insurance for Employees
		Adoption of Self-Insured Medical Reimbursement Plan
		Purchase of Group Term Life Insurance
		Authorization of Employee Death Benefit
		Agreement Regarding Death Benefits
		Purchase or Lease of Company Car
		Authorization of Payment of Standard Mileage Allowance to Employees
		Business Meal Expense Allotment for Employees
		On-Premises Meals and Lodging for Employees
		Authorization of Corporate Credit and Charge Cards for Employees
		Reimbursement of Actual Travel and Entertainment Expenses to Employees Under Accountable Reimbursement Plan
		Reimbursement of Actual Travel and Entertainment Expenses to Employees Under Nonaccountable Reimbursement Plan
		Authorization of Per Diem Travel Allowance for Employees
		Board Approval of Stock Bonus or Stock Option Plan

Chapter 17	Corporate Retirement Plan Resolutions
CH17.RTF	Board of Directors' Adoption of Retirement Plan
	Board of Directors' Adoption of Profit-Sharing Plan
	Shareholder Ratification of Retirement Plan
Chapter 18	**Stock Dividend Resolutions**
CH18.RTF	Declaration of Cash Dividend
	Authorization of Cash Dividend Payable in Installments
	Declaration of Year-End Dividend
	Declaration of Regular and Extra Dividend
	Declaration of Accumulated Dividend to Preferred Shareholders
	Authorization of Property Dividend to Shareholders
Chapter 19	**Stock Issuance Resolutions**
CH19.RTF	Approval of the Issuance of Shares
	Sale and Issuance of Shares for Property
	Sale and Issuance of Shares for Indebtedness Canceled
	Sale and Issuance of Shares for Services
	Sale and Issuance of Capital Stock for Assets and Liabilities of a Business
	Bill of Sale and Agreement
	Issuance of Shares in Exchange for Assignment of Trademark, Service Mark, Patent, or Copyright
	Assignment
	Issuance of Shares in Return for Cash and Promissory Note

How to Locate State Corporate Filing Offices and State Laws Online

How to Find Your State's Websites for Corporate Filing and Tax Information

This section explains how you can locate your state's websites for the legal and tax rules for forming and operating your corporation. We show you how to locate state corporate offices and information online using other websites that have links for the 50 states' websites instead of providing individual Web page addresses for the individual states. One advantage of using these online links is that they are maintained and updated on a regular basis and are less likely to go out of date than links that are listed in an appendix and manually updated only with each edition of this book.

State Corporate Filing Office Website

This is the state office where you file articles of incorporation (or a similar document) to form a corporation. State filing office websites typically provide sample forms and other useful information about forming or operating a corporation in your state. Most states have sample forms that you can download or, in some cases, fill in and file online. Many of the state websites also contain links to your state's corporate tax office (for tax forms and information) and state employment, licensing, and other agencies. They also often have links to the state's business corporation act or other relevant state laws.

To find your state's business entity filing office website, go to www.statelocalgov.net. In the left pane, choose your state, then "SOS" (for secretary of state) on the pull-down menu in the "Select Topic" box for a list of links to state offices. From your state's secretary of state office, you might need to search the tabs and menus to find the filing or form information you need.

You can find a direct link to your state's filing office at the website of the National Association of Secretaries of State (NASS) at www.nass.org. Register on the site (for free), then select "Issues," then Business Services," then "Corporate Registration" in the left pane, then choose your state to go to the main page for your state's business entity filing office.

State Tax Office Website

This is the state office website where you can find state corporate (and individual) tax information and forms applicable in your state. Some states impose an annual corporate tax or fee.

To find you state's tax office website, go to the Federation of Tax Administrators website at www.taxadmin.org/fta/link/forms.html, then click on your state in the map to go to your state's tax agency website.

How to Find Your State's Business Corporations Act Online

To find your state's Business Corporation Act (BCA) or similarly titled corporation law, you can use any of the following methods:

- Check your state's corporate filing office website. Many states provide an online version of their business corporation act (or similarly titled corporation laws).

- Look up your state's corporations laws using Nolo's State Law Resources page at www.nolo.com/legal-research/state-law.html (under "Legal Research," then "State Law Resources").

- Type "<your state's name> Corporation Act" or "<your state's name> corporation laws" into your browser's search box. This usually leads to a link to your state's business corporation act.

- Visit a local law library, a law school library that is open to the public, or a large public library with a substantial business collection. Ask the research librarian for help looking up your state's business corporation act. ●

Corporate Minutes Forms

Corporate Tax Resolutions

Resolutions to Amend Corporate Articles and Bylaws

Corporate Hiring and Appointment Resolutions

Director Conflict of Interest Resolutions

Resolutions for Loans to the Corporation

Resolutions for Loans by the Corporation to Insiders

Employee Fringe Benefits and Business Expense Reimbursement Resolutions

Corporate Retirement Plan Resolutions

Stock Dividend Resolutions

Stock Issuance Resolutions

Meeting Summary Sheet

Name of Corporation:

_____

Year: 20_____

Type of Meeting: ☐ Annual/Regular or ☐ Special

Meeting of: ☐ Directors or ☐ Shareholders

Date: _____, 20_____ Time: _____

Place: _____

Meeting Called by: _____

Purpose: _____

_____

Committee or Other Reports or Presentations: _____

Other Reminders or Notes: _____

Notice Required: ☐ Written ☐ Verbal ☐ Not Required

Notice Must Be Given by Date: _____

Notice of Meeting Given to:

Name	Type of Notice*	Location or Phone Number	Date Notice Given	Date Acknowledged Receipt

*Types of Notice: written (mailed, hand-delivered); verbal (in person, telephone conversation, answering machine, voice mail); email; fax

Call of Meeting

To:

Secretary: _____

Corporation: _____

Corporation Address: _____

_____

The following person(s):

Name	Title	No. Shares
_____	_____	_____
_____	_____	_____
_____	_____	_____

authorized under provisions of the bylaws of _____,

hereby make(s) a call and request to hold a(n) _____ meeting

of the _____ of the corporation for the purpose(s) of:

_____

_____

_____

_____

_____.

The date and time of the meeting requested is: _____

_____.

The requested location for the meeting is _____

_____,

state of _____.

The secretary is requested to provide all proper notices as required by the bylaws of the corporation and any other necessary materials to all persons entitled to attend the meeting.

Date: _____

Signed: _____

Acknowledgment of Receipt of Notice of Meeting

I received notice of a(n) _____ meeting of the _____

_____ of _____ on _____

_____, 20____. The notice of meeting stated the date, time, place, and purpose of the

upcoming meeting.

    The notice of meeting was:

    ☐ received by fax, telephone number _____

    ☐ delivered orally to me in person

    ☐ delivered orally to me by phone call, telephone number _____

    ☐ left in a message on an answering machine or voice mail, telephone number _____

_____

    ☐ delivered by mail to _____

    ☐ delivered via email, email address: _____

    ☐ other: _____

_____

_____

_____

Dated: _____

Signed: _____

Printed Name: _____

Please return to:

Name: _____

Corporation: _____

Address: _____

Phone: _____ Fax: _____

Meeting Participant List

Name of Corporation:

_____

Type of Meeting: ☐ Annual/Regular or ☐ Special

Meeting of: ☐ Directors or ☐ Shareholders

Meeting Date: _____, 20_____

Meeting Participants *(list names in alphabetical order):*

Name: _____

Address: _____

_____ Telephone: _____

☐ Director:_____

☐ Shareholder: Number and Type of Shares: _____

☐ Officer: Title: _____

☐ Other (Position and Reason for Attendance): _____

Name: _____

Address: _____

_____ Telephone: _____

☐ Director

☐ Shareholder: Number and Type of Shares: _____

☐ Officer: Title: _____

☐ Other (Position and Reason for Attendance): _____

Name: _____

Address: _____

_____ Telephone: _____

☐ Director

☐ Shareholder: Number and Type of Shares: _____

☐ Officer: Title: _____

☐ Other (Position and Reason for Attendance): _____

Notice of Meeting of

_____

A(n) _____ meeting of the _____ of

_____ will be held at

_____,

state of _____, on _____, 20____ at ____:____ ___.M.

The purpose(s) of the meeting is/are as follows:

_____

_____

_____

_____

_____

_____

_____

_____

_____

_____

_____

_____.

If you are a shareholder and cannot attend the meeting and wish to designate another person to vote your shares for you, please deliver a signed proxy form to the secretary of the corporation before the meeting. Contact the secretary if you need help obtaining or preparing this form.

_____

Signature of Secretary

Name of Secretary: _____

Corporation: _____

Address: _____

Phone: _____ Fax: _____

Proxy

The undersigned shareholder of _____ authorizes

_____ to act as his/her proxy and to

represent and vote his/her shares at a(n) _____ meeting of

shareholders to be held at _____,

state of _____, on _____, 20____ at ____:____ __.M.

Dated: _____

Signature of Shareholder: _____

Printed Name of Shareholder: _____

Please return proxy by _____, 20_____ to:

Name: _____

Title: _____

Corporation: _____

Address: _____

City, State, Zip: _____

Fax: _____   Phone: _____

Certification of Mailing

I, the undersigned acting secretary of _____,

hereby certify that I caused notice of the _____ meeting of the

_____ of _____,

to be held on _____, 20____, to be deposited in the United States mail,

postage prepaid, on _____, 20____, addressed to the

_____ of the corporation at their most recent addresses as shown

☐ on the books of this corporation

☐ as follows:

_____

_____

_____

_____

_____

_____

_____

_____

_____

_____

_____

_____

_____

_____

_____

A true and correct copy of such notice is attached to this certificate.

Dated: _____

Signed: _____

Printed Name: _____

Minutes of the Annual Meeting of Shareholders of

_____

An annual meeting of the shareholders of the corporation was held on _____,

20_____ at _____:_____ __.M., at _____ , state of _____

_____, for the purpose of electing the directors of the corporation and for the

transaction of any other business that may properly come before the meeting, including _____

_____

_____.

_____ acted as chairperson, and

_____ acted as secretary of the meeting.

The chairperson called the meeting to order.

The secretary announced that the meeting was called by _____

_____.

The secretary announced that the meeting was held pursuant to notice, if and as required under
the bylaws of this corporation, or that notice had been waived by all shareholders entitled to receive
notice under the bylaws. Copies of any certifications of mailing of notice prepared by the secretary of the
corporation and any written waivers signed by shareholders entitled to receive notice of this meeting were
attached to these minutes by the secretary.

The secretary announced that an alphabetical list of the names and numbers of shares held by all
shareholders of the corporation was available and open to inspection by any person in attendance at the
meeting.

The secretary announced that there were present, in person or by proxy, representing a quorum of
the shareholders, the following shareholders, proxyholders, and shares:

Name   Number of Shares

_____   _____

_____   _____

_____   _____

_____   _____

_____   _____

_____   _____

Minutes of Special Meeting of Shareholders of

_____

A special meeting of the shareholders of the corporation was held on _____,

20_____ at _____:_____ ___.M., at _____,

state of _____, for the purpose(s) of _____

_____

_____

_____.

_____ acted as chairperson, and

_____ acted as secretary of the meeting.

    The chairperson called the meeting to order.

    The secretary announced that the meeting was called by _____

_____.

    The secretary announced that the meeting was held pursuant to notice, if and as required under the bylaws of this corporation, or that notice had been waived by all shareholders entitled to receive notice under the bylaws. Copies of any certificates of mailing of notice prepared by the secretary of the corporation and any written waivers signed by shareholders entitled to receive notice of this meeting were attached to these minutes by the secretary.

    The secretary announced that an alphabetical list of the names and numbers of shares held by all shareholders of the corporation was available and open to inspection by any person in attendance at the meeting.

    The secretary announced that there were present, in person or by proxy, representing a quorum of the shareholders, the following shareholders, proxyholders, and shares:

Name	Number of Shares
_____	_____
_____	_____
_____	_____
_____	_____

The secretary attached written proxy statements, executed by the appropriate shareholders, to these minutes for any shares listed above as held by a proxyholder.

The following persons were also present at the meeting:

Name   Title

_____   _____

_____   _____

_____   _____

_____   _____

_____   _____

The secretary announced that the minutes of the _____

meeting held on _____, 20_____

☐ had been distributed prior to

☐ were distributed at

☐ were read at

the meeting. After discussion, a vote was taken and the minutes of the meeting were approved by the shares in attendance.

The following annual and special reports were presented at the meeting by the following persons:

_____

_____

_____.

The chairperson announced that the next item of business was the nomination and election of the board of directors for another _____ term of office. The following nominations were made and seconded:

Name(s) of Nominee(s)

_____

_____

_____

_____

_____

The secretary attached written proxy statements, executed by the appropriate shareholders, to these minutes for any shares listed above as held by a proxyholder.

The following persons were also present at the meeting:

Name   Title

_____   _____

_____   _____

_____   _____

_____   _____

_____   _____

The secretary announced that the minutes of the _____

meeting held on _____, 20_____

☐ had been distributed prior to

☐ were distributed at

☐ were read at

the meeting. After discussion, a vote was taken and the minutes of the meeting were approved by the shares in attendance.

The following annual and special reports were presented at the meeting by the following persons:

_____

_____

_____

_____

_____

_____

_____

_____

_____

_____

_____

_____

_____

_____.

On motion duly made and carried by the affirmative vote of _____

shareholders in attendance at the meeting, the following resolutions were adopted by shareholders

entitled to vote at the meeting: _____

_____

_____

_____

_____

_____

_____

_____

_____

_____

_____

_____

_____

_____

_____

_____

_____

There being no further business to come before the meeting, it was adjourned on motion duly made and
carried.

_____

_____, Secretary

Minutes of the Annual Meeting of Directors of

_____

An annual meeting of the directors of the corporation was held on _____,

20_____ at ____:____ ___.M., at _____

___, state of _____, for the purpose of reviewing the prior year's business

and discussing corporate operations for the upcoming year, and for the transaction of any other business

that may properly come before the meeting, including:

_____

_____

_____

_____.

_____ acted as chairperson, and

_____ acted as secretary of the meeting.

The chairperson called the meeting to order.

The secretary announced that the meeting was called by _____

_____.

The secretary announced that the meeting was held pursuant to notice, if and as required

under the bylaws of this corporation, or that notice had been waived by all directors entitled to receive

notice under the bylaws. Copies of any certificates of mailing of notice prepared by the secretary of the

corporation and any written waivers signed by directors entitled to receive notice of this meeting were

attached to these minutes by the secretary.

The secretary announced that the following directors were present at the meeting:

Name of Director

_____   _____

_____

_____

_____

_____

_____

The above directors, having been elected to serve on the board for another _____ term by the shareholders at an annual meeting of shareholders held on _____, 20_____, accepted their positions on the board. The secretary then announced that the presence of these directors at the meeting represented a quorum of the board of directors as defined in the bylaws of this corporation.

The following persons were also present at the meeting:

Name   Title

_____   _____

_____   _____

_____   _____

_____   _____

_____   _____

The secretary announced that the minutes of the _____ meeting held on _____, 20_____

☐ had been distributed prior to

☐ were distributed at

☐ were read at

the meeting. After discussion, a vote was taken and the minutes of the meeting were approved by the directors in attendance.

The following reports were presented at the meeting by the following persons:

_____

_____

_____.

The chairperson announced that the next item of business was the appointment of the officers and of standing committee members of the corporation to another _____ term of office. After discussion, the following persons were appointed to serve in the following capacities as officers or committee members or in other roles in the service of the corporation for the upcoming year:

The secretary next took the votes of shareholders entitled to vote for the election of directors at the meeting, and, after counting the votes, announced that the following persons were elected to serve on the board of directors of this corporation:

Names of Board Members

_____

_____

_____

_____

_____

On motion duly made and carried by the affirmative vote of _____ shareholders in attendance at the meeting, the following resolutions were adopted by shareholders entitled to vote at the meeting: _____

_____

_____

_____

_____

_____

_____

_____

_____

_____

_____

_____

_____

_____

There being no further business to come before the meeting, it was adjourned on motion duly made and carried.

_____

_____, Secretary

Name   Title

_____   _____

_____   _____

_____   _____

_____   _____

The next item of business was the determination of compensation or fringe benefits to be paid or awarded for services rendered the corporation by employees and staff. After discussion, the following employee compensation amounts were approved by the board to be paid for the upcoming fiscal year to the following employees of the corporation:

Name   Type and Amount of
                                                  Compensation or Benefit

_____   _____

_____   _____

_____   _____

_____   _____

On motion duly made and carried by the affirmative vote of _____ directors in attendance at the meeting, the following resolutions were adopted by directors entitled to vote at the meeting:

_____

_____

_____

_____

There being no further business to come before the meeting, it was adjourned on motion duly made and carried.

_____

_____, Secretary

Minutes of Special Meeting of Directors of

_____

A special meeting of the directors of the corporation was held on _____,

20_____ at ____:____ __.M., at _____,

state of _____, for the purpose(s) of _____

_____

_____

_____.

_____ acted as chairperson, and

_____ acted as secretary of the meeting.

The chairperson called the meeting to order.

The secretary announced that the meeting was called by _____

_____.

The secretary announced that the meeting was held pursuant to notice, if and as required under the bylaws of this corporation, or that notice had been waived by all directors entitled to receive notice under the bylaws. Copies of any certificates of mailing of notice prepared by the secretary of the corporation and any written waivers signed by directors entitled to receive notice of this meeting were attached to these minutes by the secretary.

The secretary announced that the following directors were present at the meeting, representing a quorum of the board of directors:

Name of Director

_____

_____

_____

_____

_____

_____

The following persons were also present at the meeting:

Name   Title

_____   _____

_____   _____

_____   _____

_____   _____

_____   _____

The secretary announced that the minutes of the _____

meeting held on _____, 20_____

☐ had been distributed prior to

☐ were distributed at

☐ were read at

the meeting. After discussion, a vote was taken and the minutes of the meeting were approved by the directors in attendance.

The following reports were presented at the meeting by the following persons:

_____

_____

_____

_____

The secretary announced that the next item of business was the consideration of one or more formal resolutions for approval by the board. After introduction and discussion, and upon motion duly made and carried by the affirmative vote of _____ directors in attendance at the meeting, the following resolutions were adopted by directors entitled to vote at the meeting:

_____

_____

_____

There being no further business to come before the meeting, it was adjourned on motion duly made and carried.

_____

_____, Secretary

Waiver of Notice of Meeting of

_____

The undersigned _____ waive(s) notice of and consent(s) to the

holding of the _____ meeting of the

_____ of _____

held at _____,

state of _____, on _____, 20_____ at _____:_____ ___.M.,

for the purpose(s) of: _____

_____

_____

_____

_____

_____

_____

_____

_____

_____

_____

_____.

Dated: _____

Signature   Printed Name

_____   _____

_____   _____

_____   _____

_____   _____

_____   _____

Approval of Corporate Minutes of

_____

The undersigned _____ consent(s) to the minutes of the

_____ meeting of the _____

of _____

held at _____,

state of _____, on _____, 20____ at ____:____ __.M.,

attached to this form, and accept(s) the resolutions passed and decisions made at such meeting as valid

and binding acts of the _____ of the corporation.

Dated: _____

Signature   Printed Name

_____   _____

_____   _____

_____   _____

_____   _____

_____   _____

Cover Letter for Approval of Minutes of Paper Meeting

Date: _____

Name: _____

Mailing Address: _____

City, State, Zip: _____

Re: Approval of Minutes

Dear _____:

I am enclosing minutes of a meeting of the _____ of

_____ that show approval of one or more

specific resolutions. Each resolution contains the language of an item of business approved by the

_____.

Since these items were agreeable to the _____, we did not

hold a formal meeting to approve these decisions. We are now finalizing our corporate records and

preparing formal minutes that reflect prior corporate decisions.

To confirm that these minutes accurately reflect the past decisions reached by the _____

_____, please date and sign the enclosed Approval of Corporate Minutes form and

mail it to me at the address below. If you have corrections or additions to suggest, please contact me so

we can hold a meeting or make other arrangements for formalizing and documenting these changes.

Sincerely,

_____

Enclosures: Minutes and Approval of Corporate Minutes Form

Please return to:

Name: _____

Corporation: _____

Mailing Address: _____

City, State, Zip: _____

Phone: _____ Fax: _____

Written Consent to Action Without Meeting

The undersigned _____ of _____

hereby consent(s) as follows: _____

_____

_____

_____

_____

_____

_____

_____

_____

_____

_____

_____

_____

_____

_____

_____

_____

_____

_____

Dated: _____

Signature   Printed Name

_____   _____

_____   _____

_____   _____

_____   _____

Authorization of Treasurer to Open and Use Accounts

The treasurer of the corporation is authorized to select one or more banks, trust companies, brokerage companies, or other depositories, and to establish financial accounts in the name of this corporation. The treasurer and other persons designated by the treasurer are authorized to deposit corporate funds in these accounts. However, only the treasurer is authorized to withdraw funds from these accounts on behalf of the corporation.

The treasurer is further authorized to sign appropriate account authorization forms as may be required by financial institutions to establish and maintain corporate accounts. The treasurer shall submit a copy of any completed account authorization forms to the secretary of the corporation, who shall attach the forms to this resolution and place them in the corporate records book.

Authorization of Treasurer to Open and Use Specific Corporate Account(s)

The treasurer of this corporation is authorized to open the following account(s) in the name of the corporation with the following depositories:

Type of account: _____

Name, branch, and address of financial institution:

_____

_____

_____

Type of account: _____

Name, branch, and address of financial institution:

_____

_____

_____

The treasurer and other persons authorized by the treasurer shall deposit the funds of the corporation in this account. Funds may be withdrawn from this account only upon the signature of the treasurer.

The treasurer is authorized to complete and sign standard authorization forms for the purpose of establishing the account(s) according to the terms of this resolution. A copy of any completed account authorization form(s) shall be submitted by the treasurer to the secretary of the corporation, who shall attach the form(s) to this resolution and place them in the corporate records book.

Authorization of Corporate Account and
Designation of Authorized Signers

The treasurer of this corporation is authorized to open a _____

account in the name of the corporation with _____

_____.

Any officer, employee, or agent of this corporation is authorized to endorse checks, drafts, or other evidences of indebtedness made payable to this corporation, but only for the purpose of deposit.

All checks, drafts, and other instruments obligating this corporation to pay money shall be signed on behalf of this corporation by _____ of the following: _____

_____

_____

_____

_____

_____

_____

_____

_____

_____.

The above institution is authorized to honor and pay any and all checks and drafts of this corporation signed as provided herein.

The persons designated above are authorized to complete and sign standard account authorization forms, provided that the forms do not vary materially from the terms of this resolution. The treasurer shall submit a copy of any completed account authorization forms to the secretary of the corporation, who shall attach the forms to this resolution and place them in the corporate records book.

Authorization of Rental of Safe Deposit Box

The treasurer of the corporation is authorized to rent a safe deposit box in the name of the corporation with an appropriate bank, trust company, or other suitable financial institution, and to deposit in this box any securities, books, records, reports, or other material or property of the corporation that he or she decides is appropriate for storage and safekeeping in this box.

Adoption of Assumed Name

It was decided that the corporation should do business under a name that is different from the formal name of the corporation stated in its articles of incorporation. The assumed name selected for the corporation is _____.

The secretary of the corporation was instructed to register the assumed corporate name locally and/or with the secretary of state or similar state or local governmental offices as required by law.

Board Approval of Proposed Contract

The board was presented a proposed contract to be entered into between the corporation and

_____ for the purpose of _____

_____

_____

_____

_____ _____

_____.

together with the following attachments:

_____

_____

_____

_____

_____.

Next, a report on the proposed contract was given by_____

_____, who made the following major points and concluded with

the following recommendation: _____

_____

_____

_____

_____.

After discussion by the board, _____

_____

_____, it was decided that the transaction of the business covered by the

contract was in the best interests of the corporation, and the proposed contract and attachments were

approved by the board.

The _____ was instructed to execute the contract submitted

to the meeting in the name of and on behalf of the corporation, and to see to it that a copy of the

contract executed by all parties, together with all attachments, be placed in the corporate records of the

corporation.

Approval of Lease

A proposed lease agreement between _____ and

_____ for the premises known as

_____

_____

_____

was presented to the board for approval.

The lease covered a period of _____, with _____

rental payments of $_____.

After discussion, it was decided that the lease terms were commercially reasonable and fair to the corporation and that it was in the best interests of the corporation to enter into the lease.

The board approved the lease and all the terms contained in it, and the secretary of the corporation was instructed to see to it that the appropriate officers of the corporation execute the lease on behalf of the corporation and that a copy of the executed lease agreement be attached to this resolution and filed in the corporate records book.

Purchase of Real Property

The board discussed the purchase of real property commonly known as _____

_____

_____

_____.

     The president announced that the property had been offered to the corporation for sale by the owner at a price of $_____. After discussing the value of the property to the corporation and comparable prices for similar properties, it was agreed that the corporation should

_____

_____

_____

_____

_____

_____.

     It was also agreed that the corporation shall seek financing for the purchase of the property on the following terms:_____

_____

_____

_____

_____

_____

_____.

     The president was instructed to see to it that the appropriate corporate officers prepare all financial and legal documents necessary to submit the offer _____ to the seller and to seek financing for the purchase of the property according to the terms discussed and agreed to by the directors.

Authorization of Sale of Real Property

After discussion, the board agreed that the president of the corporation is authorized to contract to sell real property of the corporation commonly known as _____

_____

_____.

on the following general conditions and terms:

_____

_____

_____

_____

_____

_____

_____

_____

_____

_____

_____

_____.

The president of the corporation and any other officers of the corporation authorized by the president are empowered to execute all instruments on behalf of the corporation necessary to effectuate and record a sale of the above property according to the terms approved by the board in this resolution.

Delegation of Authority to Corporate Employee

After discussion, it was agreed that the following employee shall be granted authority to perform the tasks or transact business by and on behalf of the corporation, or to see to it that such tasks are performed for the corporation under his or her supervision as follows:

_____

_____

_____

_____

_____

_____

_____

_____

_____

_____.

The employee also shall be granted the power to perform any and all incidental tasks and transact incidental business necessary to accomplish the primary tasks and business described above.

Director Ratification of Employee's Acts

After discussion, it was agreed that the following acts, business, or transactions are hereby adopted, ratified, and approved as acts of the corporation and are accepted as having been done by, on behalf of, and in the best interests of the corporation:

_____

_____

_____

_____

_____

_____

_____

_____

_____

_____

_____

_____

_____

_____

_____

_____

_____

_____.

Board Ratification of Contract

After discussion, it was agreed that the contract dated _____ entered into between

_____ and _____ ,

in the name and on behalf of the corporation, for the purpose of

_____

_____

_____

_____

_____

_____

_____

_____

_____

_____

_____

_____

_____

_____

is hereby adopted, confirmed, and ratified, and is approved as being in the best interests of the

corporation and its business.

Rescission of Authority of Employee

After discussion, it was agreed that prior authority granted to _____

on _____ for the purpose of _____

_____

_____

_____

_____

_____

_____

_____

_____

_____

_____

_____

_____

_____

_____

_____

_____

was no longer necessary to the interests of the corporation and that any and all authority granted under

this prior approval of authority is hereby rescinded and no longer in effect.

Shareholder Ratification of Decisions or Acts

After discussion, it was agreed that the following decisions, acts, resolutions, and proceedings of the board of directors and/or employees of this corporation as specified below, are approved and affirmed by the shareholders of this corporation as necessary to the business of and in the best interest of this corporation:

_____

_____

_____

_____

_____

_____

_____

_____

_____

_____

_____

_____

_____

_____

_____

_____

_____

_____

Certification of Board or Shareholder Action

The undersigned, duly elected and acting _____ of

_____, certifies that the attached resolution was

adopted by the _____ as follows:

    [ ] at a duly held meeting at which a quorum was present, held on _____

    [ ] by written consent(s) dated on or after _____

and that it is a true and accurate copy of the resolution, and that the resolution has not been rescinded or modified as of the date of this certification.

Date: _____

Signed: _____

Name/Title: _____

Affidavit of Corporate Decision Making

STATE OF _____

COUNTY OF _____

Before me, a Notary Public in and for the above state and county, personally appeared

_____ who, being duly sworn,

says:

    1. That he/she is the duly elected and acting _____ of

_____, a _____ corporation.

    2. That the following is a true and correct copy of a resolution duly approved by the

_____ of the corporation, as follows:

    [ ] at a duly held meeting at which a quorum was present, held on _____,

    [ ] by a sufficient number of written consents dated on or after _____

    _____

    _____

    _____

    _____

    _____

    _____

    3. That the above resolution has not been rescinded or modified as of the date of this affidavit.

Signed: _____

Name/Title: _____

Sworn to and subscribed before me this _____ day of _____, 20___.

Notary Public: _____

My commission expires: _____

NOTARY SEAL

Acknowledgment

STATE OF _____

COUNTY OF _____

I hereby certify that on _____, before me, a Notary Public, personally

appeared _____, who acknowledged

himself/herself to be the _____ of _____ and

that he/she, having been authorized to do so, executed the above document for the purposes contained

therein by signing his/her name as _____ of

_____.

Notary Public: _____

My commission expires: _____

NOTARY SEAL

S Corporation Tax Election

The board of directors considered the advantages of electing S corporation tax status for the corporation under Section 1362 of the Internal Revenue Code. After discussion, which included a report from the treasurer that the corporation's accountant had been consulted and concurred with the board's decision, it was agreed that the corporation shall elect S corporation tax status with the IRS _____ _____.

It was further agreed that the treasurer of the corporation be delegated the task of preparing and filing IRS Form 2553 and any other required forms in a timely manner so that the S corporation tax election will be effective starting with the _____ tax year of the corporation. The treasurer was further instructed to have all shareholders and their spouses sign the shareholder consent portion of IRS Form 2553.

S Corporation Shareholders' Agreement

The undersigned shareholders and spouses of shareholders of _____
represent and agree as follows:

The board of directors has approved a resolution authorizing the corporation to elect S corporation
tax status with the IRS under Section 1362 of the Internal Revenue Code, to be effective for the corporate
tax year beginning _____.

To help preserve and maintain the effectiveness of this S corporation tax status, the undersigned
agree that they shall not transfer, sell, assign, convey, or otherwise dispose of their shares, or any interest in
these shares, if such disposition would result in the corporation no longer being eligible for S corporation
tax status with the IRS.

The undersigned further agree to sign any consent forms or other documents necessary to elect
and obtain S corporation tax status with the IRS in a timely matter as requested by the treasurer of the
corporation.

The undersigned further agree that, even if a proposed transfer or other disposition of shares does
not jeopardize the corporation's S corporation tax status, no such transfer or disposition shall take place
until the proposed shareholder and the proposed shareholder's spouse consent to the corporation's
S corporation tax status, and sign an agreement that contains substantially the same terms as this
agreement.

This agreement may be terminated by the consent of a majority of the outstanding shareholders of
this corporation. Any person who breaches this agreement shall be liable to the corporation, its officers,
directors, shareholders, spouses of shareholders, and any transferees of shareholders or their spouses, for
all losses, claims, damages, taxes, fines, penalties, and other liabilities resulting from the breach of this
agreement.

This agreement shall bind all parties, their successors, assigns, legal representatives, heirs, and
successors in interest. The undersigned shall ensure that any such successors and representatives shall
be given a copy of this agreement prior to, or at the same time as, the delivery of any share certificates
to them. A conspicuous legend shall be placed on all share certificates of the corporation indicating that
the shares are subject to restrictions on transferability and that the holder may obtain a copy of these
restrictions at any time from the secretary of the corporation.

Dated: _____

Signature	Printed Name
_____	_____
_____	_____
_____	_____
_____	_____

Accumulation of Corporate Earnings

After discussion, the board resolved that it was necessary to retain the following earnings in the corporation to provide for the following reasonably anticipated needs of the business:

_____

_____

_____

_____

_____

_____

_____

_____

_____

_____

_____.

The treasurer of the corporation reported that the corporation's accountant had been consulted and agreed that the above accumulations should qualify as reasonable needs of the business under Internal Revenue Code Section 537(a).

The above accumulations of corporate earnings were approved, and the treasurer was instructed to see to it that these accumulations of corporate earnings are made.

Qualification of Shares Under
Internal Revenue Code Section 1244

The board discussed the advisability of qualifying the shares of this corporation as Section 1244 stock as defined in Section 1244 of the Internal Revenue Code, and of operating the corporation so that it is a small business corporation as defined in that section.

It was agreed that the president and treasurer of the corporation are, subject to the requirements and restrictions of federal and state securities laws, authorized to sell and issue shares of stock in return for the receipt of an aggregate amount of money and other property, as a contribution to capital, and as paid-in surplus, which does not exceed $1,000,000.

It was also agreed that the sale and issuance of shares shall be conducted in compliance with Section 1244 so that the corporation and its shareholders may obtain the benefits of that section.

The above officers are directed to maintain such records pursuant to Section 1244 so that any shareholder who experiences a loss on the transfer of shares of stock of the corporation may determine whether he or she qualifies for ordinary loss deduction treatment on his or her individual income tax return.

Approval of Independent Audit of
Corporate Financial Records

After discussion, it was agreed by the board that the accounting firm of _____ _____ was selected to perform an independent audit of the financial records of the corporation for the _____ fiscal year and to prepare all necessary financial statements for the corporation as part of its independent audit.

The treasurer was instructed to work with the auditors to provide all records of corporate finances and transactions that may be requested by them, and to report to the board on the results of the audit upon its completion.

Approval of Corporate Tax Year

The chairperson informed the board that the next order of business was the selection of the corporation's tax year. After discussion and a report from the treasurer, which included advice obtained from the corporation's accountant, it was resolved that the accounting period of this corporation shall end on the _____ of each year.

Payment and Deduction of Organizational Expenses

The board considered the question of paying the expenses incurred in the formation of this corporation. A motion was made, seconded, and unanimously approved, and it was resolved that the president and treasurer of this corporation are authorized and empowered to pay all reasonable and proper expenses incurred in connection with the organization of the corporation, including, among others, filing, licensing, and attorney and accountant fees, and to reimburse any directors, officers, staff, or other persons who have made or do make any such disbursements for and on behalf of the corporation.

It was further resolved that the treasurer is authorized to elect to deduct and amortize the foregoing expenses, pursuant to, and to the extent permitted by, Section 248 of the Internal Revenue Code of 1986, as amended.

Approval of Amendment to Articles of Incorporation

RESOLVED, that Article _____ of the articles of incorporation be _____
as follows:

_____

_____

_____

_____

_____

_____

_____

_____

_____

_____

_____

_____

_____

_____.

Approval of Restatement of Articles of Incorporation

RESOLVED, that the articles of incorporation be amended and restated to read as follows:

_____

_____

_____

_____

_____

_____

_____

_____

_____

_____

_____

_____

_____

_____

_____

_____

_____.

Amendment of Articles Form

To: _____

Articles of Amendment

of

_____

One: The name of the corporation is _____.

Two: The following amendment to the articles of incorporation was approved by the board of

directors on _____ and was approved by the shareholders on

_____:

_____

_____

_____

_____

_____

_____

_____

_____.

Three: The number of shares required to approve the amendment was _____,

and the number of shares that voted to approve the amendment was _____.

Date: _____

By:

_____

_____, President

_____

_____, Secretary

Approval of Amendment of Bylaws

RESOLVED, that _____ of the bylaws of the corporation is

_____ as follows:

_____

_____

_____

_____

_____

_____

_____

_____

_____

_____

_____

_____

_____

_____

_____

_____

_____

_____.

Approval of Hiring of Corporate Employee

After discussion, the directors approved the hiring of _____ to

the position of _____ in the employ of the corporation.

It was agreed that this employment would be subject to the following terms and conditions and

would be compensated with the following amounts and benefits:

_____

_____

_____

_____

_____

_____

_____.

It was agreed that the above individual is particularly qualified for employment and entitled to the

compensation associated with this position with the corporation for the following reasons:

_____

_____

_____

_____

_____

_____

_____

_____.

Approval of Bonuses and Salary Increases

The board considered the question of salary increases and bonuses to employees of the corporation. After discussion, the board approved the following salary increases and bonuses, to be paid for the upcoming fiscal year to the following persons:

Name and Title

Salary or Bonus

_____ $_____

_____ $_____

_____ $_____

_____ $_____

_____ $_____

The above salary amounts or bonuses shall be paid as follows:

_____

_____

_____

_____

_____

_____

_____

_____

_____

_____

_____.

Shareholder Ratification of Employee Pay

After discussion, the following annual compensation, increase in annual compensation, or authorization of bonus amount(s), paid to the following corporate _____,
was ratified by the shareholders of this corporation:

Name and Title   Salary or Bonus

_____ $_____

_____ $_____

_____ $_____

_____ $_____

_____ $_____

The above salary amounts or bonuses shall be paid as follows:

_____

_____

_____

_____

_____

_____

_____

_____

_____

_____

_____ .

Approval of Independent Contractor Services

After discussion, the board authorized and approved the services specified below to be performed by
_____ according to the following terms:

_____

Appointment of Corporate Officers

The board of directors appoints the following individuals to serve in the following corporate offices, at the annual salaries shown next to their names.

Name   Salary

President: _____ $_____

Vice President: _____ $_____

Secretary: _____ $_____

Treasurer: _____ $_____

Each officer shall have such duties as are specified in the bylaws of the corporation and as may be designated from time to time by the board of directors. An officer shall serve until his or her successor is elected and qualified to replace him or her as officer.

Authorization of Payment for Attending Meetings

After discussion, it was agreed that all of the following _____

be paid the following amounts for each day, or fraction of a day, during which they attend a meeting of

the board of directors or shareholders of the corporation.

Name and Title	Per Diem Amount
_____	$_____
_____	$_____
_____	$_____
_____	$_____
_____	$_____

It was also discussed and agreed that the following _____ be

_____ the following reasonable and necessary travel expenses incurred

to attend meetings of the board of directors and/or shareholders of the corporation:

Name and Title	Per Meeting Travel Expense Allotment
_____	$_____
_____	$_____
_____	$_____
_____	$_____
_____	$_____

Annual Director or Officer Stipend
for Attendance at Meetings

After discussion, it was agreed that the following _____ be paid

the following annual amounts, which include a yearly travel allotment, for traveling to and attending

regular and special meetings of the _____ of this corporation:

Name and Title	Annual Stipend and Travel Allotment
_____	$_____
_____	$_____
_____	$_____
_____	$_____
_____	$_____

No Compensation for Attending Corporate Meetings

After discussion, it was agreed that no salary, commission, per diem fee, travel allotment, or other amount shall be paid to the directors of this corporation for traveling to or attending meetings of this corporation or for furnishing services to the corporation in their capacity as directors. However, no director shall be prevented from receiving compensation, fees, or other payment for services or work performed for the corporation as an officer, employee, independent conractor, agent, or in any other nondirector capacity for the corporation.

Indemnification and Insurance for Directors and Officers

The corporation shall indemnify its current directors and officers _____ _____ to the fullest extent permitted under the laws of this state. Such indemnification shall not be deemed to be exclusive of any other rights to which the indemnified person is entitled, consistent with law, under any provision of the articles of incorporation or bylaws of the corporation, any general or specific action of the board of directors, the terms of any contract, or as may be permitted or required by common law.

The corporation may purchase and maintain insurance or provide another arrangement on behalf of any person who is a director or officer_____ against any liability asserted against him or her and incurred by him or her in such a capacity or arising out of his or her status as a director or officer, whether or not the corporation would have the power to indemnify him or her against that liability under the laws of this state.

Board Approval of Transaction Benefiting a Director

The next item of business considered by the board was:

_____

_____

_____

_____

_____

_____

_____ .

It was understood that the following directors have a material financial interest in this business as follows:

Name   Scope of Personal Interest

_____   _____

_____   _____

_____   _____

After discussion, it was agreed that the approval of this business was fair to the corporation. Therefore, it was approved by the votes of the directors present at the meeting as follows:

Name of Director   Vote

_____   _____

_____   _____

_____   _____

Directors' Written Consent to Transaction
Benefiting a Director

The undersigned approve the following item of business:

_____

_____

_____

_____

_____.

     Prior to signing this form, the undersigned understood that the following director(s) had a material financial interest in this business as follows:

Name of Director   Scope of Personal Financial Interest

_____   _____

_____   _____

_____   _____

_____   _____

     It was agreed that the approval of this business was fair to the corporation.

Date: _____

Signature: _____

Name: _____, Director

Date: _____

Signature: _____

Name: _____, Director

Date: _____

Signature: _____

Name: _____, Director

Date: _____

Signature: _____

Name: _____, Director

Shareholder Approval of Transaction
Benefiting a Director

The next item of business considered by the shareholders was:_____

_____

_____

_____

_____.

It was understood that the following person(s) has/have a material financial interest in this business as follows:

_____

_____

_____

_____

_____

_____.

After discussion, it was agreed that the approval of this business was fair to the corporation. Therefore, it was approved by the votes of the shareholders present at the meeting as follows:

Name of Shareholder   Vote

_____   _____

_____   _____

_____   _____

_____   _____

_____   _____

Shareholder Written Consent to Transaction Involving a Director

The undersigned approve the following item of business:

_____

_____

_____

_____

_____.

    Prior to signing this form, each of the undersigned understood that the following person(s) has/had a material financial interest in this business as follows:

Name of Director/Shareholder	Position	Personal Financial Interest
_____	_____	_____
_____	_____	_____
_____	_____	_____
_____	_____	_____

    It was agreed that the approval of this business was fair to the corporation.

Date: _____

Signature: _____

Name: _____, Shareholder

Date: _____

Signature: _____

Name: _____, Shareholder

Date: _____

Signature: _____

Name: _____, Shareholder

Date: _____

Signature: _____

Name: _____, Shareholder

Authorization of Loan at Specific Terms

It was announced that the officers of the corporation have received a loan commitment from the following bank, trust company, or other financial institution on the following terms:

Name of Lender: _____

Loan Amount: $_____

Terms of the Loan:

_____

_____

_____

_____

_____

_____

_____.

    It was resolved that the proposed terms of the loan are fair and reasonable to the corporation and that it would be in the best interests of the corporation to borrow the funds on the terms stated above.

    It was further resolved that the following officers are authorized to execute the notes and documents on behalf of the corporation necessary to effect the above loan:

Officer Name	Title
_____	_____
_____	_____
_____	_____
_____	_____
_____	_____

Authorization of Maximum Loan on General Terms

It was resolved that it was in the best interests of the corporation to borrow up to the following amount of funds from the following bank, trust company, or other financial institution:

Name of Lender: _____

Loan Amount: $_____

The following officers were authorized to sign the appropriate notes and documents on behalf of the corporation necessary to borrow an amount that does not exceed the amount noted above on terms reasonable to the corporation:

Officer Name   Title

_____   _____

_____   _____

_____   _____

_____   _____

_____   _____

Unlimited Authorization of Loans for Business Needs

It was resolved that the following officers of the corporation are authorized to borrow on behalf of the corporation from one or more banks or other financial institutions such amounts as they decide are reasonably necessary to meet the needs of the business of the corporation:

Officer Name   Title

_____   _____

_____   _____

_____   _____

_____   _____

_____   _____

_____   _____

Authorization of Line of Credit

It was resolved that it would be in the best interests of the corporation to obtain a line of credit for borrowing funds from _____.

    The following officers were authorized to complete all necessary forms, documents, and notes and to pledge as security corporate assets necessary to obtain and utilize the line of credit:

Officer Name

Title

_____

_____

_____

    It was further decided that the authority granted by this resolution be limited and that the officers not be allowed to borrow funds against the line of credit that exceed _____.

Authorization of Line of Credit With Cap
on Each Transaction

It was resolved that it would be in the best interests of the corporation to obtain a line of credit for the

borrowing of funds from _____.

    The following officers were authorized to complete all necessary forms, documents, and notes

necessary to obtain and utilize the line of credit to allow borrowing by the corporation in an aggregate

amount that does not exceed $_____.

Officer Name   Title

_____   _____

_____   _____

_____   _____

    It was further resolved that the amount borrowed under the line of credit in one transaction shall

not exceed $_____ unless any excess amount is specifically approved by further

resolution of the board of directors.

Authorization of Loan Terms Secured
by Corporate Property

It was resolved that the following officers of the corporation are authorized to borrow the sum of

$_____ on behalf of the corporation from _____:

Officer Name   Title

_____   _____

_____   _____

_____   _____

The above officers are authorized to execute a promissory note for the above amount under the

following terms together with a mortgage, deed of trust, or security agreement and other documents

necessary to secure payment of the note with the pledge of the following property:

Property Used as Security for Note:

_____

_____

_____

Terms of Note:

_____

_____

_____

_____

_____

_____

_____

Resolution Approving Loan to Corporation

It was resolved that it is in the best interests of the corporation to borrow the following amount(s) from the following individuals:

Amount   Name of Lender

$_____   _____

$_____   _____

$_____   _____

$_____   _____

$_____   _____

The terms of _____ loan were included in a promissory note presented for approval at the meeting. The board determined that these terms were commercially reasonable. The board also determined that corporate earnings should be sufficient to pay back the loan(s) to the lender(s) according to the terms in the note(s), and that such repayment would not jeopardize the financial status of the corporation.

Therefore, the board approved the terms of _____ note and directed the treasurer to sign _____ note on behalf of the corporation. The secretary was directed to attach a copy of _____ note, signed by the treasurer, to this resolution and to place the resolution and attachment(s) in the corporate records book.

Promissory Note:
Installment Payments of Principal and Interest
(Amortized Loan)

For Value Received, _____, the borrower, promises to pay to

the order of _____, the noteholder, the principal amount

of $_____, together with simple interest on the unpaid principal balance from the date

of this note until the date this note is paid in full, at the annual rate of _____%. Payments shall be

made at _____

_____.

Principal and interest shall be paid in equal installments of $_____,

beginning on _____, 20___ and continuing on _____

until the principal and interest are paid in full. Each payment on this note shall be applied first to accrued

but unpaid interest, and the remainder shall be applied to unpaid principal.

This note may be prepaid by the borrower in whole or in part at any time without penalty.
This note is not assumable without the written consent of the noteholder, which consent shall not be
unreasonably withheld. This note is nontransferable by the noteholder.

If any installment payment due under this note is not received by the noteholder within

_____ of its due date, the entire amount of unpaid principal

and accrued but unpaid interest due under this note shall, at the option of the noteholder, become

immediately due and payable without prior notice from the noteholder to the borrower. In the event of

a default, the borrower shall be responsible for the costs of collection, including, in the event of a lawsuit

to collect on this note, the noteholder's reasonable attorneys' fees as determined by a court hearing the

lawsuit.

Date of Signing: _____

Name of Borrower: _____

Address of Borrower: _____

City or County and State Where Signed: _____

Signature of Borrower: _____, Treasurer on Behalf of _____

Promissory Note:
Installment Payments of Principal and Interest
(Amortized Loan) Secured by Corporate Property

For Value Received, _____, the borrower, promises to pay to the

order of _____, the noteholder, the principal amount of

$_____, together with simple interest on the unpaid principal balance from the date of this

note until the date this note is paid in full, at the annual rate of _____%. Payments shall be made at

_____.

Principal and interest shall bepaid in equal installments of $_____, beginning

on _____, 20____ and continuing on _____ until the

principal and interest are paid in full. Each payment on this note shall be applied first to accrued but

unpaid interest, and the remainder shall be applied to unpaid principal.

This note may be prepaid by the borrower in whole or in part at any time without penalty. This note

is not assumable without the written consent of the noteholder, which consent shall not be unreasonably

withheld. This note is nontransferable by the noteholder.

If any installment payment due under this note is not received by the noteholder within

_____ of its due date, the entire amount of unpaid principal and accrued but

unpaid interest due under this note shall, at the option of the noteholder, become immediately due and

payable without prior notice from the noteholder to the borrower. In the event of a default, the borrower

shall be responsible for the costs of collection, including, in the event of a lawsuit to collect on this note,

the noteholder's reasonable attorneys' fees as determined by a court hearing the lawsuit.

Borrower agrees that until such time as the principal and interest owed under this note are paid in

full, the note shall be secured by the following described mortgage, deed of trust, or security agreement:

_____

_____.

Date of Signing: _____

Name of Borrower: _____

Address of Borrower: _____

City or County and State Where Signed: _____

Signature of Borrower: _____, Treasurer on Behalf of _____

Promissory Note:
Installment Payments of Principal and Interest
(Amortized Loan) With Balloon Payment

For Value Received, _____, the borrower, promises to pay to the

order of _____, the noteholder, the principal amount of

$_____, together with simple interest on the unpaid principal balance from the date of

this note until the date this note is paid in full, at the annual rate of _____%. Payments shall be

made at _____

_____.

    Principal and interest shall be paid in equal installments of $_____, beginning

_____, 20____, and continuing on the _____, except

that a final payment of the remaining unpaid principal amount, together with all accrued but unpaid

interest, shall be paid on _____. Each payment on this note shall be

applied first to accrued but unpaid interest, and the remainder shall be applied to unpaid principal.

    This note may be prepaid by the borrower in whole or in part at any time without penalty.

This note is not assumable without the written consent of the noteholder, which consent shall not be

unreasonably withheld. This note is nontransferable by the noteholder.

    If any installment payment due under this note is not received by the noteholder within

_____ of its due date, the entire amount of unpaid principal and accrued but unpaid interest

due under this note shall, at the option of the noteholder, become immediately due and payable without

prior notice from the noteholder to the borrower. In the event of a default, the borrower shall be

responsible for the costs of collection, including, in the event of a lawsuit to

collect on this note, the noteholder's reasonable attorneys' fees as determined by a court hearing the

lawsuit.

Date of Signing: _____

Name of Borrower: _____

Address of Borrower: _____

City or County and State Where Signed: _____

Signature of Borrower: _____, Treasurer on Behalf of _____

Promissory Note:
Periodic Payments of Interest
With Lump Sum Principal Payment

For Value Received, _____, the borrower, promises to pay to the order of _____, the noteholder, the principal amount of $_____, together with simple interest on the unpaid principal balance from the date of this note until the date this note is paid in full, at the annual rate of _____%. Payments shall be made at _____

_____.

Interest shall be paid in equal installments of $_____, beginning on _____, and continuing on the _____ until _____, 20___, on which date the entire principal amount, together with total accrued but unpaid interest, shall be paid by the borrower.

This note may be prepaid by the borrower in whole or in part at any time without penalty. This note is not assumable without the written consent of the noteholder, which consent shall not be unreasonably withheld. This note is nontransferable by the noteholder.

If any installment payment due under this note is not received by the noteholder within _____ of its due date, the entire amount of unpaid principal and accrued but unpaid interest due under this note shall, at the option of the noteholder, become immediately due and payable without prior notice from the noteholder to the borrower. In the event of a default, the borrower shall be responsible for the costs of collection, including, in the event of a lawsuit to collect on this note, the noteholder's reasonable attorneys' fees as determined by a court hearing the lawsuit.

Date of Signing: _____

Name of Borrower: _____

Address of Borrower: _____

City or County and State Where Signed: _____

Signature of Borrower: _____, Treasurer on Behalf of _____

Promissory Note:
Lump Sum Payment of Principal and Interest
at Specified Date

For Value Received, _____, the borrower, promises to pay to the

order of _____, the noteholder, the principal amount of

$_____, together with simple interest on the unpaid principal balance from the date of

this note until the date this note is paid in full, at the annual rate of _____%. Payments shall be

made at _____

_____.

The entire principal amount of the loan, together with total accrued but unpaid interest, shall be

paid by the borrower on _____. Any payment made by the

borrower prior to the due date specified above shall be applied first to accrued but unpaid interest, and

the remainder shall be applied to unpaid principal.

This note may be prepaid by the borrower in whole or in part at any time without penalty.

This note is not assumable without the written consent of the noteholder, which consent shall not be

unreasonably withheld. This note is nontransferable by the noteholder.

In the event of a default, the borrower shall be responsible for the costs of collection, including, in

the event of a lawsuit to collect on this note, the noteholder's reasonable attorneys' fees as determined by

a court hearing the lawsuit.

Date of Signing: _____

Name of Borrower: _____

Address of Borrower: _____

City or County and State Where Signed: _____

Signature of Borrower: _____, Treasurer on Behalf of _____

Promissory Note:
Lump Sum Payment of Principal and Interest
on Demand by Noteholder

For Value Received, _____, the borrower, promises to pay to the order of _____, the noteholder, the principal amount of $_____, together with simple interest on the unpaid principal balance from the date of this note until the date this note is paid in full, at the annual rate of _____%. Payments shall be made at _____

_____.

The entire principal amount of the loan, together with total accrued but unpaid interest, shall be paid within _____ of receipt by the corporation of a demand for repayment by the noteholder. A demand for repayment by the noteholder shall be made in writing and shall be delivered or mailed to the borrower a the following address: _____ _____. If demand for repayment is mailed, it shall be considered received by the borrower on the third business day after the date when it was deposited in the U.S. mail as registered or certified mail.

Any payment made by the borrower prior to the due date specified above shall be applied first to accrued but unpaid interest, and the remainder shall be applied to unpaid principal.

This note may be prepaid by the borrower in whole or in part at any time without penalty. This note is not assumable without the written consent of the noteholder, which consent shall not be unreasonably withheld. This note is nontransferable by the noteholder.

In the event of a default, the borrower shall be responsible for the costs of collection, including, in the event of a lawsuit to collect on this note, the noteholder's reasonable attorneys' fees as determined by a court hearing the lawsuit.

Date of Signing: _____

Name of Borrower: _____

Address of Borrower: _____

City or County and State Where Signed: _____

Signature of Borrower: _____, Treasurer on Behalf of _____

Promissory Note:
Variable Schedule of Payments
of Principal and Interest

For Value Received, _____, the borrower, promises to pay to the

order of _____, the noteholder, the principal amount of

$_____, together with simple interest on the unpaid principal balance from the date of

this note until the date this note is paid in full, at the annual rate of _____%. Payments shall be

made at _____

_____.

    Principal and interest shall be paid as follows:

_____

_____

_____.

    The borrower shall make a final payment in the amount of all remaining principal and all accrued

but unpaid interest on _____.

    This note may be prepaid by the borrower in whole or in part at any time without penalty.
This note is not assumable without the written consent of the noteholder, which consent shall not be
unreasonably withheld. This note is nontransferable by the noteholder.

    If any installment payment due under this note is not received by the noteholder within

_____ of its due date, the entire amount of unpaid principal and accrued but unpaid

interest due under this note shall, at the option of the noteholder, become immediately due and payable

without prior notice from the noteholder to the borrower. In the event of a default, the borrower shall

be responsible for the costs of collection, including, in the event of a lawsuit to collect on this note, the

noteholder's reasonable attorneys' fees as determined by a court hearing the lawsuit.

Date of Signing: _____

Name of Borrower: _____

Address of Borrower: _____

City or County and State Where Signed: _____

Signature of Borrower: _____, Treasurer on Behalf of _____

Approval of Corporate Loan to Insider

It was resolved that the _____ approved the following loan to the following person under the following terms:

Name and Title of Borrower: _____

Principal Amount of Loan: $_____

Rate of Interest: _____%

Term of Loan: _____

Payment Schedule:

_____

_____

_____

_____

It was further resolved that the above loan could reasonably be expected to benefit the corporation and that the corporation would be able to make the loan payments without jeopardizing its financial position, including its ability to pay its bills as they become due.

It was further resolved that the loan approved by the board was being made solely in connection with the performance of services rendered (or to be rendered) the corporation by the borrower and, in particular, as a reward for increasing the productivity of the corporation during the preceding fiscal _____ year(s) in her/his position as _____.

Promissory Note:
Monthly Installment Payments of Principal and Interest
(Amortized Loan)

For Value Received, _____, the

borrower(s), promise(s) to pay to the order of _____, the

noteholder, the principal amount of $_____, together with simple interest on the unpaid

principal balance from the date of this note until the date this note is paid in full, at the annual rate of

_____%. Payments shall be made at _____.

Principal and interest shall be paid in equal installments of $_____, beginning on

_____, 20____ and continuing on _____ until

the principal and interest are paid in full. Each payment on this note shall be applied first to accrued but

unpaid interest, and the remainder shall be applied to unpaid principal.

This note may be prepaid by the borrower(s) in whole or in part at any time without

penalty. This note is not assumable without the written consent of the noteholder, which consent

shall not be unreasonably withheld. This note is nontransferable by the noteholder.

If any installment payment due under this note is not received by the noteholder within

_____ of its due date, the entire amount of unpaid principal and accrued but unpaid interest

of the loan shall, at the option of the noteholder, become immediately due and payable without prior

notice by the noteholder to the borrower(s). In the event of a default, the borrower(s) shall be responsible

for the costs of collection, including, in the event of a lawsuit to collect on this note, the noteholder's

reasonable attorneys' fees as determined by a court hearing the lawsuit. If two persons sign below, each

shall be jointly and severally liable for repayment of this note.

Signature of Borrower #1: _____

Name of Borrower #1: _____

Address: _____

City or County, State Where Signed: _____

Date of Signing: _____

Signature of Borrower #2: _____

Name of Borrower #2: _____

Address: _____

City or County, State Where Signed: _____

Date of Signing: _____

Promissory Note:
Installment Payments of Principal and Interest
(Amortized Loan) Secured by Property

For Value Received, _____, the

borrower(s), promise(s) to pay to the order of _____, the

noteholder, the principal amount of $_____, together with simple interest on the unpaid

principal balance from the date of this note until the date this note is paid in full, at the annual rate of

_____%. Payments shall be made at _____.

Principal and interest shall be paid in equal installments of $_____, beginning on

_____, 20____ and continuing on _____ until

the principal and interest are paid in full. Each payment on this note shall be applied first to accrued but

unpaid interest, and the remainder shall be applied to unpaid principal.

This note may be prepaid by the borrower(s) in whole or in part at any time without penalty.

This note is not assumable without the written consent of the noteholder, which consent shall not be

unreasonably withheld. This note is nontransferable by the noteholder.

If any installment payment due under this note is not received by the noteholder within

_____ of its due date, the entire amount of unpaid principal and accrued but unpaid

interest of the loan shall, at the option of the noteholder, become immediately due and payable without

prior notice by the noteholder to the borrower(s). In the event of a default, the borrower(s) shall be

responsible for the costs of collection, including, in the event of a lawsuit to collect on this note, the

noteholder's reasonable attorneys' fees as determined by a court hearing the lawsuit. If two persons sign

below, each shall be jointly and severally liable for repayment of this note.

Borrower(s) agree(s) that until such time as the principal and interest owed under this note are

paid in full, the note shall be secured by the following described mortgage, deed of trust, or security

agreement: _____.

Signature of Borrower #1: _____

Name of Borrower #1: _____

Address: _____

City or County, State Where Signed: _____

Date of Signing: _____

Signature of Borrower #2: _____

Name of Borrower #2: _____

Address: _____

City or County, State Where Signed: _____

Date of Signing: _____

Promissory Note:
Installment Payments of Principal and Interest
(Amortized Loan) With Balloon Payment

For Value Received, _____, the

borrower(s), promise(s) to pay to the order of _____, the

noteholder, the principal amount of $_____, together with simple interest on the unpaid

principal balance from the date of this note until the date this note is paid in full, at the annual rate of

_____%. Payments shall be made at _____.

    Principal and interest shall be paid in equal installments of $_____, beginning

on _____, 20____ and continuing on _____,

except that a final payment of the remaining unpaid principal amount together with all accrued but

unpaid interest shall be paid on _____. Each payment on this note shall

be applied first to accrued but unpaid interest, and the remainder shall be applied to unpaid principal..

    This note may be prepaid by the borrower(s) in whole or in part at any time without penalty.
This note is not assumable without the written consent of the noteholder, which consent shall not be
unreasonably withheld. This note is nontransferable by the noteholder.

    If any installment payment due under this note is not received by the noteholder within

_____ of its due date, the entire amount of unpaid principal and accrued but unpaid

interest of the loan shall, at the option of the noteholder, become immediately due and payable without

prior notice by the noteholder to the borrower(s). In the event of a default, the borrower(s) shall be

responsible for the costs of collection, including, in the event of a lawsuit to collect on this note, the

noteholder's reasonable attorneys' fees as determined by a court hearing the lawsuit. If two persons sign

below, each shall be jointly and severally liable for repayment of this note.

Signature of Borrower #1: _____

Name of Borrower #1: _____

Address: _____

City or County, State Where Signed: _____

Date of Signing: _____

Signature of Borrower #2: _____

Name of Borrower #2: _____

Address: _____

City or County, State Where Signed: _____

Date of Signing: _____

Promissory Note:
Periodic Payments of Interest
With Lump Sum Principal Payment

For Value Received, _____, the

borrower(s), promise(s) to pay to the order of _____, the

noteholder, the principal amount of $_____, together with simple interest on the unpaid

principal balance from the date of this note until the date this note is paid in full, at the annual rate of

_____%. Payments shall be made at _____.

Interest shall be paid in equal installments of $_____, beginning on

_____, 20_____ and continuing on _____

until _____, on which date the entire principal amount, together with

total accrued but unpaid interest, shall be paid by the borrower(s).

This note may be prepaid by the borrower(s) in whole or in part at any time without penalty.

This note is not assumable without the written consent of the noteholder, which consent shall not be

unreasonably withheld. This note is nontransferable by the noteholder.

If any installment payment due under this note is not received by the noteholder within

_____ of its due date, the entire amount of unpaid principal and accrued but unpaid

interest of the loan shall, at the option of the noteholder, become immediately due and payable without

prior notice by the noteholder to the borrower(s). In the event of a default, the borrower(s) shall be

responsible for the costs of collection, including, in the event of a lawsuit to collect on this note, the

noteholder's reasonable attorneys' fees as determined by a court hearing the lawsuit. If two persons sign

below, each shall be jointly and severally liable for repayment of this note.

Signature of Borrower #1: _____

Name of Borrower #1: _____

Address: _____

City or County, State Where Signed: _____

Date of Signing: _____

Signature of Borrower #2: _____

Name of Borrower #2: _____

Address: _____

City or County, State Where Signed: _____

Date of Signing: _____

Promissory Note:
Lump Sum Payment of Principal and Interest at Specified Date

For Value Received, _____, the borrower(s), promise(s) to pay to the order of _____, the noteholder, the principal amount of $_____, together with simple interest on the unpaid principal balance from the date of this note until the date this note is paid in full, at the annual rate of _____%. Payments shall be made at _____.

The entire principal amount of the loan, together with total accrued but unpaid interest, shall be paid by the borrower(s) on _____. Any payment made under this note shall be applied first to accrued but unpaid interest, and the remainder shall be applied to unpaid principal.

This note may be prepaid by the borrower(s) in whole or in part at any time without penalty. This note is not assumable without the written consent of the noteholder, which consent shall not be unreasonably withheld. This note is nontransferable by the noteholder.

In the event of a default, the borrower(s) shall be responsible for the costs of collection, including, in the event of a lawsuit to collect on this note, the noteholder's reasonable attorneys' fees as determined by a court hearing the lawsuit. If two persons sign below, each shall be jointly and severally liable for repayment of this note.

Signature of Borrower #1: _____

Name of Borrower #1: _____

Address: _____

City or County, State Where Signed: _____

Date of Signing: _____

Signature of Borrower #2: _____

Name of Borrower #2: _____

Address: _____

City or County, State Where Signed: _____

Date of Signing: _____

Promissory Note:
Lump Sum Payment of Principal and Interest
on Demand by Noteholder

For Value Received, _____, the

borrower(s), promise(s) to pay to the order of _____, the

noteholder, the principal amount of $_____, together with simple interest on the unpaid

principal balance from the date of this note until the date this note is paid in full, at the annual rate of

_____%. Payments shall be made at _____.

The entire principal amount of the loan, together with total accrued but unpaid interest, shall be

paid within _____ of receipt by the borrower(s) of demand for repayment by the

noteholder. A demand for repayment by the noteholder shall be made in writing and delivered or mailed

to the borrower(s) at the following address: _____

_____. If demand for repayment is mailed, it shall be considered received by the

borrower(s) on the third business day after the date when it was deposited in the U.S. mail as registered or

certified mail.

Any payment mader under this note shall be applied first to accrued but unpaid interest, and the

remainder shall be aplied to unpaid principal.

This note may be prepaid by the borrower(s) in whole or in part at any time without penalty.

This note is not assumable without the written consent of the noteholder, which consent shall not be

unreasonably withheld. This note is nontransferable by the noteholder.

In the event of a default, the borrower(s) shall be responsible for the costs of collection, including,

in the event of a lawsuit to collect on this note, the noteholder's reasonable attorneys' fees as determined

by a court hearing the lawsuit. If two persons sign below, each shall be jointly and severally liable for

repayment of this note.

Signature of Borrower #1: _____

Name of Borrower #1: _____

Address: _____

City or County, State Where Signed: _____

Date of Signing: _____

Signature of Borrower #2: _____

Name of Borrower #2: _____

Address: _____

City or County, State Where Signed: _____

Date of Signing: _____

Promissory Note:
Variable Schedule of Payments of Principal and Interest

For Value Received, _____, the

borrower(s), promise(s) to pay to the order of _____, the

noteholder, the principal amount of $_____, together with simple interest on the unpaid

principal balance from the date of this note until the date this note is paid in full, at the annual rate of

_____%. Payments shall be made at _____.

Principal and interest shall be paid as follows:

_____

_____

_____.

The borrower(s) shall make a final payment in the amount of all remaining principal and all

accrued but unpaid interest on _____.

This note may be prepaid by the borrower(s) in whole or in part at any time without penalty.

This note is not assumable without the written consent of the noteholder, which consent shall not be

unreasonably withheld. This note is nontransferable by the noteholder.

If any installment payment due under this note is not received by the noteholder within

_____ of its due date, the entire amount of unpaid principal and accrued but unpaid

interest of the loan shall, at the option of the noteholder, become immediately due and payable without

prior notice by the noteholder to the borrower(s). In the event of a default, the borrower(s) shall be

responsible for the costs of collection, including, in the event of a lawsuit to collect on this note, the

noteholder's reasonable attorneys' fees as determined by a court hearing the lawsuit. If two persons sign

below, each shall be jointly and severally liable for repayment of this note.

Signature of Borrower #1: _____

Name of Borrower #1: _____

Address: _____

City or County, State Where Signed: _____

Date of Signing: _____

Signature of Borrower #2: _____

Name of Borrower #2: _____

Address: _____

City or County, State Where Signed: _____

Date of Signing: _____

Release of Promissory Note

The undersigned noteholder, _____

_____, in consideration of full payment of the promissory

note dated _____ in the principal amount of $_____, hereby

releases and discharges the borrower(s), _____

, _____ from any claims or obligations on account

of the note.

Date: _____

Name of Noteholder: _____

By: _____, Treasurer

Signature: _____

Authorization of Group Health, Accident, or Disability Insurance for Employees

After discussion of the importance of promoting employee-company relations by providing

_____ insurance to employees, it was agreed that the corporation

shall purchase _____ insurance policies as part of a group plan

provided by _____.

The following employees shall be eligible to participate in and receive

_____ insurance under the plan: _____

_____

_____

_____

_____

_____

_____

_____

_____

_____

_____

_____.

Adoption of Self-Insured Medical Reimbursement Plan

After discussion, it was decided that it would be in the best interests of the corporation to reimburse all eligible employees for expenses incurred by themselves and their dependents for medical care expenses that are not covered by health or accident insurance, subject to specific exceptions as further discussed by the board. With the intention that the benefits payable under this plan shall be excluded from the employees' gross income under Internal Revenue Code Section 105, it was decided:

Following are the eligibility requirements for participation in the medical reimbursement plan: _____

_____

_____

_____

_____

_____

_____

The corporation shall reimburse any eligible employee no more than $_____ in any fiscal year for medical care expenses.

Reimbursement under this plan shall only be made by the corporation to the extent that such reimbursement or payment is not provided under a medical, health, or other type of insurance policy, whether owned by the corporation or another person or entity, or under any health or accident wage continuation plan. If there is such an insurance policy or wage continuation plan in effect, the corporation shall be relieved of liability for reimbursement to the extent of coverage under such policy or wage continuation plan.

Any eligible employee who wishes to receive benefits under this plan shall submit to the secretary of the corporation, at least monthly, all bills for medical care for verification by the corporation prior to payment. If the employee fails to supply such medical bills in a timely manner, the corporation may, at its option, decide not to pay the bills in question.

This plan may be discontinued at any time by vote of the board of directors, provided that the corporation shall be obligated to pay any qualifying medical bills for services provided to an employee prior to the date of discontinuation of the plan.

The _____ shall determine and resolve questions regarding coverage under this plan, except that reimbursement claimed by this officer shall be administered and decided by _____.

Purchase of Group Term Life Insurance

The board discussed the advisability of providing corporate employees with the benefit of group term life insurance. After discussion, it was decided that all full-time employees with a minimum of _____ year(s) of service with the corporation shall receive life insurance coverage in the amount of $_____.

Authorization of Employee Death Benefit

It was agreed that the corporation shall contractually commit itself to pay to the named beneficiary(ies)

of _____, who is/are employees of the corporation, the

sum of $_____ if the employee(s) is/are still employed by the corporation at the time

of his/her/their death(s) or has(have) retired from the employ of the corporation in accordance with

the corporation's retirement plan. A copy of the agreement regarding death benefits is attached to this

resolution.

Agreement Regarding Death Benefits

This is an agreement between _____, referred to below as the corporation, and _____, referred to below as the employee. In consideration of valuable services performed and to be performed by the employee, the corporation hereby agrees to pay a death benefit of $_____ to _____, hereafter referred to as the beneficiary, if the beneficiary survives the employee, in the event the employee dies _____.

The foregoing death benefit shall be paid by the corporation to the beneficiary according to the following schedule: _____.

The employee may change the designation of a beneficiary named in this agreement by submitting a written statement to the secretary of the corporation naming the new beneficiary.

Date: _____

Signature of employee: _____

Name of employee: _____

Date: _____

Name of corporation: _____

By: _____

Name/Title of officer: _____

Purchase or Lease of Company Car

After discussion, the board decided that it would be in the best interests of the corporation for it to _____ a total of _____ car(s) for use by the following corporate employees:

_____

_____

_____

_____

_____

_____.

The board further agreed that the amount spent to _____ car(s) for the above employee(s) would be limited to the following maximum amounts: $_____.

It was further agreed that the use of the cars by employees would be subject to the following terms:

_____

_____

_____

_____

_____.

The treasurer was authorized to spend corporate funds for the _____ of vehicles after verifying that the amounts expended do not exceed the monetary limits set by the board. The treasurer is directed to see that procedures are established to ensure that use of the car(s) by employee(s) meets any additional terms set by the board.

Authorization of Payment of Standard Mileage Allowance to Employees

After discussion, it was agreed that the corporation shall pay the current federal standard mileage rate to the following employees of the corporation for their business use of their automobiles while working for the corporation:

_____

_____

_____

_____

_____

_____

_____

_____

It was agreed, and the treasurer of the corporation was instructed, to reimburse any of the above employees on a _____ basis according to the above rate, after receiving a statement from the employee showing the dates, places, business purpose, and mileage accumulated on the employee's automobile during the period.

Business Meal Expense Allotment for Employees

After a discussion of the business necessity for the corporation to pay for the meals of its employees while meeting with present or prospective clients and customers of the corporation or others with whom employees wish to discuss corporate business, it was agreed that the following employees of the corporation are authorized to spend up to the following monthly amounts to cover expense of meals while dining away from the premises of the corporation and discussing corporate business:

Name   Allotment

_____ $_____

_____ $_____

_____ $_____

_____ $_____

_____ $_____

_____ $_____

The treasurer was instructed to communicate these spending limits to the above employees and to instruct them to submit monthly receipts for reimbursement to the treasurer when they wish to be reimbursed for off-premises business meals. The treasurer was further instructed to reimburse employees for these expenditures after verifying that they do not exceed the employee's monthly allotment and that the expenses were reasonable and directly related to the business purposes of the corporation.

Copies of all reimbursed receipts for employee and client or customer meals shall be kept by the treasurer and placed with the financial records of the corporation.

On-Premises Meals and Lodging for Employees

After discussion, it was decided that the corporation will provide on-premises _____

_____ to the following employees of the corporation:

_____

_____

_____

_____

_____

_____

_____

_____ .

It was agreed that the furnishing of these benefits was for the convenience of the corporation's business and that the continued presence of the above employee(s) on the premises of the corporation was indispensable to the corporation's business and was a required condition of employment for the above employee(s).

Authorization of Corporate Credit and
Charge Cards for Employees

After discussion, it was agreed that to facilitate the transaction of business necessary to the corporation, the treasurer of the corporation is authorized and instructed to issue credit cards and/or charge cards for the following corporate accounts for use by the following corporate employees.

It was further agreed that employees shall not exceed the spending allocation limits shown next to their names below:

Name	Acc't. No./Name	Maximum Amount
_____	_____	$_____
_____	_____	$_____
_____	_____	$_____
_____	_____	$_____
_____	_____	$_____
_____	_____	$_____
_____	_____	$_____
_____	_____	$_____
_____	_____	$_____

Such credit cards and/or charge cards shall be used solely by employees to incur expenses that are reasonable and necessary to the business of the corporation.

The treasurer was further instructed to monitor credit card and/or charge card purchases and receipts incidental to the card privileges hereby authorized, and, if appropriate, to revoke the card privileges of any employee who exceeds any spending limits imposed by the board or uses the card for personal expenses or expenses that are not reasonable or necessary for the accomplishment of the ongoing business of the corporation.

Reimbursement of Actual Travel and Entertainment Expenses to Employees Under Accountable Reimbursement Plan

After discussion, it was agreed that the corporation shall adopt an accountable plan for the reimbursement of business-related travel and entertainment expenses paid by corporate employees while traveling away from home on business of the corporation. It was agreed that the treasurer of the corporation be instructed to reimburse the following corporate employees for their reasonable and necessary travel and entertainment expenses while performing services for the corporation on the terms noted below:

Name

Title

_____   _____

_____   _____

_____   _____

It was further agreed that, prior to any reimbursement, the employee be required to substantiate by receipts or other records, within a reasonable amount of time as set by the treasurer in accordance with IRS regulations, the date, type, amount, and business purpose of each expense, and any other information required for the expenses to be deductible by the corporation under Sections 162 and 247 of the Internal Revenue Code.

Upon providing proper substantiation, an employee shall be reimbursed for these expenses within _____. If the treasurer determines that an employee has been reimbursed for expenses that have not been properly substantiated, the treasurer shall see to it that the employee pays back the amount of unsubstantiated reimbursement within _____ _____ of the treasurer's determination.

It was further agreed that reimbursement of the above expenses to the above employees shall be subject to the following additional terms:

_____

_____

_____

_____.

Reimbursement of Actual Travel and Entertainment Expenses to Employees Under Nonaccountable Reimbursement Plan

After discussion, it was agreed that employees of the corporation should be reimbursed by the treasurer of the corporation for reasonable and necessary travel and entertainment expenses incurred and paid by employees while performing their duties for the corporation away from home.

It was agreed that the amounts so reimbursed shall be paid to employees by way of compensation such that the employees would be required to report such reimbursements as income on their individual tax returns.

The board agreed that any reimbursement by the treasurer shall be subject to the following terms, conditions, and limitations:

_____

_____

_____

_____

_____

_____

_____.

The treasurer was instructed to communicate to employees the terms and conditions of this resolution and the requirement that they report as income and pay taxes on any reimbursements made under this nonaccountable employee business expense reimbursement plan.

Authorization of Per Diem Travel Allowance for Employees

After discussion, the board agreed that the corporation shall pay its employees a per diem allowance of _____ in addition to their regular salary and other compensation while traveling away from home on business for the corporation.

It was further agreed that any part of the allowance paid in excess of the allowable federal per diem rate for the locality where the employee stops or stays over would be required to be included in the employee's income for tax purposes.

Board Approval of Stock Bonus or Stock Option Plan

The corporate treasurer presented to the board a stock _____

plan for the benefit of employees of the corporation. After a discussion of the importance of rewarding

employee loyalty and encouraging employee loyalty and productivity through the maintenance of such a

plan, the stock _____ plan was approved by the board and a copy

of the plan was attached to this resolution by the secretary of the corporation.

     The secretary was instructed to submit a copy of the plan to the shareholders for approval.

     After shareholder consent to the plan is obtained, the treasurer is instructed to implement the

stock _____ plan and to take any and all actions necessary to the

establishment and maintenance of the plan.

Board of Directors' Adoption of Retirement Plan

The board of directors discussed the importance of fostering employee incentive and loyalty and the desirability of assisting employees in setting aside funds for their retirement. The corporate treasurer gave an oral presentation of the favorable tax benefits that could accrue to employees in establishing and maintaining a qualified retirement plan and presented an outline of provisions of the qualified master or prototype retirement plan being presented to the board for approval.

Copies of the following documents were distributed to each director for review and approval:

_____

_____

_____

_____

_____

_____.

After a review of these documents and additional discussion by the board, it was resolved that the _____ plan submitted at this meeting is approved for adoption by this corporation, per the terms of the plan agreement and other documents attached to this resolution.

It was further resolved that, because the adoption of this plan was a significant corporate decision involving the long-term expenditure of corporate funds, the attached plan documents shall be submitted for ratification by the shareholders of the corporation.

The appropriate officers of the corporation are directed to sign all documents and perform other acts necessary to establish and implement the retirement plan, and the corporate treasurer is instructed to make contributions on behalf of employees, file tax reports and returns, and distribute employee notice forms as may be required under the plan in a timely manner.

Board of Directors' Adoption of Profit-Sharing Plan

After a discussion of the importance of allowing employees to share in the profits of the corporation and a review of the provisions of a profit-sharing plan presented to the board by the corporate treasurer, it was agreed that the profit-sharing plan presented to the board, a copy of which is attached to this resolution, is approved.

It was further agreed that the trust agreement with _____ provided for in the plan, a copy of which is also attached to this resolution, is also approved.

It was further agreed that copies of the above-referenced profit sharing plan and trust agreement be submitted for shareholder approval.

The treasurer of the corporation is authorized to execute the trust agreement on behalf of the corporation and to take any additional steps necessary to effectuate and implement the profit-sharing plan approved by the board and shareholders, including certifying to the trust company as to the effectiveness of all board and shareholder resolutions relating to the plan and trust agreement.

Shareholder Ratification of Retirement Plan

After discussion, the shares _____

_____ ratified

the board resolution and plan documents attached to this resolution that establish and implement a

_____ plan on behalf of the employees of the corporation.

Name of Shareholder   Shares Owned

_____   _____

_____   _____

_____   _____

_____   _____

_____   _____

_____   _____

_____   _____

_____   _____

_____   _____

_____   _____

_____   _____

_____   _____

_____   _____

_____   _____

Declaration of Cash Dividend

The board of directors resolves that the corporation shall pay a dividend to persons who are listed as owners of its _____ shares on its books as of _____ in the amount of $_____ per share.

The treasurer announced that he/she had consulted the corporation's accountant and the corporation would, after giving effect to the dividend, meet all applicable financial and legal tests under state law for the payment of dividends to shareholders.

The treasurer of the corporation is instructed to mail a corporate check drawn in the appropriate amount to each shareholder entitled to the dividend no later than _____ , addressed to each shareholder at the last address shown for the shareholder on the books of the corporation.

Authorization of Cash Dividend Payable in Installments

After a report by the treasurer of the corporation that the retained earnings and profits of the corporation

as of _____ totaled $_____, the board agreed that a dividend

of $_____ per share on the outstanding _____ shares of the corporation

is declared for all shareholders of record as of _____.

    The board further agreed that the above dividend be paid on the following dates in the following

installments:

Date	Installment Amount
_____	$_____
_____	$_____
_____	$_____
_____	$_____
_____	$_____
_____	$_____
_____	$_____
_____	$_____
_____	$_____
_____	$_____
_____	$_____
_____	$_____
_____	$_____
_____	$_____

Declaration of Year-End Dividend

The treasurer of the corporation presented a balance sheet of the corporation as of the last day of the fiscal year ending _____ that shows the corporation has retained earnings of $_____. The treasurer reported that the corporation's accountant has certified that the balance sheet fairly reflects the financial condition and assets and liabilities of the corporation.

   After examining the balance sheet and determining that the corporation could pay the dividend noted below and still be able to pay its bills as they become due in the normal course of business, as well as meet other legal requirements necessary for the declaration and payment of dividends under state law as reported by the treasurer, the board agreed to pay a dividend of $_____. This dividend is to be paid out of the net earnings of the corporation on _____ to shareholders of record on the books of the corporation as of the close of business on _____.

Declaration of Regular and Extra Dividend

After discussion and a report from the treasurer that the earnings and profits of the corporation were sufficient, it was agreed that a regular _____ dividend be declared and paid on or by _____ to the holders of shares as shown on the records of the corporation as of the close of business on _____, as follows:_____

_____

_____

_____

_____

_____.

It was further agreed that surplus of earnings and profits warranted the declaration and payment of an additional dividend. After discussion, the following additional dividend was approved by the board:

_____

_____

_____

_____

_____

_____

_____

_____

_____

_____

_____

_____

_____.

Declaration of Accumulated Dividend
to Preferred Shareholders

The board of directors, after examining a balance sheet for the fiscal year ended _____

presented by the treasurer of the corporation, determined that earnings were sufficient for the payment

of a dividend to holders of cumulative preferred stock of the corporation of record as of the close of

business on _____, in the amount of $_____ per share,

which dividend represents the payment of unpaid dividends that have accumulated on these shares since

_____.

Authorization of Property Dividend to Shareholders

The board discussed and agreed to the following facts:

1. Corporate profits of $_____ are currently invested and represented in the following pieces of property owned by the corporation:

_____

_____

_____

_____

_____

_____.

2. Ownership and use by the corporation of the above property is no longer necessary to the business and purposes of the corporation.

3. The shareholders of the corporation have expressed to the appropriate corporate officers a willingness to accept their proportionate shares of the property in a joint conveyance from the corporation to the shareholders, rather than having their interests reduced to money through a sale of the property to others before being distributed to them.

The board further agreed that the president and treasurer of the corporation are authorized and instructed to convey the above property jointly to the following shareholders, in the proportions set forth below, as _____:

Name	Percentage
_____	_____%
_____	_____%
_____	_____%
_____	_____%

Approval of the Issuance of Shares

After discussion, it was agreed that the corporation shall issue the following number of

_____ shares _____

to the following persons in exchange for payment of the following:

Name	Number of Shares	Payment	Value
_____	_____	$_____	$_____
_____	_____	$_____	$_____
_____	_____	$_____	$_____
_____	_____	$_____	$_____
_____	_____	$_____	$_____
_____	_____	$_____	$_____
_____	_____	$_____	$_____
_____	_____	$_____	$_____
_____	_____	$_____	$_____
_____	_____	$_____	$_____
_____	_____	$_____	$_____
_____	_____	$_____	$_____
_____	_____	$_____	$_____
_____	_____	$_____	$_____
_____	_____	$_____	$_____
_____	_____	$_____	$_____
_____	_____	$_____	$_____
_____	_____	$_____	$_____

The president and treasurer are instructed to issue share certificates to each of the persons in accordance with the above terms upon receipt by the corporation of the payment for the shares and after preparing all papers necessary to complete and document the transfer of the payment to the corporation.

Sale and Issuance of Shares for Property

After discussion by the board of directors, it was

    RESOLVED, that this corporation shall sell and issue shares of its stock _____

_____ to the following persons in consideration of property actually received,

as follows:

Name	No. Shares	Description of Property	Value of Property
_____	_____	_____	$_____
_____	_____	_____	$_____
_____	_____	_____	$_____
_____	_____	_____	$_____
_____	_____	_____	$_____
_____	_____	_____	$_____
_____	_____	_____	$_____
_____	_____	_____	$_____
_____	_____	_____	$_____
_____	_____	_____	$_____
_____	_____	_____	$_____
_____	_____	_____	$_____
_____	_____	_____	$_____

    RESOLVED FURTHER, that the board of directors of this corporation determines that the fair value of

such property to this corporation in monetary terms is the value shown above.

    RESOLVED FURTHER, that the appropriate officers of this corporation are directed to take such

actions and execute such documents as are necessary to sell and issue the shares listed above.

Sale and Issuance of Shares for Indebtedness Canceled

After discussion by the board of directors, it was

RESOLVED, that this corporation shall sell and issue shares of its stock _____

in consideration of indebtedness cancelled, as follows:

Name	No. Shares	Description of Indebtedness Cancelled	Amount of Indebtedness Cancelled
_____	_____	_____	$_____
_____	_____	_____	$_____
_____	_____	_____	$_____
_____	_____	_____	$_____
_____	_____	_____	$_____
_____	_____	_____	$_____
_____	_____	_____	$_____
_____	_____	_____	$_____
_____	_____	_____	$_____
_____	_____	_____	$_____
_____	_____	_____	$_____
_____	_____	_____	$_____
_____	_____	_____	$_____
_____	_____	_____	$_____

RESOLVED FURTHER, that the board of directors determines that the fair value of the indebtedness to this corporation canceled in return for the issuance of the above shares in monetary terms is the dollar amounts shown above.

RESOLVED FURTHER, that the officers of this corporation are authorized to sign documents on behalf of the corporation and take any other action necessary to sell and issue the shares listed above.

Sale and Issuance of Shares for Services

After discussion by the board of directors, it was

RESOLVED, that this corporation shall sell and issue shares of its stock
_____ in payment of services or labor _____,

for the corporation as follows:

Name	No. Shares	Description of Services	Value of Services
_____	_____	_____	$_____
_____	_____	_____	$_____
_____	_____	_____	$_____
_____	_____	_____	$_____
_____	_____	_____	$_____
_____	_____	_____	$_____
_____	_____	_____	$_____
_____	_____	_____	$_____
_____	_____	_____	$_____
_____	_____	_____	$_____
_____	_____	_____	$_____
_____	_____	_____	$_____
_____	_____	_____	$_____

RESOLVED FURTHER, that the board of directors determines that the fair value of such services

or labor _____ for this corporation in monetary terms is the

amount(s) shown above.

RESOLVED FURTHER, that the officers of this corporation are directed to execute documents and take

other actions necessary to sell and issue the shares listed above.

Sale and Issuance of Capital Stock for Assets and Liabilities of a Business

The chairperson announced that the following persons have offered to transfer to this corporation the assets and liabilities of a business, listed in Schedule A attached to this resolution, in return for the number of shares _____ listed opposite each of their names:

Name	No. Shares	Description of Business Interest	Value of Business Interest
_____	_____	_____	$_____
_____	_____	_____	$_____
_____	_____	_____	$_____
_____	_____	_____	$_____
_____	_____	_____	$_____
_____	_____	_____	$_____
_____	_____	_____	$_____
_____	_____	_____	$_____
_____	_____	_____	$_____

After discussion, it was

RESOLVED, that in the judgment of the board of directors of this corporation, the value of the business offered is $_____.

RESOLVED, that the officers of the corporation are authorized to accept the offer on behalf of this corporation, and it was further

RESOLVED, that the officers execute and deliver to each offerer a certificate representing the number of shares of stock listed opposite each of their names above, and take all other action necessary to purchase the business and transfer title of the business to this corporation. The officers are further directed to sell and issue shares to the offerers in return for the transfer of the business according to the terms of this resolution.

Bill of Sale and Agreement

This is an agreement between _____ , referred to below as "transferor(s)," and _____ , referred to below as "the corporation."

In return for the issuance of _____ shares of stock of the corporation, transferor(s) sell(s), assign(s), and transfer(s) to the corporation all right, title, and interest in the following property:

All the tangible assets listed on the balance sheet attached to this Bill of Sale, and all stock in trade, goodwill, leasehold interests, trade names, and other intangible assets except _____ _____ of _____

_____

_____.

In return for the transfer of the above property to the corporation, the corporation agrees to assume, pay, and discharge all debts, duties, and obligations that appear on the date of this agreement on the books and owed on account of said business and as reflected on the attached balance sheet except _____ . The corporation agrees to indemnify and hold the transferor(s) of said business and their property free from any liability for any such debt, duty, or obligation, and from any suits, actions, or legal proceedings brought to enforce or collect any such debt, duty, or obligation.

The transferor(s) hereby appoint(s) the corporation as representative to demand, receive, and collect for itself any and all debts and obligations now owing to said business and hereby assumed by the corporation. The transferor(s) further authorize(s) the corporation to do all things allowed by law to recover and collect any such debts and obligations and to use the name(s) of the transferor(s) in such manner as it considers necessary for the collection and recovery of such debts and obligations.

Date: _____

Signature(s) of prior business owner(s):

_____

_____ , Transferor

_____

_____ , Transferor

Date: _____

_____ , Corporation

_____

_____ , President

_____

_____ , Treasurer

Issuance of Shares in Exchange for Assignment of Trademark, Service Mark, Patent, or Copyright

The chairperson announced that _____ offered to

assign to the corporation all of his/her/their rights to a _____ related to

the following invention, trademark, service mark, or original work: _____

_____

_____

in return for the issuance of the following number of _____ shares

_____ as follows:

Name	No. Shares	Identification of Patent, Trademark, Service Mark, or Copyright (date and reference number)
_____	_____	_____
_____	_____	_____
_____	_____	_____
_____	_____	_____
_____	_____	_____
_____	_____	_____
_____	_____	_____
_____	_____	_____
_____	_____	_____
_____	_____	_____

The board agreed that the acquisition of the above patent, trademark, service mark, or copyright was in the best business interests of the corporation and that the fair value of these rights to the corporation is $_____.

The secretary is directed to see that the shares listed above are issued to _____ _____ after he/she/they execute(s) and deliver(s) to the corporation all legal documents necessary to assign his/her/their rights in the above _____ to the corporation. The secretary also shall see to it that a copy of a properly executed assignment of rights in the patent, trademark, service mark, or copyright is forwarded for filing to the U.S. Patent and Trademark Office or the U.S. Copyright Office and to any appropriate state offices or agencies.

Assignment

_____, for consideration received, hereby

assign(s) all right, title, and interest in _____No. _____ dated

_____to _____.

Date: _____

Signature(s) of assignor(s):

_____

Name: _____, Assignor

_____

Name: _____, Assignor

Notarization

State of _____)

County of _____)

      On _____, 20____ before me personally appeared

_____, the person(s) who signed this

instrument and acknowledged that he/she/they is/are the person(s) who signed the instrument on

his/her/their own behalf.

_____, Notary Public

NOTARY SEAL

Issuance of Shares in Return for Cash and Promissory Note

After discussion, it was agreed that the treasurer of the corporation is instructed to sell and issue

_____ of _____ shares _____

to _____ for a purchase price of $_____ , to

be paid as follows: a cash payment of $_____ prior to the issuance of the shares, with

the remaining balance of $_____ to be paid according to the terms of a promissory note

executed by _____ , secured by a pledge of the

stock purchased, with interest at _____ % per annum.

Index

 **Keep Up to Date**

 Go to **Nolo.com/newsletters/index.html** to sign up for free newsletters and discounts on Nolo products.

- **Nolo Briefs.** Our monthly email newsletter with great deals and free information.

- **BizBriefs.** Tips and discounts on Nolo products for business owners and managers.

- **Landlord's Quarterly.** Deals and free tips just for landlords and property managers, too.

- **Nolo's Special Offer.** A monthly newsletter with the biggest Nolo discounts around.

 Don't forget to check for updates at Nolo.com. Under "Products," find this book and click "Legal Updates."

Let Us Hear From You

 Comments on this book? We want to hear 'em. Email us at feedback@nolo.com.

CORMI5

 **Online Legal Forms**

Nolo offers a large library of legal solutions and forms, created by Nolo's in-house legal staff. These reliable documents can be prepared in minutes.

Create a Document

- **Incorporation.** Incorporate your business in any state.
- **LLC Formations.** Gain asset protection and pass-through tax status in any state.
- **Wills.** Nolo has helped people make over 2 million wills. Is it time to make or revise yours?
- **Living Trust (avoid probate).** Plan now to save your family the cost, delays, and hassle of probate.
- **Trademark.** Protect the name of your business or product.
- **Provisional Patent.** Preserve your rights under patent law and claim "patent pending" status.

Download a Legal Form

Nolo.com has hundreds of top quality legal forms available for download—bills of sale, promissory notes, nondisclosure agreements, LLC operating agreements, corporate minutes, commercial lease and sublease, motor vehicle bill of sale, consignment agreements and many, many more.

Review Your Documents

Many lawyers in Nolo's consumer-friendly lawyer directory will review Nolo documents for a very reasonable fee. Check their detailed profiles at **www.nolo.com/lawyers/index.html**.

Nolo's Bestselling Books

 **Tax Savvy for Small Business**
$39.99

 **Incorporate Your Business**
$49.99

 **Working With Independent Contractors**
$34.99

 **Consultant & Independent Contractor Agreements**
$34.99

Every Nolo title is available in print and for download at Nolo.com.

Looking for a Lawyer?

Find a Business Attorney

- *Qualified lawyers*
- *In-depth profiles*
- *A pledge of respectful service*

When you need sound legal advice for your business, you don't want just any lawyer—you want an expert in the field, who can give you and your family up-to-the-minute advice. You need a lawyer who has the small business experience and knowledge to answer your questions accurately and efficiently.

Nolo's Lawyer Directory is unique because it provides an extensive profile of every lawyer. You'll learn about not only each lawyer's education, professional history, legal specialties, credentials and fees, but also about their philosophy of practicing law and how they like to work with small business clients.

All lawyers listed in Nolo's directory are in good standing with their state bar association. Many will review Nolo documents, such as a will or living trust, for a fixed fee. They all pledge to work diligently and respectfully with clients—communicating regularly, providing a written agreement about how legal matters will be handled, sending clear and detailed bills and more.

www.nolo.com

The photos above are illustrative only. Any resemblance to an actual attorney is purely coincidental.